THE AMERICAN WAY

NO STRIKE LAWS
RIGHTWINGERS CONSPIRACY
ROMAN STYLE WARS

LIVE FREE OR DIE - NO AMERICAN WALLS

FAST EDDIE X WILLS

authorHOUSE®

AuthorHouse™
1663 Liberty Drive, Suite 200
Bloomington, IN 47403
www.authorhouse.com
Phone: 1-800-839-8640

First published by AuthorHouse 10/6/2008

ISBN: 978-1-4343-7454-7 (sc)

Library of Congress Control Number: 2008906264

Printed in the United States of America
Bloomington, Indiana

This book is printed on acid-free paper.

THE FOLLOWING ARE MOSTLY CURRENT AND PAST EVENTS THAT I HAD TO RESPOND TO AS CITIZEN OF THE UNITED STATES AND AS A HUMAN BEING. THE DAILY NEWS SHOWS THAT UPSET ME AS AN AMERICAN COMBAT WAR VETERAN. I AM AN AFRICAN- AMERICAN VIETNAM COMBAT WAR VETERAN, WHO WAS BUMMED OFF AN AIRPLANE, AND WAS TOLD TO STAY IN BANGKOK, THAILAND UNTIL I COULD HITCH A RIDE BACK TO THE STATES. I HAD EXTENDED IN VIETNAM AND WAS EARLY DISCHARGED HONORABLY. AS I THINK ABOUT THE PAST AND THE RACISM OF THE MILITARY IT ALL BECAME CLEAR. REPARATIONS FOR THE DESCEN-DANTS OF SLAVES ARE A MUST. THE SO-CALL STRICKLAWS AND DRUG LAWS SHOULD BE ABANDONED, BECAUSE THEY ARE VERY BIAS, JUST AS BIAS AS THE REASONS TO KEEP THE MEXICAN INDIANS FROM ROAMING THE LAND OF THEIR ANCESTORS. THE SAME AS THE PALESTINIANS FIGHT WITH THE FORMER ROMANS WHO ARE IN POWER IN ISRAEL AND DO NOT WANT TO SHARE AFTER THE OVERTAKE HUNDREDS OF YEARS AGO. THE WHITE GOVERNMENT GIVES ANY WHITE PERSON ANY BANK LOAN TO DO WHATEVER, AND A MORE QUALIFIED AFRICAN-AMERICAN WITH GOOD BACKGROUND AND CREDIT CAN NOT EVEN GET A SMALL BUSINESS LOAN,

CONSPIRACY TO FAIL IN THE NAME OF LAWS, WHETHER BANKING OR OTHER LAWS, IT IS MEANT TO KEEP THE POOR AND ESPECIALLY THE POOR DESCENDANTS OF AMERICAN SLAVERY IN THE BACK OUT HOUSE, AND I REFUSE.

BEING BORN TO DESCENDANTS OF SLAVES IN THE DEEP GREAT SOUTHERN STATE OF GEORGIA, ONE OF THE ORIGINAL THIRTEEN STATES OF THE UNITED STATES WAS NOT EASY, EVEN THOUGHT, MY GRANDFATHER FOUND A WAY TO BECOME ONE OF THE FIRST BUSINESS MEN IN ATLANTA AFTER RECONSTRUCTION, AND THE EMANCIPATION DECLARATION OF THE UNITED STATES. WE MADE A WAY AND I AM STILL TRYING TO EXPRESS THE NEED FOR RECOGNITION OF ALL OF MY DESCENDANTS DEATHS, PAIN, AND SEPARATION OF ONES SELF FROM A FAR AWAY LAND CALL AFRICA. WE ARE THE LOST PEOPLE TODAY AS WERE THE LOST PEOPLE OF ISREAL, AND BOTH WERE BLACK PEOPLE THEN AND NOW, BY THE SAME SYSTEM OF ROMAN AND BRITISH LAWS. THEY IN ISREAL HAD MOSES TO BRING THE WORD AND WE HAD MASTER FARD MUHAMMAD TO FREE THE MIND FOR INDEPENDENCE FREE OF BUSINESS. IF THE PEOPLE OF THE UNITED STATES PERMIT THE SKIN HEADED NEO-NAZI PARTY OF AMERICA, THE AMERICAN KLANSMEN, AND LOU DOBBS PROMOTE A FENCE AND WALL ACROSS AMERICA IN THE NAME OF TERRORIST, THEN I BELIEVE THAT MY PEOPLE AND ANY OTHER DARK SKIN PERSON ARE IN BIG TROUBLE. THEY ARE TALKING ABOUT A NATIONAL ANTI- TERRORIST BILL THAT THE TRICKY BUSH ADMINISTRATION' S PATROIT LAW WILL HAVE THE YOUNGER CHILDREN AND YOUNG AMERICANS BE REQUIRED TO HAVE THIS SPECIAL DRIVER LICENCE THAT THE GOVERNMENT CAN TRACK EVERYTHING YOU DO, FROM FLYING, BANKING, OR ANYTHING ELSE. IT REMIND ME OF WHAT THEY DID DURNING AND AFTER WORLD WAR TWO, YOU CASKED TO PRODUCE SOME TYPE OF INDENTI-

FICATION, AND THAT WOULD DENY THE FREEDOMS AND LIBERTIES THAT WAS MADE FOR CAUCASIANS, AND NOW WITH THESE DIFFERENT COLOR HUMANS IN AMERICA, THE WHITE MAN WANT TO KEEP CONTROL OF IT'S POPULATION THAT IS DARK. THE LIGHT HUMANS ALWAYS JUST WALK, RIDE, OR FLY PAST MOST PROFILES IN THE UNITED STATES.

I DID NOT ASK TO BE BORN TO DESCENDANT OF GREAT AFRI-CANS FROM AFRICA, WHO WERE KIDNAPPED, BOUND, AND CHAIN TO BE BROUGHT TO THE UNITED STATES TO CULTIVATE AND TO SERVE A BUNCH OF CRIMINALS AS THEIR SLAVES. THE SLAVE MASTER'S DESCENDANTS WHO ARE CARRYING ON THE HATE, AND NOT ALL ARE THE SAME, BUT TODAY WITH THE CORPORATE DISCRIMINATION, IN THE NAME OF FREEDOM AND CAPITALISM, THE AMERICAN PEOPLE'S GOVERNMENT NEED TO FESS -UP AND MAKE A WRONG RIGHT, JUST AS THE SOME OIL STATES OF THE MIDDLE EAST AND ELSE WHERE TO MAKE SURE THEIR PEOPLE ARE ON THE INSIDE OF THE WEALTH. GIVE THE DIRECT DESCENDANT OF SLAVES HEALTH CARE, HOMES, AND EDUCATE ALL OF THE CHILDREN ALL THE WAY THROUGH HIGHER EDUCATION INSTITUTIONS FOR FREE, EVEN IF INSTITUTIONS HAVE TO BE BUILT TO ACCOMMODATE THE NUMBERS, LIKE DOCTOR MARTIN LUTHER KING, JUNIOR SAID," IF THERE CONTINU-OUSLY BE ENOUGH FINANCES FOR WARS AND REBUILDING EUROPE AND NOW IRAQ PEOPLE AFTER THE PERSONAL VENDETTA OF THE BUSH CHENEY ATTACK ON IRAQ. THE BUSH CONSERVATIVES WANTS TO TEACH IRAQUIS ENGLISH AND THEY DO NOT WANT TO TEACH THE DESCENDANT OF SLAVES ENGLISH, AND WE ARE NATURAL BORN CITIZENS AND PAY TAXES TO HELP EVERYONE EXCEPT THE VICTIMS OF THE UNITED STATES SLAVE SYSTEM. THE DESCENDANT OF THE SLAVE MASTER WANTS TO CONTINUE TO IGNORE US, AND ALL THEY WANT TO DO TO MY LOST PEOPLE IS TO

LOCK THEM UP AND THROW THE KEY AWAY. CHAIN AND BOUND US AND THINK WE WILL NOT FIGHT, AND WHEN WE DO THEY WANT TO JAIL, DRUG, AND BEAT THEM TO SUBMISSION TO THE JAILER. HUMAN RIGHTS VIOLATIONS ARE A BIG PART OF THE AMERICAN SOCIETY, AND THE OUTSIDE WORLD THINK THAT THIS IS SUCH A GREAT COUNTRY, UNTIL THEY COME AND SEE THE SERVATUDE OF THE LOST BLACKS TO WHITES FOR A JOB.

TODAY THE UNITED STATES GOVERNMENT WANT TO TELL THE MEXICANS NOT TO SPEAK THEIR SPANISH CONQUISTADOR'S LANGUAGE, AND SPEAK THE ENGLISH CONQUEST'S LANGUAGE, AND IT IS NOT FAIR AND PROBABLY NEVER WILL BE, UNLESS THE PEOPLE OF THESE UNITED STATES ARE ONE PEOPLE AND NOT BLACK, WHITE, ASIA, OR OTHERS. THAT IS WHAT THEY TOLD THE CAPTURED AFRICANS WHO WERE BOUND AND CHAINED TO SLAVE SHIP AND BROUGH TO A NEW LAND. THE YOUNG PEOPLE WANT TO IGNORE THE HISTORY OF THIS LAND AND HOW IT EVOLVED. WE HAVE ALL OF OUR PROBLEMS FOR PROTECTING ISREAL, WHEN THE NAZI, KLAN, AND SKIN HEADS DO NOT LIKE ANY JEW, BUT THEYWILL HAVE SEX WITH EACH OTHER, BECAUSE THEY ALL LOOK ALIKE TO SOME ONE WHO WERE BOUND, CHAIN, WHIP, AND WORKED SUN UP TO SUN DOWN, THEN TELL PEOPLE THAT IS A LAZY NIGGER, IS WHY THE LAZY WHITE SLAVE MASTER'S DESCENDANTS HAS TO COME AND MAKE THE REPARATION COME TRUE. THEY ARE REALLY SCARED OF LOSING A LOT OF THE WHITE WOMEN TO THE BLACK ASS. THE AMERICAN WAY.

MY FAMILY HAS TRACED ONE SIDE OF MY FAMILY ANCESTRY BACK TO THE END OF THE 1700 IN VIRGINIA. I HAVE FAMILY WHO HAS FOUGHT OR HAS SERVED IN MOST OF THE WARS

DURING AND SINCE THE CIVIL WAR OF THE UNITED STATES. FREEDOM AND HONOR HAS BEEN THE TRADITION AS WELL AS DEATH. FORTY ACRES AND A MULE WAS A LIE AND SO IS SOCIAL SECURITY. REPARATION CAME THE CLOSEST TO BEING A REALITY DURING THE CLINTON GORE ADMINIS-TRATION, UNTIL THE RIGHT WING GANG OVERTHREW THE UNITED STATES CONSTITUTION AGAIN, IN THE NAME OF STATUS QUO, AS THE CURRENT APPOINTED BUSH CHENEY ADMINISTRATION CALL THEM.

AFTER THE 2000 PRESIDENTIAL ELECTION I WENT BACK INTO MY SHELL KNOWING THE VOTER FRAUD STILL EXIST IN THE NAME OF HANGING CHADS, INCOMPLETE PUNCH CARD THAT VOTERS OF DEMOCRATIC AREA HAD VOTED AND STILL WITH THE WORDS OF THE ORIGINAL UNITED STATES CONSTITUTION STATES THAT "...ONE MAN ONE VOTE...." AFTER THE EMANCIPATION PROCLAMATION AND THE SO-CALL FREEDOM OF HUMANS WHO HAD BEEN IN BONDAGE SINCE 1500'S JAMESTOWN, VIRGINIA, THE PLACE THAT THE QUEEN OF ENGLAND AND THE BUSHES CELEBRATED THE RUN AWAY CRIMINALS OF ENGLAND FOUND A LAND THAT EVENTUALLY HAD TO HAVE A BRITISH- AMERICAN WAR TO SEPARATE FROM THE RACIST KING JAMES, OF GREAT BRITAIN.

IF A PUNCH CARD WAS PUNCH THAT WAS WHAT THE VOTER WANTED AND NOT FOR THE RACIST UNITED STATES SUPREME COURT CHIEF JUSTICE TO COME AWAY FROM "TRICKY" DICK CHENEY'S MEETING TO DISCARD THE VOTERS INTENT AND DECLARE A BUSH- CHENEY PRESIDENTIAL WINNER. AL GORE HAD OVER A MILLION VOTES THAN BUSH AND THEN THIS HAPPEN, AFTER THE CLINTON ADMINISTRATION HAD BECOME MORE CONSCIOUS OF THE PEOPLE OF THE UNITED STATES THAN ANY BEFORE HIM. TODAY I THINK THEY HAVE

NEW VOTING MACHINES AND I HOPE THEY HAVE ENOUGH IN ALL PRECINTS TO ACCOMMADATE THE MASS OF VOTERS FOR THE 2008 ELECTION AN BEYOND.

SINCE THIS SEMI-REVISION AND THE PRIMARIES WERE WON BY SENATOR BARACK OBAMA, SENATOR CLINTON WANTS TO COUNT VOTERS IN FLORIDA AND MICHGAN AFTER THEY WERE PENALIZE FOR MOVING UP TO JANUARY. SENATOR CLINTON AND HER HUSBAND HAVE LOST AND NOW WANT THE VOTES IN THE TWO STATES TO BE COUNTED, WHEN NONE OF THE ORIGINAL CANIDATES COULD CAMPAIGN IN THOSE STATES. EVERYWHERE SENATOR OBAMA CAMPAIGNED HE WON A LOT OF VOTERS WHO WERE IN THE CLINTON'S CAMP FOR YEARS, AND THE CLINTONS HAS THE NAME, SO THEY CANNOT SAY THAT THEY HAVE MORE POPULAR VOTES AND THEY SHOULD BE THE NOMINEE. SENATOR OBAMA PLAYED BY THE RULES AND IS LEADING AND HE SHOULD BE THE NOMINEE, AND THE CLINTONS NEED TO LICK THEIR WOUNDS AND CONSOLIDATE TO WIN THIS COMING ELEC-TION. THE DEMOCRATIC NATIONAL RULES COMMITTEE MET YESTERDAY AND I THINK DID A NOBLE AND PUBLIC MEETING TO SEAT THE REBEL STATES OF FLORIDA AND MICHGAN.

IT CAME OUT IN THE MEETING THAT THE REPUBLICAN MAJORITY MOVED THE PRIMARY UP WITHOUT ANY REGARD TO THE RULES OF THE DEMOCRACTS. FORMER GOVERNOR JEB BUSH AND HIS FAMILY'S GANG PUT ANOTHER SLUG IN THE GAME OF POLITICS FOR THE RACIST RIGHTWINGERS. THE DEMOCRATS WERE OUT VOTED, BUT THE BILL HAD A PROVI-SION FOR NEW VOTING MACHINES WITH A PAPER TRAIL AND THAT IS MOST IMPORTANT, AND THOSE MACHINES SHOULD BE NATION WIDE, EVEN IF CONGRESS HAS TO HELP BUDGET TO HAVE FAIR AND EQUAL ELECTION IN THE UNITED STATES FOR ONCE.

THE ONLY REASON WHY THEY WANTED TO IMPEACH FROMER PRESIDENT CLINTON FROM OFFICE CAUSE THEIR WERE MORE AFRICAN-AMERICANS IN AND OUT OF THAT WHITE HOUSE, WHO WERE NOT MAIDS, MASONS, DRIVERS, VALET, OR OTHER SERVITUDE EMPLOYMENT AFTER THE SLAVERY AREA. THEY WERE STILL SLAVES BUT NOT REFERRED TO AS SUCH. THERE ARE STRICKLAWS TO KEEP THE IGNORANT DESCENDANTS OF SLAVES AND THE IGNORANT PEOPLE WHO CAME AND CREATED THIS SO-CALL GREAT SOCIETY OF THE UNITED STATES IN JAIL AND PRISONS UNTIL DEATH. THERE SHOULD BE NO MORE VOTER FRAUD.

THE FIRST ADDRESS AFTER THE OVERTHROW BUSH TOLD THE MEDIA AND THE AMERICAN PEOPLE THAT THE SURPLUS OF THE CLINTON ADMINISTRATION WILL BE SPENT AND THAT HE WANTED TO BE KNOWN AS A " WAR PRESIDENT", AND HE AND TRICKY DICK CHENEY WENT ON TO CORRUPT AND DESTROY THE AMERICAN WAY. THERE WERE NO BIDDING JUST TRICKY DICK'S HALLIBURTON OFF SHORE CORPORA-TION TO SUPPLY OUR TROOPS EVERYTHING, AND THEN HE, PARTNERS, AND THE BUSHES WILL LICK THEIR LIPS ALL THE WAY TO THE BANK. IF THE ELECTION 2000 WERE LEGIT, THEN I PROBABLY WOULD NOT HAVE BEEN DISCONTENT FOR THE RIGHT WINGERS, AND THE SOFT WHITE DEMOCRATS WHO HAD NOT QUESTION ENDLESSLY WITH THE MEDIA, WHO ACCEPTED THE LIES AND WOULD NOT INVESTIGATE THE ISSUES OF SADDAM HUSSEIN 'S ARSENAL UNDER A NO FLY ZONE THAT THE SPY PRESIDENT BUSH AND COLON POWELL ESTABLISHED AFTER THEY TRICKED SADDAM TO INVADE KUWAIT IN 1991. THE IRAQ WAR HAS BEEN GOING ON SINCE SADDAM SENT HIS AIR FORCE TO IRAN, WHERE THE UNITED STATES WOULD NOT DESTROY THEM. THE LATEST INVA-SION WAS FOR THE SO-CALL HIT THAT SADDAM PUT ON HIS FATHER, AFTER HIS FATHER TRICKED HIM INTO WAR WITH

IRAN, AND NOW THE BUSH-CHENEY WANT TO INVADE IRAN ON THE PRETEXT OF NUCLEAR WEAPONS. WHAT ABOUT PAKISTAN AND IT'S DICTATOR?

HE IS BEING FED LOTS OF UNITED STATES CURRENCY, JUST AS SADDAM WAS DURING THE REAGAN-BUSH YEARS OF DECEIT. SECRECY IS THE PROTOCOL AND MY PEOPLE OF UNITED STATES SLAVERY ARE STILL BEING DISPLACED AND PUT IN THE BACK GROUND, JUST AS KING DAVID, SOLOMON, AND THE REST OF HEBREWS THAT WERE SAVED FROM ETHIOPIA, AFRICA, AFTER MOSES LEAD THEM THERE FOR SAFETY FROM THE ROMAN EMPIRE. THIS BOOK WILL ADDRESS ALL OF THIS AS IN 2007 THEY WOULD NOT HELP THE HURRICANE KATRINA VICTIMS WHO HAD TO SUFFER FROM THE ALL MIGHTY CREATOR'S DISTANT FOR THE STATUS QUO OF THE UNITED STATES. BARBARA BUSH RACIST SOLE SAYS THOSE PEOPLE DOES NOT NEED HELP, CAUSE THEY DID NOT HAVE ANYTHING BEFORE, BUT HELP SOME THIRD WORLD COUNTRY TO SHOW COMPASSION IS DEVILISH.

WHEN THE INVASION OF IRAQ HAPPENS I HAD TO DO SOMETHING, AS I WAS WRITING PATENTS AND STUDYING OTHER FIELDS.

THE POPE CAME ON TELEVISION AFTER BUSH CHENEY'S LIES THAT CAUSE THE UNITED NATION INSPECTORS TO LEAVE THEIR JOB OF FINDING WEAPONS OF MASS DESTRUCTION, WHEN EVERYDAY SADDAM WAS TURNING OVER EVERY WEAPON HE HAD AND BUSH-CHENEY WAS NOT INTERESTED AFTER THEY ENGINEERED THIS OIL WAR TO CAUSE HARDSHIP ON EVERY AMERICAN, I.E., THE RICH AND POOR PEOPLE ALIKE, THE MIDDLE CLASS BECAME THE WORKING POOR AND I HOPE THAT THIS BOOK WILL MAKE THIS HUMAN RELATIONSHIP BECOME BETTER, AND HOW TO OVERCOME THE LIES OF THE CRUCIFIXION OF JESUS CHRIST.

WHEN I STARTED THESE NOTES OF CURRENT EVENTS THAT I DID NOT AGREE WITH THE IMAGES OR THE MESSAGES, I HAD ON HOW THE LAWMAKERS CREATE LAWS TO DISCREDIT THE UNITED STATES LOST CHILDREN OF THE ALMIGHTY CREATOR OF THE EARTH AND ALL THE INHABITANTS, AND THE SURROUNDING UNIVERSE. TODAY NOVEMBER 26.2007, ON THE RACIST RUPERT MURDOCH' S FOX STATION, THIS MORNING PEOPLE WERE TALKING ABOUT THE GREAT SENATOR BARACK OBAMA' STATEMENT ABOUT THE SPACE PROGRAM, AND THE GUY SHOWS, I DO NOT KNOW HIS NAME, SAID YOU HAVE TO HAVE A SPACE PROGRAM TO FIGHT THE ALIENS IN SPACE. IT HIT ME HOW BRAIN WASH IS THIS GUY OR HE IS SELLING THE LIES OF THE RIGHT WING. THE GREAT MISSISSIPPI SENATOR TRENT LOTT HAS DECIDED TODAY THAT HE IS STEPPING DOWN AS THE WHIP. TRICKY DICK CHENEY IS HOSPITALIZE AND I BELIEVE THEY ALL HAVE HEARD THAT THIS BOOK IS COMING OUT AND THERE ARE A FEW LINES ABOUT ALL OF THESE PEOPLE AND MUCH MORE.

TODAY'S NEWS ALL OF THE NOBEL PRIZE WINNERS WAS AT THE WHITE HOUSE, AS TRADITION USUALLY DICTATES, AND AL GORE WAS AWARDED ON THIS YEAR ON THE SO-CALL GLOBAL WARNING THEORY. THE SLICK PRESIDENT JOKES THAT THE SUPREME COURT AWARDED AL GORE'S NOBEL PRIZE TO HIM. HIS FATHER AND TRICKY DICK CHENEY ARE ALL UN-AMERICAN OR IS IT THE AMERICAN WAY?

THE REPUBLICAN UTUBE DEBATE NOVEMBER 28,2007 TALKS ABOUT A FENCE ACROSS AMERICAN SOUTHERN BORDER, AFTER RONALD REAGAN PLEADED TO USSR GORBCHAVCH TO TEAR DOWN THE BERLIN WALL, NOW THE POLICY OF AMERICA WANT TO BUILD WALLS TO KEEP THE PEOPLE FROM THEIR ANCESTRAL HOME, NOW UNITED STATES, AND

ISRAEL IS DOING THE SAME TO KEEP THE PALESTINE'S, JESUS CHRIST'S PEOPLE, SEPARATED TO KEEP THE DESCENDANTS OF THE ROMAN EMPIRE'S PEOPLE WHO DID NOT WANT TO RETURN TO THE COLD HILLS AND MOUNTAINS OF ITALY. THEY ARE PEOPLE AND IS THE ONLY REASON THE BUSH CHENEY ADMINISTRATION IS WILLING TO CAUSE WORLD WAR THREE. THE SO-CALL LIGHT ROMAN HEBREWS, WHO ADOPTED THE RELIGION AFTER THE MIRACLES AND THE CRUCIFION OF THE HOLY MESSIAH. THE ROMANS WHO HAD CONQUERED THE LAND FOR ALMOST FIVE HUNDRED YEARS START PRACTICING THE ORIGINAL AFRICAN HEBREWS, AND THEY FAVORED THE HALF BREEDED MOSES AND ALL OF THE BLACKS OF ISRAEL WHO ESCAPE THE ROMAN PERSECU- TION TO EITHIOPIA, NORTH AFRICA UNTIL THE 1980' S WAR THERE HAD ISREAL SO CONCERN THAT THEY HAD FLIGHTS TWENTY FOUR HOURS ADAY. THEY ARE IN THE GHETTOS OF ISREAL TODAY, YOU NEVER WILL SEE ANY OF THESE ROMAN MEDIA PEOPLE SHOW THIS, JUST AS YOU VERY SELDOM SEE MY PEOPLE HERE IN THE UNITED STATES.

SENATOR JOHN MCCANN, THE RACIST AIRMAN, WHO WAS CAPTURED TORTURED AND HELD BY THE VIETNAMESE FOR A NUMBER OF YEARS, AND NOW HE IS RUNNING AS A REPUBLICAN PRESIDENTIAL CANDIDATE, IS WITH BUSH TO CONTINUE THE SURGE AND PRESENCE IN IRAQ, JUST TO MAKE THAT COUNTRY A MODERN DAY COLONY. THIS DID NOT HAPPEN WITH VIETNAM AND IT WILL NOT WORK IN IRAQ. IT WAS ABOUT DESTROYING ANOTHER DARK SOVER- EIGN NATION. BUSH CHENEY DID NOT WANT BIN LADEN AND HIS FORCES; AND THEY TOOK THE CONGRESS MANDATE AND ATTACK IRAQ, WHEN SADDAM DID NOT PERMIT THE PEOPLE WHO ATTACK AMERICA ON SEPTEMBER 1, 2001, IN HIS COUNTRY AND NOW IT HAS BACKFIRED ON THE RIGHT WINGERS WHO STOOD BY THE BUSH CHENEY DOCTRINE,

KNOWING THAT SADDAM COULD NOT HAVE HAD THE FREE MOVEMENT UNDER A NO FLY RULE, THAT WAS IMPREMENT AFTER THE GULF WAR. WE HAVE BE IN IRAQ SINCE 1991 AND WE ARE STILL THERE AS WE TRY TO PROCEDE TO PUBLICATION. TODAY IS JANUARY 2008 AND THAT THIS IS THE 17TH YEAR OF WAR WITH AND IN IRAQ. IT IS LONGER THAN WE STAYED IN VIETNAM AND THAT SHOULD BE A CRIME TO CONTINUE TO CONQUER THOSE PEOPLE LAND, AND CHENEY AND BUSH'S ASSOCIATES HAS SIGNED DEALS WITH THE PUPPET GOVERNMENT THEIR TO MAKE EVEN MORE BILLIONS THERE. THAT IS THE AMERICAN WAY, IN THE NAME OF TERRORIST, AND THE BLACKS ARE ALWAYS BETRAYED AS TERRORISTS AND THE BAD GUY, AND WE ARE THE WORLD AND THE ORIGINAL HUMAN SPIES OF GOD'S CREATION. THEY LIE ABOUT THE NUBIANS HELP THE ORIGINAL BLACK HEBREWS OF ISREAL FROM THE ATTACK OF THE ASSYRIANS, AND THEY WANT YOU TO BELIEVE THAT IT WAS GOD'S WORD, WHEN IT WAS GOD'S SOLIDERS FROM NORTH AFRICAN EGYPT THAT RID ONE HUNDREND AND EIGHTY – FIVE ASSYRIANS KILL AND SAVE ISREAL. WE HAVE TO FIND A WAY TO UNDERSTAND AND LIVE TOGETHER, WITHOUT THE HATE OF THE CONSERVATIVE RIGHT WINGERS SKIN HEAD NEO NAZI KLANSMEN, IN THE NAME OF THE BLACK JESUS CHRIST OF NAZARRETH.

THE LESSIONS LEARNED FROM THE NORTH AFRICAN GENERAL HANNIBAL OF CARTAGE, NORTH AFRICA ELEPHANT GROUND TROOPS WHO INVADED THE ROMANS BY LAND THROUGH THE ALPS AND HIS TACTICS HAS CHANGE THE WAY GENERAL SINCE THEN UP AND UNTIL TODAY. IT WAS DONE BECAUSE OF THE THREAT FROM THE ROMANS WHO THOUGHT THAT SINCE THEY HAVE LEARNED HOW TO BUILD BOATS THAT THEY WOULD BLOW GENERAL HANNIBAL TRICK THEM AND CONQUERED THE WHOLE OF

ROME, WHICH IS CALL ITALY TODAY. HANNIBAL'S NAVY WAS DECOY AND IS STILL THE FIRST TO CONQUER THE ALL OF THE SO-CALL EUROPEAN IGNORANCE OF THE WORLD. TO THE BUSHES-CHENEY IRAQ WAR, WE HAVE TO TRY AND BE A BETTER HUMANS ON EARTH OR THE CREATORS, WHO ARE CIRCLING THE UNIVERSE AND SEE HOW THE SUPREME BEING OF THE EARTH, WHO HAS FOUND A WAY TO GO TO THE BOTTOM OF SEAS AND IS IN THE SKY SEARCHING FOR THE CREATOR HAS COME.IN MOST MOVIES THE STORIES OF ROMANS AND CARTGAGE HAS AN IMAGE PROBLEM; THERE-FORE, I WOULD BE PLEASE TO DO A MOVIE OF ROMANS AFTER THEY LEARNED TO BUILD BOATS AND INVIE THE GREAT GENERAL HANNIBAL OF CARTGAGE, NORTH AFRICA.

JOHN MC CAIN BECAME THE REPUBLICAN NOMINEE AND HE AND PRESIDENT BUSH ARE ALREADY HAVING THOSE PRIVATE KLANISH MEETINGS TO RAISE FUNDS IN THE DARK OF SOME RANCH IN ARIZONA, AS HE DO NOT WANT TO BE SEEN WITH THE PRESIDENT, AND NEITHER DOES MOST OF THE REPUBLICAN CANIDATES WHO ARE RUNNING AWAY AFTER THEY BACK HIS ADMINISTRATION'S LIES AND TREA-SONAL ACTS AGAINST THE PEOPLE OF THE UNITED STATES OF AMERICA. BUSH GOES TO HONOR ISREAL'S ANNEXING OF PALESTINIAN'S LAND AFTER THE 1948 WAR. HE THEN WENT OVER TO HIS AND TRICKY DICK CHENEY'S FRIENDS IN SAUDI ARABIA TO BEG FOR MORE OIL WHEN IN REALLY HE WAS REALLY SECURING THE FUNDS HE AND THE VICE PRESIDENT WILL RECEIVE AFTER THEY LEAVE OFFICE AS PROBABLY THE WORST ADMINISTRATION IN THE HISTORY OF THE TAKE OVER OF LAND, THAT WE CALL THE UNITED STATES OF AMERICA.

GOD IS NOT PLEASED WITH THE TREATMENT OF THE POOR. HE SAID THE WELL TO DO HAS TO SEE THAT THE LESS WELL

TO DO IS NOT TO GO HUNGRY. THE AMERICAN GROCERY STORES THROW AWAY MORE FOOD THAT COULD FEED NEIGHBORHOODS OF PEOPLE, BUT BECAUSE OF CAPITALIZATION THAT WILL THROW IT TO THE RATS. THEY WILL NOT EVEN PERMIT THEIR EMPLOYEES TO CARRY HOME THE LEFTOVERS WITH OUT CHARGE. TODAY THEY WANT TO ELIMANATE THE ELEPHANTS FOR THEIR IVORY TUFFS. THEY COULD TRANCALIZE THE BEAST, BUT THE RATHER KILL THE MOST GRACEFUL LARGE CREATURE OF GODS CREATION ON EARTH. THE AMERICAN WAY STARTS NOW.

STRIKELAWS HAS TO CHANGE NO LOCKING THE IGNORANTS UP FOR PETTY CRIMES, THEN FORCE TO DO FELONY TIME SHOULD END, IT IS TOTALLY RACIST AND A HUMAN RIGHTS VIOLATION.

08-10-03

STRIKELAWS-BUSH-CHENEY'S APPOINTMENT HAS HURT THE PEOPLE AND THE CONSTITUTION. THIS FOLLOWING ACT ANGERED ME TO START WRITING ON TO TOP OF THE INVASION OF IRAQ.

The anti-Christ Pope John Paul on the hot and burning Europe, really southern Asia, he ask the blind followers of the devil (pope), and the roman empire descendants to keep praying for rain, G-D will make them suffer more and more for continued depiction and the continued misleading of GOD'S children IN ORDER to continue the demise of his creation, the humans. Pope, Bushes, Sharon, and Blair of Britain. They worship the bomb and the superiority over the people of color, all against GOD'S will.

THE UNITED STATES SUPREME COURT. JUDGE KENNEDY ADVOCATING RE-SENTENCING GUILD LINES BECAUSE THE

SENTENCING IS TO LONG, WHAT A CHANGE, AFTER ALL THE GENOCIDE OF THE SLAVES AND THEIR DESCENDANTS. OUR FOREFATHERS CAME OVER IN THE BOWER OF SLAVE SHIPS; NOW DIE IN THE HELL HOLES OF AMERICAN PRISONS. BOB DOLE, ORRIN HATCH OF UTAH, AND SOME TIMED BILL CLINTON ALL SOUTHERN WHITE MEN, CLINTON SOME HOW OVER CAME SOME OF THE BIAS OF HIS SOUTH OF THE MASON-DIXON LINE RACISM HE WAS BROUGHT UP TO BELIEVE .HE DID SOME GREAT THINGS AS PRESIDENT, BUT HE IS STILL ONE OF THE GOOD OLD BOYS CLUB MEMBER, WHO IS A JOHN BROWN TYPE, AND THEY HUNG HIM FOR HELPING TO FREE SLAVES. WE NEED TO END STRIKELAWS OF ALL TYPES, THE RACIST FORMER GOVERNOR OF GEORGIA'S TWO STRIKELAWS IS NO PLACE IN AMERICA AND ESPECIALLY WHEN THE MOST DISPLACED PEOPLE OF DESCENDANT OF SLAVES ARE DOING HARD LABOR FOR FREE, AND SO-CALL DEBT TO SOCEITY. THERE SHOULD NEVER BE AN IGNORANT PERSON TO PRISON FOR DECADES FOR STEALING A CAR OR SOME-THING LESS, EVEN IF THEY HAVE DONE OF PETTY CRIMES THAT HAS BEEN MOVED UP TO SOME TYPE OF FELONY. I BET YOU IF YOU EDUCATE INSTEAD OF SLAVE LABOR IN UNITED STATES PRISONS THEN OUR SOCEITY COULD BE A MUCH BETTER SOCEITY, MUCH MORE THAN MOST SOCEITIES IN THE WORLD, BUT THAT IS THE AMERICA WAY.

PRESIDENT WILLIAM JEFFERSON CLINTON, FORMER PRESI-DENT OF THE UNITED STATES WAS BROUGHT TO JUSTICE FOR BEING A MODERN DAY JOHN BROWN, IN THE NAME OF COMMITTING A SEX ACT IN HIS WHITE HOUSE OFFICE. THE RIGHT WING KEN STARR, THE KLANSMAN THAT WAS GIVEN THE FEDERAL RESERVE TO CONVICT A SITTING PRESIDENT FOR LIES, WHEN EVERYONE OF THE CONGRESS PEOPLE, SENATORS, AND THE PROSECUTORS, WHO MAKES IT A LIVING ON LIES. THEY HAVE THE POLICE LIE AND THE

POLICE CAN DO WHATEVER TO ANY SO-CALL MINORITY AND THE JUSTICE DEPARTMENT WILL PROTECT AND SERVE THEM. THE AMERICAN WAY.

PRESIDENT GEORGE WALKER BUSH (GWB) SAID OF HIS CRITICS THIS WEEK "PURE POLITICS" : IN OTHER WORDS THEY OVER-THREW THE 2000 PRESIDENTIAL ELECTION PROCESS FOR MAKING LAWS BY JUDICIAL APPOINTMENTS TO KEEP THE PEOPLE OF COLOR IN LINE IN THE NAME OF THE LAW AND VOTER FRAUD. THE BUSH CHENEY ADMINISTRATION IS NOT THE FIRST PRESIDENT ELECTED AND TOOK OFFICE BECAUSE THEIR PEOPLE CONSPIRED AND SUCCESSFULLY COMMITTED VOTER FRAUD IN THE NAME OF THE LAW.

IF HITLER AND HIS REGIME WAS KNOW AS THE THIRD REICH THEN FOURTH REICH SINCE THEIR (NIXON-BUSH2) ADMIRER ADOLPH HITLER, WHO WAS PRACTICING THE ROMAN EMPIRE MATTERS, CONTINUED ARIAN DOMINATION OF THE DESTITUTE AND ANY PEOPLE OF COLOR. THE CAUCASIANS ARE ALL BROTHERS TO PROTECT THE CAUCASIAN BITCH TO KEEP THAT LIGHT COMPLETION ROLLING AND SUPERIOR. I LIKE ALL THE BEAUTIFUL WOMEN OF THE WORLD AND THEY FROWN ON IT AND I DO NOT GIVE A DAM.

08-21-22-03

WELCOME TO THE HUMAN RACE, AND THE LIGHTER HUMAN HAS LEARNED AND GAINED POWER THROUGH THE GUN POWDER AFTER THE ROMANS AND THE OTHER EUROPEAN CRUSADERS TO THE PRESENT COMBINATION OF GREAT BRITAIN AND THE AMERICAN COMBINATION, WHICH WAS NOT HAPPY WHEN PRESIDENT CLINTON SOLVED THE CROATIAN CONFLICT, COMMITTING GENOCIDE, AS DID NIXON AND NIXON'S CLONES (REAGAN-BUSH) , ALL REPUB-

LICANS, ADMIRERS OF ADOLPH HITLER. THE CROATIANS WERE EXTERMINATING THE BELIEVERS OF ISLAM BY THE SO-CALL CHRISTIANS.

DICK CHENEY-GEORGE HUBERT WALKER BUSH (GHWB) WAR FOR ISRAEL, IN THE NAME OF SAVING THE PEOPLE OF IRAQ FROM A DICTATOR, HIS SON CAME IN TO BE A WAR PRESIDENT AND TO STRIP THE TREASURY OF SURPLUSES, TO A DEBT AS LARGER OR LARGER THAN BUSH2'S GODFATHER RONALD REAGAN, AFTER CLINTON HAD CREATED WELFARE FOR WORK, AND OVERCAME THE DEBT THAT THE REAGAN-BUSH YEARS OF IGNORING THE POOR PEOPLE FROM THE DESCEN-DANTS OF AMERICAN SLAVERY, JUST AS THE FRONT MAN PRESIDENT GWB IS JUST ALL MIXED UP WITH THIS ILLEGAL WAR. THE ROMAN EMPIRE, BRITISH EMPIRE, AND NOW THE AMERICAN EMPIRE IS ALIVE AND WELL. THESE ARE DESCEN-DANTS OF THE CRUCIFIERS OF G-D'S ONLY BEGOTTEN SON JESUS CHRIST OF NAZARETH AND THE AMERICAN SLAVE TRADE.

CHIEF JUSTICE OF THE SO-CALL GREAT STATE OF ALABAMA COURT IN CONTEMPT FOR NOT REMOVING THE TEN COMMANDMENTS MONUMENT FROM THE COURT HOUSE, IN THE NAME OF JESUS CHRIST, WHO WAS WITH OUT A DOUBT BLACK. CHIEF JUSTICE MOORE IS/WAS SUSPENDED FORVIOLATING THE SEPARATION OF CHURCH AND STATE CLAUSES OF THE UNITED STATES CONSTITUTION. MOST OF THESE CHURCHES PREACHES HATE AND NOT LOVE FOR ANOTHER HUMAN. THE CONSERVATIVES RIGHT WINGERS OF THE UNITED STATES.

08-23-03

DOCTOR MARTIN LUTHER KING, JR'S FOURTH ANNIVERSARY, HIS WIFE REPEATED HIS STATEMENTS ON THE BIG AMERICAN LIE, "I REFUSE TO BELIEVE THAT THE GREAT BANK OF OPPORTUNITY HAS NO FUNDS..."FOR THE POOR, AND ESPECIALLY THE DESCENDANTS OF AMERICAN SLAVERY SHOULD RECIEVE ALL TYPES OF HELP FROM THE GOVERNMENT THAT ENSLAVED THE BEST AFRICA HAD CENTURIES THAT THE SLAVE TRADE COMMENCE AND UNTIL IT WAS CEASED.

AS BUSH AND COMPANY (CHENEY, ASHCROFT, AND RUMSFIELD), ON ORDERS OF THE GREAT AMERICAN SPY FATHER GHWB, WHO WILL GO TO HIS GRAVE WITH THE SECRETS OF SO MUCH, JUST AS HIS UNDERLING CASE TO PROTECT REAGAN AND ANDY NORTH'S CONTRA CONFLICT, AND TO CONTINUE THE GREAT ROMAN EMPIRE, I.E.. FEED THE BLACKS TO THE WOLFS/LOINS, THE LIGHTER HUMAN SUPERIORITY COMPLEXION PROBLEM. THE CAIN AND ABLE, THE LIGHTER VERSES THE DARKER BROTHER.

THE FOX TV SHOW COPS SHOWS HOW THE LAW ENFORCERS CAN NOT BE TRUSTED TO FOLLOW THE LAW, AND ESPECIALLY THE FOURTH AMENDMENT, THE NO KNOCK LAW IS STILL ENFORCED WITH A TAP AND A CRASH THROUGH SOMEBODY' DOOR FOURTH MOSTLY AN ILLEGAL SEARCH THAT COULD AND DO AT TIME YIELD SOMETHING, THEN PROSECUTOR HAS TO COACH THE OFFICER HOW TO LIE TO MAKE SOME CHARGES STICK, AND ESPECIALLY TO SOME POOR DESCENDANT OF AMERICAN SLAVERY. LOCK THEM UP INSTEAD OF EDUCATION, AND THAT KEEPS THE FOURTH REITH, THE CONTINUATION OF FIRST REITH ROMANS TO THE HITLER'S THIRD. THIS WHOLE BUSH ADMINISTRATION TO OVER THROW THIS U.S. CONSTITUTION IN THE NAME

TERRORIST IS A SHAME AND SHOULD BE TREATED AS TREASON.

A STING IN NEW ORLEANS ON PROSTITUTION, RIDICULES COP ARREST AS A "CRIME OF NATURE." WE HAVE TO LIVE FREE OR DIE.

08-24-03

GEOGHAN, JOHN, PETAFILE PRIEST OF BOSTON CONVICTED OF MOLESTATION OF CHILDREN, WAS KILLED BY AN INMATE YESTERDAY. THE ROMAN CATHOLIC RELIGION WAS/IS BASE ON RACE SUPERIORITY AND CELEBRICY OF MEN AND WOMEN; AND NOT THE RELIGION OF THE ALMIGHTY G-D'S CREATION. JESUS SAID THEY WOULD CREATE A RELIGION IN HIS NAME IN VEIN, AND THE CRUCIFIERS DID AND TWO THOUSAND YEARS LATER BRAINWASHING IS CONTINUING, IN THE NAME OF JESUS.

RACIST CHIEF JUDGE IN ALABAMA, PRIEST KILLED, MANY MORE PRIESTS ARE UP TO GO TO JAIL, AND THE GOVERN-MENT IS WITH THEM NO MATTER WHAT; AND ALL RACIST TO KEEP THE SO-CALL STATUS QUO. SEX OFFENDERS LIST THAT THESE GOVERNMENT HAS THAT THEY HAVE TO REGISTER IN NEIGHBORHOOD WHAT ABOUT THE CATHOLIC CHURCH WITH THE CRUCIFIED JESUS IMAGE, ONLY REMIND PEOPLE OF HISTORY, THAT THE ROMAN EMPIRE WILL NOT PERMIT ANY PEOPLE OF COLOR TO BE IN SUPERIORITY OUT FRONT IMAGES, THEY DESTROYED AND IMAGE OF AN AFRICAN PERSON THAT EXISTED BEFORE JESUS AND AFTER, AND ANY OF SO-CALL EUROPEAN NATION TO BE CONQUERED AGAIN, BY LIKES OF HANNIBAL-RULER OF CARTHAGE, AFRICA.

THIS WEEK ON ABC-TV, A REPORT THAT THE BUSH –CHENEY'S ADMINISTRATION RETURNED TO THE U. N. FOR HELP IN JUSTIFYING INVADING IRAQI. BUSH-CHENEY'S WAR. THEY ARE STARTING TO ROB THE US TREASURY SURPLUS, FROM THE CLINTON ADMINISTRATION AND RETURN TO PRESIDENT REAGAN'S VOO DOO ECONOMICS AND DEBT. BY A PARTISAN VOTES OF REPUBLICANS TO REBATE THOSE WHO HAD ALREADY GOTTEN TAX BREAKS, THOSE PAID THE HIGHEST TAX WOULD RECEIVE THE MOST OF THE SURPLUS, JUST WHERE THERE COULD NOT BE ANY MONEY FOR REPARATIONS OR ANY OTHER SOCIAL PROGRAM TO HELP THE POOR AND UNEDUCATED PEOPLE OF THE UNITED STATES. THEY DID NOT WANT TO HAVE A SURPLUS FOR THE PEOPLE OF THE UNITED STATES, YET THEY SAY THEY ARE AMERICAN PATRIOTS. THEY TRICKED COLIN POWELL WITH FALSE DATA TO JUSTIFY WAR BECAUSE OF WEAPONS OF MASS DESTRUTION (WMD), THEN SENT HIM AGAIN TO TRY TO CONVICED THE U.N., AFTER THEY SAID FUCK THE U.N. TO END THEIR SEARCH FOR WEAPONS OF MASS DESTRUCTION. THEY ARE NOT SAY THIS TO MUSHARRAF OF PAKISTAN WHO HAS NUCLEAR BOMB, BECAUSE THEY ARE USING HIM AS THEY DID SADDAM HUSSEIN WITH THE IRAN WAR. WE CAN NEVER GET OF LOSING IRAN AND THE THING NOW IS TO MAKE UP AN EXCUSE TO ATTACK ANOTHER SOVERIGN NATION. WE AS A NATION NEEDS TO STOP ESCALATING ALL OF THESE WARS WITH OUR GANG OF VOLUTEERS, WITH THE HELP OF GREAT BRITAIN AND OTHER EUROPEAN, BUT THIS IS THE AMERICAN WAY.

CLINTON HAD DID A LOT TO CHANGE THE ATTITUDES TOWARDS SOME POSSIBILITIES FOR THE RICH AND POOR TO HAVE A CHANGE, BUT HE WERE FLIP/FLOP ON LOT OF ISSUES, BECAUSE OF HIS HERITAGE. THEY DO NOT WANT SPECIAL PROSECUTOR NOW FOR THE LIES OF THE BUSH

CHENEY ADMINISTRATION, BUT WHEN CLINTON HAD A NICE NATURAL BLOW JOB AND LIED ABOUT, THE REPUBLICANS AND THE WEAK DEMOCRATS WENT ALONG WITH IMPEACHMENT HEARING AND NOW NANCY PELOSI' S HUSBAND MOST PROBABLY INFLUENCE HER NOT TO HOLD IMPEACHMENT HEARINGS ON SPY GATE, IRAQ GATE, OR ANYTHING ELSE THIS ILLEGAL BUSH CHENEY ADMINISTRATION HAS DONE AND IS CURRENTLY DOING AS I EDIT THESE THOUGHTS TO THE HUMAN RACE. THEY SPENT UNTOLD DOLLARS, IN THE BILLIONS IN THE NAME OF JUSTICE AND THE LAW TO PROSECUTE AND IMPEACH CLINTON THE SAME AS THEY DO WHEN PEOPLE OF COLOR COME INTO POLITICAL POWER. BUSH CHENEY ADMINISTRATION STARTED ON LIES AND CONTINUES TO LIE AND THE REPUBLICANS WHO WERE CRYING OUT LOUD EVERYDAY FOR ETHIC IN GOVERNMENT, ARE NOT CRYING OUT LOUD NOW IN THIS TRICKY ADMINISTRATION SINCE PRESIDENT RICHARD NIXON. I STILL HEAR ORRIN HATCH, TRENT LOTT, HYDE, AND ALL OF THE OTHERS DURNING THE DEMOCRACTIC MAJORITY, AND NOW THE REPUBLICANS ARE THE MAJORITY THEY LOCK THE DEMOCRATS OUT OF THERE CHAMBERS AND THE NEWS MEDIA REPORTS ON IT ONE TIME AND PERMIT THINGS OF THIS TYPE GO OFF INTO THE WIND.

NOW WELCOME ALL CAUCASIANS TO THE POLITICAL POWER/MILITARY. ARNOLD SCHARNEGGAR IS GOVERNOR OF CALIFORNIA. JOHN EDWARDS TOWN HALL MEETING FOR PRESIDENT, ON ABC THIS WEEK", BUSH SLOGAN "NO CHILD LEFT BEHIND" A JOKE, THEY TOOK THE SURPLUS AND GAVE TO THEIR CRONIES THE TAX REFUND AND NOT BUILD ANY NEW SCHOOLS BECAUSE IT CAUSE TOO MUCH, THE REPUBLICANS FUCKED THE PEOPLE AGAIN. FIRST TIME BUSH2 FUCKED THE FDIC INSURANCE TO RETURN THE SENOR CITIZENS THEIR MONEY THAT SEEM TO DISAPPEAR

FROM THE SILVERADO BANK, IN COLORADO. EVERYWHERE GWB GOES MONEY DISAPPEARS. I IN VIE HIM, CAUSE I NEED TO BE TRUSTED TO BE PRESIDENT OF A BANK AND HELP ALL THE POOR NEEDYPEOPLE AND YOU WILL HAVE SOME RETURN WITH DISCRETION. IT WOULD BE KIND OF LIKE A ROBIN HOOD. AS I EDIT WHAT I THOUGHT ABOUT NO CHILD LEFT BEHIND WAS A JOKE THEN, BUT NOW THE WHOLE OF CONGRESS AGREES. MY ENSIGHT IS AN AMERICAN ONE AND I HAVE BECOME PROUD OF IT LATELY.

CBS' 60 MINUTES TODAY-BOB SIMON REPORTED ON DETAINING FOREIGNERS QUANTANAMO BAY, CUBA AFTER 9-11-2001 WITH OUT CHARGES, PHONE CALLS, JAIL, BEATEN, TORTURED, AND DEPORTED, JUST BECAUSE THEY ARE MUSLIMS, SOME WERE TERRORIST, IT IS/WAS RIDICULOUS JAPANESE DETAINMENT OVER AGAIN. THERE IS DEFINITELY TWO AMERICAS, TWO ISRAEL, TWO OF MOST WHEN THERE ARE MULTI- COMPLEXIONS. JOHN ASHCROFT DID NOT WHAT TO APPEAR, BUT TWO MONTHS LATER WENT TO HIS REPUB-LICAN CONGRESS, WHERE HE WOULD NOT RECEIVE NO CRITICISM TOWARDS VISA LAWS THAT WAS/IS AGAINST THIS NATION'S FREEDOM; ESPECIALLY WHEN THE BUSH ADMINIS-TRATION WALKED OUT OF SOUTH AFRICA'S RACIAL CONFER-ENCE WITH ISRAEL AND THEN THE WORLD TRADE CENTER DISASTER. I REALLY BELIEVE THAT OUR POLICIES TO PROTECT THE ROMAN DESCENDANTS, WHO CALL THEMSELVES ISRAELIS, AND DO NOT WANT TO RECOGNIZE THE FIVE HUNDRED YEARS OF SLAVERY AND THE CONTINUED LOSS PEOPLE OF THE UNITED STATES SLAVERY, YET THEY WANT THE WHOLE WORLD TO MOURN THE HITLER'S GENOCIDE OF PEOPLE WHO WERE PRACTICING AN AFRICAN RELIGION (HEBREW), BUT ARE JUST MUCH RACIST TO THE AFRICAN-AMERICANS AS THE KLAN, WHO IS THE AMERICAN HITLER LIKE GROUP BEFORE HITLER WAS BORN. WHEN WORLD

WAR TWO ENDED THE UNITED STATES PERMITTED HITLER'S GENERALS AND THEIR FAMILIES TO COME TO THE UNITED STATES, THEREFORE, THEY WERE UNITED HERE WITH THE AMERICAN KLU KLUX KLAN, AND THAT IS AMERICAN WAY OF PROTECTING EVERY EUROPEAN BEFORE AND AFTER THE WORLD WAR TWO. WE DO NOT OWN ANY MEDIA COMPANY AND WHEN WE DO SOME CAUCASIAN COMES ALONG WITH A LOT OF MONEY AS A CAPITALIST AND BY THE ONE AND ONLY AFRICAN-AMERICAN MEDIA COMPANY; THEREFORE, WE STILL DO NOT CONTROL ANY OUTLET TO HONOR THE PEOPLE OF SLAVERY EVERY YEAR, JUST THE JEWS AND THERE GENOCIDE OF WORLD WAR TWO. THE AMERICAN WAY.

THE AMERICAN NEO-NAZIS BUSHES AND COMPANY OVER THREW THE 2000 PRESIDENTIAL ELECTION, WITH THEIR BROTHERS HELP U.S.S.CT. CHIEF JUDGE (REHNQUIST), WHO WAS ON HIS DEATH BED SEDATED AND WAS WHEEL IN TO APPOINT A PRESIDENT AFTER THE HALF PUNCH CARDS WERE THROWN OUT; THEREFORE, INVALIDATING VOTER OF THEIR VOTE AND APPOINTING THE BUSH CHENEY AS PRESI-DENT. THE SO-CALL ROMAN JEWS WHO IS IN POWER ARE NOT THE DESCENDANTS OF ABRAHAM.

08-25-03

TODAY THE OTHER NIGGERA, DOCTOR CONDOLESA RICE, CHIEF OF STAFF OF THE PRESIDENT, TO COVER HER BOSS (GWB) ON THESE NAZI TACTICS. THEY (WHITEHOUSE) SAID THEY WOULD GET SADDAM HUSSEIN, NOT THE IRAQI PEOPLE, BUT THEIR SOVEREIGN LEADER. THE WAR WAS NOT NECES-SARY WHEN WE HAD HIM IN NO FLY ZONES SINCE 1991. THERE WAS NO WAY SADDAM COULD HAVE BUILD ANY WEAPONS OF MASS DESTRUCTION, NO MATTER WHAT THE CENTRAL

INTELLIGENT AGENCY (CIA) CHIEF SAYS, AND EVENTUALLY CAUSING COLON POWELL TO GO TO THE UNITED NATIONS AND PROMOTE A LIE THAT THE BUSH CHENEY ADMINISTRATION KNEW WERE A LIE. COLON TOOK IT AND STAY ON UNTIL THE RE-ELECTION AND RESIGNED. LOYALTY TO THE BUSHES AND HE WAS FUCKED, JUST AS IN MOST MOVIES THE BLACK SHEEP IS THE FIRST TO BE SACRIFICED.

NOW THE ELECTION OF 2004 IS CLOSING IN, AND BODY BAGS COMING IN FROM THE IRAQ WAR AND THE ADMINISTRATION ORDER THE MEDIA NOT TO FILM THEM AS WAS DONE IN VIETNAM. IT WAS DONE AND PUT IT ON THE BACK BURNER, JUST AS THE AMERICAN DESCENDANT OF SLAVES AND THE TRUE DESCENDANTS OF SOLOMON AND ALL OF THE OTHER BIBLICAL KINGS OF THE HEBREWS, WHO ARE IN GHETTOS. THE SHARON, BUSHES, BLAIR, AND THE ENGINEER RACIST OF THEM ALL CHENEY ARE A THREAT TO WELL BEING OF THE UNITED STATES. VIETNAM WAS NOT RIGHT, BUT IT WAS AGAINST ALL THE PEOPLES, NOT LIKE HERE IN IRAQI. NOW THEY HAVE TO TRY AND EXPLAIN WHY WARRIORS OF THE U. S. MILITARY HAS TO POLICE. BUSH IN TEXAS WANTED POLICE TO DO EVERYTHING EXCEPT TALK OF HIS BAD BANK LOAN ROBBERIES, COLORADO AND NOW THE FEDERAL RESERVE SURPLUSES OF THE CLINTON ADMINISTRATION, AND NOW TEAMING UP WITH STEVE FORBS TAX CUTS :IN ORDER NOT TO HAVE MONIES FOR REPARATIONS OF THE DESCENDANTS OF SLAVES, LIKE MYSELF.

JOHN KERRY ROASTED HER IN AN IMMEDIATE RESPONSE.

08-27-03

THE REMOVER OF THE TEN COMMANDMENTS MONUMENT IN ALABAMA, AFTER THE GRAND DRAGON CHIEF JUDGE

MOORE WAS SUSPENDED. THE SO-CALL CHRISTIAN COALI-
TION HAVE THE KLAN BELIEVING CAUCASIANS TO COME
AND SUPPORT THIS CONTEMPT OF THE FEDERAL LAWS OF
DISCRIMINATION. THEY LAY ON THE CONCRETE IN THE
NAME OF JESUS; AND, IT IS RIDICULES TO USE THE HOLY
MESSENGER NAME IN VAIN TO PROTECT THE LIGHTER
COMPLEXED HUMANS. LAME DARK HUMANS, BUT HONOR,
LAVE AND TREASURE ANY BEAST, TO BE THE GREAT BEAST
MASTER. LOVE THY BEAST NOT THEIR DARK NEIGHBORS.
THE BUSH ADMINISTRATION'S BELIEFS, RIGHT ALONE WITH
THE JUDGE MOORE'S OPINIONS.THERE IS " NOTHING MORE
FREIGHTING THAN IGNORANCE IN ACTION", COMMENTARY
BY BRAIN GRUMBLE-REAL SPORTS.

08-30-03

THE WAR IN IRAQI NEWS TODAY, HAS SENATOR JOSEPH
BIDDEN, A WHITE SENATOR OF DELEWARE, GOES ALONG
WITH THE WAR AS SO MANY OTHERS IN THE DEMOCRATIC
PARTY. ALL ARE IN THE WHITE FOLKS PARTY WHEN IT
COMES TO THE U.S. CONSTITUTION AND TO KEEP THE
STATUS QUO ON TOP WITH THE MILITARY TO GO TO WAR
ON FALSE PRETENSE. DICK CHENEY'S AND BUSH PULL THE
WOOL OVER THE HEAD OF CONGRESS, BECAUSE CONGRESS
DID NOT THINK TO INVESTIGATE THE SOURCES OF THE
CIA INFORMANT. MILITARY POWER KEEP EVERY THING
IN CHECK, EVEN WHEN THERE IS A BLACK FACE IN THE
CROWD TO MAKE IT SEEMS TO SOMEONE THAT'S BLIND AND
CANNOT SEE. WANT OTHER NATIONS TO SUMMIT TROOPS
TO AN ILLEGAL WAR, BUSH, CHENEY, AND SHARON'S WAR.
DOCTOR MARTIN LUTHER KING, JUNIOR "I HAVE THE
DREAM" SPEECH, IS STILL REVELANT YEARS AFTER HIS
DEATH, AND THE GENUINE EQUALITY WAS NOT THEN AND

IS NOT NOW. SAME AS THE WAR IN IRAQI AND IN PALES-
TINE, THE BIRTH PLACE OF THE ALL MIGHTY MESSENGER
JESUS CHRIST, THE ROMAN, BRITISH, UNITED STATES, AND
RUSSIAN EMPIRES CONTROL WITH THE MILITARY, AND TO
KEEP THE PEOPLE WHO FOLLOWS JESUS MESSAGE TO THE
HUMANS, IS A LARGE PART OF THE ISLAM BELIEFS.

09-08-03

CNN CROSSFIRE-PRESIDENT CANDIDATE-STATES THAT THE
AMERICAN TROOPS THAT HAD TO FIGHT THE BUSHES AND
THE CHENEY'S PERSONAL WAR ON A SOVEREIGN NATION,
AFTER DICK CHENEY SOLD HIS AND BUSHES OIL EQUIP-
MENT TO SADDAM. TRICK DICK CHENEY CAME UP UNDER
THE TRICKY DICK NIXON, NIXON RULES AND DICTATOR-
SHIP DESIRES IS AT AN ALL TIME HIGH, TO TRY AND KEEP
EVERY PERSON OF COLOR AS A LESSER PERSON AS THE
LIGHTER COMPLEXION. SHE SAID THAT THE TROOPS HAVE
THEIR FAMILY MEMBERS TO SEND TOILET TISSUE, BECAUSE
THE POLITICIANS RATHER TAX CUT REFUND FOR THEIR
SUPPORTERS, RATHER THEY PAID MORE OR NOT , IT WAS/IS
RACIST AND ANTI AMERICAN, THIS BUSH-CHENEY ADMIN-
ISTRATION. BUSH ROBBED THE SILVERADO BANK IN COLO-
RADO. THE AMERICAN PEOPLE DID NOT VOTE FOR HIM,
HE DID NOT WIN THE POPULAR VOTE, THE BIG DICTATOR
U.S.S.CT. APPOINTED THEIR GOLDEN BOY TO CARRY ON THE
DISPARITIES OF THE PEOPLE OF COLOR, NO MATTER WHAT
LANGUAGE.

09-15-03

COMPTON, CALIFORNIA, ELEMENTARY SCHOOL NAMED AFTER THE FORMER PRESIDENT BILL CLINTON. CNN CARRIED THE WHOLE NEWS DEAL. RACIST RUPERT MURDOCK FOX STATIONS DID NOT GIVE ANY AIR TIME TO THE FORMER PRESIDENT THAT REACHED OUT TO ALL TYPES OF INDIVID-UALS, NO MATTER OF RACE, GENDER, OR RELIGION. NBC NEWS CARRIED A BRIEF PART OF HIS SPEECH, UNTIL WHAT IS GOOD FOR OUR COUNTRY INTERRUPTED THE CLINTON STORY, AND THEN THEY CUT IT. THE MEDIA IS OVERWHELM-INGLY RACIST. IT IS A LITTLE BETTER THAN EARLIER DAYS OF NO BLACKS ON THE SCREEN, AND CNN IS THE BEST. TED TURNER IS THE BEST AFTER HAVING TO HAVE SOME TYPE OF AWAKENING.

09-23-03

JOHN ASHCROFT, U.S. ATTORNEY GENERAL, SAID TWO DAYS AGO WHILE ON HIS HATRED FOR PEOPLE OF COLOR TOUR TO INCARCERATE THE ALREADY ILLEGAL SENTENCING TO BE MAXIMIZE, UNLESS THE ACCUSED AGREE WITH THE STATE; IN MOST CASES A PERSON PROBABLY HAS SOME TYPE OF CONVICTION AND OF COLOR COMPLEXION YOU DO NOT HAVE A CHANCE. ASHCROFT HAS MADE US KNOWLEDGE-ABLE DESCENDANTS OF SLAVES TO HAVE NO HOPE FOR OUR CHILDREN'S IF THEY SO HAPPEN TO HAVE A LEGAL PROBLEM. BUSH SPEECH TO UNITED NATION YESTERDAY MENTION ABOUT THE SLAVE TRADE OF YESTERDAY AND TODAY. LIKE HE IS CONCERN, HE AND HIS FAMILY CREATES HAVOC IN ORDER TO ROB THE FEDERAL RESERVE AND TREAT ANY ONLY ELSE WHO SHOULD TRY AND FAIL, TO DIE UNDER THE TEXAS LAW, HANG THE NIGGER AND SPIC AT

THE NEAREST TREE MENTALITY. AT THE UNITED NATION SPEECH YESTERDAY HAD THAT GUN HO ATTITUDE WHEN HE AND HIS ADMINISTRATION FUCKED THE WHOLE AMERICAN SOCIETY, IN SO MANY WAYS AND FRONTS: FOR THE LOVE OF THE MONEY AND POWER. I HAD ALMOST STARTED FEELING LIKE THAT THIS COUNTRY WAS BEGINNING TO TREAT PEOPLE AS PEOPLE, AS BILL CLINTON TRIED TO MEND BRIDGES FROM SO MANY CENTURIES BEFORE BY HIS FORE FATHERS. RECOGNITION OF REPARATIONS, PROFILING, SECOND CHANCES FOR CHILDREN'S RIGHTS, THE RIGHTS OF SOME TYPE OF REHABILITATIONS FOR INCARCERATED INDIVIDUALS AND ABOLISHMENT OF THE ROCKEFELLERS DRUG LAWS, ALL OVER THE COUNTRY THE TWO, THREE, AND OTHER STRICKLAWS ARE PURE AND SIMPLE RACIST TO IT'S CORE.

09-29-03

BUSH ADMINISTRATION DOES NOT WANT AN INDEPENDENT INVESTIGATION, BECAUSE THE GREAT WHITE /EUROPEANS SCHEME TO STACK THE DECK I.E. LEGAL/ILLEGAL SET OF THE SO-CALL CONSTITUTION RACIST LAWS TO KEEP PEOPLE IN JAIL AND THROWING AWAY THE KEY, TO HAVING ATTORNEY GENERAL JOHN ASHCROFT TO DENY/HIDE THE REQUEST FROM THE CENTRAL INTELLIGENT AGENCY (CIA) TO INVESTIGATE THE WHITE HOUSE FOR ILLEGAL LEAKS IN BUSH PUPPY PIT (WHITE HOUSE.) ADMINISTRATION, INCLUDING HIS OWN JUSTICE DEPARTMENT, NOT THE U.S. PEOPLE JUSTICE DEPARTMENT, BUSH'S USE/ ILLEGAL RACIST JUSTICE DEPARTMENT TO KEEP THE STATUS QUO/EUROPEAN DESCENDANTS TO KEEP THE PEOPLE OF COLOR DOWN, IN THE NAME OF THE LAW I.E. TEXAS LAW, HANG THE NIGGER. DARKIE/INDIAN OR WHAT EVER TERM, AT THE NEAREST

TREE, TEXAS JUSTICE. BUSH TOLD THE WORLD THAT HE WAS GOING TO ADMINISTRATE TEXAS LAW, TO ALL PEOPLE OF COLOR, IN THE NAME TERRORIST AND HIGHER PROFILING, IN THE NAME OF THE COMMUNISTS, MARXIST, AND OTHER CATEGORIES THAT THEY MIGHT CREATE TO SCARE OTHER WHITE PEOPLE TO BE ON THE LOOK OUT FOR THE NIGGERS/ NELSON MANDELA BUSH ADMINISTRATION JUSTICE DEPART-MENT WAS ASKED, BACK IN JULY 2003, TO INVESTIGATE HIS BOSS'S WHITE HOUSE, NOT PEOPLE'S AND JOHN ASHCROFT HIDE IT IN SECRET PLACES, UNTIL NOW. IN JULY 2003 UNTIL TODAY TWO MONTHS TO COME OUT AND THE NEWS ORGA-NIZATIONS BRING IT TO THE LIGHT AND THE DEMOCRATS HAS TO FIGHT THE MAJORITY REPUBLICANS TO HAVE AN INDEPENDENT COUNSEL. TODAY THE CHRISTIAN COALI-TION'S, SO-CALL "SPRIT OF MONTGOMERY TEN COMMAND-MENTS TOUR" CROSS THE COUNTRY/SOUTHERN STATES TO KEEP THE TEN COMMANDMENTS IN THE COURT HOUSES TO PROMOTE SOMETHING, IF IT IS TRUE, THEN THEY SIN, THE UNITED STATES SINS AND DECEIVE THEMSELVES AND ANY ONE ELSE THAT WAS DESCENDANTS OF SLAVES, TO LEARN ENGLISH WHERE THEY IGNORANT ASSES CAN COMMUNI-CATE, OUR HERITAGE AND RELIGION NAME WAS DIFFERENT, BUT THEIR SO-CALL CHRISTIAN VALUES, AFTER THEY CRUCI-FIED THE HOLY MESSIAH JESUS CHRIST, WHO WERE BLACK, TO HANG MY PEOPLE HERE IN THE UNITE STATE KLU KLUX KLAN, IN BARROW COUNTY THE OTHER DAY AND NOW THEIR BROTHERS CHRISTIAN COALITION) AT THE GEORGIA CAPITAL TODAY, THE 29TH. OF SEPTEMBER 2,2003

10-10-03,

BIRTHDAY WAS NOT THE BEST BUT INTERESTING, GOT INTO IT WITH THIS CLUB PUNCH LINE" OWNER RON, HE

WANTED SALE BUT I TOLD HIM THAT IF HE DID NOT OWN THE BUILDING, THAT IT WON'T GO, DO NOT THINK THAT HE LIKED IT. WE CONTINUED ON ABOUT SOMETHING ELSE AND I ALL OF A SUTTON I SAID " ALL THAT WOP SHIT", THEN A LITTLE HELL BROKE OUT AND HE ALL OF A SUTTON NIGGER THIS NIGGER THAT, FOR HIS IGNORANT ASS THINKS THAT NIGGER IS THE SAME AS WOP. I TRIED TELL THE IGNORANT CRACKER, WHETHER ITALIAN OR NOT PHILSTEINS, JESUS CRUCIFIERS DESCENDANTS, CALL THEMSELVES CHRISTIANS, KILL AND BLOW – UP THE WHOLE WORLD TO PROTECT THAT VERY WELL ESTABLISH LIE THAT EVER BEEN SINCE JESUS CHRIST'S CRUCIFIXION. IT IS NOT THE SAME. W O P WITH OUT PAPERS, THE ORIGINAL PEOPLE OF THIS LAND ARE THE ONES WITH OUT PAPERS, AND THE IGNORANT PEOPLE WHO THOUGHT THAT IS AS BAD AS BEING CALLED A NIGGER, IT IS NOT NEAR THE SAME AS NIGGER, IT IS CRACKER SHIT, TRANSFORMING MORE LIES TO SOCIETY; AND, THEIR PEOPLE THINKING THAT IT IS THE SAME. IT IS A DIVISION AN IGNO-RANT PEOPLE WHO CAME OVER AFTER WORLD WAR TWO AND RESENTED TO BE KNOW AS AN IMIGRANT IN THE AMERICA WITH OUT PAPER, IT WAS SHAMEFUL TO THEM WHEN OUT IN SOCIETY, AND THEY THOUGHT IT WAS JUST AS SHAMEFUL AS BEING A NIGGER AND IT COULD NOT REALLY COMPARE AGAINST PEOPLE OF COLOR.

BUSH- CHENEY ON THE CONQUISTADORS JUSTIFICATION OF TAKING OVER AN AFRICAN- DESCENDED SOVEREIGN PRESI-DENT OF IRAQ SADDAM HUSSEIN, THE AMERICANS WHO LOST/LOSING THERE LIVES AS BUSH ADMINISTRATION IS OUT DOING DAMAGE CONTROL, AS HIS FATHER IS GUILD THE WAY TO COVER-UP, TRICKY DICK'S CENTRAL INTELLI-GENT AGENCY (CIA) CHIEF. THERE DESCENDANTS ROBBED, LIE, TRICK, DECEIVED, KILLED THE AMERICAN INDIANS, WHILE SLAVERY OF MY DESCENDANTS AND THE ORIEN-

TALS. THE WAR WAS VERY PERSONAL, THEY HAD DISARMED SADDAM BACK IN 1991 AND HE CELEBRATED WHEN BILL CLINTON DEFEATED GEORGE W H BUSH.

AN AMERICAN ENGLISHMAN WITH ALL THOSE NAMES, THERE WHOLE FAMILY WAS CROOKS, ROBBERS, KILLERS, AND IN THE NAME OF THE UNITED STATES CONSTITUTION, THAT WAS ADOPTED FOR ARIAN SOCIETY, WHAT EVER THERE RELIGION THAT ARE THE SAME, TO CONTROL ALL PEOPLE, ESPECIAL THE PEOPLE OF COLOR, RICHARD NIXON WANTED TO CARRY ON THE ARIAN FIGHT, THE AS JULIUS CAESAR, HITLER, NIXON, HOOVER, AND NOW THE BUSH'S FIGHTING AS SO-CALL CHRISTIAN SOLDIERS, DESTROY ANY AND ALL PEOPLE OF COLOR AND THE ONES THAT PRACTICE AFRICAN DESCENDANTS RELIGION, THE HEBREW JUDEA RELIGION. I KNOW SOUTHERN SO-CALL JEWS MOVES TO RURAL AREAS, THEY DO NOT CLAIM THAT BECAUSE THEY KNOW THE TRUTH, THAT THEIR COMPLEXION SHOWS THAT THEY ARE AN ARIAN DESCENDANT PEOPLE, THE LIGHTER OF THE HUMAN SPIES.

10-15-03

COURT TV NANCY GRACE ON JOHANN WOODWARD, AN ENGLAND LADY CONVICTED OF MURDERING A BLACK CHILD AND JUDGE IMMEDIATELY VACATED THE CONVICTION AND PERMITTED TO RETURN TO ENGLAND. THIS IS A PERFECT EXAMPLE OF THE BRITISH AND THE AMERICAN CONSERVATIVE CONFEDERATE BELIEF THAT A BLACK LIFE IS NOT WORTH THE FOOD THAT THEY FEED THEIR BEASTLY DOGS. A BLACK IS NOT ALLOW TO HURT ANY CAUCASIAN AND ESPECIALLY THE WOMEN, AND THAT WAS INBREEDED INTO THE SLAVES FROM ONE GENERATION TO ANOTHER. IT

IS NOT OPEN LIKE IT WAS THEN, BUT IF YOU SERVIVE AND GO TO A COURT THE JUDGE AND MOSTLY, AN ALL WHITE JURY WILL CONVICT WHEN THEY KNOW THAT IS NOT THE CORRECT PERSON, BUT THEIR MENTALITY IS THAT SOME NIGGER HAS TO PAY , AND IN THE JURY ROOM THE COHERSION OF THE JURY FOR A CONVICTION OR THEY CAN NOT WALK THEIR OWN STREETS. THERE IS NO JUSTICE FOR A BLACK MAN TODAY.

KOBE BRYANT DAY IN COURT, TWO SETS OF DRAWS AND SET-UP CONTINUES. RACISM IS VERY STRONG AND CAUCASIANS WANT ALL OF THEIR WOMEN TO STAY WITH THERE OWN OR GET A DOG, AND NOT TO HAVE BLACK ASSES, PURE RACISM. WE ARE HUMANS AND TODAY PEOPLE HAS TO LEARN FOR THEMSELVES INSTEAD OF BELIEVING THEIR RACIST PARENTS

$87 BILLION DOLLARS TO IRAQ WHEN PEOPLE OF THE UNITED STATES, VOTED FOR BUSH WAR SCARED TO GO AGAINST BUSH CHENEY WHITE PEOPLE'S PARTY, TELL THE NIGGER, POOR CRACKERS, AND ANY BODY ELSE ANYTHING AND DO OTHER THINGS. WHY IS IT THEY DO NOT WANT BLACK AMERICANS TO SUCCEDE IN THE UNITED STATES, AFTER OUR ANCESTORS WERE DEMORALIZED AND WAS MADE TO BE A SLAVE AND SERVANT FOR SOME WHITE MAN, AND NOW THEY CAN FINE MONIES FOR A WAR THAT SHOULD NOT HAVE BEEN, JUST TO TRY AND PLEASE A PEOPLE AFTER THEIR COUNTRY WAS CHOOSEN TO TEST THE NEW BOMBS AND PLANES OF THE UNITED STATES. THERE HAS TO BE A TESTING OF ALL NEW WEAPONS AND STARTING A WAR EVERY FEW YEARS AFTER ONE HAS ENDED. THE AMERICAN WAY.

TWO AMERICANS KILLED IN GAZA AND BUSH WANT TO BLAME AFRICAN DESCENDANT YASSAR ARAFAT, PRESIDENT

OF PALESTINIAN ARMY FOR THE KILLINGS. BUSH, CHENEY, AND SHARON ARE THE NEO-NAZIS FOR CONTROL OF THE ENTIRE WORLD. STEP BY STEP AND THEN THEY WILL TRY TO CONTROL THE ORIENTALS AND THAT WILL BE HELL ALL OVER THE WORLD. CHINA HAS REJECTED ANY MILITARY ACCESS TO IT'S PORTS, AND THE UNITED STATES CAN NOT CONTEST CHINA, AS THE BUSH CHENEY WAR ADMINIS-TRATION HAS MADE US TO BE HATED MORE NOW THAN ANYTIME IN MODERN HISTORY. SENATOR JOE BIDDEN AND OTHERS SAYS THIS IS THE WORST AMERICAN ADMINISTRA-TION EVER.

10-19-03

LT. GENERAL WILL BOYKIN'S-ANOTHER OF BUSH'S FRONT SO-CALL CHRISTIAN SOLDIERS STATES ALL THIS WEEK THAT GOD PUT BUSH IN AS PRESIDENT AND THAT ALL THE OTHERS ISLAM IS DEVILS.... THEY ABORTED THE U.S. CONSTITUTIONS BY THE U.S.S. CT. AS SUPREME TO KEEP AND DIRECT/ ORDERED THAT BUSH BE DECLARED THE WINNER AND PRESIDENT IN 2003.

TODAY'S CBS'S 60 MINUTES" ON NATION BUILDING THAT THE AMERICANS BILLIONS ON TOP OF BILLIONS AND PEOPLE OF BOSNIA STILL ARE SEPARATED. THE CONGRESS OF THE UNITED STATES WILL GIVE ANY AND EVERYTHING TO MAKE SOME TYPE OF RESTITUTION FOR THERE NATION BUILDING IN IRAQ AND NOT HERE MY GREAT AND MORE GREAT BLACK. BACK, IN MOZART, BOSNIA. AFRICAN DESCENDANTS RELIGION COMPARED TO A EUROPEAN RELIGION (CHRIS-TIAN). HITLER'S DREAM IS STILL THE ALIVE AND HE WAS DESCENDANT OF THE ROMANS WAY, THE BUSHES ARE IN THE FAMILY.

11-06-03

DEMOCRATIC SELLOUT ZELL MILLER ENDORSE G. W. BUSH AND BUSH SIGNED THE BILL TO SENT MONEY TO IRAQ TO HELP IRAQ PEOPLE, WHEN HE DOES NOT CARE OR WANT TO HELP THE AMERICAN PEOPLE, ESPECIALLY THE POOR AND BLACK PEOPLE. ZELL AND BUSH NO SOCIAL PROGRAMS FOR THE AMERICAN POOR, WHO PAYS/HAVE PAID TAXES AND IGNORED BY THIS HITLER DESCENDED BUSHES ADMINIS-TRATION RAM LAW, JUDGES, AND ROB ALL THE BANKS AND MUTUAL FUNDS IN THE NAME OF AMERICAN CITIZENS. LIES AND MORE LIES ABOUT CARING ABOUT THE AMERICAN PEOPLE, WHICH REALLY MEAN AMERICAN WHITE PEOPLE. LIKE PAT BUCHANAN SAID "THE FALL OF THE WEST". DICTA-TORSHIP ON IT'S WAY. THERE WILL BE NO BLACK AMER-ICAN PRESIDENT AGAINST THE PRINCIPLE OF THE ROGUE ENGLISHMEN, THE AMERICANS AS THEY ARE NOW KNOW AS AND THE ARE NOT GOING TO GIVE THE KEYS TO NO SLAVE DESCENDANT PERSON.,

11-07-03

CNN-WOLF BLITZER, ON EDWIN WILSON'S ARMS DEALER CONVICTION WAS A FRAUD BY THE GOVERNMENT, SAYS THE JUDGE. WILSON HAS SERVED TWENTY YEARS, THE CIA AND THE POLITICAL SIZED PROSECUTION IS ABSOLUTELY RIDICULES. PROSECUTORS PLAY STATISTICAL GAMES WITH PEOPLE LIVES. THE AMERICAN WAY. PRINCE CHARLES WAS HAVING SEX WITH HELPER, AND THE BRITAIN'S DID NOT PERMIT THE PRESS TO WRITE ABOUT IT, FREEDOM OF PRESS, SPEECH, AND RELIGION IS WHY THIS AMERICAN COMMON LAW DIFFERENT FROM THE KING'S LAW.

LORI BROWN AND A CO WORKER WERE KILLED IN A MODEL HOME REAL ESTATE KILLINGS, ROBBERY OR SOMETHING MONDAY THIS WEEK. THE COBB POLICE GAVE THIS BLOND YOUNG WOMAN HONORS, PROTECTING THE WHITE BITCHES, NEVER WOULD HAPPEN IF IT WAS BLACK BITCHES.

11-11-03

AL GORE IN WASHINGTON SPEECH YESTERDAY THE TENTH, VERY LITTLE WAS HEARD IN THE NEWS MEDIA, BUT HE WHO BEAT PRESIDENT G.W. BUSH IN POPULAR VOTES AND THE U. S. SUPREME COURT DICTATED THAT BUSH BE SEATED AS PRESIDENT OF THE UNITED STATES IN 2000 ELECTION. GORE SAID THAT THE BUSH ADMINISTRATION IS OVERTHROWING THE CONSTITUTION BY ALL THE SECRECY THAT IS BEING DONE BY THIS BUSH ADMINISTRATION, THERE ARE UNDOING THE FREEDOM OF INFORMATION AND ASHCROFT'S HIDING ANY AND EVERYTHING BUSH AND FRIENDS OF THEM UNDER THE TABLE, FROM ENRON, CHENEY CLAIMING ELECTIVE PRIVILEGE OF MEETING OF CIVILIANS, IRAQ, CIA EXPOSURE OF BUSH ENEMIES WIFE, AND SO MANY OTHER THINGS THAT THIS BUSH ADMINISTRATION NEED TO HAVE AN INDEPENDENT COUNSEL, WHICH ASHCROFT BY THE MEDIA IN THE DARK, AND THE PEOPLE REPRESENTATIVES OF THE REPUBLICANS IS SENDING ALL OF US UP THE RIVER TO DICTATORSHIP; AND AL GORE SAID"… OF THE PEOPLE FOR THE PEOPLE, AND FOR THE PEOPLE…" IS NOT BEING SERVED BY THIS PRESENT ADMINISTRATION.

11-12-03

THE STUDENTS OF LONG ISLAND, N. Y. WHO SODOMIZE STUDENTS AT A FOOTBALL CAMP IN PENNSYLVANIA, RULE TODAY THAT THEY WILL BE TRIED AS JUVENILES, HAD THE BEEN BLACK OR CHILDREN'S OF COLOR THEY WOULD HAVE BEEN TRIED AS ADULTS A AND THE BOOK THROWN AT THEM. THE AMERICAN WAY.

BUSH AND THE SENATE ON A THIRTY HOURS CONTINUING DEBATE ON PUSHING JUDICIAL NOMINEES THROUGH TO CONTINUE THE STACKING OF FEDERAL JUDGES WHO ARE RIGHT WING AND PREJUDICE TOWARD AFRICAN – AMERICANS AND THAT IS SO-CALL PRO-CHOICE OR PRO-CAUCASIAN BABIES TO BOOST THE CAUCASIAN COMPLEXION. NOT ONE THE SENATORS OR CONGRESSMEN IN THE HOUSE OF REPRESENTATIVES ARE GOING TO PAY OR SUPPORT ONE BABY.

11-22-03

NO SMOKING IN NEW YORK, NEW YORK! RACIST LAWS CONTINUES UNTIL MOST OR ALL THE BLACK PEOPLE ARE INCARCERATED OR DEAD, THEIR MASTER PLAN. THEY CARE ABOUT PEOPLE LIVES, GIVES ME A BREAK. THEY DO NOT CARE ABOUT AFRICAN-AMERICANS (AA) HER E IN AMERICA AND OUR FORE FATHERS WERE THE SLAVES, THAT WAS KIDNAPPED, TORTURED, KILLED, MAIMED, SCANDALIZED, AND DEPRIVED OF MOST, SO-CALL RIGHTS, AND IS DEHUMANIZED INN THE NAME OF ANYTHING, TERRORIST, MARXIST, COMMUNISM, DUMBEST, DEPRIVED YOUR HERITAGE IN THE HUMAN CHAIN FROM GOD, NOT WHETHER YOU WERE E BORN HERE OR THERE, THIS EXTENSIONS OF

THE ROMAN EMPIRE, LEAD BY GEORGE HUBERT WALKER BUSH AND RICHARD CHENEY, WITH GWB'S VIEW OF TEXAS JUSTICE, "HANG THE NIGGER AT THE NEAREST TREE", THE AMERICAN WAY. BUSH AND BLAIR THIS PAST WEEK TO PLAN THEIR PROTECTION POSTURE AS THE WORLD IS LEAD IN TO COMPLETE CHAOS. MONEY AND OIL IS/WAS THE MOTIVATION AND NOT HUMAN RIGHTS FOR ILLEGAL THE BUSH ADMINISTRATION.

AFTER THE JENA 6 MARCHES TO FREE SIX BLACK STUDENTS AFTER A NOOSE, A HANGMAN'S ROPE, SYMBOL OF HATE, JUST AS THE CRUCIFIX THAT BLACK JESUS CHRIST WAS CRUCIFIED. TODAY AS I TRY TO FINISH, MORE NOOSE NEWS IN NEW YORK NEWS 12-04-07, AFTER THE COLUMBIA UNIVERSITY AND MANY MORE ACROSS AMERICA THE LAST YEAR. THE CHRISTIAN CHURCH PREACHES IT TO THEIR CONGREGATION AND RAISES THEIR CHILDREN TO HATE THE DARK/ COLORFUL MAN.

12-05-03

CINCINNATI, OHIO HAS THE DEATH OF ANOTHER BLACK MAN, THIS PAST MONDAY, THE SECOND IN THE PAST YEAR OR TWO IN POLICE CUSTODY. THIS WAS ON VIDEO AND A LAW SUIT IS NOW PENDING. INTOXICATION DOES NOT MEAN THAT A POLICE CAN KILL AN AFRICAN- AMERICAN AT WILL, WHILE THEIR GREAT CONSPIRACY TO LOWER THE BLACK POPULATION ANY AND EVERYWHERE ON EARTH, AND IN MANY CASES WITH BLACK OFFICIALS BLESSING IN THE NAME OF TERRORIST. THE MASTER TERRORIST IS THE SO-CALL GREAT DESCENDANTS OF THE ROMAN EMPIRE, HITLER AND NOW BUSHES AND CHENEY.

TODAY ROMANS WANT TO RELIEVE THE CITIZENS OF THE UNITED STATES OF THEIR TEN CENTS COIN. THE ROMANS (REPUBLICANS) WANT SELL RONALD REAGAN AS THE GREATEST INSTEAD OF FRANKLY D. ROOSEVELT, WHO IS CURRENTLY ON THE TEN CENTS COINS. RIDICULES RACIST AT IT'S HIGHEST FORM AMERICAN STYLE, THE AMERICAN WAY.

BROWN WAS KILLED BY OFFICER CRENSHAW AFTER KILLING BROWN BACK IN 2000, MAY. STORY ON WEBTV SAYS THE MEDICAL EXAMINER FULTON COUNTY, CALLED THE KILLING AN ACCIDENT, NOT HOMICIDE BECAUSE THE POLICE DID LIKE IT TO BE CALLED A HOMICIDE

12-15-03

BUSH AND CHENEY HAS WHAT THEY THEIR PERSONAL WAR WITH IRAQ TO CONQUER THE GAS AND OIL OF IRAQ AND KUWAIT, WITH GEORGE W. H. , BUSH , THE ONE AND ONLY TRICKY DICK RICHARD M. NIXON PRESIDENTIAL CENTRAL INTELLIGENT AGENCY CHIEF AND VICE PRESIDENT TO THE ONE AND ONLY GREAT WHITE POWER MAN PRESIDENT RONALD REAGAN, PUT SADDAM TO SLEEP WITH THE REUNION OF IRAQ PORTS (KUWAIT), BECAUSE GEORGE SENOR GAVE SADDAM THE OK TO INVADE, BUT THAT WAS THE TRICK.

TRICKED SADDAM INTO INVADING KUWAIT AND THEN WENT TO WAR, BECAUSE SADDAM HAD TRUSTED BUSH SENIOR AND THEY DID BIG BUSINESS, NOT AS BIG AS HE DIRECTED HIS SON AND CHENEY. BUSH PRESS COVERAGE IS TRYING TO FOOL THE AMERICAN PEOPLE WITH A BUSH OF BULLSHIT RATIONAL TO JUSTIFY HIS WAR IN IRAQ WHEN THE SADDAM NOR IRAQ WAS TREAT TO THE UNITED STATES,

AND MOST DEFINITELY THAT IRAQ DID NOT, AND BUSH AND TONY BAIR OF BRITAIN KNEW SADDAM DID NOT HAVE ANY WEAPONS OF MASS DESTRUCTION. THERE ARE OTHER NATIONS THAT HAS THEIR DICTATORS AND BUSH ADMINISTRATION IS NOT GOING TO ATTACK THEM WITH OUR TROOPS, BECAUSE THERE IS NO GAS OR OIL.

BUSH AT HIS LAST PRESS CONFERENCE THIS MORNING, LIES ABOUT HIS CONCERNS OF THE IRAQ PEOPLE WHEN HE DOES NOT HAVE CONCERNS OF THE AMERICAN PEOPLE. FEDERAL RESERVE MONIES TO BUSH ADMINISTRATIONS TAX TO THE RICHEST OF THE RICHEST. WANT TO PUT THE IRAQ INVASION ON THE SEPTEMBER 11,2001 ATTACK, BECAUSE THEY HAD WALKED OUT OF THE WORLD RACIAL CONFERENCE IN SOUTH AFRICA EARLIER IN 2001, WHEN THE BUSH AND CHENEY WALK OUT OF THE CONFERENCE WITH ISRAEL, BECAUSE OF THE RELATIONSHIP OF THE TWO FORMER DEFENSE MINISTERS I.E. DICK CHENEY AND ARIA SHARON, KEEPER OF THE POWERS OF THE ROMAN EMPIRE TO THE BRITISH EMPIRE TO THE COMBINATION OF ALL SO-CALL EUROPEANS EMPIRE AND THE AMERICAN EMPIRE TO GO FOR DICTATORSHIP PF ALL BLACKS AND DARK PEOPLE OF THE WORLD ARE ENDANGER.

BUSH SAYS HE CAN NOT TRUST SADDAM TO THE AMERICAN PEOPLE, BUT WE CAN NOT TRUST THE BUSHES AND CHENEY AND THAT INCLUDE JAMES BAKER WHO ENGINEERED THE OVERTHROW OF THE UNITED STATES CONSTITUTION AND THE CONSERVATIVE RACIST COURT APPOINTED GEORGE W. BUSH INSTEAD PF THE PERSON WHO THE AMERICAN PEOPLES CHOOSE AL GORE. GORE OVER HAD OVER A MILLION VOTES MORE THAN BUSH IN 2000 ELECTION. IF THE PEOPLE'S PRESIDENT HAD NOT BEEN PUT ASIDE IN THE NAME OF TIME LIMIT ON THE COMPLETION OF THE COUNT AND DECISION

OF THE ELECTIONS FOR PRESIDENT, THEIR WOULD NOT HAVE BEEN THE WORLD TRADE CENTER BOMBING, BECAUSE GORE WOULD NOT HAVE WALKED OUT WITH ISRAEL AND ISRAEL POSSIBLY NOT HAD WALKED OUT OF THE CONFERENCE BECAUSE GORE AND CLINTON HAD CAME THE CLOSEST AS ANYBODY TO HAVING PEACE IN THE MIDDLE EAST.

12-28-03

THE BUSHES AND CHENEY WERE NOT ELECTED IN 2000.

-NOW IS 2007 RUSSIAN PUTAN WAS ELECTED BY LIMITING THE PEOPLE OF RUSSA; S VOTE, JUST BUSH CHENEY AND WE AS AMERICAN HAVE TO NOT PERMIT ANYTHING LIKE THE 2000 PRESIDENTIAL ELECTION EVER HAPPEN AGAIN. CHINA IS STRENGTHEN CAUSE THEY KNOW WHAT DICTATORS DO AND THAT WAS THE SAME AS MUSHARRAF OF PAKISTAN DID THIS WEEK , WAS TO LIFT MARSHALL LAW, TAKE HIS ARMY UNIFORM OFF, AND DECLARED HIMSELF PRESIDENT AND BUSH CHENEY WANTED TO BOMB IRAQ , AND NOW IRAN. WE THE PEOPLE ARE IN BIG TROUBLE AND I HOPE OBAMA IS ELECTED AS WE COME DOWN TO DECEMBER 2007. MY VISION WAS CORRECT AND BUSH CHENEY SHOULD BE BROUGHT UP FOR WAR CRIMES FOR DENYING MY PEOPLE REPARATIONS

12-30-03

JOHNSTOWN, PENNSYLVANIA COUNTY REPUBLICANS PUTTING ADS TO REPLACE THE LONG TIME DEMOCRATS. THIS IS A LARGE CONSPIRACY THAT IS BEING LEAD BY THE REPUBLICAN PARTY LEAD BY VICE PRESIDENT DICK CHENEY ALL OVER AMERICA, STARTING WITH THE CALIFORNIA

RECALL OF GREG DAVIS. IT SHOULD BE AGAINST THE CONSTI-
TUTION THAT THEY ARE TRYING TO GET RID OF BECAUSE IT
IS GETTING CLOSE TO BEING A BLACK OR WOMAN BEING
PRESIDENT AND THE SO-CALL PROTECTORS OF OUR U. S.
CONSTITUTION IS NOT READY TO GIVE THE CONTROLS OVER
TO THE PEOPLE AS IT WAS ORIGINALLY SUPPOSE TO DO.

01-02-04

THE EMPIRE'S SO-CALL LEADER PRESIDENT G.W. BUSH GIVING
ACCOLADES TO ONE OF HIS GENERALS BILL FIST, CHAIR OF
THE SENATE, FOR HIS BRISANCE IN CONNING THE ARRP
PRESIDENT TO MISLEAD THE SENIORS TO BELIEVE THAT
THIS PRESIDENCY IS FOR THE SENIORS IN ORDER FOR THE
REPUBLICANS TO RAM A SO-CALL PRESCRIPTION DRUG BILL
THROUGH THE SENATE FOR THE PRESIDENT TO SIGN.

01-04-03

CBS 60 MINUTES- OVER SENTENCES FOR DRUG CASES, AND
JUDGES BY THE DOZENS ARE CRITICIZING THE MANDATORY
SENTENCES, MANDATED BY CONGRESS, THE ONE FOR THE
PEOPLE FOR THE PEOPLE, LOCK THEM UP AND THROW THE
KEY AWAY BECAUSE CITIZENS, WHITE CITIZENS ESPECIALLY.
BRENDA VALENCIA, IN FLORIDA SPRUNG THIS FOR SENTENCES.
JUDGE IN EAST SAINT LOUIS SAYS THAT HIS STATE GIVE THE
HARDEST SENTENCES IN THE COUNTRY, AND NINETY – NINE
PERCENT OF THE THEM CAN BARELY AFFORD AN ATTORNEY
AND HE HAS NOT SEEN VERY FEW KING PENS. CONGRESSMAN
GRASSLEY, THE ARIAN RACIST WHO IS DOING HIS PART IN
THIS WORLD'S GENOCIDE CONTINUES WITH THE HUMAN
RIGHTS VIOLATION SENTENCES IN THE WORLD. THE SAME

IS AS NELSON MANDELA AND HIS COMRADES, FOR FORTY YEARS OF COMPLETE TORTURE.

IT'S ALL ABOUT THE MONEY. THE LIGHTER COMPLEX TED HUMAN RULES ARE NOT TO PERMIT NO BLACK ASSES HAVE ANY OF WHAT THEY (CAVE PEOPLE) WORSHIP, CAPITAL (MONEY). SINCE THE SO-CALL EMANCIPATION PROCLAMATION THE CRACKERS SAY THEY WILL MAKE A LAW FOR ANY REASON TO KEEP SLAVE DESCENDANTS NOT TO HAVE CAPITAL, LAND, OR THE WILL TO ACHIEVE IT, SCARE YOU TO DEATH IF YOU ARE WEAK. CLOSE BARS EARLY AND THE NIGGER SUPPOSE TO GO TO SLEEP WHILE THE CRACKERS GET DRUNK, WOMEN. LYNCHING; LIKE HANGING JUDGE LYNCH, JESSICA LYNCH'S RELATIVE. THAT IS WHY SHE WAS GIVEN MILLIONS AND FREED FROM ACTIVE DUTY, RACIST GOVERNMENT AND THE WHITES IS GOING TO SUFFER BUT NOT LIKE THE BLACKS

01-09-04

PAUL O'NEILL FORMER TREASURE SECRETARY AND THE FIRST AND ONLY DESCENDANT FROM THE GEORGE W. BUSH ADMINISTRATION, SAID OF BUSH CABIN MEETINGS AS GHOST LIKE, DEAD MOST LIKELY COMICAL, ON NIGHTLY NEWS NBC. HAS BOOK OUT AND HARSH AS HE IS SUPPOSE TO BE OR IS, I BET HE DID NOT GET INTO RACISM AND THE GRAND CONSPIRACY TO BE THE GREATEST BANK ROBBER SINCE Hitler

01-13-04

CNN WOLF BLITZER'S SITUATION ROOM SHOW-GEORGE SORES, AUTHOR AND FORMER NAZI SURVIVOR STATES THAT

G.W.BUSH, PRESIDENT TEAM BUSH TALK REMIND HIM OF HITLER REGIME AND HE IS A HOLOCAUST SURVIVAL. HE HAS BOOK OUT ON THE SUBJECT. TERRY CHAIRMAN OF THE DEMOCRATS WAS ON THE SHOW WITH THE CHAIRMAN OF THE REPUBLICAN PARTY WHO IS TRYING TO TRICK THE PEOPLE AND CREATE A MILITARY STATE IN THE UNITED STATES, THE CONTINUATION OF RICHARD NIXON'S DREAM.

DAVID FRUM, AUTHOR" AN END TO EVIL' ON WOLF BLITZER, TO END EVIL BY THE DEVIL BUSH ADMINISTRATION TRYING TO CARRY THE UNITED STATES.

02-19-04

FOX NEWS –ROGER WILLIAMS UNIVERSITY'S RACE BASE SCHOLARSHIP PROGRAM IS A PERFECT EXAMPLE OF THE IMBEDDED RACISM IN AMERICA AND THROUGH OUT THE ROMAN EMPIRE PEOPLES.

PAUL BREMER, THE FRONT MAN OF THE BUSH-CHENEY IN IRAQ SPEECH TODAY. THE BUSH-CHENEY HAS KILLED OUR CITIZENS AND THE IRAQ'S FOR OIL MONEY AND RACISM THAT IS THE ROMAN EMPIRE MENTALITY. CHENEY DIRECT ALL ACTIVITIES AND DECISIONS, IS FRONTING REAL WELL BUT WATERGATE TWO IS ON IT'S WAY, IT HAS THE BUSH – CHENEY'S, SO-CALL INDEPENDENT INVESTIGATION, WE WILL SEE IF IT SHOWS BIAS TOWARD THE KILLING OF OUR CITIZENS OR WILL THEY OUTRIGHT CRITICIZE THE ADMINISTRATION ATTACKING A SOVEREIGN NATION (IRAQ) WHEN IT WAS/IS CLEAR THAT THE ONLY THREAT IRAQ WAS TO THE STATE OF ISRAEL AND IRAQ WAS UNDER NO FLY ZONE. SADDAM HAD SUPPOSED TO HAVE PUT A HIT ON HIS FORMER FRIEND AND PRESIDENT GEORGE W. H. BUSH AND CHENEY SOME TWELVE YEARS EARLIER. PAUL BREEMER NOW PUTTING OUT NEW

LIES ABOUT IRAQIS KILLING MORE TERRORIST THAN THE AMERICANS.

THIS WAR, (IRAQ), THAT THIS SILLY BUSH WANT TO GO DOWN AS A WAR PRESIDENT, PROBABLY GO DOWN AS HIS FATHER'S BOSS RICHARD NIXON, WHO STARTED THIS AMERICAN HITLER ATTITUDES ABOUT GOLD AND RACISM.

02-26-04

THE PIMP LAW, FRIENDS DOING TIME FOR THIS SAME LAW, BUT THIS TIME IT WAS USED FOR MARCUS DIXON A TEENAGE KID HAVING SEX WITH EACH OTHERS. IT SHOWS HOW LAWS ARE MADE AND IMPLEMENTED FOR THE BLACK PEOPLE. EUROPEANS KIDNAPPPED, RAPED, CHAIN, BOUND, AND KILLED MY PEOPLE AND THERE WAS NO LAW FOR IT, THEN THEY CREATE A LAW AFTER THEY HAVE DID THERE DIRT AND ESTABLISH A NEW COUNTRY ON SOMEBODY'S ELSE LAND. THEY DO NOT WANT ANY BLACK PEOPLE OWNING LAND IN AMERICA. THE SLAVE LAW AND THEY OWE US AND SO WAY HAS TO BE MADE TO PAY US LIKE THEY PAY THE IRAQ PEOPLE AND OTHERS THROUGHOUT THE TWENTY-CENTURY. GEORGIA AND OTHERS SHOULD ABOLISH THE LAW WHEN THERE IS LAWS ON THE BOOKS PERTAINING TO YOUNG PEOPLE YOUNGER THAN SIX-TEEN. TEENS NEED TO UNDERSTAND SEX AND RESPONSIBLE SEX, BECAUSE IT IS NOT EASY FOR CHILDREN TO RAISE CHILDREN JUST BECAUSE A HUMAN RELATE TO EACH OTHER SOON IN LIFE, BUT IT IS NOT ON THE FARM WHERE ONE CAN PLANT FOOD TO EAT AND LIVE IN ONE ROOM SHACKS.

OPRAH'S INTERVIEW WITH MARCUS DIXON FOR RAPE OF THIS WHITE GIRL FEBRUARY 10, 2003 AND BOTH WERE HONORABLE STUDENTS IN SCHOOL. HE WAS ACQUITTED OF

RAPE, BUT GEORGIA LAW GAVE HIM TEN YEARS FOR AGGRA-
VATED RAPE OF A MINOR, RACIST LAW FRO THE PROTEC-
TION OF WHITE GIRLS HAVING SEX WITH BLACK GUYS. THE
JURORS KNEW THAT THE WHITE GIRL WAS A LIE AND DID
NOT CONVICT, AND IF THEY KNEW THAT THE SENTENCE
WAS SO HARSH THAT THEY WOULD NOT CONVICT EVEN
FOR THAT CHARGE. THIS IS "THE AMERICAN WAY", AND
ESPECIALLY IN THE SOUTH. THE PROSECUTOR IS A BLATANT
RACIST. SCARED THAT HER FATHER WOULD FINE OUT. HER
INTERVIEW ON THE SHOW SHE SAYS SHE DOES NOT THINK
ABOUT IT AND THAT IS ANOTHER LIE.

THIS ABSOLUTELY THE SAME THING HAPPEN IN ALABAMA,
WHEN THEY CHANGED THE INGRIENCE FOR COCA- COLA.
IT WAS CHANGED BECAUSE SOME BLACK WAS HAVING SEX
WITH A WHITE GIRL AND WAS CAUGHT BY A SHERIFF. THE
MAN RAN AND THE SHERRIFF WAS SURE HE HAD SHOT THE
MAN THAT HE CONCLUDED THAT HE HAD DRUNK TOO
MANY COCA-COLA AND MADE A DEAL WITH THE COMPANY
TO CUT THE BASE OUT OF THE SOFT DRINK.

 HOWARD STERN BANNED.

THE 911 WHITE HOUSE SO-CALL COMMISSION BOB KERRY
MAY RESIGN IF NOT ABLE TO INTERVIEW THE PRESIDENT
AND THE VICE PRESIDENT CHENEY.

BRITAIN PRIME MINISTER TONEY BLAIR WAS SPYING ON THE
SECRETARY GENERAL KOFFI ANAN.

ROSIE O'DONNELL MARRIED HER LONG TIME GIRLFRIEND.
FLEW TO SAN FRANCISCO, BECAUSE OF PRESIDENT BUSH'S
PROPOSAL FOR ALTERING THE ALREADY ALTERED UNITED
STATES CONSTITUTION. ANOTHER AMENDMENT TO SPECIF-
ICALLY TO STATE THAT MARRIAGE IS BETWEEN A MAN AND

A WOMAN IS NOT FEASABLE.ROSIE AND THE ONES THAT IS LIKE HER WHETHER IT IS A MALE OR FEMALE, ARE GODS CHILDREN; BUT THEY ARE THE DEVILISH ONES (HYBRIDS), FROM ALL SPECIES INCLUDING HUMANS, THE SUPPOSE/ ARE THE SUPREME BEING, AMENDMENTS TO KEEP THE DIFFERENT HUMAN COMPLEXIONS SEPARATE. DEVILISH. THE ONLY ADMENDMENT TO THE CONSTITUTION SHOULD BE TERM LIMITS OF FEDERAL JUDGES. PROSECUTORS SHOULD NOT BE A POLICTICAL ARM OF A PRESIDENT, CAUSE CONVIC- TION STATISTICS BECOME CORRUPTION OF THE LAWS THAT THEY ARE TO UPHOLD.

THE START OF BUSH-CHENEY'S 9/11 COMMISSION ERA ENDED AND THE BUSH ADMINISTRATION DID NOT LIKE THE RECOMMENDATIONS OF THE HAMILTON BAKER LEAD COMMISSION. BUSH WANTS TO BE A DICTATOR UNDER DEMO- CRATIC LAWS. THEY DID NOT LISTEN AND BE PATIENT WHEN THE UNITED NATION COULD NOT FIND ANY WEAPONS OF MASS DESTRUCTION, AND THEY KNEW THERE WERE NONE. BUSH CHENEY DID NOT TRY TO RETALIATE AGAINST THE PEOPLE WHO WERE RESPONSIBLE FOR THE ATTACK AT THE WORLD TRADE CENTER, THEY USED THEIR AUTHORITY FROM CONGRESS TO GO INTO IRAQ ILLEGALLY, JUST AS ILLEGALLY AS HIS ADMINISTRATION BEING APPOINTED AS PRESIDENT OF THE UNITED STATES AND CALL IT DEMOCRACY.

02-26-04

THE DENIED ACCESS HAS STARTED THE SAME WAY THAT THE WATERGATE COMMISSION STARTED, RICHARD M. NIXON AND HIS MEN GEORGE W. H. BUSH, RUMSFIELD'S, BUSH 11, REAGAN AND THE OTHER DICK CHENEY. GOD BLESSES AMERICA. PERMANENT JUDGES SHOULD NOT BE PERMA-

NENT, ENGLISH LAWS, NAMES, AND HATRED FOR THE DARK COMPLEXION, NOT ALL BUT THE POWER STRUCTURE, KEEPS THE CASS SYSTEM IN TACK, IN THE NAME OF THE UNITED STATES CONSTITUTION.

THE CNN'S LARRY KING AND THE LOS ANGELES TIMES DEMOCRATIC PRESIDENTIAL DEBATE NIGHT.

PRIEST CONFESSING CHILD MOLESTATION AND HOMOSEXU-ALITY.

02-28-04

AMERICA'S MOST WANTED FEATURED THIS GARCIA GUY ON BILLBOARDS ACROSS THE AMERICA WEST, TEXAS JUSTICE, I.E. BLACK MEXICAN. KILLER, MONEY MAN AND A NIGGER TEXAS STYLE, I.E. "HANG THE NIGGER AT HE NEAREST TREE.

INJUSTICE BEING STACK BY THE REPUBLICANS INSTEAD OF HON ABLE MEN WITH A BLIND EYE TO PEOPLE AND THAT IS A DIFFICULT THING, BUT WITH SUPERIORITY COMPLEXION OF THE HUMAN RACE THE ONLY RACE OF HUMANS, VERY NARROW MINDED HUMAN'S LIGHTEST BEING. THEY THINK THEY ARE THE WIZ, ONLY WIZ IS THE GUN POWDER AND ALCOHOL TO CONQUER PEOPLE, LAND, BANKS, AND WHAT-EVER ELSE THAT MAKE THEM TRY TO CONTINUE TO FOOL ALL THE PEOPLE ALL THE TIME, JUST AS WATERGATE TO BUSH ADMINISTRATION IS ON THEIR WAY TO DOOM DAY, BECAUSE THEY DO NOT WANT TO GO TO THEIR APPOINTED COMMIS-SION WITH OUT TIME LIMITS THROUGH A BUNCH OF NEGO-TIATIONS, THAT IS NOT "THE AMERICAN WAY"; BUT IT IS THE SYSTEM OF INJUSTICE TO ALL THE AMERICAN CITIZENS WITHOUT PREJUDICE, THEY WILL DIE AND GO TO HELL, JUST

THE FORMER CENTRAL INTELLECT DIRECTOR CASEY, WHO WHEN ON TO COMMIT SUICIDE IN THE NAME OF A BRAIN TUMORS, THAT WAS THE PERFECT TIME TO DECEASE AND PROTECT THE UNITED STATES CONSTITUTION AND RONALD REAGAN'S SO –CALL THE LATEST GREAT WHITE MAN WITH BIG RED CHEEKS, SANTA CLAUSE.

02-29-04

CBS' 60 MINUTES", STORY OF NORTH KOREA'S CHILDREN, IN YOU KIM'S NORTH KOREA, HISTORY THAT IS TAUGHT TO THEIR HIGH SCHOOL STUDENTS IS THE ANN FRANK DIARY, AND THEY REALIZE HISTORY OF THE WORLD, EVEN A LITTLE UNDER CONTROL, THERE REALLY IS A TRUE DESIRE TO PULL A HITLER TYPE CONTROL OF ALL DARK COMPLETED PEOPLE, TO THE WORLD ORDER OF THE AMERICAN AND UNITED KINGDOM HAVE AND ENJOY ALL THAT IS GOOD AND THE REST TAKE THE LEFT OVERS. ONE CHILD SAID IN AMERICA THE PEOPLE ARE USED TO INCARCERATION BY THE CONTROL-LING ROMAN EMPIRE MENTALITY, THAT HITLER AND NOW BUSH – CHENEY-BLAIR THAT GIVING ORDERS TO PROTECT THE QUEEN AND THE UNITED STATES CONSTITUTION, TO KEEP ORDER FOR THE LIGHTER OF THE HUMANS.

 ALSO ON THIS SAME SHOW ABOUT THE FEDERAL BEAU OF INVESTIGATION AND THEIR WAY TO OBTAIN FALSE CONFES-SIONS FROM SO-CALL SUSPECTS.

03-01-04

TOMBSTONE IS A BIG PART THE HISTORY OF THE "AMERICAN WAY", WYATT EARP AND BAT MASTERSON IS/WAS THE LAW AND THE OUTLAW, RACIST LAWS. JESSE JAMES AND THE

CONFEDERATE FOUGHT THE RAILROAD WITH THE FORDS WHO RUNS THE WORLD TODAY. THEY ROBBED BANKS AND THEIR FAMILIES OWN ALL TYPES OF LAND AND BUSINESSES, BUT WANT TO LOOK DOWN ON A POOR PERSON TODAY. THEY WERE ALL SOUTHERN RACIST AND SO ARE MOST OF THEIR DESCENDANTS TODAY. THERE SHOULD BE NO STRIKE LAWS .

HOWARD STERN REMOVAL BY CLEAR CHANNEL, AND PRESSURED BY THE REPUBLICANS (WHITE PEOPLE PARTY), WHAT EVER HAPPEN TO THE UNITED STATES CONSTITUTION 'S FREEDOM OF SPEECH? IMAGES AND PERCEPTIONS, BY LARRY FLICK IS WHAT THE ROMAN EMPIRE IS CONTINUING AS THE "AMERICAN WAY", BY LARRY FLICK. THE BILL MAHER SHOW GUESS SAY THAT " THIS IS A NATION OF LAWS", REFERRING TO THE HOMOSEXUAL MARRIAGE FRENZY THAT IS GOING ACROSS THE NATION. THE REPUBLICANS AND THE UNITED KINGDOM CONTINUES THIS BIG BIG BIG LIE ABOUT JESUS AND HIS COMPLEXION IS STILL BEING DISTORTED,; EVEN IN THIS HUMAN MIND CONTINUALNESS OF SPACE AND SATELLITE, THAT PRODUCES DATA ACROSS THE WORLD IN SECONDS, WHICH IS CLARIFYING THE HUMAN GROWTH FROM THE DARK. GOD SAYS THAT EVERYTHING, INCLUDING THE HUMAN WAS STARTED IN THE DARK.

THIS GUY ON THE BILL MAHER SHOW SAYS, "WHY DON'T RAISE AND PAY THE TAX AND GET THE FINANCIAL PROBLEM".

RALPH NADLER WAS A GUESS ON BILL MAHER AND SAYS THAT BUSH IS JUST A BIG CORPORATE CONGLOMERATE THAT IS VERY INSENSITIVE TO THE PEOPLE OF THE UNITED STATES.

03-04-04

CNN'S WOLF BLITZER, CYNTHIA TUCKER, ATLANTA CONSTI-
TUTION, DEBATE WITH THAT LARRY ELDER, A BLACK SO-
CALL CONSERVATIVE TALK SHOW HOST IN LOS ANGELES,
THAT IS BRAIN- WASH HOUSE NIGGER IS AMAZING. "MOVE
ON. ORG", AN INDEPENDENT GROUP THAT WANTED TO RUN
THIS AD TO SHOW THESE LITTLE WHITE KIDS WORKING IN
MILLS AND FACTORIES TO PAID OFF THIS TRILLION DOLLAR
DEBT THAT THIS BUSH ADMINISTRATION IS GOING TO LEAVE
THE BABY BOOMERS, THAT IS PEOPLE LIKE ME THAT WAS
DRAFTED, UNWILLINGLY, INTO VIETNAM CONFLICT. RACIST
DAN RATHER AND THE CBS FAMILY DID NOT WANT TO
RUN THIS AD THROUGH THE SUPER BOWL. THIS THE SAME
NETWORK THAT THE REPUBLICANS PRESSURED NOT TO RUN
THE STORY OF RONALD REAGAN DURING CHRISTMAS 2003,
BECAUSE THIS ADMINISTRATION IS CRYING ON THIS SO-CALL
GREAT WHITE MAN, THAT SUPPORTED AND PRESSURED THE
SOVIET UNION TO TEAR DOWN THAT BERLIN WALL TO FREE
THE WHITE GERMANS TO ADD TO THIS UNITED EUROPE, HE
IS BETRAYED AS GREAT PRESIDENT AND ALL HE DID WAS
TO LEAVE US DEBT, JUST AS HIS SON GEORGE W. BUSH IS
INTENDING TO DO WITH US TODAY.

03-06-04

DEMOCRACY FOR THE WORLD-CHENEY-BUSH

'REVOLVE" RELIGION OF THE NEW TESTAMENT IN A BOOK,
TOA TEENAGER, WHITE TEENAGER ESPECIALLY WHITE
TEENAGERS, ABOUT ALL THE LIES THAT WENT INTO THAT
VERSION OF THE KING JAMES VERSION OF THE BIBLE, I.E. THE
ROMAN EMPIRE IS STILL ALIVE TO PROTECT THE GREATEST

LIES OF THE HUMAN RACE, THE CRUCIFIXION OF THE HOLY MESSIAH JESUS CHRIST OF BETHLEHEM.

ABC EVENING NEWS STORY ABOUT THIS AND OTHER STORIES THIS EVENING.

SOME OF THE ARTICLES AND THEIR VIEWS DOES NOT NECESSARLY BE THAT OF THIS AUTHOR.

AN ARTICLE THAT CAME OUT ON THE INTERNET TODAY-12-05-07 THAT WANT TO SHARE WITH YOU AS I EDIT SOME OF THE EVENTS AND RESPONSE TO THEM:

Before I began this post I would like to offer any one this shocking-truth

In video format by request sent to your e-mail box

Now for the post:

A Bomb Shell

This work is a revelation of the Africans who wrote the theosophical

Documents that became the Christian Bible of ancient Greece, Europe, and the world.

For over two thousand years, the world has known and credited the Jewish people

As the creators of the foundational concepts and documents that became the doctrines

Of Judaism for Jews, Christianity for the Europeans, and Islam for the Arabs.

However, few people have gone beyond this knowledge to verify whether it is true

That the Jewish people created the foundational concepts, doctrines, and documents

In the Bible or not.

One of the most simple arguments supporting the fact that the Jewish

People did not write create the ideas or write the documents of the Bible is their

Inability to tell the world where and how these documents originated. Another is their

Inability to tell the world who truly wrote these documents besides the false authors

They assigned to the documents.

As a major part of the revelation in this work therefore, I would like to establish that

The Jewish people did not create the foundational concepts or the theosophical

Documents that became the foundations of world religions.

WOW! NOW THAT'S A MAJOR BOMB!

With that in mind I'm forced to dig for myself and this is what I found.

The Christian dispensation is believed to have been ushered in by the birth of a child, and the portrait of that child in the Roman Catacombs as the child of Mary is the youthful Sun-God in the Mummy

Image of the child-king, the Egyptian Karast, or Christ. The alleged facts of our Lord's life as Jesus the Christ, were equally the alleged facts of our Lord's life as the Horus of Egypt, whose very name signifies the Lord. ... The Jesus Christ with female paps, who is the Alpha and Omega of Revelation, was the Iu of Egypt, and Iao of the Chaldeans. Jesus as the Lamb of God, and Ichthys the Fish, was Egyptian. Jesus as the Coming One; Jesus born of the Virgin Mother, who was overshadowed by the Holy Ghost, Jesus born of two mothers, both of whose names are Mary; Jesus born in the manger—at Christmas, and again at Easter; Jesus saluted by the three kings, or Magi; Jesus of the transfiguration on the Mount; Jesus whose symbol in the Catacombs is the eight-rayed Star—the Star of the East; Jesus as the eternal Child; Jesus as God the Father, re-born as his own Son; Jesus as the child of twelve years; Jesus as the Anointed One of thirty years; Jesus in his Baptism; Jesus walking on the Waters, or working his Miracles; Jesus as the Caster-out of demons; Jesus as a Substitute, who suffered in a vicarious atonement for sinful men; Jesus whose followers are the two brethren, the four fishers, the seven fishers, the twelve apostles, the seventy (or seventy-two in some texts) whose names were written in Heaven; Jesus who was administered to by seven women; Jesus in his bloody sweat; Jesus betrayed by Judas; Jesus as Conqueror of the grave; Jesus the Resurrection and the Life; Jesus before Herod; in the Hades, and in his re-appearance to the women and to the seven fishers; Jesus who was crucified both on the 14th and 15th of the month Nisan; Jesus who was also crucified in Egypt (as it is written in Revelation); Jesus as judge of the Dead, with the sheep on the right, and the goats on the left, is Egyptian from first to last, in every phase from the beginning to the end

Many other historians make the same claim that Jesus Christ was An African (Egyption)

Concept taken from the tombs of north Africa.

Moses, does not acknowledge Jesus as a true participant in the concept and reality of God. As a result, there is no New Testament in the Hebrew Bible. It can be found only in the protestant and catholic Bibles.

According to Kersey Graves author of the book The Worlds 16 Crucified Saviors Jesus Christ had the same attributes as many other created Gods thousands of years before him

For researches into oriental history reveal the remarkable fact that stories of incarnate Gods answering to and resembling the miraculous character of Jesus Christ have been prevalent in most if not all the principal religions heathen nations of antiquity; and the accounts and narrations of some of these deific incarnations bear such a striking resemblance to that of the Christian Savior -- not only in their general features, but in some cases in the most minute details, from the legend of the immaculate conception to that of the crucifixion, and subsequent ascension into heaven -- that one might almost be mistaken for the other.

YES BUT WHAT DIFFERENCE DOES IT MAKE, CAN BELIEVEING IN JESUS CHRIST HURT ME OR MY FAMILY ?

IN CONCLUSION:

This topic was bought up because absolutely critical to the white supremacy system of religious thought was the formation of the image of a white man as the "son" of God.

This white male image then was referred to as" Christ"

the brain-computer functions most fundamentally on logic circuits, at deep unconscious levels it automatically computes that God, the father, is also a white male.

If God is other than white, he would have produced a Black (or other non-white) son.

Thus, any person programmed to accept the Christian religion, whether conscious of it or

Not, has the image and concept of God as a white man in the logic network of his/her brain-computer.

Bottom of Form

WE SHALL CONTINUE THE ORIGINAL MANUSCRIPT:

03-07-04

CBS"60 MINUTES" THE MOST OPEN GAY (HOMOSEXUAL) PRIEST GENE ROBINSON AND IS MARRIAGE TO A WOMAN IN AMERICA, THE MAIN REASON FOR ALL THE GAY MARRIAGES IS THE CATHOLIC CHURCH. THE ROMAN EMPIRE BIG LIE THAT SO-CALL SAINT AUGUSTINE, WHOM LAID DOWN THE CLERIC LAW.

CONSPIRACY LAW IS A BUNCH OF PSYCHOLOGY THAT UNFAIRLY AND SHOULD BE CONSIDERED ILLEGAL. THE WAY THAT I WAS RAISED, IS THAT I DO NOT BELIEVE ANYTHING I HEAR, AND HALF OF WHAT I SEE. SO IF YOU TELL ME THAT YOU WANT TO WHIP SOMEBODY'S ASS, THAT IS A CONSPIRACY TO HARM, BUT TO WHAT EXTENT I.E. IF YOU ACTUALLY DO BEAT SOMEBODY UP, THEN YOU HAVE COMMITTED A CRIME OF ASSAULT OR MAYBE TO PROTECT YOURSELF AS SELF DEFENSE; BUT TO THINK, SAY, BOSE, THAT YOU HAVE INTENTION OF COMMITTING A CRIME IS NOT ILLEGAL.

03-12-04

THE PEOPLE THAT STOP WORSHIPING DIFFERENT FALSE IDOLS, THE SUN, COW, AND STARTED FOLLOWING THE WORD OF JESUS IN EGYPT, AND THE RELIGION WAS ISLAM, NOT TO WORSHIP HIM OR NO MAN, WORSHIP GOD THE CREATOR OF THE HEAVENS AND EARTH. THE SAME ONES THAT ORDERED THE CAPTURE AND CRUCIFIXION OF JESUS, THE ROMANS, WOULD SENT PAUL BACK AND FORTH TO ROME TO KEEP THEM ABREAST OF THEIR COLONY AS JESUS BELIEVERS LIVE AND PAST ON THE WORD OF GOD THROUGH JESUS OF NAZARETH. THE ROMANS DESTROYED JESUS IMAGE INSTEAD OF THE WORD OF GOD. JESUS SAID THAT THEY WOULD LIE AND THEY LIED, AND THEY ARE STILL LYING WITH PASSION. MEL GIBSON'S NEW MOVIE ABOUT THE SUBJECT ' PASSION', IS PERFECT PROOF THAT THE IMAGES AND THE TRUE WORDS OF GOD THROUGH THE HOLY MESSIAH JESUS WILL BE CONTINUED DISTORTED BY THE DESCENDANTS OF THE GREEK AND THE ROMANS.

03-14-04

ALL WEEK THE DICTATORS (WHITE PEOPLES PARTY), RICHARD M. NIXON'S OUTLOOK, RACIST PHILOSOPHY, AND OUTRIGHT BRAIN WASH ALL WHITE PEOPLE TO APPLY LAWS, WHETHER NEEDED OR NOT, DOES MAKE A DIFFERENCE JUST TO KEEP THE STATUS QUO IN THE AMERICAN CASS SYSTEM, I. E. SEPARATE BUT EQUAL, BUT IT DOWN TO OUTRIGHT BLATANT DESTRUCTION OF ALL THE PEOPLE OF COLOR, YOU HAVE TO REMEMBER THAT NIXON WAS PUSHING THE ALMIGHTY UNITED STATES SUPREME JUSTICES TO MAKE LAWS FOR A NATION POLICE FORCE THAT THE FUTURE DICTATOR WILL

NEED TO RETURN TO SLAVERY OR DEATH UNDER THE UNITED STATES MILITARY ORDERS.

THE BUSH ADMINISTRATION IS NOT TALKING ABOUT RACIAL PROFILING OF THE DESCENDANTS OF AMERICAN FORCE LABOR (SLAVERY), BECAUSE THEY DO NOT EVER RECOGNIZE AND PAY MONIES TO THE DIRECT DESCENDANTS OF SLAVES; WHERE AS, WILLIAM JEFFERSON CLINTON, THE PREVIOUS ADMINISTRATION WERE TURNING TO GIVE A LITTLE CONFIDENCE TO PEOPLE, EVEN THOUGH HE WAS RAISED AS A WHITE SUPREMIST, HE BECAME EDUCATED AND SAW THE LIGHT TO MAKE A DIFFERENCE FROM HIS SLAVE MASTER'S ANCESTORS TREATMENT OF THE KIDNAPPED AFRICANS AS HUMAN LIFE AND SEGREGATION AFTER THE EMACIPATION PROCLAMATION. BUSH AND CLINTON'S ANCESTORS DID NOT HAVE, NOR DO MOST OF THEM HAVE THE HEART TO INSTITUTE REPARATIONSTODAY IN BOTH HOUSES OF CONGRESS. ALL OF THE GRAND DRAGONS ARE THERE, IN THE NAME OF THE LAW. ALL YOU HAVE TO DO IS GO BACK TO THE WESTERN MOVIES, AND THAT IS PURELY DOCUMENTAL OF THESE SO –CALL ANGLO-SAXTON LAWS, AND THEY "HANG THE NIGGER AT THE NEAREST TREE" IS ALSO PRESIDENT GEORGE W. BUSH'S FAVORITE LINE, "GIVE THEM TEXAS JUSTICE. HE USED IT MENTALLY, AND AFTER THE AFTERMATH THE WORLD TRADE CENTER DISASTER, AND I STRONGLY BELIEVE THAT THEY INSTITUTED THE ENVIRONMENT FOR THIS HORRIBLE LOST OF LIFE AND ATTACK ON US AFTER WALKING OUT OF THE WORLD SUMMIT IN SOUTH AFRICA IN 2001.

 IT ALL STARRED WITHIN THE FIRST MONTH AFTER INAUGURATION, THEY DROPPED BOMBS ON A SOVEREIGNS NATION (IRAQ) AND WALKED OUT OF THE WHOLE WORLD NATIONS RACIAL CONFERENCE WITH THE RACIST ISRAELITES. THE

IRAQ WAR WAS FOR HIS FATHER'S FAILED ASSASSINATION, BY SADDAM AND TO RELIEVE THE MAJOR TREAT TO ISRAEL. THE SOVIET JEW BELIEVERS WAS FLOWN OUT OF THE SOVIET UNION AND PLACED ON PALESTINIAN'S LAND AND OTHER LAWS THAT WAS CONQUERED THROUGH THE WAR GAME. IT IS, OR SHOULD BE THE MOST OUTRIGHT HUMAN RIGHTS VIOLATIONS, WHICH BUSH-CHENEY PEOPLES DO NOT RESPECT NOR GIVE DAM WHAT YOU, ME, OR NO OTHER BLACK ASSES LIVING THINK. BUSH – CHENEY ARE THE REAL TERRORIST OF MANY NATIONS, FOR MANY MILLENNIUMS, AND THIS PIECE OF DOCUMENT, THE UNITED STATES CONSTI-TUTION, HAS TO DEFEAT THESE CROOKED BUSH ADMINIS-TRATION EVER IN THE HISTORY OF THESE UNITED STATES.

ALL WEEK THEY (REPUBLICANS PARTY) HAS BEEN TRYING TO GET HIM TO APOLOGIZE, FOR SAYING THAT THEY SHOULD GO UP FOR IMPEACHMENT, NOT THEY CRYING FOUL AND I AM ELATED THAT JOHN KERRY HAS ENOUGH BALLS TO STAND UP AND FIGHT THESE DEVILS THAT IS TRYING TO CONTINUE TO RUIN THIS COUNTRY'S PROGRESS OF RACIAL TORRANCE. ALL THEY WANT IS TO STACK THE COURTS WITH BIAS, RACIST, AND CORRUPT JUDGES THAT WILL KEEP EVERY-THING IN LOCAL COURTS, BECAUSE THEY HAVE A SAYING IN LOCAL COURTS TO KEEP GOVERNMENT OUT, IN ORDER FOR THEM TO KEEP THEIR DESCENDANT OF SLAVE POPULATION BLIND AND UNEDUCATED. THEY DO NOT WANT ANY JUDGES (LIBERAL) MAKING LAWS, JUST WANT THEM TO FOLLOW THE EXISTING LAWS, NOW IT DOES NOT SEEMS LIKE DEMOCRACY TO PEOPLE LIKE ME, WHO HAS FOUGHT IN THE VIETNAM WAR AND PEOPLE WANT TO DISCARD THAT UNNECESSARY CONFLICT, THAT HAS A GRANITE WALL IN WASHINGTON, D.C., OF ALL THE LIVES THAT WAS LOST, LIKE THEY ARE TRYING TO DO WITH SLAVERY. SENATOR TRENT LOTT AND OTHERS WISH THAT JIM CROW LAWS WERE STILL IN EFFECT.

THEY HOPE THAT THERE WILL NEVER BE A SURPLUS FOR REPARATION FOR THE DEPRIVED PEOPLE OF GOD, WHO ARE THE DESCENDANT OF SLAVES THAT WAS AND STILL ARE BEING MISTREATED TODAY. THAT THE FUTURE GENERATION OF DESCENDANTS OF SLAVES NOT TO PUSH THERE BUTTONS FOR MONIES OWED FOR OVER A CENTURY, IT IS NOT THAT YOU HAVE MONIES OF YOUR OWN SHOULD NOT HAVE ANYTHING TO DO WITH THE DEBT THAT THE UNITED STATES GOVERNMENT OWN TO THE DIRECT DESCENDANTS OF SLAVES. THERE SHOULD BE AN ADMENDMENT TO THE UNITED STATES CONSTITUTION FOR THIS PURPOSE OF THE UNITED STATES LOST PEOPLE, WHO ARE CONSTANTLY FILLING THE PRISONS OF THE COUNTRY, INSTEAD OF BEING EDUCATED AS THE WHITE PEOPLE WHO PAY THE MOST TAXES GETS THE LARGER PIECE OF THE PIE. THE UNITED STATES GOVERNMENT AND IT'S LARGEST CORPORATION HAS TO SUBMIT TO THIS EFFORT. IF WE BRING A LAW SUIT FOR THE BROKEN PROMISE THAT WAS THE LAW OF THE LAND, AND THERE SHOULD NOT BE ANY TYPE OF STATUE OF LIMITATIONS, CAUSE THAT WILL NOT SOLVE OUR PROBLEMS IN AMERICA, EVEN THOUGH, WE HAVE CAME A LONG WAY ON OUR OWN, BUT THE PRISONS ARE FULL OF IGNORANCE AND HOPE GOD CAN SET MY DISPLACED PEOPLE.

THE REPUBLICANS SCARED AL GORE TO DEATH WITH THE BIG RAT COMMERCIAL AND HE NEVER RECOVERED AFTER THAT, EVEN THOUGH, HE DID WIN THE POPULAR VOTE. HE DID NOT HAVE THE BALLS TO FIGHT CHENEY-BUSH'S GANG. THE SIGNIFICANCE OF THE COMMERCIAL AD WAS THAT HE WAS A NIGGER LOVING BIG RAT, AND HE DID NOTHING. HIS FELLOW TENNESEE SENATOR FRED THOMPSON GAVE HIS OWN STATE TO BUSH, THEN THEY SAID GOOD BYE "NIGGER LOVERS".WE HAVE OUR WHITE HOUSE PURELY WHITE,

GENERAL COLIN POWELL AND DOCTOR CONDOLISA RICE DO NOT COUNT.

CHENEY-BUSH IS TRYING TO LIMIT AND STONE WALL HIS APPOINTED COMMISSION TO INVESTIGATE THE WORLD TRADE CENTER DISASTER, BY HAVING SOME TYPE OF TIME LIMIT FOR THE AMERICAN PEOPLE AND THE ROMAN AND JEWISH NEWS MEDIA IS RIGHT ALONG WITH THE WHITE PEOPLE'S PARTY, BUT LIKE I SAID AFTER THE ENRON SHREDDING TO PROTECT THE CHENEY- BUSH FAMILY PEOPLE FROM BEING APART OF THIS HORRIBLE ROBBERY, THEY SHOULD BE IMPEACHED. TRICKY DICK CHENEY IS IN CONTROL, BUT WATERGATE TWO IS ON IT'S WAY, AND ESPECIALLY IF FOR SOME UNFORTUNATE WAY THAT THEY BECOME ELECTED AGAIN, MAY GOD BLESS AMERICA IF THAT HAPPENS, BECAUSE I FEEL THAT DICTATORSHIP WILL BE THE LAW OF THE LAND. THEY WILL ROB ALL KNOWN BANK ACCOUNTS, AS THEY ARE DURING NOW WITH THE UNITED STATES OF AMERICA'S TREASURY MONIES, THAT IS IN THE FEDERAL RESERVE AND IN WALL STREET SCAMS OF FUNDS, I .E. THE WORKERS WORKED FOR NOTHING, THE BIGGEST TRICK OF THE TRICKY DICKS OF AMERICA.

ARIAN SHARON, PRIME MINISTER OF ISRAEL'S CHIEF ADVISOR GRISS, WANTS TO CONTINUE BLAMING THE PALENTINANS WHO ARE THE DISTORTED, DISENFRANCHISED, ROBBED OF THEIR LANDS, AND NOW THEY ARE BLAMED TO BLOCK THIS S0-CALL ROAD MAP TO PEACE, BY BUSH CHENEY ADMINISTRATION IS THE MOST KLU KLUX KLANIST AND NAZIS ATTITUDE THAT YOU CAN THINK OR SPEAK OF, I E. YOU LOOKED AT A WHITE BITCH, UNDER JIM CROW LAWS OF SOUTHERN STATES AND THEY HANG YOUR BLACK SOLE, "TEXAS JUSTICE".

" STOP THE TERRORIST THE MAN SAID THIS MORNING, ON CNN'S RELIABLE SOURCES, COME IN WITH ALL YOUR GUNS AND WEAPONS, TAKE ALL OF OUR MONIES, RAPE OUR WOMEN, TAKE YOUR LAND, AND THEN CALL YOU THE TERRORIST. THEY ARE THE GOVERNMENT SUPPOSE TO BE FOR THE PEOPLE OF THESE UNITED STATES, BUT AFRICAN-AMERICANS IN SLAVERY WERE NOT CONSIDERED HUMAN; THEREFORE, YOU WERE NOT CONSIDERED PEOPLE AND THEIR ANCESTORS, IN POWER OF THE GOVERNMENT LIVES TO KEEP THAT STATUS QUO, NO MATTER WHAT. CIVIL CHAOS AND DESTRUCTION OF PEOPLE OF COLOR, IN THE NAME OF LAW, BIAS AND CORRUPT LAWS THAT WILL READ, MONEY OR NO MONEY YOU ARE A DARKIE; THEREFORE YOU DO NOT MATTER. THE MONIES THAT THE REPUBLIC SPENT FOR THEIR LIES TO HARASS AND TRICKED THE DEMOCRATS TO HOLD IMPEACHMENT HEARINGS FOR WILLIAM JEFFERSON CLINTON, JUST AS HIS FORE FATHER THOMAS JEFFERSON, FOR HAVING A SEX ACT IN THE WHITE HOUSE, WILL YOU PLEASE EXPLAIN WHEN DID THE WHITE PEOPLES WHITE HOUSE WORRY ABOUT SEX ACTS? REMEMBER WHAT THE FROMER BRITISH SUBJECTS DID TO THE AMERICAN INDIANS, SOUTH AFRICANS, AND ABAREGIAN OF AUSTRALIANS. WE AS A NATION SUPPORT THIS BECAUSE THIS HOW WE ARE THE UNITED STATES AND THEY TOOK OUR HOME LAND IN AFRICA, AND THEY DO NOT WANT TO PAY. WANT BUILD WALLS ACROSS THE SOUTHERN BORDER TO KEEP HUMANS FROM ROAMING THEIR ANCESTOR'S LAND. WE IMPORT THE EASTERN EUROPEANS AFTER REAGAN HELP TORN DOWN THE BERLIN WALL AND CANNOT ALLOW THE MEXICANS TO COME ACROSS THE RIO GRAND. TEXAS, ARIZONA, AND CALIFORNIA ARE ALL MEXICO.

ON WOLF BLAZER TODAY DONALD RUMS FIELD TALK ABOUT HUMAN RIGHTS, HOW CAN HE USE THOSE WORDS AFTER

HE AND JOHN ASHCROFT ARE TAKING PEOPLE ACROSS OCEANS TO CONTAIN THEM IN CUBA, NO RIGHTS, NO ATTORNEYS, JUST EXISTING, AND HE WANT TO MENTION THOSE WORDS.

CBS' 60 MINUTES, UNSAFE PRESCRITION DRUG LIE THAT TRENT LOTT AND THE REST OF THE WHITE PEOPLE'S PARTY, BECAUSE THE AMERICAN SENIORS GO TO CANADA AND MEXICO TO BUY DRUGS. THEY DO NOT GET THE MONEY FROM THE SENORS, AND MULTIMILLION DOLLARS TO THE PHARMACIES FROM THE GOVERNMENT. THEY ARE EXTORTING THE CANADA'S DOCTORS AND THEIR PHARMACIES. THE FEDERAL DRUG ADMINISTRATION HAS ORDERS FROM GEORGE W. BUSH'S ADMINISTRATION ORDERS CONGRESS TO PROPOSE HELP TO PROTECT THE CITIZENS. BUSH'S MEDICARE PROPOSE BILL GIVES MEDICARE TO KEEP THE SENIORS PAYING THEIR MONIES, CONGRESSMAN BURTON ON THE SHOW SAYS THAT THE PRESIDENT RECEIVED MONIES AND OTHER PERKS.

03-17-04

DICK CHENEY'S IRAQ WAR, THAT HAS KILLED SIX HUNDRED AMERICANS AND COUNTING. DICK IN CALIFORNIA GROOMING GOVERNOR ARNOLD SCHWARZNEGGER, THE EUROPEAN BORN GOVERNOR OF CALIFORNIA, SPOKE ON THE TERRIBLE BLAST, THAT BROUGHT DOWN THE LEBANON HOTEL IN BAGHDAD, IRAQ, THE TERRORISTS WILL NOT DISCOURAGE AMERICANS FROM ROBBING THE PEOPLE OF IRAQ OF IT'S OIL AND FINANCES. IT IS A SHAME AND ESPECIALLY WHEN IRAQ WAS NOT A THREAT TO US AMERICANS, CALLING PEOPLE THUGS, BECAUSE THEY (WHITE FOLKS) USED TO CALL MY PEOPLE THE SAME, WHEN THEY MOVED

INTO SO-CALL WHITE NEIGHBORHOODS ACROSS AMERI-
CANS. HE IS ANGRY, UPSET, AND ALL HIS NIXON RACIST
ATTITUDES ARE OUT HE CAN NOT STAY IN THE VICE PRESI-
DENTIAL ROLE CAUSE, BUDDY BOY BUSH CAN NOT HANDLE
THE CRITICISM ABOUT A WAR HE ONLY WANTED TO DO WAS
TO KILL SADDAM FOR HIS FATHER.

POLYGAMY RELATIONSHIPS THAT IS MARRYING TEENAGERS,
YET THEY WANT TO GIVE TEN YEARS HARD TIME TO PIMPS
AND TEENAGERS THAT HAS SEX, BUT IN UTAH SEX WITH
FAMILY MEMBERS, "THE AMERICAN WAY ", TWO SEPARATE
LAWS FOR THE PEOPLE OF AMERICA. THE SCAR BOUGH
SHOW ON CNN'S NIGHT SHOW, WITH JESSICA WHO ESCAPE
WITH TWO TEENAGER GIRLS BEFORE THEY ARE FIFTEEN
AND READY TO PRODUCE CHILDREN FOR THE WHITE RACE,
WARREN HATCH, SENATOR FOR THE GREAT STATE OF UTAH
IS THE UNDIVIDED LEADER

03-28-04

RICHARD CLARK SAID THAT HE KNEW THAT BUSH'S DOG
WAS SENT OUT TO DEMORALIZE HIM FOR NOT BEING LOYAL
TO THE REPUBLICANS. RICHARD CLARK IS LOYAL TO THE
AMERICAN CONSTITUTION AND LET THE CHIPS FALL WHERE
THEY MAY. SECRECY IS WHAT THE SOVIET UNION AND
HITLER'S GERMANY WAS ABOUT. BILL FRIST, THE MAJORITY
LEADER OF THE SENATE, IS CONSTITUTIONAL. ONE OF THE
DOGS OUT TOO PROTECT THE LIE INSTEAD OF THE UNITED
STATES

THE AMERICAN WAY

03-20-04

CHENEY-BUSH STILL IS STONE WALLING THE AMERICAN PEOPLE IN THE NAME OF THE UNITED STATES CONSTITUTION, IN THE NAME OF PARTY LOYALTY INSTEAD OF FOR THE PEOPLE BY THE PEOPLE. THEY SHOULD BE IMPEACHING FOR THE CONTINUED DESPAIR AND THE OUT RIGHT ROBBERY OF THE FEDERAL RESERVE. SILVERADO AND HALLIBURTON ARE JUST THE START AND HOPEFULLY THE LAST PUBLIC ROBBERY I.E. CRIME DOES PAID.

THE 2004 RELEASE OF MOVIE ABOUT WOMEN SUFFRAGE AND WOODROW WILSON'S PRESIDENCY, THE MOVIE" IRON JAWED ANGELS" BY HILLARY SWANK, IS EXCELLENT PORTRAYER OF THE MOVEMENT OF WHITE WOMEN FOR ALL WOMEN, EVEN

THOUGH BLACKS, MEN OR WOMEN, COULD NOT VOTE. IF
EVER ANY PEOPLE OF COLOR GAIN A MAJORITY OR ATTEMPT
TO CLAIM A MAJORITY OF THE UNITED STATES POPULA-
TION, THERE WILL BE A WHITE DICTATOR AND THERE IS NO
NATION WILL BE ABLE TO COME TO THE RESCUE THE BLACKS,
INDIANS, AND THE MEXICAN FROM BEING SENT BACK TO
THE PLANTATION. FOR SOME THEY ARE ON A PLANTA-
TION TODAY WITH SLAVE WAGES. TO HAVE A SYSTEM THAT
WHITE FARMER GET ALL THE SUBSIDIES FROM THE GOVERN-
MENT, AND CONTINUE TO IGNORE THE AFRICAN- AMER-
ICAN FARMERS. THE BLACK FARMERS PROTEST IN GEORGE
WASHINGTON CITY AND CONGRESS IGNORE THEM AND
THERE WAGONS IN THE STREETS, BECAUSE IF CONGRESS
DOES NOT GIVE THEM A PIECE OF THE FARMERS HAND TO
THE WHITE FARMER THE FARM AND THEIR CHILDREN GOES
UNDER,THEN THE WHITE FOLKS CAN BUY UP THEIR LANDS
TO BUILD SUBDIVISIONS AND APARTMENTS IN THE NAME OF
GENERATING GROWTH IN THIS ECONOMY. THE AMERICAN
WAY.

AMERICA IS SENDING THE UNEDUCATED DESCENDANTS OF
SLAVES TO PRISONS AS YOUNG ADULTS. THERE FAMILIES ARE
THE VICTIMS OF THE AMERICAN SLAVE SYSTEM AND ARE
HANDED DOWN SECOND HAND HOMES, PROJECTS THAT
WERE BUILT TO ACCOMADATE THE FROMER SLAVES AND
SHARECROPPERS AFTER THEY WERE SUPPOSE TO BE FREE.
MOST STAYED BECAUSE THEY DID NOT HAVE ANYWHERE
TO GO TO RAISE THEIR CHILDREN AND MANY WERE ELDERS
THAT WORK FROM SUN UP TO SUN DOWN, JUST TO LIVE
ON THE SLAVE MASTER'S FARM AFTER THE EMANCIPA-
TION PROCAMATION. WHITE AMERICA TAKE ANY WHITE
FAMILY AND TAKE CARE OF THEM AS LONG AS THEY WERE
NOT JEWS.PUTTING THEM IN GENERAL AMERICAN PRISON
POPULATION AND OUT OF SIGHT AND OUT OF MIND TO THE

REGULAR POPULATION OF THE UNITED STATES AND THE WORLD.

NOW DAYS WHITE AMERICANS TALKS OF A REVOLVING DOOR AND THE WHITE COURTS RECOGNIZED ANY WHITE KID WHO MIGHT GET LOCKED –UP WITH AN ENGLISH NAME THEN MOSTLY LIKELY THEY WILL BE RELEASED, AND AN EX-SLAVE WITH HIS SLAVE MASTER'S NAME, THE JUDGE OF THE COURT KNOWS HE IS A FROM SLAVE OF THIS PLANTA-TION OR THAT PLANTATION, THE SENTENCING OF PETTY CRIMES AND GIVEN LIFE SENTENCES, NO MATTER HOW MANY TIMES THE IGNORANCE OF SLAVERY DESCENDANT CHILDREN SHOULD BE A HUMAN RIGHTS VIOLATION, BUT WHO WILL ENFORCE THAT IF THE AMERICAN POLITICANS DO NOT FESS –UP, BUT WANT TO SEND UNTOLD BILLION OF CASH AMERICAN DOLLARS TO IRAQ FOR THE LIES OF THE BUSH ADMINISTRATION. THIS AN AMERICAN THING AND THE YOUNG AMERICAN POLITICANS HAS TO MAKE THIS A PART OF THE UNITED STATES BUDGET, THEN BELIEVE CRIME WILL GO DOWN AND DOWN. EDUCATE FROM BIRTH UNTIL COLLEGE, TUTORS AND WHATEVER ELSE IS NEEDED, AND WE CAN DO THIS , JUST LOOK AT THE TAX REBATE AND ALL OF BILLION THAT HAS BEEN SENT TO IRAQ, NO TO MENTION AFGANISTAN, WHERE WE SHOULD HAVE STAYED, BUT A WANT TO BE WAR PRESIDENT WITH RIGHTWING CONGRESS THAT SHOULD BE ASHAME OF THEMSELVES TO HURT AMERICA JUST NOT TO SUPPORT REPARATION TO THE PEOPLE OF THE UNITED STATES. OUR ANCESTORS DID NOT ASK TO COME TO AMERICA, THEY WERE KIDNAPPED AND KILLED TO BE SOLD INTO BONDAGE, AND NOT KIDNAPPING IS A SERIOUS CRIME BECAUSE THEY DO NOT WANT TO BE KIDNAPPED TODAY. MOST WHITES DID NOT HAVE AN EDUCA-TION, SO YOU CAN BET THE BLACKS OF THE UNITED STATES SLAVERY DID NOT AND COULD NOT TEACH THEIR CHIL-

DREN EITHER. AMERICA OWES US AND IT IS TIME FOR SOME TYPE OF REPARATIONS TO RECTIFY THE HARM DONE TO THE DESCENDANTS OF THE UNITED STATES SLAVE SYSTEM, AS THEY HAVE DONE TO THE JAPANESE, KOREANS, INDIANS, AND WE NEED TO BE COMPENSATED. WITH THE REPUBLICANS IN POWER OUR CHANCES ARE A LITTLE SLIM, BUT IT IS TIME FOR THOSE RACIST CHILDREN TO COME ON BOARD IN THIS TECHNOLOGY SOCIETY.

BLACK FARMERS

SENATOR WIFE WAS ENGINEER FOR THE SUFFRAGE MOVEMENT AND HE TURNED AGAINST HER, BUT DID NOT STOP HER FROM GOING TO JAIL AND MAKING HISTORY FOR THE WHITE WOMEN AFTER THE AMENDMENT TO ABOLISH SLAVERY ON THE BOOKS, BUT NOT ACTUALITY. NOW BUSH-CHENEY WANT TO BRAIN WASH CONGRESSIONAL OF CONGRESS TO AMENDMENT THE CONSTITUTION OF THE UNITED STATES, FOR GAY MARRIAGES, CRACKERS.

THE AMERICAN WAY

03-20-04

CHENEY-BUSH STILL IS STONE WALLING THE AMERICAN PEOPLE IN THE NAME OF THE UNITED STATES CONSTITUTION, IN THE NAME OF PARTY LOYALTY IN STEAD OF FOR THE PEOPLE BY THE PEOPLE. THEY SHOULD BE IMPEACHING FOR THE CONTINUED DESPAIR AND THE OUT RIGHT ROBBERY OF THE FEDERAL RESERVE. SILVERADO AND HALLIBURTON ARE JUST THE START AND HOPEFULLY THE LAST PUBLIC ROBBERY I.E. CRIME DOES PAID.

THE 2004 RELEASE OF MOVIE ABOUT WOMEN SUFFRAGE AND WOODROW WILSON'S PRESIDENCY, THE MOVIE" IRON JAWED ANGELS" BY HILLARY SWANK, IS EXCELLENT PORTRAYER OF THE MOVEMENT OF WHITE WOMEN FOR ALL WOMEN, EVEN THOUGH BLACKS, MEN OR WOMEN, COULD NOT VOTE. IF

EVER ANY PEOPLE OF COLOR GAIN A MAJORITY OR ATTEMPT TO CLAIM A MAJORITY OF THE UNITED STATES POPULATION, THERE WILL BE A WHITE DICTATOR AND THERE IS NO NATION WILL BE ABLE TO COME TO THE RESCUE THE BLACKS, INDIANS, AND THE MEXICAN FROM BEING SENT BACK TO THE PLANTATION. FOR SOME THEY ARE ON A PLANTATION TODAY WITH SLAVE WAGES. TO MAKE SOME WHITE FARMER GET ALL THE SUBSIDIES FROM THE GOVERNMENT CONTINUE TO IGNORE THE AMERICAN FARMERS, WHERE THE WHITE FOLKS CAN BUY UP THEIR LANDS TO BUILD SUBDIVISIONS AND APARTMENTS IN THE NAME OF GENERATING GROWTH IN THIS ECONOMY.

BLACK FARMERS

A SENATOR WIFE WAS ENGINEER FOR THE SUFFRAGE MOVEMENT AND HE TURNED AGAINST HER, BUT DID NOT STOP HER FROM GOING TO JAIL AND MAKING HISTORY FOR THE WHITE WOMEN, AFTER THE AMENDMENT TO ABOLISH SLAVERY ON THE BOOKS, BUT NOT ACTUALITY. NOW BUSH-CHENEY WANT TO BRAIN WASH CONGRESS TO AMENDMENT THE CONSTITUTION OF THE UNITED STATES, FOR GAY MARRIAGES, CRACKERS.

03-28-04 CONTINUE

FBI FILES ON JOHN KERRY AND THE REPUBLICANS OF THE VIETNAM ERA HAS BEEN STOLEN GERALD NICOSIA, OF SAN FRANCISCO, HOME WAS PROFESSIONALLY BURGLARIZED, ACCORDINGLY TO CNN WEB PAGE TODAY.

A PROSECUTOR RECOMMENDS THAT ISRAEL'S PRIME MINISTER TO BE INDICTED FOR BRIBERY. IS IT NEW ELECTION

TIME FOR DICK CHENEY'S RACIST PARTNER IN INHUMAN SITUATION AGAINST THE DARK PEOPLE OF THE WORLD?

AZIZE RANTISI, OF PALESTINIAN'S HAMAS, SPEAKING AT THE UNIVERSITY, SAYS THAT BUSH IS THE ENEMY OF GOD. THE VETOED A RESOLUTION IN THE UNITED NATION THAT CONDEMNED ISRAEL FOR Its LATEST ATTACK,

THIS IS WHAT I WAS SAYING PREVIOUSLY ABOUT THE CAUSE OF THE SEPTEMBER 11, 2001 WORLD TRADE CENTER CREMATION. THEY VETOED IT AGAINST THE AMERICAN PEOPLE'S WISHES. SHARON AND CHENEY BROUGHT ALL THESE ENEMIES AGAINST US AS A NATION, THESE TWO SHOULD BE BROUGHT UP ON WAR CRIMES BY UNNECESSARY BOMBING IRAQ FIR ISRAEL, THE ONLY STATE THAT IRAQ THREATEN, IT WAS NOT A THREAT TO THE UNITED STATES. LIKE RICHARD CLARK SAID IN HIS BOOK AND THIS MORNING THAT BUSH DID NOT LIKE TO READ AND HE DID NOT KNOW ANYONE OR ANY FOREIGN POLICES, HE DEPENDED ON DOCTOR RICE, COLON POWELL, AND HIS UNCLE DICK CHENEY FOR HIS FOREIGN POLICES. ARAFAT COULD NOT HAVE MEETINGS ANYMORE WITH THE UNITED STATES BECAUSE OF THE PRIME MINISTER SHARON AND HIS EQUALLY RACIST CARRYOVER OF THE ROMAN EMPIRE.

THE GREAT FORMER PRESIDENT OF THE UNITED STATES, JIMMY CARTER, BOOK "PALESTINE PEACE NOT APARTHEID" BECAME A BEST SELLER OF 2007, SHOULD BE A ROAD MAP TO PEACE IN THE REGION, ALONG WITH THE ROAD MAP TO PEACE THAT IS AGREED UPON EXCEPT FOR THE BUSH CHENEY ADMINISTRATION WHO WILL NOT DO ANYTHING TO BRING THE ISRAELIS AND THE PALESTINIANS TO TWO STATES. JERUSALEM IS THE CAPITAL OF PALESTINE AND THE ROMAN ISRAELIS WANT TO BUILD NEW SETTLEMENTS, AFTER BUILDING A WALL AND DISBANDING OTHER SETTLE-

MENTS. HIS VIEWS ON MIDDLE EASTERN AFFAIRS SHOULD BE THE STANDARD. BUSH CHENEY DO NOT CARE FOR NO BLACK ASS UNLESS THEY ARE KISSING THEIR BUTT.

THIS WEEK BUSH CHENEY HAD A CONFERENCE OF THE ARABIC LEAGUE, EXCEPT FOR IRAN IN WASHINGTON. PRESIDENT G.W. BUSH STILL LOOK DUMB FOUNDED, AS VICE PRESIDENT "TRICKY DICK" CHENEY WAS DOING MOST OF THE NEGOTIATING FOR TWO DAYS, THAT LEAD TO ANOTHER PROMISE THAT BUSH IS NOT AND CAN NOT BE SINCERE ABOUT THIS SUBJECT OF PEACE, WHEN ALL HE WANT TO BE IS A WAR PRESIDENTS BUSH CHENEY. HE SAID IN HIS FIRST SPEECH TO THE NATION, AS WELL AS THE CLINTON SURPLUS WILL BE SPENT AND SPENDING DID HE DO, AND IS CONTINUING TO DO IN THE NAME OF THE STATUS QUO. AMERICA DO NOT NEED ANY SENATOR OR REPRESENTATIVE WHO HAVE BACKED BUSH'S IDEALS IN THE NAME OF BEING A REPUBLICAN. THEY BETRAY AMERICA. THEY LOCKED THE DEMOCRATS OF HOUSE CHAMBERS, AS IF IT WAS THEIR HOME AND NOT THE CITIZENS REPRESENTATIVES HOME. THE CONSPIRACY CONTINUES UNTIL THE AMERICAN PEOPLE CAN OVER COME THE RELIGIOUS RIGHT BELIEFS OF HATE, DESPAIR, ABORTION, AND THE SEPARATION OF THE PEOPLE OF COLOR. AMERICA HAS TO OVERCOME THOSE BIAS BELIEFS THAT ARE ENFORCED IN THE SO-CALL CHURCHES.

03-29-04

HATFIELD, THE AMTRAK POISON SCIENTIST WHOM WAS ACCUSED AS A PERSON OF INTEREST, BY THE ATTORNEY GENERAL ASHCROFT, WAS IN FEDERAL COURT TODAY AND THE JUDGE GAVE HIM THE RIGHT TO INTERVIEW THE JUSTICE DEPARTMENT OFFICIALS THAT SLANDERED HIS NAME. THE

JUDGE IS EXPECTED TO THROW THE CASE OUT. ASHCROFT AND CHENEY IS THE GRAND DRAGONS OF THE KLU KLUX KLAN, AND TO HAVE THE PATRIOT ACT TO DECLINE OUR RIGHTS AS CITIZENS PRIVACIES IS ON LINE WITH THE SOVIET UNION AND HITLER'S GERMANY.

CHAOS IN IRAQ

TODAY OUR SOLDIERS ARE IN BIG TROUBLES TODAY, JUST TO PROTECT ISRAEL. CHENEY-SHARON-BUSH OIL WAR HAS THE UNITED STATES HATED MORE TODAY THAN EVER BECAUSE OF DICK CHENEY AND HIS BOY BUSH. ED BRADLEY ASKED DOCTOR RICE LAST NIGHT ON 60 MINUTES, WHY IS THERE MORE ATTACKS IN THE UNITED STATES THIRTY MONTHS AFTER 9/11 THAN BEFORE 9/11, AND SHE COULD NOT ADMIT THAT HER ADMINISTRATION DO NOT COMMUNICATE WITH PEOPLE OF AFRICAN DECENT I.E. ARAFAT AND OTHERS AS DID THE CLINTONS AND GORES, WHO HAD ALMOST PULLED A PRESIDENT JIMMY CARTER AND PRESIDENT OF EGYPT ANWAR AL- SADAT PEACE DEAL THAT FREED THE LAND AND THERE HAS BEEN PEACE EVERY SINCE. ISRAEL IS CONTINUING TO INVITED BELIEVERS TO ISRAEL AND IT'S SMALL LAND SPACE. TAKING MORE OF THE PALESTINIANS LAND IS KEEPING UNREST AND WAR.

04-05-04

WHY IS BUSH-CHENEY UNLIMITED TIME AT 9/11 COMMISSION PRIVATELY? THE INVASION OF IRAQ IS THE PERFECT ROMAN EMPIRE THINKING OF CONQUERING TO TEST WEAPONS OF THE UNITED STATES. NOW WE HAVE A LARGE PROBLEM COMING IF BUSH-CHENEY WINS ELECTION 2004.

THE COURT APPOINTMENTS WITH A WIN OF THE REPUBLI-
CANS CONTROL OF ALL THREE BRANCHES OF GOVERNMENT
WILL REALLY BE CHAOTIC HERE WITH ALL THE RIGHTS
AND FREEDOMS ARE DECLINING AND WILL CONTINUE
IF BUSH-CHENEY WINS. TEDDY KENNEDY, SENATOR FROM
MASSAC HUES, SAID, " IRAQ IS THE BUSH ADMINISTRATION'S
VIETNAM". DICK CHENEY AND PUPPET BUSH SAID FUCK THE
UNITED NATION, GERMANY, AND THE FRENCH,' WE WILL
GO IT ALONE AND CHARGE THE AMERICAN TAX PAYER FOR
ANOTHER TEN TO FIFTEEN YEARS, 1991-UNFORESEEN OCCU-
PATION OF A SOVEREIGN NATION, THEY (CHENEY, SHARON,
AND BUSH), WANTED SADDAM AND DESTROYED IT EVEN
MORE THAN HIS FATHER. THE IRAQ WAS ABOUT PROTECTING
ISRAEL. CONDOLISA RICE APPEARANCE B TE 911 COMMIS-
SION THIS THURSDAY, IS BEING PREPARED BY THE VICE PRES-
IDENT CHENEY AND NOT THE PRESIDENT BUSH, BECAUSE
IT IS NOT PERSONAL INVOLVED, THIS DICK CHENEY'S PRESI-
DENCY AND NOT GEORGE W. BUSH'S. ALL THE PICTURES
COMING ACROSS THE TELEVISION MEDIA I S SIMILAR TO THE
PICTURES OF ISRAEL'S DEMOLITION AND DEMORALIZING OF
THE PALESTINIANS, AFRICAN DESCENDANT HUMAN'S DARK
POPULATION AROUND THE WORLD. THE ROMAN DESCEN-
DANTS WHO ADOPTED THE HEBREW JUDAISM RELIGION IS
BAD FOR THE WORLD, EVEN MORE THAN THE AGAINST GOD
RELIGION OF THE CRUCIFIERS CATHOLICS. GOD SAYS MAN
SHOULD NOT BE ALONE WITHOUT A WOMAN, AUGUSTINE
BRAIN WASHED AND INSTITUTED THE LAWS OF CELIBATE
AND DIVISION OF THE HUMAN POPULATION.

04-06-04

RWANDA, AFRICA 'S GENOCIDE BY THE WESTERN NATIONS
CAME OUT TODAY ACROSS ALL NEWS MEDIA, BY A CANA-

DIAN GENERAL, WHO WAS THERE AND HAD INFORMED THE UNITED NATIONS MONTHS BEFORE. GENOCIDE CONTINUES TODAY AFTER OVER TWENTY- FIVE HUNDRED YEARS. TED KENNEDY, OF THE STATE OF MASS CUTES, SAID TODAY THAT PRESIDENT BUSH HAS THE LARGEST CREDITABILITY GAP SINCE RICHARD M. NIXON'S PRESIDENCY.

04-07-04

JOE BIDDEN, SENATOR OF DELAWARE, ON FOX NEWS TODAY, SAYS THAT BUSH SAID WE HAVE TO TAKE AN AMERICAN FACE OFF OF THIS IRAQ WAR", BIDDEN SAID SURE YOU ARE RIGHT, BUT HOW CAN YOU WHEN THE SOON TO BE DIPLOMAT IS TO RUN THINGS THERE. HOW COULD BUSH SAY SOME THING LIKE THAT AFTER HE WAS DETERMINED TO BOMB IRAQ AND ALL OF IT'S PALACES THAT OIL MONEY BROUGHT AND PAID FOR, AND NOW TAKE IT AWAY FROM THE AFRICAN DESCEN-DANT PEOPLE. BUSH STARTED D.A.R.E., PATRIOT ACT, AND THE IRAQ WAR; ALL IS AGAINST THE AFRICAN DESCENDANT PEOPLES, HERE IN AMERICAN AND ABROAD.

DO NOT FORGET DARFOR, SUDAN GENOCIDE OF IT'S OWN PEOPLE, WHETHER THEY ARE CALLED ARAB OR AFRICAN, WHICH IS THE SAME EXCEPT FOR RELIGION AND THE CASS SYSTEM OF THE LIGHT IS NEARER TO THEIR CAUCASIAN COUNTER PART.

04-09-04

NBC DATELINE- RACIAL PROFILING, FOURTEEN MONTHS INVESTIGATION, SHOWS THAT AMERICA POLICE FORCES PROFILE TWO TO THREE TIMES MORE TRAFFIC STOPS FOR NON MOVING VIOLATIONS AND JULIAN BOND OF THE

N.A.A.C.P. SAID THIS IS A FIRST TIME ANYONE HAS DID THIS TYPE OF STUDY. CINCINNATI, OHIO KID WAS STALKED AND HARASSED OVER TWENTY TIMES BEFORE THEY KILLED THIS MAN AND SETTLED OUT OF COURT FOR FOUR MILLION DOLLARS TO THE KID'S FAMILY. THAT IS THE NORMAL ACROSS THE NATION. VEGAS TO NEW YORK IT IS THE SAME KILL ALL BLACK MALES AS POSSIBLE AND SAVE ALL THE WHITE CHILDREN POSSIBLE IS THE PROTOCOL ACROSS THE WORLD AND THAT INCLUDE IRAQ AND THE PALESTINIANS.

04-10-04 –FIGHT FOR RE-ELECTION OF 2004

THE WHOLE BUSH ADMINISTRATION SHOULD BE FIRED AT THE ELECTION TIME. JOHN THE RACIST ASHCROFT IS IN THE HOT SEAT NOW AFTER MAKING SO MANY RACIST THOUGHTS TO UNDERMINE THE UNITED CONSTITUTION ALONG WITH HIS SO KNOWLEDGE IN CRIME, THE VICE PRESIDENT DICK CHENEY. THE 9/11 COMMISSION WILL HAVE HIM THIS COMING WEEK AND HIS FORMER ADVISOR WILL TESTIFY THE DAY BEFORE THAT ASHCROFT AND BUSH ADMINISTRATION DID NOT FOCUS AN ANY THING BUT TO PROTECT KEN LAY AND ENRON'S SWINDLE OF IT'S WORKERS PENSION, AND THE THERE NAMES WAS ALL OVER ENRON'S ROBBERY. ALL OF THE SHREDDED PAPERS WAS TO PROTECT THE PRESIDENCY OF THE UNITED STATES, SECRECY IS STILL THE THEME OF THIS ADMINISTRATION.

04-15-04

THE BUSH- CHENEY'S WAR IN IRAQ IS BACK FIRING IN THE ROMAN EMPIRE (U.S.)'S FACE. BUSH SPEECH TUESDAY ALL HE WAS SAYING, THE JEWS THIS OR THAT. THE UNITED STATES

POPULATION IS A VERY DIVERSE IN THE MIX OF HUMAN COMPLEXIONS AND ATTITUDES. SENATOR JOHN KERRY SAID THAT BUSH "UNJUST WAR HAS MADE NATIONAL GUARD INTO ACTIVE DUTY". THE IRANIAN DIPLOMAT WAS KILLED TODAY, BECAUSE HE WERE IN MEETINGS WITH THE UNITED STATES IN ORDER TO PLEAD WITH THE IRANIAN GOVERN-MENT NOW AFTER THEY ARE CATEGORIZED AS ONE OF THE "EVIL EMPIRE", NOW BUSH-CHENEY WANT HELP BY IRAN WITH THE SITUATION FALLUGA, IRAQ WITH HOLY SHEIK THAT IS DEFYING THIS ILLEGAL OCCUPATION BY THESE RACIST BANK ROBBERS WHO CONTINUES ROB THE MINERALS OF THE AFRICAN CONTINENT AND SOUTHERN ASIA, JUST THE UNITED KINGDOM IS CONTINUING TODAY TAKING THE GOLD AND DIAMONDS FROM ALL OF AFRICA.

SADDAM HUSSEIN MIGHT HAVE HIS WAYS OF TORTURE AND THAT IS NOT ANY REASON TO GO TO WAR WITH A SOLVE RING NATION, BECAUSE THEY HAVE BELIEFS DIFFERENT THAT THE CRUCIFIERS OF JESUS CHRIST, THE ROMAN EMPIRE CONTINUES UNDER A NEW DAY AND FACE AND IT IS IN THE MIDDLE EAST HAS IT HAS BEEN FOR THE LAST TWENTY –FIVE HUNDRED YEARS AGO. THE PEOPLE OF THE UNITED STATES IS WAKING –UP AND BUSH –CHENEY WILL NOT SURVIVE THIS CATEGORIZATION THEY HAS AND IS CAUSING THE PEOPLE OF THE UNITED STATES. THE DRAFT IS PROBABLY IS GOING TO LEAD TO DRAFT AFRICAN DESCENDANTS AGAIN FOR THE UNSTABLENESS IN IRAQ THAT BUSH- AND CHENEY SHOULD BE IMPEACHED FOR THIS WAR CRIMES, AND SHARON OF ISRAEL, BLAIR OF THE UNITED KINGDOM SHOULD ALSO BE INDICTED FOR WAR CRIMES.

04-22-04

MICHAEL JACKSON IS INDICTED TODAY FOR MOLESTATION OF A CHILD. THEY SAY, " YOU CAN INDICT A HAM SAND-WICH" IS JUSTICE IN AMERICA? THE SYSTEM OF JUSTICE HAS STARTED WITH AN INDICTMENT. THE GRAND JURY PROCEED-INGS WERE VERY BIAS AND SHOULD BE LOOKED INTO VERY SERIOUSLY. ONE SIDEDNESS JUST DOES NOT SEEM TO BE FAIR AND AMERICAN JUSTICE IS NOT FAIR WHEN THEY (PROS-ECUTORS) DECIDE, IN THEIR OFFICES THAT THEY WANT YOU TO BUILD ON THEIR CAREERS NOT WHETHER YOU ARE INVOLVED OR NOT IN ANY CRIMES.

04-28-04

THE UNITED STATES SUPREME COURT- HEARD ARGU-MENTS ON THE ENERGY TASK FORCE V. THE SIERRA CLUB, ON FREEDOM OF INFORMATION ACT THAT SHOULD MAKE THOSE TRANSCRIPTS SHOULD BE MADE AVAILABLE, IF NATION SECURITY IN NOT ESTATE OR BLACK OUT, THIS WAS YESTERDAY. TODAY HONORABLE JUSTICES HEARS THE 'WAR POWERS ACT" AND RACIST PRESIDENT GEORGE BUSH, "TRICKY DICK" CHENEY AND JOHN ASHCROFT'S TERM "ENEMY COMBATANT" TO DENY PEOPLE THE RIGHT TO HAVE COURT PROCEDURES, THIS BUSH ADMINISTRATION HAS MUCH MORE SECRECY THAN THE TRICKY RICHARD NIXON. WOLF BLITZER TODAY WITH JOHN DEAN, NIXON'S FORMER WHITE HOUSE COUNSEL AND HE SAID THAT SECRECY, WORST THAT WATERGATE. JOHN DEAN NEW BOOK IS ON SALE. TRICKY DICK CHENEY NOW IS THE PRESIDENT BABY BUSH FOLLOWED ALONG. ENEMY COMBATANT " IS A NEW TERM CREATED BY THE RACIST OVERSEERS OF THE UNITED STATES CONSTITUTION, "LOCK THEM UP AND THROW AWAY

THE KEY" AND HANG THEM AT THE NEAREST TREE", TEXAS JUSTICE AS BABY BUSH SAYS TO THE SO CALL TERRORIST AFTER THAT 9/11 DISASTER. JUSTICE SANDRA DAY O'CONNOR, ASKED THAT IN OTHER WORDS YOU COULD KEEP THEM FOR TWENTY OR TWENTY-FIVE YEARS", AND THIS IS WITHOUT A HEARING, AND THESE ARE AMERICAN CITIZENS.

12-05-07

TODAY THE UNITED STATES SUPREME COURT HELD HEARING ABOUT HABEAS CORPUS FOR THE GUANTAMO BAY, CUBA DETAINEES. THERE HAVE NEVER BEEN HABEAS FOR ALIENS", SCALIA SAID. THE DECISION WILL BE OUT MOST PROBABLY IN JUNE 2007

04-29-04-

TREASON ACTS SHOULD BE CARRIED AFTER THE BUSH CHENEY ADMINISTRATION. BUSH LIES AND THE RIGHT WING CONSPIRACY COMPELLED AND COVERED UP THE TREASONABLE ACT. THE AMERICAN WAY.

9/11 COMMISSION MEETS WITH BUSH AND CHENEY TODAY, WITH NO RECORDING, NO TRANSCRIPTS AND JUST PLAIN OLD STONE WALLING. AT PRESS CONFERENCE HE COULD NOT ANSWER THE FAMILIES OF THE 9/11 VICTIMS, WHY THERE WERE NO TRANSCRIPTS? NO ANSWER.

02-02-04 AMBASSADOR JOE WILSON, BOOK" THE POLITICS OF TRUTH", BUSH-CHENEY BLEW THE COVER OF HIS CENTRAL INTELLIGENCE AGENCY'S WIFE. RACIST ROBERT NOVAK, SPY FOR THE KLAN AND THE NAZIS SPREAD THESE LIES ACROSS WASHINGTON, D.C., BECAUSE JOE WILSON BLEW

COVER OF THE BUSH ADMINISTRATION. IN THE LAND OF 'FREEDOM OF PRESS" BUSH ADMINISTRATION HAS FEAR IN THE NEWS MEDIA TO WRITE ABOUT STORIES NOT FAVORABLE TO THE BUSH ADMINISTRATION, NOW THAT SOUNDS TO BE IMPEACHABLE, SINCE THEY CRUCIFIES PRESIDENT CLINTON FOR A SEX ACT, THIS ON "MEET THE PRESS" THIS MORNING. PATTERN OF DECEPTION" AND PARTISAN POLITICS IN CONGRESS IS A CRIME", THE REPUBLICANS ARE GUILTY OF COVER UP. CHENEY LIED TO CONGRESS IN ORDER TO START THIS IRAQ WAR AND NOW WILSON AND HIS WIFE IS THE TARGET OF THE GANGSTERS IN THE WHITE HOUSE, THE SAME ONES THAT OVERTHREW THE ELECTION 2000, IN ORDER TO DO THIS.

CONSPIRACY TO PUT THE UNITED STATES AT WAR FOR ISRAEL AND OIL MONEY-FASCISM IS ALIVE AND WELL IN AMERICA AND CHENEY-BUSH ARE THE OUT FRONT LEADERS OF THIS REPRESSIVE MOVEMENT IN RACIST AMERICA.

CHRIS MATTHEWS SHOW TODAY, ON DICK CHENEY, THE MOST POWERFUL VICE PRESIDENT IN THE HISTORY OF THE UNITED STATES, WITH HIS SECRET CHAMBERS AND SECRET MATING IN THE WHITE HOUSE IS COMING.

05-03-04

SHARON, PRIME MINISTER OF ISRAEL, WHOSE INITIATIVE TO GIVE UP LAND IN THE GAZA STRIP WAS DEFEATED YESTERDAY AND TODAY HE REJECTS THE NOTION TO RESIGN, AFTER HE HAD KILLED HIS PREDECESSOR, AND CALLED FOR NEW ELECTIONS ALL THE TIME UNTIL DEATH WAS DONE. NOW HE HAS PLANNED FOR BUSH-CHENEY REELECTION AND IT IS BACK FIRING HE AND BUSH.

MARCUS DIXON, IS/WAS THE GEORGIA HIGH SCHOOL STUDENT CONVICTED ON THE PIMP LAW OF UNDER AGE TEENAGER'S CONVICTION, THAT WAS CREATED FOR PIMPS, HAS BEEN OVERTURNED FOR THE TEENAGER, BUT THERE WERE OTHER CONVICTIONS, WITH SENTENCES THAT DID NOT FIX THIS CRIME OF CONSENUAL SEX, AND BOND HAS BEEN GRANTED. THERE MANY LAWS, BUT SINCE RECON-STRUCTION OF THE UNITED STATES AFTER THE CIVIL WAR, AND THE EMANCIPATION RIGHTS FOR SLAVES TO BE FREED AND ISSUED AN ACRE AND A MULE. ACONTRACT WITH AMERICA THAT I WANT SETTLED. THIS HAS TO BE DONE AN IN SOME CASES THE MENTAL ILL MUST HAVE AN OVER-SEER TO MAKE SURE THEY HAVE THE SOME TREATMENT OF REVIVAL OF BEING POOR AND DEMORALIZE TO THE POINT OF INSANITY.

KERRY IN NEW MEXICO WITH BILL RICHARDS, CLINTON ADMINISTRATION, TALK OF ONE MILLION MORE HIGH SCHOOL GRADUATES AND BUSH OUT IN OHIO PREACHING TAXING THE RICH TO PAY, THAT IS NOT ENOUGH TO PAID FOR HIS PROGRAMS TO HELP NIGGERS, THE ORDINARY CITI-ZENS WILL HAVE TO PAY FOR KERRY'S PROGRAMS, BUT WHO IS PAYING FOR ALL THE WAR PROGRAMS, INCLUDING RUMS-FIELD'S INFORMERS THAT CONFIDENCE THE UNITED STATES GOVERNMENT THAT GEORGE W. BUSH, FOR THE ESSENTIAL DECISION TO FOOL THE AMERICANS, WHILE TONY BLAIR DID THE SAME TO THE BRITISH EMPIRE ROLLING ON. BUSH RHETORIC IS ALL-RACIST. BILL CLINTON, FORMER PRESI-DENT, RAISED TAXES TOOK AWAY WELFARE AS WE KNOW IT ", BUILD SURPLUSES AND REPARATIONS NEGOTIATIONS AND TALK IN THE WHITE HOUSE OR SHOULD I SAY SLAVE HOUSE, NOW THAT IS WHAT I CALL A HUGE CHANGE UNDER UNITED STATES OF AMERICA'S COMMON LAW SYSTEM OF GOVERNING AND KEEPING THE DARK GENOCIDE THROUGH

OUT THE WORLD, BY ANY MEANS NESS CARY ",. Bush-Cheney IS OUT FOOLING, LYING AND TRICKING THEM TO VOTE FOR HIM, IN ORDER FOR HIM AND CONGRESS CAN RAM DOWN THE THROAT THE JUDGES TO PREVENT WOMEN FROM HAVING THE CHOOSE TO DECIDE WHAT HAPPENS TO THEIR BODIES. I REMEMBER WHEN THEY USED COKE BOTTLES, COAT HANGERS, AND WHAT EVER ELSE THAT WERE AVAILABLE NOT TO HAVE A CHILD AT THAT TIME, AND SOMETIME IT CAUSED THE FEMALE HER LIFE. IT IS ALL-RACIST TO PROMOTE THE ARIAN DREAM OF WHITE PEOPLE FOREVER. FREEDOM OF PRESS IS AT STAKE IN THIS ELECTION 2004, RUPERT MURDOCK AND COMPANY TRYING TO SENSOR ANYTHING THAT DOES NOT HAVE BUSH-CHENEY IN BRIGHT LIGHT.

05-06-04

THE SCANDALS OF THE BUSH-CHENEY ADMINISTRATION HAS STARTED AND BUSH SENT CONDOLISA RICE TO SPEAK TO THE ARABS FOR AN APOLOGY FOR THE INHUMAN TREAT-MENT OF IT'S PEOPLE IN PRISONS AND GEORGE HIMSELF HAD TO FOLLOW HIMSELF, FOR SOME KIND OF PUBLIC RELA-TION PLOY TO MAKE PEOPLE THINK THAT BUSH, SHARON CHENEY) CARES ABOUT HUMAN RIGHTS, WHEN THEY ARE CONSTANTLY ABUSING HUMANS SO-CALL RIGHTS, BOTH HERE AND ABROAD. THIS WAS DONE THE PREVIOUS TWO DAYS. TODAY TOM HARKINS, SENATOR FROM IOWA, HAS CALL FOR DONALD RUMSFIELD TO RESIGN, THE FIRST TO DO SO; IN THE ALTERNATIVE BUSH SHOULD FIRE HIM AND IF BUSH DOES THIS, THE SHIT REALLY WILL IT THE FAN, BUSH AND CHENEY ADMINISTRATION IS FALLING, AND WATER-GATE TWO WILL BEGIN.

I CANNOT WAIT TO SEE WHAT THOSE ALMIGHTY REPUBLI-
CANS GOING TO DO WHEN THEIR CLANNISH MONOPOLY
SCHEME OF FOOLING THE AMERICAN PEOPLE TO STACK
RACIST JUDGES ON THE BENCH. HOW MANY BLACK JUDGES
HAS BEEN PUT FORWARD FOR CONFIRMATION? WARREN
HATCH, UTAH SENATOR DOES NOT CARES FOR ANYTHING
DARK AROUND, VERY ARIAN. A LAW SUIT IS BREAKING TO
DAY FROM AN EGYPTIAN DETAINEE, FROM SEPTEMBER 30,
2001 PICKED UP FROM HIS IN NEW JERSEY OR NEW YORK,
AND HELD IN BROOKLYN DETENTION FACILITY FOR A YEAR
WITHOUT AND TYPE OF COURT APPEARANCE, AND IT WAS
FOUR MONTHS BEFORE HE COULD MAKE A PHONE CALL
TO HIS FAMILY. THE RED CROSS-TO DAY ON WOLF BLITZER'S
SHOW OF CNN SAID THEY KNEW THE ABUSES IN IRAQ PRISON
AND THE MILITARY DID NOT REACT. THIS WAS INVASION OF
A FOREIGN SOVEREIGN NATION OF IRAQ, REGARDLESS OF Its
LEADER AND HOW HE GOVERNED.

GEORGE W. BUSH SAID THAT "WE ARE GOING TO SHOW
THEM SOME TEXAS JUSTICE" BACK IN THE BEGINNING OF HIS
WAR VENTURES. RUMSFIELD MET TODAY WITH FOUR REPUB-
LICANS AND NO DEMOCRAT SENATORS, AND NOW THAT
RACIST TEXAS TOM DELAY, HOUSE LEADER, CHANGING THE
CENSUS FOR NEIGHBORHOODS VOTING ZONES, IN OTHER
WORDS VOTER FRAUD, AND LATER FOUND GUILTY OF LIES
AND HAD TO LEAVE CONGRESS. HE AND ALL THAT VOTED
WITH HIM SHOULD BE VOTED OUT OF OFFICE AND IN THE
2006 SOME WERE. TOM DELAY WAS CHIEF AND TREASON-
ABLE AS HE WAS USING THE BUSH LINE " THE DEMOCRATS
USING AS POLITICS, ALL IS POLITICS AND THE REPUBLICANS
DO NOT HAVE THE BEST INTEREST OF AMERICANS, TRYING
TO HAVE ONE PARTY ONE VOICE, VERY UN-AMERICAN LIKE.
QUEEN NOOR, AN AMERICAN LADY WHO MARRIED THE
KING OF JORDAN AND IS THE MOTHER OF THE KING OF

JORDAN TODAY IS GUEST OF CHRIS MATTHEWS' HARDBALL", TODAY SHE SAYS TO THESE POLITICIANS THAT ARE RACIST LIVE AND KILL TO KEEP THE BIG LIE ALIVE ABOUT THE HUMAN RACE.

'ISRAEL HAS THE LONGEST OCCUPIER IN THE HISTORY OF THE WORLD," AND THAT IS THE PROOF THAT THE ROMAN EMPIRE IS CONTINUING BEHIND THE LIE ABOUT JESUS, THE HOLY MESSIAH FROM THE CREATOR OF ALL HUMANS. THE TRUTH THEY HAVE KEPT SINCE HANNIBAL OF CARTHAGE, THAT NO BLACK ASS WILL DOMINATE A LIGHT COMPLEXION PEOPLE. GWB CANNOT SAY WHY HE WILL NOT SEE YASSAR ARAFAT TO NEGOTIATE , BECAUSE DICK CHENEY AND SHARON OF ISRAEL TOLD HIM NOT TO, NEGOTIATE ABOUT TERROR QUEEN NOOR EXPLAINED IT EXACTLY. THE ISRAEL AND PALESTINIANS SITUATION SPRUNG FROM THAT CONTINUING CONFLICT THAT BUSH ADMINISTRATION REVERSED EVERYTHING THAT CLINTON HAD ACHIEVED. EVEN THOUGHT ARAFAT DID NOT GO ALONG WITH EVERY-THING WITH CLINTON, HE WAS THE LEADER AT THE TIME AN SHOULD HAVE BEEN CONSIDERED, BUT BUSH CHENEY CAME IN WITH HATE OF THE SHORT MAN, BECAUSE OF CHENEY'S PREVIOUS DEFENSE SECRETARY

RACIST OF AMERICA, MY HOME LAND AND THE ROMAN EMPIRE ARE ALL ONE AS LONG AS THERE IS A BUSH ADMIN-ISTRATION IS IN POWER. THEY FREED SHARON, PRIME MINISTER OF ISRAEL FROM HIS SCANDAL OF EMBEZZLEMENT, SHREDDED DOCUMENT AND CLEANED EVERYTHING UP BECAUSE OF THIS 2004 ELECTION DEPEND ON BUSH ADMIN-ISTRATION TO RUN UNITED STATES AS A POLICE STATE, JUST RICHARD M. NIXON HAD PREPARED, EXCEPT GOD BLESSED AMERICA WITH THE WATERGATE AFFAIR OF 1973; GOD BLESS AMERICA THE NEW BABYLON.

THE AMERICAN RACISTS ARE BEHIND A LIE ABOUT CHRIS-
TIANITY, WHICH CONTINUES TO KEEP THE DESCENDANTS
OF AMERICAN SLAVES. THEY DO NOT WANT TO FROM THE
SYSTEM THAT IS IN PLACE, THE UNITED STATES CONSTITU-
TION THAT IS CONSTANTLY BEING AMENDED AND IN THE
MOST RECENT ELECTION FOR PRESIDENT 2000, THEY OVER-
THREW THE CONSTITUTION BY USING THAT THE SUPREME
COURT IS THE ULTIMATE RULE OF JURISPRUDENT LAW
OF AMERICA. SOMEWHERE WITH AMENDMENTS TO THE
UNITED STATES CONSTITUTION, THAT WE AS A COLORFUL
NATION SHOULD ESTABLISH A TIME LIMIT FOR BEING ON
THE UNITED STATES SUPREME COURT. IT IS AMAZING WHY
THERE ARE NOT TIME LIMITS, IF IT IS TRULY "FOR PEOPLE BY
THE PEOPLE", THEN PERMIT THE PEOPLE OF AMERICA HAS A
FACE OF AMERICA ON THE UNITED STATES SUPREME COURT,
THE HIGHEST COURT OF THE LAND. THE BUSHES, OLD AND
YOUNG CREATED THIS FOR OUR COUNTRY AND THEY TREAT
IT (AMERICA) AS THEIR OWN PERSONAL EVERYTHING: THE
TIME COMES WHERE IT HAS TO STOP OR THERE WILL BE A
POLICE STATE, INCLUDING CANADA, THE SAME AS HITLER
AND JULIUS CAESAR BEFORE THEN.

THIS GUN –HO FEMALE (BITCH) JESSICA LYNCH AND HER
HUSBAND WHO WERE TORCHING THE DETAINEES IN IRAQ'S
ABUJA PRISON UNTIL IT HIT THE NEWS WITH THE PICTURES
OF THIS FEMALE SOLDIER WITH A WHIP AND A CIGARETTE IN
HER MOUTH AND SHE STANDS FIVE FEET FIVE INCHES TALL,
FROM WEST VIRGINIA, THE MAJORITY RIGHT WING RACIST
RELIGION OF THE GRAND DRAGON RACIST JERRY FARWELL.
THAT MENTALITY OF AMERICANS, AND THE BUSH ADMIN-
ISTRATION SAYS IT IS NOT OUR WAY, WHAT A LIE. JESSICA
LYNCH'S FAMILY ARE PART OF THE ORIGINAL TERRORIST
TO THE SLAVES AND INDIANS OF AMERICA. THEY TRIVED
AFTER SLAVERY DURNING THE SANCTION OF JIM CROW

LAWS, THE UNITED STATES SUPREME COURT. ANY PERSON, CITY, OR SCHOOL NAMED WITH LYNCH IN IT HONORS THE TERRORIST OF AMERICA. WHITE IMAGES FOR THE FUTURE AND DESTROY ANY BLACK IMAGES, AS IF THEY ARE THE ONLY HUMANS ON EARTH.

CONGRESSMAN CHARLES RANGEL FINALLY GOT UPSET ENOUGH TO FILE IMPEACHMENT PAPERS AND NAZI HOUSE SPEAKER TOM DELAY, MAJORITY LEADER OF THE HOUSE SCHEMES TO CHANGE VOTING ZONES AFTER THE POPU-LATION STATISTIC ARE REVEALED EVERY TEN YEARS, AND AFTER TRENT LOTT PRAISED STROM THURMAN, THE SEGRE-GATIONIST SENATOR FROM THE GREAT STATE OF SOUTH CAROLINA, RACIST STAND AGAINST, HARRY TRUMAN IN THE 1948 PRESIDENTIAL ELECTION, NOW DELANEY. THESE PEOPLE PRACTICE WHAT THEY WERE DOING AND TAUGHT SINCE CHILD HOOD. HER HUSBAND IS A SARDIS TIC CORREC-TION OFFICER AND YOU KNOW ALL, AT LEASE NINETY PERCENT OF THEM ARE BORN RACIST, AND THE STATES OF THE UNITED STATES PAST LAWS AND THROW AWAY THE KEY, BECAUSE NINETY PERCENT OF PRISON POPULATION IN AMERICA ARE PEOPLE OF COLOR.

05-11-04

VOTING RIGHTS IN THIRTY-SIX STATES ARE GIVEN TO EX-CONVICTS, IS THAT REALLY THE STATES RIGHTS? I ALWAYS TAUGHT THAT ONE NATION UNDER GOD, BUSH-CHENEY ALWAYS WANTS TO CONCEAL AND SPILT/ DIVIDE THE PEOPLE OF THIS COLORABLE NATION. BUSH WANT TO CONTINUE TO STUMP THE CAMPAIGN TRAIL ABOUT, BEING A WAR PRESI-DENT, BUT DO NOT WANT TO TAKE CREDIT FOR ALL THE ATROCITIES IN IRAQ. THE ARMIES SERVICE COMMITTEE OF

THE SENATE HELD HEARINGS TODAY, ON THE TORTURING OF IRAQ PEOPLE IN THEIR OWN LAND, NOT OUR LAND, BUT THEIR LAND. WE SHOULD NOT BE IN IRAQ AND WE NEED A NEW PRESIDENT. NBC, NIGHTLY NEWS, "FLEECING OF AMERICA", THE BUSH ADMINISTRATION IS SELLING GOVERN-MENT LAND IN THE COLORADO ROCKIES; AT BOTTOM PRICE TO MOSTLY/ ALL WHITE PEOPLE. BUSH- CHENEY IS THE ENEMY OF THE UNITED STATES PEOPLE.

05-22-04

YESTERDAY FORMER BILL CLINTON SPOKE AT THE DOLE INSTITUTE, AT THE UNIVERSITY OF KANSAS, WITH BOB DOLE IN ATTENDANCE. TODAY ON NEWS WORLD INTERNATIONAL THERE WERE COMPARISON OF SIR WINSTON CHURCHILL, AND TODAY'S LEADERS, BUSH AND BLAIR. BUSH HAS BEEN IN WASHINGTON ON THE JOB FORTY-TWO PERCENT OF THE TIME, WHILE DICK CHENEY IS THERE BEING PRESIDENT. INTERVIEWING CHURCHILL AUTOBIOGRAPHY SIR MARTIN GILBERT, BOOK "…NAG AND BITE…." BUSH MADE WAR WHEN CHURCHILL TRIED TO AVOID WAR, AND BUSH IS CLOSER TO HITLER THAN CHURCHILL.

05-23-04

CANNES' FILM FESTIVAL, IN FRANCE, A MICHAEL MOORE'S MOVIE OF GEORGE BUSH, "BUSH BASHING" FILM THAT AMERICAN BROADCAST COMPANY (ABC), SUPPOSED TO HAVE RELEASED, IS NOT BEING RELEASE BECAUSE IT IS CRITICAL TO BUSH-CHENEY ELECTION AND DICK CHENEY IS PULLING PEOPLE BALLS, AND CAUSING CENSORSHIP. COLUMBIA BROADCAST COMPANY (CBS) ALREADY PULLED

THE TRUER PICTURE OF RONALD REAGAN'S PRESIDEN-
TIAL MYTHS, EARLY THIS YEAR. OUTRIGHT CENSORSHIP IN
AMERICA TODAY SHOULD BE INTOLERABLE. HITLER LIVES
ON WITH THIS ADMINISTRATION AND IT IS THE REPUBLI-
CAN'S CONGRESSIONAL SUPPORTS, " OF THE PEOPLE FOR
THE PEOPLE, BY THE PEOPLE " IS WHAT THEY ARE SUPPOSED
TO BE REPRESENTING? QUESTIONS NOT ALLOWED.

05-25-04

AFTER THAT HITLER TYPE OF SPEECH YESTERDAY, THAT
PRESIDENT BUSH HELD TO CONVINCE THE FOOLS (RACISTS),
THAT WE SHOULD STAY AT WAR, FOR WHATEVER REASON,
AFTER ATTACKING A FOREIGN SOLVER IN COUNTRY OF
IRAQ, THAT WAS DISRUPTED FOR ANY REASON, QUALI-
FIES FOR "WAR CRIMINAL", CATEGORY, TODAY HE HAS ONE
OF SADDAM'S TORTURED PERSON FOR AMERICA TO SEE
WHAT TYPE OF MAN SADDAM IS, THIS IS THIS "GO IT ALONE
WAR PRESIDENT OF AMERICA", "TEXAS JUSTICE "MAN, THE
MAN THAT CAN NOT GO AND HANDLE THE ASIAN TOUR,
EARLIER THIS YEAR, WITHOUT THE GUIDING HAND OF THE
VICE PRESIDENT DICK CHENEY, THAT ONLY MEANS THAT
COLON POWELL WAS THE PRESIDENT OF THE UNITED STATES
FOR THE TIME THAT DICK INTRODUCED THE BABY BUSH,
THAT CONTINUES TO ROB THE TREASURY AND DENIES ANY
CONSIDERATION FOR REPARATION FOR THE DESCENDANT
OF AMERICAN SLAVES.

THE AMERICAN GOVERNMENT IS BUILDING A WALL ACROSS
AMERICA TO KEEP THE PEOPLE OF COLOR IN WHEN THEY
BRING IN THE TANKS AND START PLANTATIONS OF SLAVES
AGAIN. THE WORSHIP FORMER PRESIDENT RONALD REAGAN
AS THE GREAT MAN, WHEN HE WAS A GREAT ACTOR THAT

FOOLED THE WORLD, JUST AS THIS GEORGE W.. BUSH, THAT IS FOLLOWING THE ORDERS OF THE SO-CALL OVERSEERS OF THEIR FORE FATHERS OF SLAVE DRIVERS, AND THE BIGGEST TRICK OF THEM ALL IS COMING AND HIS FATHER G.H.W. BUSH IS THE HEAD CARE-TAKER, AND HE DOES NOT LIKE NOTHING BLACK. HE IS A YALE MAN AND KERRY IS NOT GOING TO LOW, BECAUSE HE IS YALE MAN. TAKE ALL OF YOUR WEALTH AND BECOME A SLAVE OR DIE, AND I WILL DIE. THE PEOPLE OF THIS COULD BE GREAT NATION, BUT CAN NOT BECAUSE OF ALL THE HUMAN EXPERIMENT CONTINUES, AS THEY CONTINUE TO DENY THAT THERE ARE OTHER BEING IN THIS UNIVERSE, THE ONLY THING IS, IS RACISM, BECAUSE THEY KNOW THE OTHER BEINGS ARE DARK PEOPLE, JUST AS THERE ARE IN AFRICA, THE ROMAN EMPIRE CONTINUES.

05-26-04

MISTAKE? -WRONGLY FAXED TWO COPIES TO THE DEPART-MENT OF EDUCATION- RITA RIDDLE, WHO WAS ADVISING ME THAT IT WAS NOT ANYTHING THAT THEY COULD DO WITH THE SCHOOL PROBLEM NEED TO FINE PUBLISHER, AS THOUGH MY THOUGHTS ARE OUT THERE UNREFINED AND READY TO BE PUBLISH NOW. SHE COULD STEAL MY CONCEP-TION WITH A LITTLE REFINING AND RESEARCH.

05-29-04-

STRICKLAWS NEEDS TO BE ABOLISHED, AS IT HAS PROVEN THAT IT INCARCERATED THE POOR AND UNEDUCATED.

'THE REVOLVING DOOR" TERM USED TO IMPRISON DESCEN-DANTS OF AMERICAN SLAVES, THAT WAS RATIONAL TO LOCK -UP- IMPRISON AND KEEP THEM IGNORANT OF THE

LANGUAGE AND CULTURE OF THE BRITISH EMPIRE, THE GRAND CONSPIRACY THAT WILL CALL FOR MARSHALL LAW, JUST AS HITLER AND JULIUS CAESAR AND ALL OF THE OTHER CAESARS, UNTIL THEY CHALLENGED AND THREATEN THE GREATEST GENERAL OF ALL TIME, HANNIBAL OF CARTAGE, NORTH AFRICA THREE CENTURIES BEFORE THE BIRTH OF CHRIST TO A PEASANT LADY NAME MARY.

BECAUSE OF HANNIBAL AND HIS ELEPHANT MAN ARMY AND HIS NAVY HELD THE ROMAN AT BAY, THEY WERE THINKING THAT HE WAS GOING TO COME ACROSS THE STRAIT FROM SPAIN TO ITALY AND THEY WERE GOING TO BLOW HANNIBAL'S NAVY FROM THE SEA, WHERE THEY HAD BUILT A NAVY TO RIVAL HANNIBAL'S, BUT INSTEAD HE WENT THROUGH THE ALPS AND CONQUERED ITALY AND THE ROMANS LANDS FOR TWENTY YEARS.

AFTER THAT THE ROMANS RECOVERED AND GATHERED THEMSELVES , AND PROMISE THAT NO AFRICAN OR DESCEN-DANT OF AFRICAN WOULD NEVER IMPRISON THEM AND THEIR PEOPLE AGAIN. PROTECT THE WHITE WOMEN AS THEY HAVE THEIR WAY WITH ANY FEMALE, YOUNG OR OLD.

BECAUSE OF THIS THE CRUCIFION HAPPENED. AFTER CONQUERING NORTH AFRICA AND ALL OF THE HOLY, CENTURIES AFTER HANNIBAL'S DEATH, THEY RAN INTO THIS DARK MAN WHO IS SUPPOSE TO BE HOLY AND HAS HEALING POWERS, AND THEY COULD NOT PERMIT ANYONE TO BETTER THAN A ROMAN, WHO FELL IN LOVE WITH THE MAGIC OF OLIVE OILS FROM THE OLIVE TREES OF THE HOLY LAND.

THE ROMANS WENT ON A TEAR OF THE EARTH FOR THEN UNTIL TODAY , IT HAS JUST BEEN RENAMED AS THEY WENT, AND ESPECIALLY AFTER THE CRUCIFION OF THE HOLY

MESSENGER, IT BECAME GREAT BRITAIN'S EMPIRE, NOT TO MENTION THE ORIENTALS, AND NOW IT IS THE AMERICAN AND BRITISH TO MAKE-UP THE MODERN DAY ARMY TO COMPRESS THE SO-CALL THIRD WORLD PEOPLE, AND ALL OF MINERALS OF THE LAND; THAT IS, GOLD, COOPER , AND TODAY IT IS OIL WARS.

IT IS ALL ATTACHED TO THE MOTHER LAND OF THE HUMAN RACE, AFRICA. THEY ARE ALL CAUCASIANS AND ALL ARE NOT BAD PEOPLE, UNTIL A BLACK ASS TAKE A LADY OF THEIRS THINGS SEEM TO CHANGE. THE ONES WHO DOES NOT GO ALONG ARE CALLED TRADER OF THE LIGHTER HUMAN RACE (ARIANS), THE SO-CALL SUPERIORITY OF HUMANS. THEY CONTINUE THE LIES AND DECEIT OF THE REVAMPING AFTER THE HANNIBAL WAR.

IF G-D CREATED THE HUMAN RACE IN THE DARK ON THE DARK CONTINENT OF AFRICA, THE CAUCASIANS WERE CREATED IN SOUTHERN ASIAN MOUNTAINS , THEY CALL EUROPE TODAY, THEN THEY CREATE A NEW TESTAMENT IN ORDER TO KEEP THEIR PEOPLE TOGETHER AND DIVIDE THE AFRICANS AND THEIR DESCENDANTS, AND AFRICA IS WHERE ALL OF THE GENOCIDE IS OCCURRING TODAY.

WE ARE THE EXPERIMENT OF THE CREATOR(S). EVERYDAY THERE IS THE SUN AND THE MOON, WHETHER ONE CAN SEE IT OR NOT, AND IT ALL MAKES THE EARTHLY WORLD REVOLVE, AND WE ARE STILL SEGREGATING OUR SOULS AND EVENTUALLY IT ALL COMES AND DESTROY US ALL, WHETHER RICH OF POOR.

THE SPACE PROGRAMS THAT IS POPPING -UP HAS SOME-THING TO DO WITH THE HATE THAT MAN HAS BESTOWED UPON HIMSELF. THE STATUS QUO, AS THE BUSHES AND THE RIGHT WINGERS CALL THEMSELVES, HAS TO COME OFF THEIR

SUICIDE MISSIONS OF SPACE VENTURES AND WORK TO HAVE A BETTER EARTHLY FAMILY INSTEAD OF THE DIVIDE AND CONQUER ATTITUDE THAT HAS US IN THE TECHNOLOGY FIELD TODAY, IF NOT WE HAVE STARTED OUR DEMISE. G-D EXPERIMENT HAS REACHED THE BOTTOM OF THE SEA AND IS CONTINUING TO EXPLORE THE UNIVERSE IN SEARCH OF G-D WHEN HE IS HERE AND THERE , BUT ONLY WILL APPEAR ON EARTH, THE PLACE OF THE CREATION.

THIS TWO STRIKE LAW OF RACIST ZELL MILLER IS WORST THAN OTHER STATES, RIGHT ALONE WITH THAT CONTINUED ROCKERFELLERS DRUG LAW OF NEW YORK NOT TO MENTION MICHIGAN'S. THIS RACIST SOCIETY THAT IS SUPPOSE TO BE DEMOCRATIC, BULLSHIT, EXTERMINATE ALL OR AS MANY BLACK AND DARK HUMANS AND WE WERE THE ORIGINAL HUMANS. HELP ANY CAUCASIAN ALL THEY HAVE TO DO IS GO TO CHURCH TO CREATE MORE EVIL DEVILISH PLOTS TO CONTROL THE WORLD ON THE BASICS OF COMPLEXION OF A HUMAN. THE SAME CRUCIFIX THAT THE ROMAN EMPIRE CRUCIFIED GOD'S ONLY BEGOTTEN SON JESUS CHRIST OF NAZARETH, BETHLEHEM, AND PALESTINIAN JESUS WAS BORN AND DIED. THE ARIAN IAN KEPT POWER AFTER THE CRUCIFIXIONS OF GOD'S ONLY BEGOTTEN SON AND THEY CAN NOT HIDE BEHIND JUDEA HEBREW STORY OF ABRAHAM, JESUS, SOLOMON, KING DAVID AND ALL THE PEOPLE OF THE OLD TESTAMENT WERE OF COLORFUL HUMANS THAT THEY (ARIANS) WORSHIP TODAY, IF THEY TRY TO PUSH THAT HOMOSEXUAL WEBSTER'S DEFINITION OF ENGLISH WORDS, THAT INTERRUPTED TO KEEP AFRICANS FROM MIXING WITH THE CAUCASIAN WOMEN. TODAY ORRIN HATCH, THE SO-CALL GREAT SENATOR OF THE GREAT STATE OF UTAH, RELI-GION HAS REVISED THE HOLY BOOK NOT TO MENTION THEIR UNDERCOVER PREJUDICES AGAINST ALL BLACK AND DARK PEOPLE OF GOD'S EARTH. BOTH SIDES OF THE MEDITERRA-

NEAN OCEAN WAS CONTROL BY THEFT, BUT THE ROMANS POLICE OF THE ISRAELIS AND ALL OF NORTH AFRICA WAS FORCED ON THE CRUCIFIX AS A RELIGION TO KILL AND NOT TO LOVE AS JESUS TRIED TO CARRY OUT HIS MISSION FROM GOD AND YASSAR ARAFAT AND ISLAM IS FOLLOWING THE HUMAN NATURE OF SELF PROTECTION. MY PEOPLE OF THESE UNITED STATES PAID WITH THEIR BLOOD, SWEAT, AND TEARS, AND BUSHES AND CHENEY SPEND ROB THE UNITED STATES TREASURY EVERY DAY TO STAY AHEAD OF THE BLACK AND PEOPLE OF COLOR IN THE BOTTOM AND LAST OF EVERYTHING THAT IS GOOD.

06-01-03

VICE PRESIDENT CHENEY AND THE PRESIDENT OF THE UNITED STATES SPOKE TODAY TO WIN UNITED STATES SUPREME FAVORABLE OPTIONS FOR JOSE PADILLA, BEING HELD WITH OUT ANY CONSTITUTIONAL RIGHTS, IN THE NAME OF "ENEMY COMBATANT", TERMED BY THE GRAND DRAGON ARIAN DICK CHENEY, TO DENY AMERICANS ANY RIGHTS IS A TOTAL VIOLATION OF ALL OF OUR CONSTITU-TIONAL RIGHTS, BECAUSE ALL THAT ARE PROFILED ARE PEOPLE OF COLOR, THE PEOPLE THAT THE AMERICAN RIGHT WING DOES NOT LIKE AND IS DETERMINE TO KEEP SEPARATE AND EQUAL , JUST THE PAST UNITED STATES SUPREME COURT HAS RULED IN THE DREAD SCOTT RULING , FOR THE DEPENDANTS OF AMERICAN SLAVERY. CHENEY ALSO SPEAKING AND FIGHTING FOR THE PATRIOT ACT, BECAUSE JUNIOR GENERAL JOHN ASHCROFT HAS LOST A LOT OF CREDIBILITY WITH THIS RETURN TO NO KNOCK, NO SEARCH WARRANTS, AND MORE KILLINGS BY THE UNITED STATES POLICE AND THE BLACK POLICE THAT HAS SOLD THERE SOLES FOR EMPLOYMENT HELP SOLIDIFY THE

DEPENDANTS OF SLAVE MASTERS OF AMERICA AND THE NEO-NAZI APARTHEID MONEY PEOPLE WHO CONTINUES TO DENY BLACKS AND OTHERS THEIR RIGHTS. ANDY ROONEY, OF CBS' 60 MINUTES", SAID IT CORRECTLY THAT SINCE THE THIEVES AND KILLERS THAT WAS PERMITTED TO LEAVE THEIR JAIL CELLS TO VENTURE TO OTHER COLONIES AND PAST ON THE HATRED OF AFRICANS THROUGH OUT THE WORLD, IN AMERICA WE HAVE NEVER HAD A DICTATOR AND WHEN IT IS COMING PEOPLE RIGHTS ARE DENY LITTLE BY LITTLE, AND THAT IS WHAT THE RIGHT WING HAS BEEN DOING SINCE THE WARREN COURT DECISIONS, STARTING WITH PRESIDENT RICHARD M. NIXON, EXPLOITED WITH THE ACTOR RONALD REAGAN AND HIS VICE PRESIDENT GEORGE HERBERT WALKER BUSH, NIXON'S CENTRAL INTELLIGENT AGENCY DIRECTOR. RONALD REAGAN' S DIRECTOR CASEY COMMITTED SUICIDE, IN THE NAME OF BRAIN SURGERY TO KEEP THE CONTRA SECRETS OF THE RIGHT WING AND THEY'RE SUPPOSEDLY PROTECTION OF ILL OF OUR GOVERN-MENT. SAY ONE THING AND DO ANOTHER, NEWT GINGRICH LIE HIS WAY WITH THE CONTRACT OF AMERICA, TELL THE SO-CALL LIBERAL WILLIAM J. CLINTON ANYTHING ON PUBLIC SHOWS WHERE HE GOT EMBARRASSED BY CLINTON.

06-10-04

AT THE G8 SUMMIT, AT SEA ISLAND, GA., DENIED THAT HE APPROVED THE TORTURE OF THE AFRICAN IRAQ IN THEIR PRISON. COLIN POWELL DENIED THAT HE KNEW ANYTHING ABOUT, A PRESIDENT REAGAN TYPE LIE, ABOUT TERRORIST ATTACKS WERE DOWN, WHEN THEY THAT IT WAS A LIE, UNTRUE AS CONGRESSIONAL MEMBER STATED TODAY, FOR POLITICAL GAIN IN THE POLLS THAT PRESIDENT BUSH

ADMINISTRATION HAD A LOT TO DO WITH THAT DECLINE IN 2003.

06-13-04

AFTER HONORING FORMER PRESIDENT RONALD REAGAN DEATH, AT THE AGE OF 93, FOR A WEEK, FOR BRING CAUCA-SIANS TOGETHER BY CONVINCING THE RUSSIANS (SOVIET UNION) TO COME AND JOIN THERE RACE AS ONE CONTROL-LING CONQUISTADORS, AND PERMIT THE AIDS VIRUS SPREAD THROUGH OUT THE AFRICAN CONTINENT. CREATED BY REAGAN AND HIS CENTRAL INTELLIGENT AGENCY SCIENTISTS TO CREATE AND SPREAD. TODAY DIPLOMATS, GENERALS MILITARY, AND FROM HIGH LEVEL PEOPLE HAVE JOINT TOGETHER, TO TELL THE WORLD THAT THE BUSH ADMINISTRATION HAS CARRIED THIS COUNTRY IN THE WRONG DIRECTION, AND THEY ARE MOVING TO ELECT JOHN KERRY AS COMMANDER AND CHIEF IN NOVEMBER. BUSH-CHENEY WAR CRIMINALS SHOULD BE IMPEACHED, BUT THAT WILL NOT HAPPEN, BUT I AM GLAD THAT THEY (MILITARY) AND OTHERS HAS DECIDED NOT TO HIDE AND BE SILENT ANY LONGER WITH THE PEOPLE OF THE UNITED STATES HAS TO SUFFER MORE THAN NECESSARY. THE DESCENDANTS S ARE THE REAL PROTECTORS PF THIS COUNTRY, BECAUSE WE AND THE AMERICAN INDIANS, ALONG WITH THE MEXICANS REALLY KNOW OF THESE ENGLISH PEOPLE, THAT THEY SAY ONE THING TO A BLACK AND GO OFF AND DO ANOTHER. GERONIMO'S SKULL WAS ROBBED BY PRESIDENT BUSH'S GRANDFATHER, GEORGE PRESCOTT BUSH, HE BROUGHT IT UP TO YALE, TO BE KEPT AT YALE UNIVERSITY'S PRIVATE SKULL AND BONES SOCIETY TO BE SECRET AND STAY SECRET. PRESI-DENT BUSH FATHER SAID AFTER HIS LOST TO BILL CLINTON THAT HE WOULD NOT BE WRITING ANY BOOKS. CENTRAL

INTELLECT AGENCY DIRECTOR HAD BRAIN SURGERY TO KEEP THE SECRETS OF RONALD REAGAN ADMINISTRATION. THE BUSHES CONTINUE THEIR DECEIT AND THEIR FORTUNE HUNTING WAYS AS DIGNIFIED CITIZENS. CRIME DOES PAYS AND THEY, MOST WHITE PEOPLE DOES LITTLE OR NO TIME FOR THEIR CRIMES AGAINST AMERICAN TAX PAYERS. THE RECENT UNITED STATES SUPREME COURT DECISIONS TO DEMOLISHED THE FOURTH AMENDMENT TO THE CONSTITUTION OF THE UNITED STATES. PEOPLE OF COLOR DOES NOT HAVE CHANCE, EVEN WHEN THERE ARE MORE EDUCATED THAN EVER, BUT AS PEOPLE OF COLOR IT IS THE SAME AS WAS DURING SLAVERY, SIDE WITH THE WHITES WHO ARE CURIOUS ABOUT OTHERS OF COLORS.

06-15-04

BUSH HONORED FORMER PRESIDENT WILLIAM CLINTON AND HILARY CLINTON'S PORTRAITS IN THE WHITE HOUSE. CLINTON'S PORTRAITS WERE THE FIRST EVER BY A DESCENDANT OF SLAVES, AN AFRICA AMERICAN.

06-21-04

THE BOOK BY THE FORMER BEST PRESIDENT, WILLIAM CLINTON'S "MY LIFE", WILL GO AN SALE TOMORROW. SOLDIERS CIVILIAN LAWYERS WANT PRESIDENT BUSH AND DONALD RUMS FIELD TO TESTIFY IN THE TORTURE CASES OF SOLDIERS THAT TOP RANK MILITARY AND BUSH'S ADMINISTRATION WANT TO PUT ON THE LOWER RANK, AS USUAL, THE GOOD THEY TAKE CREDIT AND THE BAD THEY PUSH IT TO THE LOWER RANK.

06-24-04

LOS ANGELES POLICE CHIEF RUSHED BACK FROM THE EAST COAST TO FACE JUSTIFYING HIS FORCE'S CONTINUING ABUSE OF BLACKS AND LATINOS BEATING TODAY OF A BLACK MAN ON LIVE TELEVISION, AND THE RACIST COMMENTATORS ON RACIST RUPERT MURDOCK'S FOX CABLE NEWS STATIONS WERE LAUGHING AND JOKING AS THE POLICE WERE BEATING AN UNARMED IN THE CUSTODY MAN. WHAT THE UNITED STATES MILITARY DONE IN IRAQ, FOLLOWING PRESI-DENT GEORGE W. BUSH'S ORDERS OF TEXAS JUSTICE, THAT HE GAVE RIGHT AFTER SEPTEMBER 11, 2001. AL GORE AND JOHN KERRY MUST HAVE GOTTEN A COPY IF THIS DOCU-MENT AS THEY ARE NOW REFERRING TO MY THOUGHTS ON THIS COUNTRY'S TREATMENT OF IT'S DESCENDANTS OF SLAVES. HITLER AND RICHARD NIXON'S SECRETS ARE ALIVE AGAIN. NIXON'S MAIN MEN GEORGE H.W.BUSH AND CHENEY. CHENEY'S TRIP EARLIER IN THE YEAR WITH THE UNITED STATES SUPREME COURT JUSTICE ANTHONY SCALIA PAID OFF TODAY, WHEN CHENEY'S NOTES ON THE ENERGY TASK FORCE DID NOT HAVE TO BE REVEALED AND WAS SENT BACK TO THE LOWER COURT TO JUSTIFY THE FREEDOM OF INFOR-MATION ACT APPLY. THE ROMAN EMPIRE COURT DOES THIS COUNTRY DISSERVICE AGAIN. "WHEN YOU ARE IN ROME DO AS THE ROMANS...", THE UNITED STATES SUPREME COURT , THE ULTIMATE OF JURISPRUDENT COMMON LAW OF THESE CONQUISTADORS , THEY ARE ANTI AMERICAS , FOR WHAT THEY JUSTIFIED IN THE 2000 ABORTION OF THE UNITED STATES CONSTITUTION, TO STACK THE COURTS , BECAUSE OF RACISM 2004. THE RACIST CONSERVATIVES WHO THREATEN THEIR OWN CHILDREN TO BELIEVE IN THE CONTINUED RACIST ATTITUDES THAT WANT TO BLOCK POSSIBLY THE GREAT HUMAN MELTING POT OF HUMANS HERE, BUT OLD FOUR CENTURY HABIT ARE HARD TO BREAK, " GRANDPA

WOULD ROLL OVER IN HIS GRAVE, IF HE KNEW WE MARRY AN AFRICAN DESCENDED MEN," JULIUS CAESAR'S DREAM IS STILL ALIVE AND WELL AROUND THE WORLD; JUST NOT AS MUCH IGNORANCE OF THE HUMAN POPULATION AND THAT IS A GOOD THING, IN TIME. FAHRENHEIT 9/11, MICHAEL MOIRÉ'S MOVIE THAT THEY ARE CONTINUING TO INSTITUTE CENSORSHIP IN AMERICA AND THE SAME TIME TALKING ABOUT FREEDOM IN IRAQ, IT DOES NOT MAKE SENSE FOR OUR CONGRESSIONAL AND SENATORS TO FALSELY REPRESENT THE PEOPLE OF THE UNITED STATES. AN AMENDMENT TO THE CONSTITUTION OF THE UNITED STATES CONSTITUTION THAT THE UNITED STATES SUPREME COURT SHOULD HAVE TIME LIMITS OF TEN YEARS. AMEND THE U.S. CONSTITUTION FOR THIS REASON AND THIS REASON ALONG, WOULD GIVE HOPE TO THIS DEMOCRACY, A TRUE DEMOCRACY, MAY GOD BLESS. FREEDOM OF PRESS GOD BLESS AMERICANS. SITUA-TION WILL SHOW THE TRUTH THESE DAYS, OF SATELLITE TECHNOLOGY.

06-27-04

THERE ARE A NUMBER OF INTEL LENT PEOPLE THAT KNOWS THE DIFFERENCE IN THE LAW AND A JUDGE OF THE SECOND CIRCUIT OF NEW YORK, HAS STATED THAT THE PRESENT PRESIDENT BUSH RISE TO POWER IS SIMILAR. JUDGE GUIDO CALABRESI, 71 YEARS OLD. BUSH IS NOT A HIT AT THE NATO MEETINGS AND THE CONSERVATIVE MEDIA IS NOT REPORTING EVERY ASPECT OF THE DISTASTE FOR THE IRAQ WAR THAT IS CHANGING THE MIDDLE EAST VERY RAPIDLY. MAY GOD BE WITH US, WHEN JOE LIEBERMAN AND ALL THE ISRAELITES SUPPORT OR THROW ALL BOMBS IN THE NAME OF PROTECTING AMERICA'S INTEREST, AND THAT IS WHY

BUSH-CHENEY WENT TO WAR IS TO PROTECT ISRAEL AND OIL FINANCES.

06-28-04

PRESIDENT CHIRAC, OF FRANCE CHILLED PRESIDENT BUSH TODAY FOR HIS COMMENTS WITH THE EUROPEAN UNION (EU). HE TALKED TO TURKEY'S LEADERS AND PROMISE THEM THEY HAD DID ENOUGH TO JOINT THE EU. GEORGE BOY CANNOT FOOL THE WORLD ALREADY KNOWS THAT HE IS IN LINE WITH HITLER.

07-01-04

"INSIDE POLITICS

, WITH JUDY WOODRUFF, SHE PULLS FOR CONSERVATIVES, BUT HAS MADE IT POSSIBLE FOR BLACKS TO STAY IN FRONT OPPOSITION TO CONSERVATIVE (NEO NAZIS), IN NEW HAMP-SHIRE REPUBLICAN CONSERVATIVE DID A COPY CAT CRIME OF TAMPERING WITH VOTES, VOTE MACHINES, AND NOW JAMMING THE CALLS TO DEMOCRATIC VOTERS, JUSTICE DEPARTMENT SUPPOSE TO BE INVESTIGATING, BUT LIKE SADDAM HUSSEIN, CONVICT ME ON LAWS THAT I CREATED", JOHN ASHCROFT AND HIS JUSTICE DEPARTMENT IS NOT GOING TO INVESTIGATE THEMSELVES. THE SAME THING HAPPEN TO GAIN THE MAJORITY, BECAUSE THEY ARE WRONG AND WILL DO WHAT IS NECESSARY TO KEEP AND MAKE NEW LAWS TO MAKE IT MORE DIFFICULT TO ATTAIN EDUCATION AND OTHER RIGHTS TO LIVE TO KEEP THE POOR, AS IS SAID IN THE BIBLE, BUT BUSH LIKE PEOPLE FUCK THE POOR. DICK CHENEY GOT AND MADE THE SPEECH TO DAY CLAIMING VICTORY IN IRAQ, IT IS. CHENEY PRESIDENCIES

NOT BUSH; BUT BOTH WILL SUFFER SOME HOW. PEOPLE HAD ENOUGH BUT THERE ARE MORE LIVES TO BE WASTED IN THAT ILLEGAL WAR.

07-09-04

YESTERDAY THE BUSHES CLOSE FRIEND AND BUSINESS PARTNER KEN LAY WAS INDICTED AND ARRESTED YESTERDAY. HE IS THE SAME GENTLEMAN THAT ROBBED ALL OF THE ENRON'S RETIRES AND ORDERED ALL OF THE SHREDDING OF FILES AND DOCUMENTS TO PROTECT THE BUSHES. KEN LAY IS INDICTED FOR THE SAME CRIME THAT GEORGE W. BUSH DID TO SILVERADO BANK, IN COLORADO BACK IN THE EIGHTIES. BUSH-CHENEY AND THEIR REPUBLICAN RACIST COLLEAGUES IS PUMPING CASH INTO RALPH NADLER'S RUN FOR PRESIDENT TO AGAIN OVERTHROW THE AMERICAN PROCESS OF VOTING. PEOPLE THAT ARE LOST AN SO-CALL UNDECIDED SIX AND ELEVEN O'CLOCK NEWS WATCHERS TO VOTE NADER INSTEAD OF KERRY, BECAUSE THEY KNOW THAT GEORGE BUSH AND DICK CHENEY ARE NOT AND SHOULD NOT BE IN THE WHITE HOUSE.

07-09-04

CREATE A WEB SITE FOR CHARGE-IN FUTURE?- PRESIDENT SADDAM HUSSEIN , OF IRAQ, HAS ATTORNEYS FROM UNITED STATES, JORDAN, LEBANON, BELGIANS , AND LIBYA, THAT WOULD BE JUSTICE THEY RULE THAT SADDAM HUSSEIN BE RELEASED, IRAQ WAS A SOVEREIGN NATION .BUSH- CHENEY INTENTIONAL MISLEAD THE AMERICAN PEOPLE, AS I HAD SAID, AND THEY SHOULD BE IMPEACHED, SHOULD HAVE NEVER BEEN A BUSH – CHENEY ADMINISTRATION, WITH

THE UNITED STATES SUPREME COURT AS A MAJOR PLAYER IN THE ELECTION, STACKING THE COURTS ; THE UNITED STATES SUPREME COURT JUSTICES SHOULD NOT GIVEN A LIFE TIME TENURE, WHEN TIME IS FLYING AND THE JUSTICES ARE STELL IN THERE THOUGHTS, THEREFORE, THEY NEED TO BE REPLACE IN A TWENTY – YEAR TERM, A CONSTITUTIONAL AMENDMENT ONLY TO THAT SPECIFY YEAR TERM . AFTER WHAT OCCURRED IN THE 2000 ELECTION A CHANGE HAS TO COME TO SAVE AMERICA.

WE ARE THE MELTING POT OF THE EARTH EXPERIMENT OF GOD. SOME ARE SHORT AND VISA VERSA, SOME RUN FAST AND OTHER DO NOT, SOME OF OUR BRAIN FUNCTION S IS FASTER THAN OTHERS AND THE HUMAN EXPERIMENT COULD EXIST IF THE WELL TO DO CONTRIBUTE BACK IN TO THEIR (HUMAN) LESSER TO DO BOTHER HOOD, OF THE HUMAN RACE, IF AMERICA WANTS A MORE UNDERSTANDABLE HUMAN HABIT OF DOMINATION. GOD CREATED US AS THE SUPREME BEING OF EARTH. ISRAEL IS THE REAL REASON THAT THE RIGHT WING DEVIOUS SIDE OF THE HUMAN BEING, THEY HAVE CAPTURE DOMINATION OF SEVENTY PERCENT OF THE HUMANS, SO WE ARE HUMANS AND THE EXPERIMENT COULD GO WITHOUT DESTROYING OUR SELVES; AND THAT IS THE REASON FOR THE SPACE VENTURES OF THE HUMANS, THE SUPREME BEING HAS CONQUERED THE BOTTLE OF THE SEA, UP IN GREAT HEIGHTS OF THE ATMOSPHERE LOOKING FOR IT'S CREATOR. THEY HAS COMMITTED GENOCIDE OF HUMANS, IRREGARDLESS OF THE HUMAN COMPLEXION, IT IS HUMAN, IT IS CO MEDICAL WHEN YOU SEE THE PICTURE AND I THE SPIRITED OF CHANGE AND AWARENESS OF THE HUMAN MIND, THAT IS INTERIOR OF THE BRAIN. HONORABLE OR NOT, THE NOT IS THE LESSER OF THE HUMAN, AS THE FOOL AND THE FOOL DOES NOT HAS A FACE, THIS IS THE HUMAN EXPERIMENT OF GOD;. IT ALL

STARTED FROM ONE HUMAN, AND THE REST OF IT IS RACIST, HATRED, DEVILISH, AND THE MOST UNPREDICTABLE MIND OF THE HUMAN MIND.

04-09-04

SENATOR ROCKERFELLER, REPORTED TODAY THAT THE CENTRAL INTELLIGENCE AGENCY, WAS FLOUT AND THE CONGRESS WOULD HAVE NEVER WENT TO WAR, FREE SADDAM HUSSEIN TO PLEASE THE MAJORITY OF THE PEOPLE THAT ARE CRYING FROM HIS RUTHER NESS OVER HIS FELLOW HUMAN, ON THE DEFENSE OF THE LIGHTER COMPLEXION OF HUMANS, AND JULIUS CAESAR WAS THE LITTLE (SHORT) PEOPLE REVOLUTION OF THE HUMAN EXPERIMENT AND WE AS HUMANS HAS A JOB, BUT RESOURCES SHOULD MAKE SURE THAT THEY, THE LESSER HUMAN DOES HAS BACKS SURVIVOR, AS LIKE IN THE PHYSIOLOGY FOR THE MENTAL ILLNESS PATIENCE'S. THE RIGHT WING CONSPIRACY, THE LIGHTEST OF THE LIGHT COMPLEXION HUMAN MIND OF GREED. THIS INTELLECT REPORT THAT IS OUT IS "HORRIBLE FAULTED ", AND IS HIGHLY CRITICAL OF GEORGE TENET, THE DIRECTOR OF THE CENTRAL INTELLIGENCE AGENCY, BUT HE WAS FOLLOWING DICK CHENEY'S ORDER TO THIS WEAK MAN, OR OTHER WISE HE WOULD HAVE BEEN REPLACED BY CHENEY, THE CONSPIRACY WAS IN HIGH GEAR WHEN HE WANTED AND MOST LIKELY BEGGED TO BE APART OF THIS GRAND CONSPIRACY CONTINUATION OF HITLER AND RICHARD NIXON; AND THE WENT TO HOLLYWOOD TO DRAFT THE GREAT ACTOR, RACIST ASS RONALD REAGAN, HONOR HIM FOR WHAT. CHENEY AND SHARON OF ISRAEL HAS PUT THE UNITED STATES IN THE POSITION CONTINUE ROMAN DREAM OF JULIUS CAESAR. THE MEDIA AND THE ADMINISTRATION WAS A POLITICAL RELATION THAT

SHOULD BE LIBERAL MINDED HUMANS TO EXIST, INSTEAD OF THE SO- CALL CONSERVATIVE, IN RHETORIC, THEY ONLY THE CASE FOR WAR, AND AS THE PRESIDENT GOT UP ON TELEVISION AND SAID AMERICA STICK WITH ME BECAUSE SADDAM PUT A CONTRACT ON HIS FATHER TO BE KILLED, WHEN HIS FATHER TRICKED SADDAM TO BELIEVE THAT HE COULD INVADE KUWAIT WITH OUT REPERCUSSIONS AND ALL HELL BROKE OUT; BUT KUWAIT WAS THE SOUTHERN PORT OF IRAQ, UNTIL THE BRITISH EMPIRE DESERTED THE CONQUERED LANDS OF THE RED SEA AND THE MEDITER-RANEAN. SADDAM IS AFRICAN DISSENTED AND SHARON, OF ISRAEL IS THE RUSSIAN DESCENDANT OF THE ROMAN EMPIRE, THE SAME ONES THAT CRUCIFIED THE OTHER HOLY MESSENGER OF GOD'S WORD AND SPIRIT. JESUS SAID THEY THE PHI STEINS WOULD USE HIS NAME IN VAIN, AND THEY CONTINUE ON IN THE NAME OF THE ROMAN EMPIRE CRUCI-FIERS THE CATHOLIC BELIEFS ARE THOSE OF THE CRUCI-FIERS OF AFRICANS, GOD SAYS HAVE MANY CHILDREN AND BE MERRY, AND THE CRUCIFIERS SAYS BE CELEBRATE, THAT IS AGAINST GOD'S LAW OF THE HUMANS AND IT WAS CREATED IN THE DARK, THEN THERE SHALL BE LIGHT TO SEE YOURSELF. FREE SADDAM AND PERMIT HIM TO BE IN THE PEOPLE RIGHTS FOR THEIR RICHES OF IRAQ, SOMEWHAT LIKE IN KUWAIT AND THE GULF NATION THAT SHARES THE WEALTH. A THOUSAND OF OUR TROOPS (HUMANS) HOME ON A MAFIA TYPE OF HIT ON SADDAM, IN THE NAME OF WEAPONS OF MASS DESTRUCTION, A BIG RIGHT WING LIE IN THE NAME OF THE MAJORITY OF VOTES FOR THE PEOPLE, BY THE PEOPLE, HAS BEEN BREACHED, AND THE LEADER DICK CHENEY HAS ANYTHING TO DO WITH IT, IT WILL CONTINUE, NEW LEADERSHIP IS NEEDED IN 2004 ELECTION, IF NO CHANGE, MAY GOD BLESS US. DICK CHENEY TOLD THE CENTRAL INTELLIGENCE DIRECTOR, GEORGE TENET, NOT TO SHOW THE OTHER REPORTS, BECAUSE THAT WOULD BE

TOO LIBERAL, AND THE MEDIA CONTINUE WITH RUPERT MURDOCK, RACIST AS AUSTRALIAN, OF THE BRITISH EMPIRE VENTURES, JUST AS THESE IN THE AFRICAN BRITISH EMPIRE WAR, THEY ARE ALL BROTHER OF THE LIGHTER HUMANS, TO BRAIN WASH THE WEAKER ONES, WOMEN TO BE IN THE CORNER OF THE LIGHTER SKIN HUMANS, RACIST.

07-12-04

NAACP HAS ASKED THE PRESIDENT BUSH TO SPEAK FOR THE PAST FOUR YEARS, AND THE RACIST BASTARD- SON OF A BITCH DENIED THE REQUEST, AND HE TRIES TO BE SEEN AS LIBERAL MINDED BECAUSE OF COLON POWELL AND CONDO LISA RICE, WHO HE CONTROLS COMPLETELY, IN THE NAME OF LOYALTY. THE RIGHT WING IS TRYING TO SCARE THE POPULATION AGAIN. THEY ARE THROWING OUT SOMETHING CALL DELAYING A PRESIDENTIAL ELEC-TION, THE SAME ONES THAT COMMITTED FRAUD TO GET BUSH-CHENEY INTO THE WHITE ILLEGALLY. A U.S. CONSTI-TUTIONAL AMENDMENT FOR EVERYTHING, CARRY ON THE SLAVERY MINDED EFFECTS OF THE DRED VS. SCOTT DECI-SION, THE RACIST RULING BY THE U. S. SUPREME COURT, THE RACIST COURT THAT THE BLACKS HAS TO CONTINUE TO SUFFER THIS DAY AND TIME. MARSHALL LAW IN THE NAME OF THE CONSTITUTION, CAUSE THESE CAUCASIANS DO NOT HAVE ANOTHER LAND TO CALL HOME AND THEY ARE NOT TO RETURN TO EUROPE, HITLER LIVES ON. WE AS A PEOPLE ARE IN BIG TROUBLE.

 RUPERT MURDOCK'S EMPLOYEES ARE STATING THAT HE REQUIRED THAT THEY BE CONSERVATIVE (RACIST) , IN ORDER TO BE EMPLOYED A FOX NETWORK. HE IS NOT A CITIZEN OF THIS COUNTRY, HE HAS THE CASH FROM HIS

SWINDLING IN AUSTRIAN. OWNING PRINT AND TELEVISION IS TOO MUCH POWELL FOR ONE INDIVIDUAL ON A SO-CALL FREED SOCIETY. CAME TO NEW YORK AND BROUGHT THE TROUBLED NEW YORK POST, AND HIS JULIUS CAESAR AND HITLER THOUGHTS GOES OUT AND HE HIS HEAD OF THE SO-CALL NEO –NAZI NESS, AND THESE SO-CALL WHITE JEWS TRYING TO BECOME RED NECKISH TO GET ALONG IN THIS RACIST SOCIETY AND THE RACIST WOMEN, THEY LOOK A LIKE AND THEY HAVE NOT FORGOT HITLER DID TO THEM FOR WORSHIPING AN AFRICAN ROOTED RELIGION.

07-18-04

THE SHARON BIAS AND HATRED OF AFRICAN DESCENDANT PEOPLE, HAD ISRAEL'S ARMY TO DESTROY THE PALESTIN-IAN'S INTELLIGENT OFFICE TODAY. THEY ARE CONTINUING TO TERRORIZE DEFENSIVE LESS PEOPLE, PALESTINE, AND THE SAME PEOPLE JESUS OF NAZARETH. ISRAEL WANTS TO DESTROY HISTORY EXCEPT THEIR ROMAN HISTORY TO BE HIGHLY PROTECTED HISTORY, WHICH INCLUDE PALESTINE. THAT IS THE SAME AS THE KLAN COME AND TERRORIST US BLACKS AND CALL US UN-AMERICAN IF YOU DO NOT AGREED WITH THE REAL TERRORIST, ISRAEL AND AMERICA. THE STORY OF "DEATH ROW RECORDS" 2001 SHOWS HOW CENSORSHIP IN AMERICA. C. LORY TUCKER, CRACKER BLACK ASS THAT COLLABORATED WITH THE AMERICAN RIGHT WING, HEADED BY BOB DOLE AND WILLIAM BENNETT, JOE LIBERIAN, AL GORES PICK FOR VICE PRESIDENT, NO WONDER HE LOST. BETWEEN JOE, BUSHES, AND NOT ASSOCIATING WITH THE PRESIDENT CLINTON, AL GORE WAS LOST AND TRYING TO SATISFY THE RIGHT WING, ORRIN HATCH WAS DEFINITELY PLEASE. LAWS TO KEEP PEOPLE OF COLOR IN A COMPLETE CONSPIRACY TO FIGHT CONSPIRACY FROM THE

AMERICAN GOVERNMENT, IN THE NAME OF THE LAW. JOHN GOTTI, JR., WAS INDICTED TODAY ON THE MOST BULL SHITISTS OF OUR LAWS, CONSPIRACY. THE PRESIDENT BUSHES HAVE ALL THREATEN SADDAM AND OTHERS, BUT THEY ARE NOT BROUGHT UP IN AN INDICTMENT. NEWT GINGRICH, FORMER CONGRESSMAN SAID A LOT OF THINGS THAT HE DID NOT / NOR INTENDED TO DO. LIED TO THE AMERICAN PEOPLE CONSTANTLY. HE AND PRESIDENT CLINTON MADE AGREE-MENTS MANY TIMES IN PUBLIC, BUT NEWT WENT BEHIND CLOSE DOORS AND THAT WAS THAT. MEDIA IGNORED IT FOR OTHER, SO-CALL UP TO DATE NEWS WORTHINESS'.

08-08-04

BUSH-CHENEY ADMINISTRATION HAS TOOK US BACKWARDS FOR THE OLD CONQUISTADORS, ROBB THE BANKS AND GOLD FILLED LANDS (AFRICA& MIDEAST), THEN LAY BACK AS A BIG MAN BIG KILLER OF THE HUMAN RACE, THEY ARE THE DEVILS OF THE HUMAN EXISTENCE OF THE LIGHTER SKIN HUMAN, THEY CREATED A CONTINENT AND CALLED IT EUROPE, WHEN IN ACTUALITY IT IS ONLY SOUTH ASIA. THE CRUCIFIERS OF THE HOLY AFRICAN SON OF GOD, JESUS THEY CALL HIM, THEY (ROMAN EMPIRE) CRUCIFIED THE HOLY MESSIAH JESUS OF NAZARETH, PALESTINE, WAS CRUCI-FIED BY THE ROMANS AND HE WAS BETRAYED BY JUDAS A HEBREW JEW.

THE BIG LIE CONTINUES AND THERE WILL CONTINUE TO BE WARS BECAUSE OF RACISM. THE PRESIDENT LAST WEEK SAID " THAT THEY HAVE TURNED THE CORNER AND IS NOT LOOKING BACK", REFERRING TO THE IRAQ WAR .THE POPE AND HIS POSITION IS THE STANDARD, ANTI- CHRIST. THEY GIVE FREELY TO ANY POOR WHITE AND HESITATE THE DARK,

BECAUSE OF ALL THE WARS, SLAVERY, AND GENOCIDE, ONE DO NOT THINK THAT THEY ARE GOING TO FREELY HELP RESTORE WHAT THEY HAVE TRIED TO DESTROY, THE DARK OF THE HUMAN BEING.

THERE IS A CHANCE THAT THE HUMANS CAN EXIST AS A GREAT CREATION OF THE ALMIGHTY CREATOR OF ALL THINGS, BUT THE LIGHT MUST SHINE AS GOD INTENDED. THE LIGHT IS THE GROWTH OF THE HUMAN MIND, BODY, AND TO FEED THE POOR AROUND THE WORLD. GROCERY STORES WOULD RATHER THROW AWAY THE COOKED FOOD OF THE DAY INSTEAD OF PERMITTING THEIR EMPLOYEES TO CARRY THE COOKED HOME INSTEAD OF FEEDING THE RATS. NOT A SO-CALL CHRISTIAN NATION. AS A NATION WE CAN DO BETTER FOR THE PEOPLE OF THIS NATION NO MATTER THE COMPLEXION, BUT THE DESCENDANTS OF SLAVES HAS TO REAP FROM THE SUCCESS OF THE NEW NATION ON EARTH, THE UNITED STATES OF AMERICA.

WE SENT FOOD AND OTHER ITEMS TO HELP IN SOME DISASTERS, BUT WE HAVE TO DO BETTER A HOME. WE AS A NATION CAN DO BETTER AND STRAIGHTEN A WRONG THAT TODAY'S POWERFUL ARE THE DESCENDANTS OF THE SLAVE TRADE AND THE SLAVE MASTERS OF THE UNITED STATES. HAND OUT CRUMBS AND MOST OF THE TIME NOT EVEN THE CRUMBS.

THE BUSH CHENEY ADMINISTRATION SHOWS THAT CRIME DOES PAY. CHENEY'S HALLIBURTON COMPANY THAT HAS HAD EXCLUSIVE CONTRACT ON EVERYTHING IN SAUDI ARABIAN, AND THE IRAQ WAR, EXCLUDED ALL BIDDERS, NO COMPETITORS, THE AMERICAN WAY. THEY ROB THE SILVERADO BANK AND LEFT THE OLD PEOPLE SUFFERING FOR THE FDIC INSURANCE TO COVER THE COVER-UP, AS WAS THE 2000 PRESIDENTIAL ELECTION TO BECOME A PRESIDENT

AND TO SET BACK AND KEEP ASLEEP THE PEOPLE OF THE UNITED STATES.

THEN IN THE NAME OF THE LAW THE LAW HAS TO IMPEACH A SITTING PRESIDENT CLINTON FOR A LIE, SO THE BUSH CHENEY NEEDS TO BE IMPEACH JUST THE OHIO SENATOR KUCINICH. ORRIN HATCH IS NOT SAYING ANYTHING NOW AS HE DID DURING THE CLINTON YEARS, BECAUSE HE LIVES A LIE EVERYDAY WITH HIS RELIGION OF HATE FOR THE DARK HUMAN, THE MORMON, SCIENCETOGY, AND OTHERS ARE KLANIST NOT GODLY. THEY ARE ANTI- CHRIST. FORBES AND ALL THE REST OF THE RECEIVERS OF THE TAX REFUND FROM THE SURPLUS SHOULD MAKE IT A RIGHT FOR MY PEOPLE, THE DESCENDANTS OF AMERICAN SLAVERY, SHOULD BE EDUCATED, HOUSED, AND MEDICALLY TAKEN CARE OF, AND THE WELL TO DO WILL KEEP HAVING. IT IS ALL-RACIST AND NOT CAPITALISM. THEY ARE ANTI- CHRIST, NO SOCIAL PROGRAMS IN THE BUDGET IS COMPLETELY RACIST AND ANTI-AMERICAN. THE RIGHT WING CONSPIRACY TO MARSHALL LAW, MAY GOD BLESS US? CONTINUE TO DECEIVE THE IGNORANT PEOPLE OF THE AMERICAN SLAVE SYSTEM.

EVERYTHING THAT IS FROM GOD EARTH AND FOR THE CREATURES OF THE EARTH WEED ADD LEAVES ARE A NATURAL VITAMIN FOR HUMANS, BUT THE DEVIL OF OUR SOCIALITY WANT TO JAIL US UNDER FALSE PRETENSIONS, THAT IS WHY THIS ELECTION MUST NOT BE IN THE HANDS OF ORRIN HATCH AND THE BUSH 2 ADMINISTRATION.

08-09-04

THE RIGHT WINGERS ARE AT IT AGAIN, LAST PRESIDEN-TIAL ELECTION OF 2000. TODAY DEBATES OF THESE PEOPLE STATING THAT THEY SERVED WITH KERRY AND HE IS NOT

HONORABLE". HONORABLE IS NOT THE THING, CAUSE BUSH IS HONORABLE ON HIS CIRCLE AND THOSE THAT NOT IN HIS CIRCLE, HE IS NOT HONORABLE AND VICE VERSA WITH KERRY, IN THAT PEOPLE CAN SEE HIM AS MORE CREDITABLE. BASED ON THOUGHTS OF GOD'S PEOPLE, THAT THE WELL TO DO MAKE WAY FOR THOSE HAS NOT. DOCTOR MARTIN LUTHER KING, JUNIOR, SAYS THAT IF THE UNITED STATES HAS FUNDS FOR THE POOR, BUILDING SCHOOLS IN IRAQ AND TEACHING THEM ENGLISH IS NOT THE WAY FOR TAX DOLLARS FOR THAT, THAT SHOULD BECOME THE LAW OF THE LAND. THE SUDANESE IN AFRICA HAS NEEDED AID FOR THE PAST EIGHTEEN MONTHS, AND YOU DO NOT SEE IT CONSTANTLY, WHEN THE BUSH CHENEY DOES NOT PLAN ON HELPING THOSE AFRICANS, WHEN THE REBELS HAS KILLED, FOR THE SAKE OF GENOCIDE, IN THE NAME OF GOLD. KILL YOUR OWN, BUT YOU ARE NOT TO TOUCH THEIR PEOPLE, BUSH SAYS WHAT RONALD REAGAN SAID, UNITE EUROPE AND POISON THE RIVERS AND CREATING AIDS. GENOCIDE. ALAN KEYS, FROM MARYLAND AND NOW MOVING TO ILLINOIS TO RUN FOR THE RIGHT WINGERS RELIGION, PAT ROBERTSON AND JERRY FARWELL'S FRONT MAN FOR WHITE PEOPLE, TO SAY… "YELL I LIKE BLACKS, I VOTE FOR ALAN KEYS, THAT IS LIKE JUDAS, HE RAN OFF COLLABORATING NG WITH THE ROMAN EMPIRE OF TODAY. THE OIL MEN GETS ON TV AND SAYS THAT HE LOOKS AT FIFTY DOLLAR A BARREL, WHEN EXXON MOBLE HAS STOLES AND CAPTURE DRILLING RIGHTS IN THE AFRICAN COAST AND GIVE THE AFRICAN NATION TEN PERCENT. ON 60 MINUTES A FEW WEEKS AGO, HAD THE STORY OF AN AFRICAN NATION THAT WAS GLAD FOR THAT PIECE OF PIE.

08-17-04

CHIVA EDMONDS, A FIRED LINGUIST, A WHISTLE BLOWER, THAT PULL THE COVER OFF FEDERAL BUREAU OF INVESTI-GATION ON IT'S COVER UP OF INFORMATION ON TERRORIST TRANSLATIONS. PAULA ZHAN, CNN NEWS ANCHOR, WITH CHARLES GRASSLEY, SENATOR OF IOWA, OS FAIRLY FRANK THAT THE FBI HAS AND STILL IS COVERING UP THEIR ILLE-GALITY OF CITIZENS AND EMPLOYEES. BUSH ADMINISTRA-TION IS AT IT AGAIN WITH THESE BIAS ADS AND COMMER-CIALS, DISTORTION OF SENATOR JOHN KERRY'S VIETNAM RECORDS, AND IT IS A GREAT POSSIBLY THAT I WAS ON ONE OF THOSE MEKONG DELTA TRIPS WITH KERRY AND HIS CREWS. GETTING OFF THOSE BOATS INTO THIGH HIGH MUD WAS NOT NO JOKE IN THE SWAMPS OF THE DELTA. THE BIG RAT COMMERCIAL THAT SCARED AL GORE SO MUCH THAT HIS ATTACK OF GEORGE W. BUSH CURTAILED AND HE LOST THE WEST VIRGINIA AND HIS HOME STATE. THEY ARE NERVOUS THAT THEY WILL NOT GET A CHANCE TO REALLY BE A LAME DUCK" PRESIDENT, WITH THE BIG GRAND DRAGON OF THE RIGHT WING, SENATOR ORRIN HATCH, THE RACIST MORMONS OR THE LATTER DAY SAINTS THAT REFER TO BLACKS AS MONKEYS AND OTHER DEROGATORY LIES, TO APPROVE ANY JUDICIAL APPOINTMENT THAT BUSHES AND CHENEY TO MAKE IT DIFFICULT TO LIVE IN AMERICA AFTER SLAVERY AND THE WARREN COURTS DECISIONS THAT ARE BEING REVERSED. THEY ARE EVEN PUSHING FOR CLARENCE ----- AS CHIEF JUSTICE OF THE SUPREME COURT OF THE UNITED STATES, NOW THAT IS WHAT YOU CALL GIVING YOU HOUSE NIGGER FACE ON HISTORY AS NOT RACIST. HE AND COLON WILL BE THE FIRST TO GO AFTER THEY RE-CONQUERED THIS LAND AND THE EARTH. THIS HUMAN SPECIES' WILL BE ON THEIR WAY OF DESTROYING WHAT THE ALMIGHTY GOD'S PLAN FOR THE SUPREME BEING OF THE EARTH, IT WILL BE

DESTROYED. HURRICANE CHARLIE OF 2004, THIS CRACKER SAYS ALL THESE GREAT MINDS AND CAN NOT TRACK THESE STORMS", THAT MIND SET OF THE ROMAN EMPIRE BEFORE THE CREATION JESUS CHRIST OF NAZARETH, BORN IN BETH- LEHEM, PALESTINE, SAME AS YASSAR ARAFAT, THE PRIME MINISTER OF ISRAEL, ARIEL SHARON, A RUSSIAN BORN HEBREW JEWISH RELIGION BELIEVER AND FOLLOWER OF THE ROMANS INSTEAD OF SALOMON AND ABRAHAM.

08-18-04

Kerry spoke TO THE VFW, IN CINCINNATI, OHIO, TO LET THEM KNOW AFTER BUSH WAS THERE EARLIER THIS WEEK, THAT BUSH PLAN TO PULL TROOPS FROM KOREA AND GERMANY WILL WEAKEN OUR STRENGTH. THIS AFTER NOON RESPONSE TO KERRY 'S SPEECH, BY SOME MARINE ON THIS POLITICAL DECISIONS BY THIS CROOK RACIST BUSH AND CHENEY ADMINISTRATION, THAT KERRY IS GOING AGAINST THE " STATUS QUO', NOW FOR AN AMERICAN BANK ROBBER TO TALK OF STATUS QUO, AMERICA IS IN BIG TROUBLE.

08-20-04

Bush is back at ranch WITH FATHER, WHO SET UP THIS WHOLE ANTI AMERICAN THING, ANTI-SADDAM THING THAT HAS OUR COULD BE GREAT NATION, BUT RACISM WILL KEEP THE EARTHLY WORLD INN DEMISE. GOD SAYS TAKE CARE OF THE DESTITUTE AND AMERICA DO NOT , INSTEAD THEY WILL POUR UNLIMITED FUNDS TO TEACH ENGLISH TO IRAQ BUT NOT MY PEOPLE OF COLOR. BUSH'S CNN LARRY KING 'S INTERVIEW HE SITS THERE AND LIE ABOUT ANY AND EVERY- THING AND IT WILL COME BACK TO HAUNT HIM. HOPE-

FULLY BY NOT GETTING ELECTED, SINCE HE IS THE FIRST APPOINTED PRESIDENT IN THE HISTORY OF THIS SO-CALL DEMOCRACY. GWINNETT COUNTY, GEORGIA WILL NOT AFFORD INDIGENT PRISONERS WITH THE BASIC DEFENSE, FOR TO SAVE COUNTY TAX PAYERS TWO MILLION DOLLARS PER YEAR. NO EDUCATION TO SENTENCED PRISONERS, THE LAW IS LOCK-EM –UP AND THROW THE KEY AWAY. THEY LOOK AT ME AS A REASON NOT TO EDUCATE A DESCEN-DANT OF SLAVES. NO FLY LIST FOR TEDDY KENNEDY AND CONGRESSMAN JOHN LEWIS NOT TO FLY, ALL DEMOCRATS. BUSH AND CHENEY HAS SCARED THE SO CALL LIBERALS ON THIS HOME LAND SECURITY TO PUT THIS SOCIETY INTO MARSHALL LAW IN THE NAME OF THE LAW. A C L U SUPPOSES TO BE FILING SUIT ON THE REASON. A SEVENTY-SIX YEAR OLD BLACK TEXAS MAN, THAT WAS A WORLD WAR TWO AND KOREAN WAR VETERAN WAS RELEASED FROM A TEXAS PRISON FOR A CRIME THAT HE DID NOT COMMIT, SAYS BET NEWS. TEXAS JUSTICE AS THE PRESIDENT OF THE UNITED STATES GEORGE W. BUSH SAID HE WAS GOING TO HAND OUT TO SADDAM HUSSEIN.

08-23-04

"TARGETED ASSASSINATION", BY THE UNITED STATES OF AMERICA OF ANYONE THAT WAS A " KINGPIN DRUG DEALER" IN ANOTHER COUNTRY AND FOR POOR PEOPLE OF AMERICA IS A RACIST LAW, THEN SENTENCES, ARE TO EXTORT OF ONES FINANCES, BY FORMER CENTRAL INTELLI-GENCE DIRECTOR AND NOW THE (1980) -THE PRESIDENT OF THE UNITED STATES GEORGE W. H. BUSH DOCUMENTARY ON TV DRAMA, MARK BOWDEN'S "KILLING OF PABLO" BY BLACK HAWK DOWN AUTHOR. THE ROCKERFELLER LAW OF NEW YORK, MICHIGAN, ALL THE STRIKE LAWS, AND ESPECIALLY

FROMER GEORGIA'S ZELL MILLER'S TWO STRIKE LAW IS THE PURE EXAMPLE THE RACISM IN AMERICA WITH ALL THE PEOPLE OF COLOR WITH FINANCE ACCESS, THAT IS, ALL THE LAWS WERE MADE FOR THE PEOPLE OF COLOR AND THE VERY FEW CAUCASIANS THAT MIGHT GET CAUGHT, JUST TO SAY SEE " WE ARE NOT PREJUDICE" THE FIRST LIE THAT THE RACIST WILL SAY. " CRACKERS (SLAVE MASTER'S DESCENDANTS) ARE A MOTHER FUCKER", AND ARE DEPRIVING EDUCATION, HOUSING, AND OTHERS SURVIVAL FROM A LOST PEOPLE THAT DID NOT ASK TO BE KIDNAPPED AND ENSLAVED, THEN LOOK APOND AS UNINTELLENT BECAUSE OF THE STRIPPING ONES SOUL TO APLEASE THE GREED AND DESIRE OF BRITISH SUBJECTS TO ESCAPE THE RULE OF A KING SHIP OF THE ANGLO SAXON LAWS OF ENGLAND, THAT WAS THE MODEL FOR THE UNITED STATES LAWS.

THOSE TWO GREAT WORD THAT IS INTERPRETED DIFFERENTLY IN THE LATIN SPANISH IDIOMS. EVERY MAN HAS FUCKED A MOTHER, NOT YOUR BIRTH MOTHER, BUT YOUR ON CHILDREN 'S MOTHER. WEBSTER DICTIONARY. MOTHER FUCKER IS NOT PROFANITY. AMERICA IS SLOWLY BECOMING A MARSHALL LAW STATE, TO CONTROL AND SEIZE ACCESS OF FORTUNES BY THOSE WHO HAVE WORKED AND SUPPOSE TO FOLLOW ALL THE LAWS THAT THE CRACKERS MADE UP TO KEEP THE "STATUS QUO'. HISTORY AND THE OVER THROW OF THE UNITED STATES CONSTITUTION WITH THE APPOINTMENT OF BUSH AND CHENEY AT CHENEY AND BUSH2 DIRECTION, AS COURTS INTERFERED WITH RECOUNT. ANOTHER GRAND SCHEME OF THE UNITED STATES HIGH COURT FOR ABORTION AND MORE PRISON TIME THAT IS AFFIRMED TO THE JUSTICE OF SOME LOCAL RAILROAD JOB IN LOCAL COURTS. THE AMERICAN WAY. AS JAMES BAKER THE POINT MAN SENT FROM BUSH FAMILY, THE SAME BUSH WHO CHANGE THE LAW TO ASSASSINATE LEGALLY, BECAUSE

OF PABLO ESCOBAR IS ABSOLUTE RIDICULOUS. BLACK AND PEOPLE OF COLOR ILLEGAL LAWS OF THE UNITED STATES. THE CRACKERS ONLY CARE FOR CASH. THE AMERICAN GOVERNMENT IS BECOMING LARGER THAN THE ROMAN EMPIRE, JUST AS THE HOUSE OF COMMON, ALL AFTER ROMAN LAWS OF DESTINATION FOR THE AFRICANS. AMERICAN SLAVERY WAS BORN AFTER THEY CRUCIFIED THE HOLY MESSIAH JESUS CHRIST.

THE Fugitive slave act of 1850 BY UNITED STATES CONGRESS, IS ENOUGH FOR THE UNITED STATES CONGRESS TO WORK OUT SOMETHING BESIDES THE PROJECT TYPE HOUSING AND THE RESERVATION GIVEN TO THE INDIANS, AND NOW THEY CAN OPERATE CASINOS ON THEIR RESERVATIONS; BUT, THE DESCENDANT OF SLAVES DID NOT HAVE THAT LUXURY. THEY WERE OFFERED AN ACRE AND A MULE AND NOW THE UNITED STATES NEEDS TO FIGURE OUT WHAT THAT IS WORTH IN TODAYS MARKET.

THEY USE IMMINENT DOMAIN LAWS TO REMOVE THE MOM AND POP STORES, AND OTHER PRIME GHETTO PROPERTY FOR SOME OTHER THAN GOVERNMENT USE OF THE LAND, WHICH EMMINENT DOMAIN LAWS WERE INTENTED FOR INTERSTATE HIGHWAY PROJECTS AND OTHER STATE ROAD PROJECT, BUT NOT FOR BUSH, FORBES, TRUMP, AND OTHERS TO BUILT A WAL-MART OR SOME EXPENSIVE HIGH RISE THAT SURELY DOES NOT HAVE THE MIDDLE CLASS TENANTS, AND THAT IS DISCRIMINTORY OF HOUSING. EASTERN IMMIGRANTS, EUROPEANS, AND OTHER ARE ALLOWED TO COME TO THE UNITED STATES TO ROB, OBTAIN GRANTS FOR SCHOOLS, HOUSING, AND LOOK DOWN ON THE LOST PEOPLE OF THE EMACIPATION OF SLAVERY. BUILT PROJECTS TO SUBSTITUTE SHARECROPPING, BUT NO EDUCATION, AND TODAY ALL JOBS ARE TAKEN BY THE SLAVE MASTER'S

CHILDREN AND THEY CREATE A SO-CALL GLASS CEILING, WHERE AND IF A BLACK OBTAIN A JOB ON WALL STREET OR ANY OTHER CORPORATION IT IS AT BEST MIDDLE LEVEL, BUT TO THE CRACKERS THAT IS BETTER THAN THE PROJECTS AND HARD LABOR, SO THE BLACKS FALL IN LINE AND FORGET WHERE THEIR PEOPLE HAVE COME FROM AND WHAT IS NEEDED TO KEEP THE YOUNG BLACKS FROM DESTROYING THEMSELVES, BECAUSE OF NO INTEREST IN AN EDUCATION THAT WILL NOT HELP THE MAJORITY. MASTER FARD MUHAMMAD, WHO CAME THROUGH GEORGIA IN THE THIRTIES TO WAKE –UP THE EX-SLAVES AND THE EX-SHARE-CROPPER PREACHED INDEPENDENCE. CROP A TREE DOWN AND SELL YOUR WOOD AND ETC.

THE UNIVERSITY OF OBERLIN IS THE FIRST DESCENDANTS OF SLAVE INSTITUTE 1858. THE HISTORY CHANNEL IS A PREFECT RESOURCE. THE DRED SCOTT LAW, BY THE UNITED STATES SUPREME COURT, "SLAVES HAS NO RIGHTS THAT A WHITE MAN IS BOUND TO RESPECT" IN 1865, ABRAHAM LINCOLN'S INAUGURAL ADDRESS-" THE WHOLE NATION MUST TAKE THE RESPONSIBILITY OF THE SLAVERY....

08-26-04

FORMER SENATOR BOB DOLE IS IN THE NEWS AGAIN, ATTACKING SENATOR JOHN KERRY ON HIS APPEARANCE BEFORE CONGRESS IN 1971 TO END THE VIETNAM CONFLICT. PRESIDENT RICHARD NIXON WAS COMMENTING ON THIS, AT THE TIME, AND NOW NIXON'S MEN, CHENEY, DOLE,, ADD OTHERS ARE TRYING TO DISCREDIT MR. KERRY. HOME LAND SECURITIES MONEY IS FOUND, BUT REPARATION MONIES FOR MY PEOPLE ARE STILL EVASIVE. THE RIGHT WINGERS HAD THE UNITES STATES SUPREME COURT TO APPOINT

BUSH AND CHENEY, AND ON INAUGURAL ADDRESS, BUSH TO TOLD THE PEOPLE THAT " THE SURPLUS WILL BE SPENT" AND IT HAS BEEN SPENT AND THE COUNTRY IS IN A RONALD REAGAN DEBT.

08-29-04"CNN'S people in the news", SAYS HIS DAUGHTER IS A LESBIAN THAT HE DOES NOT SUPPORT HER WAYS AND THAT HE VOTED AGAINST HIV AIDS TESTING, AND THAT IS BECAUSE HE AND THE RONALD REAGAN ADMINISTRA-TION IS A GRAND CONSPIRATOR IN THE CREATION OF THIS GENOCIDE DISEASE THAT STARTED OUT AS A "GAY DISEASE" AND NOW IT IS KILLING HUNDREDS OF THOUSANDS AFRI-CANS AND AFRICAN- AMERICANS GENOCIDE TO KEEP THE "STATUS QUO" AS PRESIDENT G.W. BUSH SAID A WEEK OR TWO AGO.

09-01-04

George W. BUSH ADMITTED THAT THE WAR IN IRAQ WAS A CASTASPHY SUCCESS" AND THAT WE " COULD NOT WIN THE WAR ON TERROR." BUSH KNEW THIS WIN HE GAVE THE ORDERS AND CONVINCED TONE BLAIR, PRIME MINISTER OF GREAT BRITAIN (BRITISH EMPIRE) RENAME, JUST AS THE ROMANS ARE CALLED ITALIANS NOW DAYS. ZIG ZAG ZELL MILLER WILL BE THE KEY NOTE SPEAKER AT THE REPUB-LICAN CONVENTION IN NEW YORK, TRICKY DICK CHENEY IS NOT A KEYNOTE TONIGHT, TRICK THE PEOPLE OF THE UNITED STATES IS THE DEAL WITH THE RIGHT WINGERS THAT ARE MOVING TOWARDS DICTATORSHIP IN THE NAME OF CONSERVATIVENESS. AMERICAN WAS DOING FAIRLY WELL DURING THE PRESIDENT CLINTON'S ADMINISTRATION AND THAT IS SAYING A LOT FROM AN AFRICAN – AMERICAN DESCENDANT OF SLAVES. CLINTON AS GOVERNOR AND

PRESIDENT WAS VERY CONSCIOUS AND EDUCATED ABOUT WORLD AFFAIRS.. JIMMY CARTER THE SAME AS CLINTON A SOUTHERN GENTLEMAN. ALAN KEYS SUPPOSE TO BE PLEASING CONSERVATIVES. HE BEGGED THEM TO REPRESENT THEM IN ILLINOIS, TO RUN AGAINST ABABA THE ONLY SENATE CANDIDATE. NOW KEYS IS RUBBING THOSE RACIST STATUS QUO RIGHT WINGERS TE OTHER DAY, TALKING ABOUT REPARATIONS AND HOMOSEXUALITY OF CHENEY'S DAUGHTER.

REPARATIONS IS NEEDED TO HEAL SOME OF THE OLD WOUNDS OF LYNCHING AND KILLINGS FROM THE SETTLEMENTS OF JAMESTOWN , VIRGINIA TO TODAY. THE RIGHT WINGERS ESPECIALLY, BECAUSE THEY CALL THE DEMOCRATS "LIBERALS", AND THE BUSH CHENEY HAS COMMITTED CRIMES AGAINST THE UNITED STATES, AND THAT IS BECAUSE THE PEOPLE HAD VOTED AL GORE FOR PRESIDENT AND HE HAD ALMOST A MILLION MORE VOTES THAT BUSH, YET THE SLAVE PROTECTOR SYSTEM KICKED IN AND THE CHIEF JUSTICE OF THE SUPREME COURT DICTATED THAT BUSH BE PRESIDENT OF THE UNITED STATES. WE CAN NOT SAY ANYTHING OF RUSSIANS SYSTEM OF DEMOCRATIC DICTATORSHIP THAT IS RETURNING, NOT TO MENTION CHINA.

CLINTON WAS CALLED A "NIGGER LOVER, A LIBERAL", AND WITH HE AND GORE TALKING ABOUT ALL OF THE RACIST PROFILING DURING MY LIFE, AND PARTICULAR DURING THE CLINTON GORE YEARS OF PROTEST OF THE PROFILING. BUSH CHENEY CAME IN OFFICE TO RID THE SURPLUS, IN ORDER, NOT TO HAVE THE FUNDS TO FUND ANY SOCIAL PROGRAMS FOR AMERICANS, AND ESPECIALLY THE DESCENDANT OF THE UNITED STATES SLAVE SYSTEMS. NIXON MEN ARE STILL ALIVE AND WELL, AS THEY PULL ANOTHER FAST ONE, WITH THE 2000 PRESIDENTIAL ELECTION.

KOBE BRYANT'S ACCUSER HAS LOST THEIR DESIRE TO CHARGE A BLACK MAN WITH RAPE. EVEN THOUGHT IT COULD LEAD TO UNDESIRABLE STRESS AND AT TIMES DEATH, BUT TO HAVE A RAPE SHIELD LAW, WHICH IS VERY MUCH RACIST IN AMERICA. PIMP LAW IN GEORGIA FOR SEX WITH UNDER AGE GIRLS, WHEN SINCE THE BEGINNING OF TIME HUMANS HAVE HAD INTERRELATION WITH EACH OTHER, FROM ADOLESCENT ON UNTIL OLD AGE. HUMAN NATURE IS GOD 'S LAW, BUT WHITE MAN 'S LAW WANT TO SET EXAMPLES TO FEARFULLY SCARE AFRICANS AND AFRICAN AMERICANS TO STAY AWAY FROM PEOPLE OF COLOR. THE BUSHES AND MOST ALL THE FAMILIES THAT ARE CAUCASIANS PREACH AND RAISE THEIR CHILDREN TO MARRY WITHIN YOUR RACE, I.E. SHOULD BE HUMAN RACE BUT THE ROMAN PHILOSOPHY IS NOT TO PERMIT NO PERSON OF COLOR WILL DOMINATED A WHITE MAN AGAIN. THEY HAVE THEIR OWN AND WE HAVE THEIR OWN". THAT ATTITUDE CRUCIFIED THE HOLY MESSIAH JESUS CHRIST OF NAZARETH, PALESTINE, THE SAME PALESTINE THAT THE DESCENDANTS F ROME, THAT CLAIM TO BE DESCENDANTS OF SALOMON WITH HAIR OF LAMB'S WOOL. ETHIOPIANS. 09-04-04UNITED STATES SUPREME COURT JUSTICE, SANDRA DAY O'CONNOR DISCUSSED ABOUT THE FEDERAL AND STATE SENTENCING LAWS. A SPEECH A " 10 EARTH QUAKE", SHE SAID IN MONTEREY, CALIFORNIA. JULY 23,2004.

09-10-04

POLICE LAW (LAW ENFORCEMENT) IS PROTECTING RACISM NOT THE LAW, MAKING MARSHALL LAW.

09-15-04There has been a lot on bush-Cheney incompetence THIS PAST WEEK. ISRAEL WAS THE REASON ALL OF THE LIVES AND NOW ALL THE MONIES THAT IS SUPPOSE TO BE FOR

REBUILDING IRAQ IS GOING TO SECURITY OF IRAQ AND 8 BILLION DOLLAR TO SUBSIDIZES THE DESTRUCTION OF THE ORIGINAL PEOPLE THAT WAS NOT RUN NED ACROSS THE RED SEA TO NORTH AFRICA, BEFORE AND DURING THE CRUCIFIXION OF JESUS CHRIST, THE ONLY BEGOTTEN SON OF THE ALMIGHTY, WITH GODLY POWERS TO DEMONSTRATE TO THE INFIDELS OF ROME AND GREECE, WHO CONVERTED TO HEBREW JUDAISM RELIGION OF ISRAEL, BUT THE ARE ROMANS AND ALL IMAGES OF JESUS AND ANY BLACK ASSES ARE NOT TO EXIST. ALL CAUCASIANS PICTURES AND NO OR VERY FEW THAT WAS TAKEN AND HIDDEN IN AFRICA ALONG WITH THE HOLY CONVENT THAT MOSES HAD DISCOVERED BECAUSE OF THE ROMAN EMPIRE, EVEN MOSES FATHER WAS ROMAN. TODAY PROBLEMS IS A CONTINUATION OF THAT AREA. BUSH 2 IS IN TEXAS FEELING THE HEAT OF ALL THE RICHARD NIXON TRICKS CONTINUED THROUGH EVERY REPUBLICAN ADMINISTRATION SINCE THE NIXON ADMIN-ISTRATION. NOW KITTY KELLY HAS A BOOK OUT THIS WEEK OF THE POWERFUL BUSHES USING DRUGS AT CAMP DAVID DURING IS FATHER 'S PRESIDENCY.

09-19-04

BUSH- CHENEY CONTINUE THE "WATERGATE SCANDAL" RULE, WITH THE REPUBLICANS, WHEN THEIR HANDS GET CAUGHT IN THE COOKIE JAR, ADMIT IT AND KEEP DOWN CONGRESSIONAL HEARINGS, BUSH PLAY DOWN THE JULY REPORT ON IRAQ, THAT IT WAS HEADING TOWARDS CIVIL WAR, BUSH CAN NOT HAVE THAT IN ORDER TO BECOME ELECTED FOR THE FIRST TIME: SO, THE LIES AND COVER UP BEGINS. HOW COULD THE RACIST AMERICAN PEOPLE PERMIT A KNOWN INCOMPETENT PRESIDENT THAT DID NOT GET ELECTED, BUT APPOINTED, BECOME ELECTED TO DISBAR

THE WARREN COURT RULINGS OF THE 1960"S? MARSHALL LAW IS ON IT'S WAY IF BUSH- CHENEY IS ELECTED. THEY HAVE HELPED RALPH NADER TO GET ON THE BALLIOL IN FLORIDA AND A FEW MORE STATES, IN ORDER TO WHEN THOSE STATES AND THROW THE ELECTION. THIS ELECTION IS BETWEEN THE NORTH VERSES THE SOUTH RACISM. CBS "60 MINUTES", FIRST STORY OF TODAY WAS ANOTHER BUSH-CHENEY FOUND MAN TO LIE ABOUT THE WAR IN IRAQ. HE WAS DOING WHAT THIS SO-CALL PRIME MINISTER THAT WAS IN ENGLAND,. WITH TONY BLAIR, GREAT BRITAIN'S FRONT MAN OF THE EMPIRE, AND IS TO COME HERE TO HELP FOOL THE AMERICAN PEOPLE, IN ORDER TO WIN THIS ELECTION. STACKING THE COURTS AND MAKING LAWS FOR AMERI-CANS WHO IS SUPPOSE TO HAVE NOTHING TO HIDE, THE GREAT LIE THAT THIS IS PROTECTING WHITE PEOPLE FROM THE BLACKS AND OTHER CITIZENS OF COLOR. GOD BLESSES AMERICA FROM THIS TAKE OVER ATTEMPT BY THE RIGHT WINGERS. THEY ARE PLAYING HARD BALL. WHILE THE OTHER PARTY (DEMOCRATS) ARE BEING PASSIVE AND THEY ARE IN BETWEEN BEING LABEL "LIBERALS (NIGGER LOVER", BY THE REPUBLICANS, IN THE NAME OF PROTECTING THE UNITED STATES CONSTITUTION. THEY MUST NOT WIN THIS 2004 ELECTION.

9-22-04

BUSH-CHENEY ADMINISTRATION HAS SOLD ISRAEL "SMART BOMBS", TO ATTACK IRAN. TODAY FINAL. THE NBC'S CHRIST MATTHEW 'S HARDBALL", GUEST WAS JOHN MC CAIN, RACIST SENATOR OF ARIZONA, SAID TONIGHT "THAT WE (RIGHT WINGERS) ARE GOING TO CHANGE THE CONSTITUTION" TO PUT HITLER'S SON ARNOLD SCHWARZENEGGER, THE

AUSTRIAN, WHO SWEEP THE CALIFORNIA PEOPLE TO ELECT THE "TERMINATOR".

09-29-04

SOROS, HUNGARIAN MILLIONAIRE AND NOW ERICA. HAS A MISSION TO KEEP BUSH-CHENEY NOT TO BE REELECTING. HE REMEMBERS HITLER'S FASCISM AND THIS PRESENT ADMINISTRATION IS NOW ATTACKING HIM FOR HIS STAND. HE IS ON JUDY WOODRUFF'S "INSIDE POLITICS" EXPLAINING HER BUSH LOVING SELF WHY IS HE AFTER HER CANDIDATE. Bush and Blair love is splitting. BLAIR LIED AND BACKED UP THIS HIT MAN BUSH, WITH HIS TEXAS JUSTICE FOR A MAN OF COLOR, SADDAM HUSSEIN. TODAY BUSH'S VENGEANCES FOR THE HIT PUT ON HIS FATHER, BY SADDAM, HAS COST THE AMERICAN PEOPLE THEIR LIVELY HOODS, OIL AND THE WORLD IS MUCH WORSE. THERE HAS BEEN OVER A THOUSAND NATIONAL GUARD AND REGULAR MILITARY PEOPLE, NOT TO MENTION ANY CIVILIANS ON EITHER SIDE OF BUSH- CHENEY WAR FOR PROFIT. CHENEY JUST RECEIVED A TWO MILLION DOLLAR CHECK FROM HIS COMPANY (HALLIBURTON), THEY NEED TO BE AND WILL BE IMPEACHED IF THEY FOOL THE AMERICAN PEOPLE INTO ELECTING THIS ADMINISTRATION. BLAIR AND BUSH ADMITTED THAT THEY LIED TO GO TO WAR IN IRAQ, THEN WHY EVERYONE IS NOT IN AN OUTRAGE ASSAULT TO HURRY THESE NO GOOD GANGSTERS OUT OF OFFICE EARLY? THEY WANT TO LOOK DOWN AT PEOPLE WHEN THEY ARE WORST THAN THE REGULAR POPULATION TO SURVIVE WITHIN THE SYSTEM. THEY DECLARE WAR THEN DROP BOMBS ON ANY DARK NATION.

09-30-04

BUSH-CHENEY FOLLOWING SHARON'S AND THE ISRAELIS ARMY TOWARDS THE PALATINES BOMB FIRST, OR SHOOT FIRST AND THEN ASKS QUESTIONS LATER. THEY ARE KILLING IRAQ'S CHILDREN'S AND THEN COME IN AND GIVE THEM CANDY FOR DESTROYING THERE ECONOMY AND STRUC-TURES TO SHOW ALL OF GOD'S PEOPLE OF THE BIBLE, NOT THE IMAGES BUT THE AREA S OF ABRAHAM. THESE ARE THE MODERN DAY CONQUISTADORS. LAST THEY (U.S.) GOVERN-MENT WERE HANDING OUT CASH CURRENCY. NOW THEY DO NOT WANT TO PASS BILLS AND MONIES TO THE AMER-ICAN DESCENDANTS OF SLAVES.

10-02-04

KERRY-BUSH DEBATES WAS A PLUS FOR KERRY. BUSH- CHENEY ROBBING THE UNITED STATES TREASURY, WHILE ATTORNEY JOHN ASHCROFT, UNITES STATES ATTORNEY GENERAL, WHO IS ENGINEERING THE COMPLETE COVER-UP, INCLUDING THE SHREDDING AND DELETIONS OF DISC, THE FEDERAL BUREAU OF INVESTIGATION PUT ALL HARD DRIVES OUT THE WINDOWS. DICK CHENEY JUST RECEIVE A TWO MILLION DOLLAR CHECK FROM HALLIBURTON, BUSH AND HIS FATHER WILL RECEIVE THEIRS AFTER THE COMPLETION OF THIS TAKE FROM WITHIN THE UNITED STATES. JAMES BAKER BACK ON THE CASE TO CONTROL THE DAMAGE, BUT THERE IS SO MUCH AND SO MASSIVE DAMAGE THAT HE (BAKER) HAS TO WATCH IS ASS. PROSECUTION COULD BE NEAR IF BUSH LOOSE AND ASHCROFT WILL BE RUNNING ASKING FAVORS AFTER HE SET –UP SO MANY PEOPLE, JUST BLAIR OF ENGLAND, THAT THANK GOD IF THE PEOPLE WILL WIN IF THESE RACIST ASS GO HAVE AND OUT OF THE GOVERN-

MENT, THAT IS SUPPOSE TO OVERSEE THE POOR PEOPLE OF AMERICA (U.S.), INSTEAD THEY DESTROY ANOTHER BLACK COUNTRY, AFRICAN DESCENDANTS PEOPLE IRAQ AFTER ALL THE OIL MONEY WENT TO THOSE PEOPLE, INCLUDING SADDAM HUSSEIN, NOW THE UNITED STATES AND THE BRITISH ARE DESTROYING THE RICHES . THEY WANT TO CALL THE AFRICANS TERRORIST.

10-06-04CHENEY- EDWARDS DEBATE LAST NIGHT, NOW BUSH MAJOR FOREIGN POLICY SPEECH, THIS MORNING, IS ONLY CONTINUING TO JUSTIFY THE IRAQ WAR, FOR REVENGE ON SADDAM FROM HIS FATHER, OVER ONE THOUSAND AMER-ICAN LIVES TO PROTECT ISRAEL. THIS MORNING ON TRAVIS SMILEY, PUBLIC BROADCAST RADIO, THAT THE UNITED STATES IS SCARE TO LEAVE ISRAEL ALONG. IT IS FUNNY THAT THEY TALK OF THE HOLOCAUST AND ISRAEL, BUT THEY ARE HERE SIDING WITH THE AMERICAN RACISTS TO HATE ON THE AFRICAN- AMERICAN.

10-07-04

THIS IS CALL BLACK THURSDAY FOR THE BUSH-CHENEY-TOM DELAY, FROM THE GREAT OF TEXAS AND THE MAIN CONSPIRATORS TO THE OBSTRUCT JUSTICE ON THE ENRON SCANDAL AND THE 2000 ELECTION, WHICH WAS SAFE TO SHREDDING OF DOCUMENTS TO PROTECT BUSH CHENEY AND ASSOCIATES . THE BUSH CHENEY BEING DECLARED A WINNER OF 2000 ELECTION, BY AN OLD WHITE MAN IN A WHEEL CHAIR AND ONE FOOT IN HIS GRAVE , CAME TO DECLARE BUSH WINNER AND THEN WENT RIGHT TO HIS GRAVE, IS A SCANDAL ITSELF, AND GAVE RISE TO THE ENRON SCANDAL, TEXAS WAS IN CONTROL OF EVERY BRANCH OF GOVERNMENT AND THE PEOPLE OF ENRON AND THE

UNITED STATES SUFFERED AGAIN. TOM DELAY IS GUILTY IN THE UNETHICAL NESS OF THE UNITED STATES HOUSE OF REPRESENTATIVES. COVER -UPS AND THEY STILL DID NOT HAVE TO RESIGN, EVEN THOUGHT THERE WERE CALLS FOR THAT TO HAPPEN. GOOD OL'BOY TOM DELAY HAD BEEN REBUTTED IN CONGRESS FOUR TIMES AND HE COULD NOT BE STOPPED DESTROYING THE VOTERS RIGHTS BILLS OF ANOTHER TEXAS PRESIDENT LYNDON B. JOHNSON.

THE CENTRAL INTELLIGENCE AGENCY HAS COME OUT THAT THERE WERE NOT ANY WEAPONS OF MASS DESTRUCTION IN IRAQ AND TODAY BUSH CHENEY ARE STILL IN BIG DENIAL, IN COMPLETE DENIAL THAT SADDAM DID NOT HAVE ANY WEAPONS OF MASS DESTRUCTION. THEY DENIED THE UNITED NATION INSPECTORS TO FINISH THEIR JOB, AS THEY DID NOT FIND ANY OF THE WEAPONS, BUT BUSH DECLARE THE INSPECTORS HAS TO LEAVE IRAQ, BECAUSE BOMBING WAS TO COMMENCE WITHIN DAYS. THE WAR PRESIDENT THAT HE SAID HE WANTED TO BE KNOWN AS THE PRESI-DENT OF THE UNITED STATES.

IT IS RE-ELECTION TIME AND BUSH CHENEY IS TRYING TO HOLD HIS ADMINISTRATION TOGETHER UNTIL AFTER THE 2004 ELECTION, IN ORDER, TO PUT THE PUBLIC APPEAR-ANCE THAT THEY ARE COHESIVE ADMINISTRATION, WHEN BEHIND CLOSE DOORS , COLIN POWELL HAD FOUND OUT THAT THEY HAD BETRAYED HIS NAME BY HAVING HIM GO BEFORE THE UNITED NATION TO SELL A LIE, BUT HE STAYED AND PERPETRATED A FRAUD BECAUSE OF HIS LOYALTY TO GEORGE HERBERT WALKER BUSH' S SON.

COLIN POWELL, TRICKY" DICK CHENEY, AND GHWB HAD INSTITUTED A NO FLY ZONE AND ANYONE SHOULD KNOW THAT IT WAS DIFFICULT FOR SADDAM TO HIDE ANYTHING , LESS THAT HE COULD CREATE ANY WEAPONS OF MASS

DESTRUCTION, AFTER THE 1991 GULF WAR. WE HAVE BEEN IN IRAQ FIGHTING EVERY SINCE AND THE YEARS ARE CONTINUING, AS THE RIGHT WINGERS ARE STATING THAT WE WILL BE THERE FOR MANY MORE YEARS. I BELIEVE THAT IT HAS SUPERSEDED THE YEARS OF VIETNAM.

I HAD STARTED WONDERING WHETHER I WAS WATCHING AMERICA GIVING WAY TO SOME OF IT'S WRONGS OF THE PAST, WITH ALL OF THE AFRICAN-AMERICANS WHO WERE PART OF AN AMERICAN PRESIDENT CABINET AND FRIENDS THAT WAS IMPRESSIVE, EVEN THOUGHT, THE CIA KILLED COMMERCE SECRETARY RON BROWN, AFTER BEING IN AFRICA DANCING TO THE CLOUDS , AS A UNITED STATES REPRESENTATIVE , THE A MIDNIGHT RAINEY FLIGHT INTO A DARK MOUNTAIN, AND ALL WAS IGNORED; THEN THE ELEC-TION 2000, AND ALL OF THE HATE TOWARDS OUR COUNTRY TODAY , SHOULD BE LAID SQUARELY ON THE BUSH FAMILY AND IT'S FOLLOWING REPUBLICAN PARTY FIGHTING AND DENYING THE FLORIDA VOTERS THEIR VOTE. IF THERE WERE ANY HANGING CHADS IT SHOULD HAVE BEEN COUNTED AS A VOTE, PLAIN AND SIMPLE.

WITH MY PEOPLE BEING DENIED MANHOOD UNDER THE INSTITUTION OF AMERICAN SLAVERY, AND TODAY JAILING THEIR DESCENDANT IN PRISONS ALL ACROSS AMERICA IN THE NAME OF PROTECTING THE SLAVE MASTER'S CHILDREN FROM CRIME FROM A PEOPLE THAT WERE MADE IGNORANT, BY DENYING THEM TO COMMUNICATE THEIR LANGUAGES, RELIGION, AND ROYALTY INTO SERVING AN ENGLISH, WHO TODAY IS TRYING TO CONTINUING THEIR QUEST TO HAVE EVERY MEXICAN AND THE WHOLE WORLD SPEAK ENGLISH, IN ORDER, FOR THE ENGLISH TO OVERHEAR WHAT ONE IS SPEAKING. TOOK OUR WOMEN AND RAPE TORTURED THEM AND NOW TODAY THEY ACT LIKE THEY ARE SO PROPER AND

CLEAN , WHEN THE TRUTH IS THE DESCENDANTS ARE JUST AS BAD, IT JUST IS NOT IN THE OPEN, UNTIL THEY CLOSE THE SOUTHERN BORDER IN THE NAME TERRORIST. LOU DOBBS IS A RACIST, WHO MARRIED A DARK MEXICAN AND DO YOU THINK A BUNCH OF MID-EASTERNERS ARE GOING TO GO TO MEXICO AND TRAVEL THROUGH THE DESERT WITH NO WEAPONS AND ATTACH THE SO-CALL MAIN LAND OF THE UNITED STATES. POLITICIANS IN 2007 HAS A PLAN ALONG WITH THOSE RACIST SOUTHERN TEXAS AND ARIZONA SLAVE MASTER CHILDREN. THESE PEOPLE LAND AND THEY WERE NOT INPUTTED HERE , THEY WERE DISPLACED, JUST THE PALESTINIANS.

WITH THE OVERTHROW OF THE ONE MAN ONE VOTE, IN THE NAME OF SOME ELECTORAL COLLEGE, BRING BACK MEMORIES FOR ME BEFORE THE 1964 VOTERS RIGHT BILL, AND MY PARENTS ARE THE FIRST ONES WHO VOTED, AFTER BEING DENIED IT ALL OF THEIR LIVES AND MY DESCEN-DANTS LIVES. WANT AFRICAN - AMERICAN TO ENLIST FOR THIS OIL WAR, OFFERING EDUCATION , IF YOU SURVIVE THIS SHAMEFUL WAR, MORE SHAMEFUL THAN WE WERE DURING THE VIETNAM ERA.

WITH THE DEBATES THAT WAS A FARCE TODAY, AS "TRICK" DICK CHENEY BUSH HAD TO HAVE THE QUESTION BEFORE THE DEBATE, AND WHAT DOES THAT SAY ABOUT THE ILLEGAL ADMINISTRATION. CHENEY HAD SAID THAT HE WAS NOT AWARE OF A.I.D.S AMONG AFRICAN- AMERICAN WOMEN. THEY ARE THE LATTER DAY RACIST, JUST AS LATTER DAY SAINTS, THERE IS NO SUCH THING.

10-10-04

BUSH –CHENEY ARE IN COMPLETE DENIAL AND IS INTENT ON CARRYING OUT THE SAME THING AS RONALD REAGAN, WRITE A BUNCH OF LIES FOR A SPEECH TO THE AMERICAN PEOPLE, JUST TO APOLOGIES THE NEXT MORNING WHEN PEOPLE ARE AT WORK. ROBERT NOVAK SAYS THAT THE AMERICAN PEOPLE CAN BE FOOLED, CAUSE HE SEEN IT ALL THE TIME DURING THE REAGAN YEARS.

10-17-04

DEMOCRACY ON AMERICA, BUSHES AND CHENEY STYLE, IS TOM DELAY STYLE. REDISTRICTING OF TEXAS DISTRICTS ARE ILLEGAL AND YET IT WAS DONE BY DELAY, IN ORDER, TO UNSEAT INCUMBENTS. THAT RACIST TOM DELAY SHOULD HAVE BEEN SENT HOME WHEN THE MAJORITY DID THE PEOPLE OF THE UNITED STATES DID NOT OUST HIM LAST WEEK FOR HIS UNETHICAL NESS. BUSH2 WENT TO THE ROMAN CATHOLIC CHURCH AGAIN TO DELIVER A MESSAGE FROM ROME, TRYING TO WIN THAT VOTE, IN ORDER TO KEEP HIS PRESIDENCY . MARSHALL LAW IS HIS INTENT, IN THE NAME OF A WHITE MAJORITY IN THE AMERICA THAT IS SLOWLY BUT SURELY BECOMING DARKER AND THAT WILL CAUSE A TAKE OVER OF THE MILITARY, JUST AS HITLER. MAY GOD FORBID?

10-21-04

BUSH STEADY CALLING FOR "MEDICAL LIABILITY REFORM", IN ORDER TO EXTERMINATE PEOPLE ON THE OPERATING TABLE AND HAVE NO RESPONSIBILITY TO THE PATIENT.

PEOPLE NEED SOME TYPE OF SAFE GUARD AGAINST SOME DRUNK AND DRUGGED UP DOCTOR MAKING MISTAKES THAT WERE MAIMING AND DEATH. TRICKY DICK NIXON AND REAGAN'S ARE CONTINUING THROUGH THE BUSHES. THEY ARE POINTING TOWARDS DIVISIONS AND SLAVERY. BY THE TIME ALL THE JUSTICES BEING APPOINTED AND IF CONGRESS STAYS THE SAME WE THE PEOPLE WILL BE COMPLETE SEGREGATION THROUGH MARSHALL LAW, TEXAS JUSTICE. CNN'S "INSIDE POLITICS", JUDY WOODRUFF, REPORT ON CITIZENS OVERSEAS TRYING TO VOTE IS NOT EASY, THE RIGHT WINGERS FIX IS IN, THAT SOME BALLOTS WERE SENT WITH JOHN KERRY 'S NAME CROSSED OFF. ONE SAID A BANANA REPUBLIC COULD DO BETTER THAN THAT. THERE SHOULD BE SOME JAIL TIME FOR THESE CRACKERS FOR CONTINUING TO PREVENT CITIZENS TO VOTE AND SUPPOSE TO BE NONE CITIZENS (AFRICAN AMERICAN) IS NOT TO EVER HAVE A VOTE MORE THAN ALREADY IS. ROMANS, BRITONS, AND NOW BUSHES WANTS TO CONTINUE TO KEEP THE STATUS QUO.

10-30-04

IT HAS BEEN AN EYE OPENER FOR AMERICANS THAT IS DISCUSSED WITH THIS SO CALL "WAR PRESIDENT", AS BUSH2 LIKE TO HAIL UNTO HIMSELF. WE DO NOT NEED A PRESIDENT THAT HAS PUT OUR TROOPS I N IRAQ, JUST TO HAVE REVENGE ON SADDAM BECAUSE OF SADDAM'S SUPPOSINGLY CONTRACT ON BUSH ONE. NOW THERE IS A COMPLETE VIDEO FROM OSAMA BIN LADEN, THAT LAYS IT OUT AND THE BUSH ADMINISTRATION DO NOT WANT TO RESPOND. THE RIGHT WINGERS OF THE AMERICAN CONSTITUTION IS BLATANTLY FILING LAW SUITS TO INTIMIDATE THE AMERICAN VOTERS THROUGH THE COURTS INSTEAD OF RIDING AROUND IN

TRUCKS, WITH THE CONFEDERATE FLAG FLYING HIGH, AS THEY ARE THE LAW THAT WANT TO KEEP THE STATUS QUO. 2004 PRESIDENTIAL ELECTION IS FIGHTING TO STACK THE COURTS ON AMERICANS AS A SO CALL "LAME DUCK" PRESIDENT. RACISM IS ALIVE AND WELL, AND HOPE THAT PEOPLE ARE EDUCATED ENOUGH TO VOTE BUSH OUT AT ALL COST. IRAQ DID NOT HAVE ANY THING TO DO WITH SEPTEMBER 11,2001. MAY GOD BLESS AMERICA THAT WILL GIVE HOPE FOR A MORE UNDERSTANDING WORLD, BUT BUSH CHENEY HAS MADE IT VERY DIFFICULT TO WORK WITH THE MIDDLE EAST. BUSH2 ADMINISTRATION DID NOTHING BUT MADE THE MIDDLE EAST MORE CHAOTIC.

10-31-04Bush went to another CATHOLIC CHURCH. HE IS CARRYING ON THE LIES AND DECEIT OF THE ROMAN EMPIRE AND THE CRUCIFIX OF JESUS OF NAZARETH, THE HOLY MESSIAH.. ON HIS TRIP TO NATO EARLIER THIS YEAR HIS FIRST STOP WAS ROME TO VISIT THE ANTI CHRIST POPE JOHN PAUL OF POLAND, WHO CANNOT STAY AWAKE.

11-01-04

CNN'S "LIVE CNN, DAN ROBERTS, A SUPPOSINGLY SPOKESMAN, SAID "BLACKS IN THE PAST VOTED REPUBLICAN, UNTIL THE CIVIL RIGHTS MOVEMENT," HE IS A REPUBLICAN TRYING TO IGNORE THE PAST, BEFORE THE CIVIL RIGHTS, BLACKS RARELY COULD VOTE IN ANY STATE OF THE UNITED STATES. REMEMBER THE "JIM CROW LAW" AND SLAVERY BEFORE THEN.   The ELECTORAL COLLEGE TO ELECT A PRESIDENT SHOULD BE ABOLISHING, BECAUSE IT WAS CREATED AFTER THE EMANCIPATION AND IT WAS TO MAKE SURE THAT NO DESCENDANT OF SLAVE WOULD BECOME PRESIDENT. IT WAS CREATED AS A BIAS TOOL AND IT WORK TO THE ABSO-

LUTE IN THE 2000 PRESIDENTIAL ELECTION OF THE WORST PRESIDENTIAL ADMINISTRATION IN THE HISTORY OF THE UNITED STATES. ONE MAN ONE VOTE SHOULD BE JUST AS IT WAS BEFORE THE EMANCIPATION PROCLAMATION, SLAVE OWNING RIGHTS WERE SUPPOSED TO BE ABOLISHED, THEN SHARES CROPPING LIVING BEGUN.

SHARE CROPPING WERE OFFERED TO THE SLAVES WHO WERE TOO OLD, HAD LARGE FAMILIES, MOST MIX FAMILIES, AS THE SLAVE MASTER'S CHILDREN FROM THE SLAVE WOMEN, WERE OUT IN THE SHACKS AND OUT HOUSE FOR SLAVE, AND EVENTUALLY A FEW INDEPENDENTLY BLACK FARMER STARTED TO FURIES AS INDEPENDENT BUSINESS MEN.

I AM A FARMER, EVEN THOUGH, I OVERCAME THAT FIELD OF MAKING A LIVING INTO OTHER INDEPENDENT FIELDS TO SURVIVE THE RACISM AND BIAS OF CAUCASIAN AMERI-CANS TOWARDS ME AND MY PEOPLE. WE HAVE COME FROM BEING KIDNAPPED IN AFRICA, BOUND,CHAIN, KILLED, ENSLAVED, FREED AFTER FOUR HUNDRED YEARS LOST TO OUR HERTIAGE, LANUAGE, AND NO WHERE TO GO BUT ROAM THE LAND AS WE ARE STILL DOING TODAY, AND ALL WAS AFTER THE ABOLITIONISTS AND THE UNDERGROUND RAILROAD.

SOME TYPE OF REPARATION SHOULD BE INSTITUTED INTO THE CONSTITUTION TO HAVE A BETTER NATION WITH A MELTING POT OF KNOWLEDGE FROM PEOPLE OF DIFFERENT COMPLEXION. THE MONEY FROM THE 2008 PRESIDENTIAL CANDIDATES TO GIVE IRAQ WAR AND THE REBUILDING THE WAR ZONES THAT OUR BOMBS DESTROY, SHOULD MAKE IT ABSOLUTELY A MUST TO EDUCATE, HOUSE, AND HAVE THE MEDICAL CARE. JUST AS IT IS IN THE HARVARD, YALE, AND ALL OF THE OTHER SO-CALL ELITE INSTITUTIONS, THAT ARE FILLED WITH THE DESCENDANTS OF THE SLAVE MASTERS,

AND IS GIVING FOREIGN STUDENTS FROM ASIA, PAKISTAN, AND OTHER NATIONS, WHO BECOME EDUCATED HERE AND LOOK TO THE AFRICAN-AMERICAN SLAVE DESCENDANTS AS SOME TYPE OF OUTCAST. IT IS TAUGHT IN THE INSTITUTIONS AND ALL OF THE EVENING NEWS OF THE MOSTLY UNEDU-CATED AND DRUG DEPENDANTS. IT IS THE INSTITUTION OF AMERICAN'S PROBLEM AND WE NEED TO DO MORE THAN FILL ALL OF PRISONS, JUST AS THE BRITISH DID AND THEY WERE RELEASE TO AMERICA, AUSTRALIA, SOUTH AFRICA, AND OTHER PLACES. THEY WERE PUT ON SHIPS TO LEAVE THE COUNTRY, AND THE COUNTRY'S MILITARY BACKED THEM, AS THEY WERE BRITISH SUBJECTS.

AFTER THE EMANCIPATION PROCLAMATION TO END LEGAL SLAVERY, AFTER ALL OF YOUR HERITAGE HAS BEEN DESTROYED AND YOU ARE SUPPOSE TO HAVE LAND AND A MULE, THAT BECAME THE FIRST PROMISE OF THE AMERICAN GOVERNMENT TO IT'S SLAVE SUBJECTS. WE ARE A LITTLE MORE EDUCATED AS A WHOLE. IN MY FAMILY MY PARENTS AND RELATIVES WERE NOT EDUCATED, SO TELL ME HOW COULD THEY TEACH YOU EDUCATION?

TO REPARATIONS MONIES FROM THE UNITED STATES TREA-SURY, JUST DOCTOR MARTIN LUTHER KING, JUNIOR, CALLED FOR AND INSTITUTED THE POOR PEOPLE'S MARCH THAT NEVER HAPPEN, BECAUSE OF THE INSTITUTION OF AMER-ICAN GOVERNMENT RACISM. OUR HERITAGE , LANGUAGE, AND BELIEFS, WERE TAKEN AWAY FROM US , THE ALL OF THE KIDNAPPING OF THE AFRICANS, AND THE AMERICAN GOVERNMENT NEEDS TO PAY MY CHILDREN, AND THEIR DESCENDANTS FOR THEIR CRIMES AGAINST HUMANITY, SOMETHING THE RIGHT WINGERS ARE AGAINST. THEIR TAX DOLLARS ARE NEEDED TO BE THE PRIMARY MONIES TO INSURE THIS, THEY ARE LIVING ON THE DESCENDANTS

MONIES, STOLEN LAND, AND IS CARRYING ON THE INSTITU-
TIONAL RACISM WE SEE IN THE LYNCHING OF TWENTY- FIRST
CENTURY. WE STILL DO NOT HAVE THE ENGLISH LANGUAGE,
AND THEY DO NOT HAVE THE ENGLISH OF THEIR HOME-
LAND OF ENGLISH AND IRELAND.

 THE REPUBLICANS ARE TARGETING THE BLACK VOTE TO
SUPPRESS THEM IN THIS TWENTY- FIRST CENTURY TECH-
NOLOGY, RACISM IS STILL ALIVE AND EVEN ARMSTRONG
WILLIAMS, DON KING, WHO IS DISAPPOINTING, ALLAN KEYS,
AND ALL THE OTHER PIECES OF SHIT, AS FIREBALL USE TO
SAY. NOVEMBER 3,2004IT IS NOT OFFICIAL YET, AS SOME POLL
WORKERS WENT TO BED, BUT BUSH-CHENEY DID WIN FLORIDA
AND POSSIBLE THE ELECTION. OHIO IS NOT COMPLETE A FIVE
IN THE MORNING. KERRY VOTED YESTERDAY AND MADE A
STATEMENT THAT WAS NOT STRONG AND CONFIDENT THAT
HE WOULD WIN. "NO MATTER WHO THE PEOPLE VOTE FOR
AMERICA WILL BE STRONG" , JUST THAT "CROSS BONES"
SOCIETY THAT WON OUT, THAT IS THE SAME AS RACIST.
WHITE PEOPLE ARE TOGETHER, AS REPUBLICANS TO KEEP
THE SO CALL STATUS QUO. I KNEW DEEP DOWN INSIDE THAT
KERRY WOULD NOT BEAT BUSH, BECAUSE HE JUST WAS NOT
HARD ENOUGH AND THAT HE COULD NOT GO TO HARD
AGAINST HIS FRATERNITY BROTHER. I KNEW IT WHEN THE
TRICKY PARTY (REPUBLICANS) FOUND A WAY TO DISCREDIT
HOWARD DEAN, WHO THEY DID NOT WANT TO FACE. THEY
HELPED RALPH NADER TO GET ON SOME THIRTY STATES, IN
ORDER TO HAVE THOSE OTHER WHITE FOLKS TO NOT VOTE
FOR KERRY. THE GRAND CONSPIRACY AND POLITICS IS STILL
THE DIRTIES GAME. THERE IS A INVESTIGATION OF HALLI-
BURTON AND THAT WILL LEAD TO A LOT OF HEARINGS.
THAT IS A SURPRISE FROM THE JOHN ASH CROFT'S JUSTICE
DEPARTMENT.

11-04-04

THE ELECTORS COLLEGE OF THE UNITED STATES IS A STATUS QUO OF SLAVERY. ELECTORS COLLEGE OF THE UNITED STATES CONSTITUTION IS THE CONTROL OF AND AMENDMENT THAT WAS /IS TO PREVENT ANY BLACKS A CHANCE TO BE ELECTED PRESIDENT. THE NORTH VERSES THE SOUTH IS STILL BATTLING AND THE SOUTH WON. HOW CAN A FLORIDA, OHIO, PENNSYLVANIA, AND NOT NEW YORK HAVE MORE ELECTORAL VOTES? IT SHOULD BE ABOLISH.

 BUSH2 SAID TODAY THAT HE WOULD PICK JUSTICES WHO INTERPRET THE LAW AND NOT HAVE A PERSONAL OPINIONS, HE WOULD PICK JUDGES WHO THINK AS HE DOES, NOW THAT IS A REAL OPINION. CRIME DOES PAY AND THAT IS THE AMERICAN WAY". WE WILL SEE HOW JUSTICE IS HANDED DOWN. DETAINEES IN CUBA IS TREATED WORST THAN CRACKERS TREAT DOGS. THEY LOVE THEIR DOGS, BUT NOT THE CRACKERS DARK HUMANS RELATIVES. HAVE THESE PEOPLE HERE MAKING THEM HATE AMERICANS MORE AND WE KNOW THAT ALL THESE MEN WERE NOT AGAINST ALL AMERICANS. CBS DID AN REPORT THAT CAME OUT TODAY AND THE MILITARY IS HOLDING ON TO THESE SO CALL 'ENEMY COMBATANTS". 11-06-04 NBC'S "MEET THE PRESS" BARRACK OBAMA, NEW AFRICAN AMERICAN, FATHER IS FROM AFRICA, WAS GUESS AND WAS VERY ARTICLED VERY SPOKEN. THE FOLLOWING GUESSES WERE SPEAKING ON WHOM THE DEMOCRATS NEEDED; THEY CAME UP WITH THE NEW AND ONLY BLACK SENATOR SINCE LATE NINETEENTH CENTURY.

11-28-04

NBC'S "MEET THE PRESS" HISTORICAL THAT JERRY FARWELL, AL SHARPTON, RICHARD LAND, AND SOUTHERN BAPTIST PRESIDENT, NO NAME, TOGETHER IN ONE ROOM, ONE EPIC SOLE DISCUSSING CHRISTIAN RELIGION, ON IMPOSING THE WILL OF THEIR BELIEFS ON OTHERS IS STILL CONTINUING ON TODAY.

IN ONE OF MINE PREVIOUS EXPERIENCE THEY WHAT TO INCARCERATE ALL THE DESCENDANTS OF SLAVES, THEY DO NOT WANT AN EDUCATED AFRICAN – AMERICAN, THEY ONLY MAKE AVAILABLE THE HOMOSEXUAL KING JAMES'S VERSION OF THE HOLY BIBLE. TOOK ALL OF OUR HERITAGES, LANGUAGE, WOMEN, AND THEN CALL YOU UNEDUCATED." THE AMERICAN WAY".

ALSO, ON ABC'S " THIS WEEK WITH…" THEIR RACIST INTEL-LECTUALS, SPEAKING ON BUSH'S POSSIBLE UNITED STATES SUPREME COURT'S NOMINEES, ONE SPOKE ON NO NEED TO HAVE KERRY TYPE AS A NOMINEE, NOT TO SPEAK OF ONE BEING NOMINATED, THAT " WE DO NOT NEED THAT TYPE OF SOCIAL ENGINEERING", THAT IS , NO RIGHTS FOR DARK PEOPLE OF THESE UNITED STATES.

REMEMBER THAT AFTER THE EMANCIPATION PROCLAMA-TION, THE SOUTHERN RULE MORE SO THAN TATES, "NY TIME THAT WE FINE NIGRAS'S, YOU KNOW THAT MOST WAS IGNORANT, CAN GO AND EAT, SLEEP, AND ON DOWN THE LINE, WE WILL PAST A LAW TO MAKE IT MORE DIFFICULT FOR THEM SLAVES." SHAPING WHAT ANOTHER MAN CAN OR CANNOT ACHIEVE.

12-20-04

BUSH2 HAD HIS SECOND PRESS CONFERENCE. SHOWED HIS LIES CAN NOT AND SHOULD NOT HAVE WON AN ELECTION, THAT DELEGATES SHOULD NOT EVER HAVE BEEN, BUT THAT IS THE STATUS QUO WAY OF POWER FROM THE GROWING NEED TO KEEP THE DARKMAN AS SECOND OR THIRD BEHIND THE GREEK AND ROMAN CAVEMEN. LOST DATA AND THOUGHTS ON BUSH HURT ON AMERICA. ROB THE TREASURY AND SEND MONIES TO WALL STREET. FUCKED UP. " THE AMERICAN WAY.

He said that he HAS" TO CONDITION THE AMERICAN PEOPLE" , FOR THIS ROBBERY OF TAX PAYERS PENSIONS (SOCIAL SECU-RITY).

HE HAS PUT THE NATIONAL GUARD IN THEIR CASKETS, AND THE MEDIA WAS SEDUCED NOT FILM THE CASKETS AS THEY RETURN TO THEIR FAMILIES. BUSH-CHENEY NEVER HAS CARED ABOUT HE AMERICAN POOR PEOPLE.

01-04-05

the American government HAS SPREADED FROM THE MISSED FAX TO THE DEPARTMENT OF EDUCATION, FROM THE FREE THE CHILDREN FROM HANDCUFFS OF BLACK ELEMENTARY AND MIDDLE SCHOOL AGE CHILDREN.

CRACKERS ALWAYS WANT TO LIMIT HUMAN NATURE THAT IS OF COLOR. THEY WANT TO BE LOOKED AT AS SAVERS AFTER THEY HAVE CREATED CHAOS, THAT IS THE ROMAN EMPIRE'S WAY OF SUPERIORITY TO THE WHITE /LIGHT WOMEN OF THE WORLD.

CNN'S AND OTHERS REPORT OF ETHICS IN CONGRESSIONAL HUMAN BEING, THAT IS THE LAST OF THE COLOR EXPANSION OF THE DARK TO THE LIGHTEST OF HUMAN COMPLEXIONS. CONGRESSMAN TOM DELAY IS THE TEXAS PROTECTOR OF THE BUSHES STATUS QUO. THAT IS, THEY WILL CROSS, KILL OR ANYTHING ELSE TO KEEP THIS LIGHT COMPLEXION CONTROL OF ALL THE MILITARY, MONETARY, OIL, GOLD, DIAMONDS, AND ALL THE OTHER RICHES OF GODS EARTH. THE DEVILS THEY TRULY ARE AND THAT IS GODS LAW NOT THE OF COMPLEXION SUPERIORITY. THESE ARE THE DESCENDANTS WHO CRUCIFIED THE ONLY BEGOTTEN SON OF THE ALMIGHTY GOD, THE CREATOR OF THE UNIVERSE. THEY TELL THE IGNORANT THAT JEWS KILLED JESUS, WHEN IT IS CLEAR THAT A JEW DECEIVES AND COLLABRA RATED WITH THE ROMANS, WHO WERE THE CRUCIFIERS, AS THE JEWS WERE MOSTLY UNDER BONDAGE. THE ROMAN LIE THAT IS STILL LIVING TODAY, JUST TO PROMOTE THE HOMOSEXUALS WHO ARE THE LEADERS OF THE CATHOLIC CHURCH, CARRIES ON THE LIE TO PROTECT THEIR BELOVED ROMAN MILITARY. THAT IS WHY THE CHILDREN OF THEIR CHURCHES ARE MOLESTED.

05-31-05

BUSH2 PRESS CONFERENCE THIS MORNING, WAS IN THE NAME OF TERRORIST. BUSH CHENEY IS THE LEADER OF TODAY'S RIGHT WING CONSPIRACY TO RULE THE WORLD, AND TRIES TO DISBAND THE UNITED NATION CHARTER THAT WAS CREATED TO HELP AND PROTECT THE SOVEREIGN NATIONS. ISRAEL AND THE UNITED STATES GOES AGAINST THEM REGULARLY.

PRESS CONFERENCE HIS FRIEND IS INNOCENT UNTIL FOUND GUILTY, FOR PEOPLE OF COLOR IS GUILTY UNTIL FOUND INNOCENT, DEMOCRACY THE "AMERICAN WAY"

THE AMERICAN WAY

LYING TO THE PEOPLE OF AMERICA THE ELDERLY PEOPLE TO GIVE YOUR FUTURE TO A "STOCK MARKET CRASH" THAT IS INEVITABLE TO CRASH MANY TIMES OVER.

CHENEY-BUSH SHOULD BE UP FOR TREASON? THE REPUBLI-CANS WERE CONSPIRATORS; THEY COULD NOT COMMENCE IMPEACHMENT HEARING. NANCY PELOSCI DENIED HEAR-INGS AFTER THE 2006 ELECTION AND THE LEADERSHIP CHANGE, BUT WE WILL HAVE TO WAIT UNTIL AFTER THE 2008 PRESIDENTIAL ELECTION.

06-05-05

GUANTAMO BAY, CUBA COMMISSIONERS ARE UNCONSTI-TUTIONALLY AND THE DEFENDING OFFICERS ARE SUING PRESIDENT BUSH2 AND DONALD RUMSFIELD. THE RULES ARE BIAS AND THAT IS WHAT BUSH AND CHENEY IS THE LEAD OF DEPRIVATION OF HUMAN RIGHTS, THAT IS WHY PRESIDENT JIMMY CARTER WAS NOT INVITED TO ROME FOR THE POPE JOHN PAUL'S FUNERAL.

12-06-07

JIMMY CARTER'S BOOK, "PALESTINE PEACE NOT APART-HEID", BUSH VIEWS ARE ANTI-AMERICAN AND CARTER AND FORMER VICE PRESIDENT WALTER MONDALE DO NOT SEE

HOW THE VICE PRESIDENT BECAME THE PRESIDENT AS HE IS SUPPOSE TO BE THE SITTING VICE PRESIDENT. CLINTON AND BUSH2'S FATHER, GHWB WERE ON THE PLANE THAT DENIED CARTER. THE AMERICAN WAY

CBS'60MINUTES' STORY OF COURT BATTLE OF RIGHTS. THERE IS NO JUSTICE OF PEOPLE OF COLOR AND THE PEOPLE OF ASIA KNOW THESE CRACKERS (EUROPEAN DESCENDANTS), AND THEY ARE NOT TO BE TRUSTED.

06-06-05

SURVIVING NG APARTHEID IN SOUTH AFRICA INTERVIEW WITH MAEK MASBATI, A SOUTH AFRICAN, IT'S ON CNN'S 25TH ANNIVERSARY. HE HAS A BOOK.

THE BRITAINS WHO TRICKED THE SOUTH AFRICANS WITH THE CRUCIFIX, THE SYMBOL OF THE ROMAN EMPIRE., THAT THE HOLY MESSIAH , JESUS CHRIST OF BETHLEHEM , PALESTINE, WITH THE CURLY HAIR AS SOLOMON, KING DAVID, JESUS, AND MANY MORE OF THE HEBREW FAITH, THAT IS, LAMB'S WOOL TYPE HAIR. THE ETHIOPIANS WHO HOUSE THEM AFTER THE ESCAPE WITH MOSEST, EVENUALLY LEARN THE CONVANT AND IN THE 1980'S ISREAL SENT PLANES DAY AND NIGHT TO RECURE THE HEBREW JEWS FROM CENTURIES BEFORE DESCENDANTS WHO ESCAPE THE ROMAN EMPIRE.

I HAVE HAD A CHANCE TO EXPERIENCE THAT TEXTURE OF HUMAN HAIR FROM A FORMER GIRL FRIEND. IT IS AMAZING. HER SISTER HAD HERS PERMED AND PROCESSED.

THE SUPREME ROMAN COURT TODAY HANDED DOWN A RULING ON MEDICAL MARIJUANA.

THE SUPREME COURT OF THE UNITED STATES OF AMERICA IS THE DIFFERENCE IN THE EMPIRE AMONG THEMSELVES AND NOT FOR THE PEOPLE OF COLOR, WHOSE ROOTS ARE IN THE JUNGLES OF SOUTH AFRICA UP THROUGH THE MOTHER LAND AND ACROSS THE STRAITS OF THE WHAT IS CALLED THE ATLANTIC OCEAN, INTO WHAT IS CALLED SOUTH AMERICA.. GOD SAID YOU HUMAN HAS TO LIVE OFF OF THE LAND ON EARTH, AND THAT INCLUDE THE MARIJUANA HERBAL PLANT, WHETHER COOKING IT FOR TEA OR SMOKING IT FOR MANY RELIEF'S, MENTAL AND PHYSICAL. THE CO CO LEAF IS ANOTHER OF MANY JUNGLE FRUITS AND FOOD FOR HUMANS. JUST STUDY WHAT THE GORILLAS EAT AND LIVE ON AND IT IS ALL THE LIGHTER HUMAN THAT EVOLVED OVER MANY MILLIONS OF YEARS, THROUGH THE BIOLOGY OF THE HUMAN SPERM THAT THE ALL MIGHTY CREATOR CREATED AS HIS LAST BEING OF THE EARTH, AND CALLED IT THE SUPREME BEING OF THE EARTH.

TO CO-EXIST AS HUMANS IS VERY FAR ADVANCED, SO THAT WE HAVE CAME OUT OF THE DARK INTO THE LIGHT OF THE DAY AND THE LIGHT OF THE HUMAN COMPLEXION. THAT IS THE ROOT OF COMPLEXION DISCRIMINATION, ALSO, KNOWN AS RACIAL PREJUDICE. THE LIGHTER HUMAN WANTS AND IS CONTROLLING MOST OF THE RESOURCES OF THE EARTH BY INTIMIDATION AND THE MISSILES. CHINA AND KOREA IS THE HUMAN EQUALIZER FOR HUMAN UNITY, AS THEY ARE NOT SLEEPING ON THIS HUMAN MIGRATION FROM THE SOUTH OF THE MOTHER LAND AFRICA.

NANCY GRACE, THE COURT TV COMMENTARY ANKLE, IS A BEAUTIFUL SOUTHERN WHITE WOMAN, WHO WAS A PROSECUTOR, AND SHE STILL THINKS SHE IS PROSECUTOR ON THE SHOW, SHE KEEPS HER PROSECUTOR HAT ON. MICHAEL JACKSON TRIAL SHE HAS CONVICTED HIM WITHOUT A

TRIAL OR JURY. SHE SAY'S SHE HAS BEEN RAPED AND KNOWS CHILD MOLESTERS. TODAY SHE CALLED THE KING OF POP," A SPOILED BRAT", AND THEN JESSE JACKSON, THE FAMILY SPOKESPERSON, EXPLAINED THAT THE SHERIFF AND DEPU-TIES CAME IN WITH SEVENTY-FIVE PEOPLE, DESTROYING THIS BLACKMAN'S ROYALTIES IN THE UNITED STATES OF AMERICA.. THE MORE YOUR BLACK-ASS ACHIEVE THE MORE THAT THE ROMAN RULES COME INTO EFFECT.

A CAMERA AT AN APARTMENT BUILDING IN LOS ANGELES, CALIFORNIA, WHERE A MAN GRAB A WOMAN AND THREW HER AROUND, HAS FOUND OUT THAT IT WAS A ROMANTIC COUPLE, THAT WAS FOUND CELEBRATING AN ANNIVER-SARY, STATED CBS EVENING NEWS.

06-08-05

DEBT RELIEF FROM THE BUSH 2 ADMINISTRATION, DO NOT WANT TO HELP TONY BLAIR'S VENTURE TO SAVE AFRICA AFTER HELPING TO DESTROY IT, AND DEVELOPING THE AMERICAN SLAVE SYSTEM. COTTON IS A PLANT FROM AFRICA. JUST AS IS THE HORSE ALSO ORIGINATED THERE. THE TRANSPORTATION OF THE EUROPEANS, HORSES, KIDNAPPED AFRICANS, AND OTHER VITALS TO AMERICA WERE NEEDED FOR THEIR SURVIVAL ON A NEW LAND, WHICH EVENTUALLY BECAME KNOWN AS THE UNITED STATES OF AMERICA. THE AFRICAN'S KNOWLEDGE OF THE EARTH, AND HOW TO GROW AND CULTIVATE PLANTS TO LIVE ON, WERE ESSENTIAL TO THE FUTURE SLAVE MASTERS. THE COTTON CULTIVATORS OF GHANA, AFRICA, AROUND THE AREA OF MY FAMILY'S ORIGIN, I BELIEVE IS SENEGAL, GAMBIA, AND OWN DOWN TO GHANA, CENTRAL AFRICA. ONE SIDE OF MY FAMILY BEGAN IN THE LATE 1600'S AND

EARLY 1700'S IN VIRGINGIA. THERE ARE MANY REASONS WHY THE GOVERNMENT SHOULD SUPPORT THE REPARA-TIONS FOR THE ONES WHO WERE MADE TO BE SLAVES AND MADE THE UNITED STATES WHITE PEOPLE HAVE RICHES BEYOND THEIR THIEVERY HISTORY. A ACRE AND A MULE LIE, NOW TODAY THERE NEEDS TO BE SOME TYPE OF CHANGE TO THE POOR PEOPLE, ESPECIALLY THOSE OF SLAVE SYSTEM OF THE UNITED STATES.

REPARATION OF SOME TYPE HAS TO COME A PART OF THE NEXT PRESIDENTIAL ELECTION AND THERE IS NO REPUB-LICAN CANDIDATES WHO WILL WORK TO HELP THE CORPO-RATE WORKS. THEY HAVE MORE THAN ENOUGH FOR THEIR NEXT FIFTY GENERATIONS OF CHILDREN.

THE REPARATIONS FOR THE DESCENDANTS OF THE UNITED STATES SLAVE INDUSTRY HAS TO BE ADDRESS. THEIR CLAIM TODAY AS OUR COUNTRY ARE THE RICHEST OF THE WORLD, BUT THE REPUBLICANS CONTINUE TO BUILT THE DEBT OF THE UNITED STATES, AND THE DEMOCRATS, THEY CALL TAX AND SPEND, HAVE TO COME ALONG AND RECTIFY WHAT THE REPUBLICANS HAS DONE TO BUILT THE BANK ACCOUNTS OF THE SO-CALL STATUS QUO; THEREFORE, THE UNITED STATES HAS GREAT HUMAN RIGHTS WITH ALL OF THE JAILS AND PRISONS ARE FILLED TO CAPACITY AND SOME STATES ARE CONTRACTING SOME OF THE CUSTODIAL DUTIES OF CONVICTS TO PRIVATE COMPANIES, WHO ARE PROFITING FROM THE PRISONS POPULATIONS OF PEOPLE OF COLOR AND LANGUAGES THAT ARE NOT ENGLISH. THERE ARE NO MORE SECOND CHANCES FOR PRISONER AS IT WERE BECAUSE OF THE COLOR POPULATIONS AND THE HUMAN RIGHTS VIOLATIONS OF SENTENCING AND NO EDUCATION TO BETTER A PRISONER'S MIND. THIS AMERICAN SOCIETY

DOES NOT WANT THE AFRICA-AMERICANS , WHO ARE THE DESCENDANTS OF THE AMERICAN SLAVE SYSTEM.

NIXON, REAGAN, AND BOTH BUSH ADMINISTRATIONS ARE STILL CARRYING ON THE ALL WHITE AND SEPARATE SOCIETY. REAGAN ONCE SAID HE WAS NOT A RACIST, THAT WAS BECAUSE THERE WERE NEVER ANY BLACKS IN HIS LIFE EXCEPT MAYBE HIS SERVANTS AT A PARTY, AND THE SLAVES OF THE WHITE HOUSE WHO ARE THE UP KEEPERS TODAY. BUSH FATHER PREACHED NO TAXES, HIS SON ROBBED THE TREASURY TO GIVE THE THEIR FRIENDS AND CORPORATE OWNERS A REFUND AFTER THEY HAD ALL OF THE TAX DEDUCTIONS, IT IS ANTI-AMERICAN AND THEY HAVE TO CONTRIBUTE TO THE EFFORT TO RECTIFY WHAT THE SLAVE MASTERS OF THE UNITED STATES SLAVE SYSTEM DID TO DENY ANY HELP FOR THEIR SLAVES AND THEIR SLAVES DESCENDANTS. THE WEALTHY HAS TO PAY THERE FARE SHARE OF TAX AND THIS COUNTRY COULD AFFORD ALL THAT IS NEED TO RECTIFY THE ACRE AND MULE LIE TO THE SLAVES, THAT THE AMERICAN POLITICIANS HAS THE RESPONSIBILITY TO MAKE THIS A GREAT COUNTRY. THE GROWTH OF COTTON WAS/IS VERY PROFITABLE THEN AND TODAY, AND THEY SHOULD POOL MONIES TOGETHER WITH THE INSURANCE COMPANIES, AND THE GOVERNMENT TO MAKE THIS A GREATER COUNTRY, BECAUSE THEY FINALLY FOUND AWAY TO GIVE BACK TO THE KIDNAPPED ROYAL AFRICAN, AND MADE THEM A SLAVE IN A FOREIGN LAND.

TODAY MY UNCLE IS NINETY-THREE AND HE HAS PICKED TONS OF COTTON IN GEORGIA AND NO ONE HAS OFFER HIM OR HIS FAMILY A PENNY. THEY JUST WANT TO LOCK US UP AND THROW AWAY THE KEY AND HOPE THEIR RESPON-SIBILITY WILL GO AWAY. ONE MAN ONE VOTE COULD BE THE BEST AS IT WAS IN THE BEGINNING, OTHER WISE THE

SYSTEM WILL CONTINUE TO BE BIAS TO MY PEOPLE, NOT NO IMMIGRATION PROBLEM WITH US , OUR PROBLEM ARE WITH THE AMERICAN GOVERNMENT AND IT'S ENTITLEMENT PROGRAMS THAT REPUBLICANS ARE CONSTANTLY TRYING AND ARE ELIMINATING IN EVERY ELECTION, BECAUSE THEY CALL THEMSELVES THE ELITE AND THE POOR WHITE POPU- LATION ARE MUCH SMALLER THAN IT WAS WHEN PRESI- DENT FRANKLY D. ROOSEVELT SAVE PEOPLE DURING THE STOCK MARKET CRASH OF 1929.

THE ELECTORAL COLLEGE IS A SLAVE LAW AND PEOPLE OF COLOR VOTING RIGHTS IS SUPPOSE TO EXPIRE IN THE YEAR OF 2007.WHAT DOES THAT MEAN? ALL THIS IS STACKING THE COURTS. BUSH JUDGES WAS APPROVED THIS WEEK AND LAST. ONE WHITE WOMAN, ONE BLACK WOMAN, AS WOMEN DOES NOT RELATE TO THE MEN'S CLUB, AND THET IS THE CLYB THAT RUN THE WORLD. MOST LIKELY THEIR HUSBANDS ARE CONSORACY AND IS IN THE MEN'S CLUB. YOU KNOW THE TELL THE BITCH TO SIT DOWN AND SHUT -UP. IT HAS TO BE ROUGH FOR A WOMAN TO BE IN THE MEN'S CLUB OF CONGRESS. BETCHA.

06-09-05

"THE PATRIOT LAW"

PRESIDENT OF THE UNITED STATES HAVING A PRESS STATE- MENT FROM COLUMUS, OHIO, ON WHY CONGRESS SHOULD MAKE "THE PATRIOT ACT" PERMANENTLY IS JUST THE SAME OLD SLAVEMASTER'S REASONS TO SPY AND CONTROL THEIR CITIZENS IN THE NAME OF THE LAW. CHENEY IS ENGI- NEERING ALL OF THIS FROM THE WHITE HOUSE, AS SENOR BUSH IS THE CREATOR O OF THIS TEAM TO SET BACK AMER-

ICANS IN THE NAME OF THE LAW, WHILE ALL OF THEM CONTINUE TO GO TO THE BANK.

PROBABLY THAT'S WHY THE NUCLEAR OPTION" THAT WAS THREATHEN TO UNDO THE CONSTITUTION OF THE UNITED STATES, OVER THREE JUDGES, THAT WAS NOMI-NATED BY BUSH2: THAT IS,TO STACK THE COURTS AS HIS FATHER AND RONALD REAGAN ADMINISTRATION, THAT WAS FOLLOWING INTO NIXON ADMINISTRATION NATION-IZED POLICE FORCE, THE ONLY THING THAT SLOWED IT UP BECAUSE IT HAS GAINED STREAM , IN THE NAME TERRIOST AND "THE PATRIOT ACT".

THE DEMOCRATS SAID NOT ALL OF THEM TO STAY, IT CANNOT STAY AS IS, BECAUSE "IT VIOLATES OUR BILL OF RIGHTS". ON CNN WAS THIS TAPE.

06-13-05

NOT GUILTY MICHEAL JOE JACKSON

CRACKERS EVERYSINCE COLUMUS AND THE BOSTON TEA PARTY, TO NOT TO HAVE A KING HERE ON THIS CONQUERED LAND OF NORTH AMERICA CONTINENT. NO CHURCH WARS WITH THE STATES, SEPARATION OF CHURCH AND STATE. THEY WERE ONE MAN ONE VOTE, SOMETHING THE BRITISH IS NOT AS PROTECTED OF THEIR POPULATION AS THERE IS HERE, JUST THERE IS NOT OPEN SLAVERY AS IT WAS DRAFTED IN PHILADELPHIA, PA., THE . HOME OF BENJAMIN FRANKLIN IS THE ONLY NONE PRESIDENT OF THE AMER-ICAN CURRENCY, THE ONE HUNDERD DOLLAR, OR ANY OTHER DENOMINATION OF AMERICAN CURRENCY.

THE ROMAN ATTITUDE OF GRTTING THE HEAD MONKEY MAN", AND THE AFRICAN DECENDANT PEOPLE, JUST AS

THE ONLY BEGOTTEN OF THE CREATOR, JESUS CHRIST OF NAZARET. THE CRUCIFIX IS WAVED ALL OVER THE WORLD AND IN THE HISTORY OF THE HUMAN POPULATION HAS THERE EVER BEEN THE LIGHTEST OF HUMANS, ARIANS AS THEY CALL THEMSELVES; BUT THEY ACT AS THOUGHT IT IS A PROTEST OF THE CRUCIFIX, WHEN IN REALITY IT IS A REMINDER THAT AFRICANS, I FEED YOU TO THE LIONS IN ROME AND WE HAVE CRUCIFIED YOUR HOLY MESSIAH OF ALL OF US, BUT WE ARE THE DEVIL AND WE WILL SNEAK UP ON YOU, TO KILL AND EAT ALL THE DARK BABIES THAT WERE BORN AT THE END OF THE EARTH POPULATION, EURO-PEAN EAT ALL OF THE DARK BABIES TO CREATE THIS GRAND EXAMPLE TO THE LIGHTER HUMAN(CRACKERS), NOT TO HAVE BLACK OR DARK BABIES. THE DARKEST WAS EATTEN FIRST.

ABC INVESTIGATES AMERICAN SLAVERY AND LYCHINGS. "WITHOUT SANCTIONS" IS A NEW BOOK ON LYCHINGS, A DOZEN SENATORS THAT REFUSED TO SIGN ON TO THE LESGISTORS IN CONGESS TODAY.REPARATIONS SHOULD FOLLOW THE APOLOGY. THE CLINTON ADMINISRATION WAS PUSHING IT UNTIL THE OVERTHROW OF THE UNITED STATES CONTITUTION IN THE 2000 PRESIDENTIAL ELECTION.

DICK CHENEY HAS STEPPED OUT FRONT AGAIN, AS BABY BUSH CANNOT HANDEL THE PRESSURE OF CLOSING QUAN-TALOMO, CUBA PRISON OF AMERICAN OCCUPATION OF CUBA. HE IS THE CREATOR OF THE BOMBING OF BAGDAD, IRAQ; HE IS THE RACIST OF THE RACIST JUST RONALD REAGAN. BUSH TOLERATE PEOPLE OF COLOR A LITTLE BETTER, BUT RACIST DICK CHENEY DO NOT HAVE ANY BLACKS AS HIS CLOSE FRIEND, NOT EVEN COLON POWELL. CHENEY SHOULD BE BROUGH UP FOR TREASON, JUST AS SADDAM HUSSEIN, EVEN IF HE AND BABY BUSH MAKE IT OUT OF THIS PRESIDENCY.

MARCHA CLARK, THE O.J.SIMPSON 'S PROSECUTOR, AND NANCY GRACE SHOULD NOT BE ON TELEVISION PASTING ON ALL OF THOSE THEORIES, JUST AS THE SLAVE MASTER. DO NOT LOOK AT WHITE WOMEN OR YOU WILL BE HUNG"

06-14-05

RASANJANA, IRANIAN PRESIDENT'S INTERVIEW, SHOW ON CNN SPECIAL REPORT, THAT THEY ARE THE VICTIMS OF TERRIORIST AND THAT THE UNITED STATES WAS INVOLVED WITH ALQATA AND THE WORLD TRADE CENTER. THEY HAVE NOT BEEN VOCAL, THE UNITED STATES IS IN SUPPORT OF THESE DIFFERENT ORGANIZATIONS.

CONGRESS SHOULD' ADMINISTRATION. THEY HAVE FUCKED-UP THE RELATIONSHIP THIS COUNTRY WAS INVOLVED IN UNDER THE CLINTON ADMINISTRATION.

CONGRESS SHOULD START IMPEACHMENT HEARINGS WITH ALL THE CONGRESS DID TO THE CLINTONS AND SEX IN THE WHITE HOUSE, JUST AS IT IS IN THE HALLS OF CONGRESS. THEY ARE HYPOCRITES AND THAT IS, MOST OF THEM, NO PARTY LINES, JUST CRACKER LIES (ARIAN DESCENDANTS).

CNN'S JUDY WOODRUFF RETIRED LAST WEEK, WITH HER MENTOR/CO-WORKER, BERNARD SHAW, WHO TED TURNER GENIUSES TO CHANGE THE NEWS AND TELEVISION FOR CURRENT EVENTS FOR THE WORLD OF HUMANS. TED WAS SO GREAT TO PUT AN IMAGE OF COLOR TO THE WHOLE WORLD NEW EVENTS WITH BERNARD AS CHIEF OF CNN. HE WAS THE HEAD MAN AND A OPEN MINDED AFRICAN-AMER-ICAN. THE IMAGE OF SO-CALL THIRD WORLD PEOPLE, AND TED TURNER WAS RAISED AS A SEGREGATIONIST, AND THEN LATER MARRIED JANE FONDA. A REBELLIOUS WHITE LADY,

AND ALL OF THE OTHER HUMAN DEEDS THAT THE TED HAS AND CONTINUE TO INFLUENCE THE NEWS MEDIA EXECUTIVES, AND TED MOST LIKELY WAS BEING INFLUENCED BY THE GREATEST HUMANIST CONSCIOUSNESS OF FORMER PRESIDENT JIMMY CARTER, HABITAT FOR HUMANITY.

THIS DEMOCRACY CAN WORK WITHOUT A DICTATOR DESIRES ON THE PEOPLE OF THE UNITED STATES. RUMSFIELD IS GETTING TESTY IN HIS INTERVIEW TODAY, QUESTIONING THE IRAQ WAR AND OTHER MATTERS. GENERAL MYER IS NOT THERE TODAY, HE SENT HIS VICE CHAIRMAN GENERAL TO FACE THE MEDIA'S QUESTIONS OF CLOSING GUANTAMO BAY, CUBA. THE RECRUITMENT REQUEST AFTER THEY HAVE WENT TO WAR JUST TO REPLACE SADDAM HUSSEIN AND TAKE CONTROL OF IT'S OIL, NOT BECAUSE OF WEAPONS OF MASS DESTRUCTION, AND NOT THAT HE WAS IN A SECRET NUCLEAR BUILD UP THAT THE INSPECTORS OF THE UNITED NATIONS (U.N.) COULD NOT FIND.

BUSH- CHENEY RAN THEM OUT OF IRAQ, JUST TO BOMB AND NOW NEARLY TWO THOUSAND OF OUR AMERICAN CITIZENS HAS DIE, BECAUSE OF THEIR COMMITMENT TO SECURE OUR COUNTRY AND NOT TO DIE FOR NOTHING.

REVENGE ON SADDAM AFTER HE HAD AN ASSASSINATION PLOT ON FRIEND GHW BUSH PRESIDENCY AND BEFORE, BECAUSE PRESIDENT GHW HAD GIVEN SADDAM PERMISSION TO ANNEX KUWAIT, WHICH WAS IRAQ BEFORE IT WAS TAKEN AWAY. THE INVASION ON KUWAIT AFTER THE IRAN IRAQ WAR, THE WORLD FROWN ON IT AND PRESIDENT GHW BUSH TURNED ON HIM AND WE RAN SADDAM BACK INTO HIS BORDER LINE OF IRAQ, IN WHAT WAS CALLED THE GULF WAR. I SAID THEN THAT WE WERE GOING TO BE THERE A LONG TIME JUST IN VIETNAM. SINCE 1991 UNTIL TODAY AND COUNTING WE ARE STILL IN IRAQ, AND IT STARTED WITH A

BUSH AND IS BEING CONTINUE BY A YOUNGER BUSH, WITH CHENEY AS VICE PRESIDENT INSTEAD OF SECRETARY OF DEFENSE.

BUSH2 ADMINISTRATION SHOULD GO UP FOR TREASON, INCLUDING COLON POWELL, WHO WENT ALONG WITH HIS SPY PARTNER, GEORGE HUBERT WALKER BUSH, THAT HE PUT ON ONE SIDE OF HIS SON AND DICK CHENEY ON THE OTHER, TO COMMIT TREASON ON THIS COUNTRY, WITH THE CONSPIRACY OF THE SENATE AND THE HOUSE OF REPRE-SENTATIVES. IN THE END IT CAME OUT THAT THEY HAD TRICKED COLON POWELL TO GO TO THE UNITED NATION TO LIE ABOUT INFORMATION ON SADDAM. HOW COULD THE CONGRESS GIVE A PRESIDENT THE BACKING WITHOUT GOING INTO THE BACK GROUND AND WHETHER THE INTEL-LIGENCE WAS TRUE? THAT IS WHY MOST OF THE REPUB-LICANS CONSPIRED WITH BUSH AND CHENEY TO BRING AMERICA INTO DESTROYING ANOTHER AFRICAN-DESCEN-DANT NATION.

THE SENATE IS THE KING'S RIGHTS THAT THE MILITARY HAS TO REPORT TO. THE PRESIDENT'S WAR, WHICH IS WHAT HE TOLD US WHEN HE AND CHENEY WAS APPOINTED AS DICTATOR OF THE UNITED STATES, IN THE NAME OF DEMOC-RACY.

8-30-05

HURRICANE KATRINA TOOK ALL OF THE GULF COAST AND THE RACIST SAYS HOW COULD THAT HAPPEN, JUST TO SHOW YOU THAT THEY UNDER ESTIMATE GOD THROUGH EVERY LYNCHING, POVERTY, AND JAILING OF ALL THE PEOPLE OF COLOR POSSIBLE, AND THANK GOD FOR DNA RELEASE OF

ALL OF THESE BLACK, SUPPOSE TO BE KILLING AND RAPING OF WHITE WOMEN.

THE GULF COAST RACIST IS NOT SUPERIOR; THEY ARE CHILDREN OF GOD GONE ASTRAY. THE CREATOR OF THE HEAVENS AND THE EARTH IS SUPERIOR, EVEN THOUGHT, WE BEING IN THE IMAGE OF GOD, WE CAN HAVE THAT ATTITUDE UNTIL YOU HAVE TO PLAY GOD BY UNNECESSARILY TAKING OF A LIFE.

THEY WERE CRYING ABOUT LOOTING WHEN THEY WERE THE ONES DEPRIVE BEFORE GOD GAVE THEM SOME RELIEF. FROM THE EMANCIPATION PROCLAMATION AND THE FREEING OF SLAVES THAT THE DESCENDANTS STILL ARE NOT REALLY FREE. MENTALLY NOT FREE, MATERIALIST NOT FREE, AND THE DESCENDANTS OF THE SLAVE MASTERS ARE RAISED TO KEEP THE UNDER CLASS. THEY WILL FEED A SMELLY DOG OR CAT BEFORE THEY WOULD FEED ANY HOMELESS, WHETHER THEY WERE UNEDUCATED, DRUNKEN, AND TODAY DRUG ADDICT THERE NEEDS TO BE SOME LAND TO HOUSE THESE PEOPLE INSTEAD OF PRISONS AND THE INSANE HOUSE, AND TODAY THE GOVERNMENTS ARE CLOSING THOSE AND THE PEOPLE ARE SLEEPING UNDER INTERSTATES, CHURCHES, AND ANY STREET ALLEY IN THE URBAN CITIES. SOME MAKE BE COULD BE TAKEN TO FARMS TO BE HOUSED AND WORK SOME OF JOBS THAT SOME OF THE MEXICANS HAVE, BUT AT A HIGHER COST OF HOUSING AND THEY COULD EAT SOME OF WHAT IS FARMED.

FARM SUBSIDIES SHOULD BE TIED TO MAKING SURE THE DESCENDANT OF SLAVES WHO WOULD WANT TO LEAVE THE HOMELESS SHELTERS TO THE FARM LAND AND THE GOVERNMENT ARE ALREADY OVER PAYING THE LARGE WHITE FARMER MORE THAN THEY SHOULD, AND THE

BLACK FARMER'S ARE LEAVING THE FARM FASTER THAN THE WHITE FARMER.

09-02-05

REGULAR People ARE LIVING THE WORDS OF THE DOCTOR AND SON OF GOD, THE REVEREND DOCTOR MARTIN LUTHER KING JUNIOR'S 1963 MOUNTAIN TOP SPEECH ON THE MALL OF WASHINGTON, D.C, WAS A GREAT DAY FOR DESCENDANTS OF UNITED STATES' SLAVE SYSTEM.

THE OLD TRICKY DICK CHENEY AND HIS PROJECT GEORGE W. BUSH DON 'T GIVE DAM ABOUT ANY MAN OF COLOR, NOT TO MENTION DESCENDANTS OF SLAVES, THEY WILL SPENT MONIES AND TRENT LOTT, CHENEY, BUSH 1&2, HAS BETRAYED THE PEOPLE OF THE UNITED STATES. STACKING OF SO-CALL CONSERVATIVE JUDGES, WHICH IS ANOTHER WORD FOR HATING THE DESCENDANTS OF SLAVES, AND ALL OF THE PEOPLE OF COLOR THAT WAS HERE AND CAME AFTER MY PEOPLE ARE IN A GLASS CEILING, I.E. NO MATTER HOW EDUCATED YOU CAN ONLY GO SO HIGH IN THE CORPO-RATE STRUCTURE. THERE ARE ALWAYS A VERY FEW EXCEP-TIONS TO EVERY RULE. EVERYONE CAN NOT BE AN INDEPEN-DENT BUSINESS MAN LIKE MY GRANDFATHER, WHO WAS IN THE ENERGY BUSINESS, BUT THE MORE THAT BELIEVE THEY CAN TAKE VERY LITTLE AND SUCCEED THE BETTER. THE CAPITALIST SYSTEM IS SET FOR IDEALS, BUT THE LAWS ON LICENSING, PATENTS, BANKING, AND OTHER CONTROL OF CAPITAL IS SET-UP AGAINST THE AVERAGE PERSON OF COLOR.

PRESIDENT BUSH VISITED THE GULF COAST TODAY, AFTER THE HURRICANE THAT VISITED THIS CHURCH GOING CROWD OF HATE ON A SUNDAY, AND I KNOW DICK PATTED

HIM ON THE ASS AND TOLD HIM TO GO FOOL THE PEOPLE OF THE UNITED STATES AGAIN. HE STARTED IN MOBILE, ALABAMA, MISSISSIPPI, AND FINALLY THE CITY OF NEW ORLEAN CITIZENS STILL TRAPPED AND ALL WERE DESCENDANTS OF SLAVES.

THE PEOPLE OF THIS POOR AMERICA AREA WAS NOT A PRIORITY. THEY ARE PROTECTING THEIR CLIENTELE FORTUNE WHO HAS INVESTED IN OIL, AT THIRTY AND FORTY DOLLARS A BARREL. OIL IS GOING UP AND BUSH WILL NOT DO A JIMMY CARTER AND OPEN RESERVES TO HELP THE PEOPLE OF AMERICA. THE REPUBLICAN CONTROL OF ALL BRANCHES OF GOVERNMENT IS VERY DANGEROUS TO THE UNITED STATES. THE HEAD OF THE OIL MEN GOT ON THE NEWS TODAY. HE TOLD THE INVESTORS TO INVEST THEIR MONIES INTO THE OIL BUSINESS. HE SAID IT WOULD GO OVER FIFTY DOLLARS A BARREL.

TODAY THE CONSPIRACY BETWEEN BRITAIN AND THE UNITED STATES, TO INVADE UNDER FALSE PRETENSE TO KILL SADDAM HUSSEIN IS ONLY FOR OIL AND NOT BECAUSE HE HAS OBTAINED WEAPONS UNDER A NO FLY ZONE, WHICH WAS SET IN PLACE TO CONTROL HIS MOVEMENTS AND NOT TO GO INTO BAGHDAD. BUSH 41'S FATHER, CHENEY, AND POWELL WERE SMART BACK THEN, AND NOW THEY WANT TO JUSTIFY IT ALL THESE YEARS LATER, THE WHOLE REPUBLICANS AND MOST OF THE RACIST DEMOCRATS SHOULD PAY A PRICE, AND THE CONGRESS SHOULD NEVER BACK A WAR RESOLUTION AGAIN ON A WHIM.

NEW ORLEANS, LOUISIANA IS UNDER SIEGE AND UNDERWATER. RUSSELL SIMONS'S BUS WENT WITH ALL TYPE OF SUPPLIES, THE AMERICAN GOVERNMENT FAIL THE AMERICAN PEOPLE, THAT IS, PEOPLE OF COLOR AND THE POOR WHITES IN THE MELTING POT FOR A SHORT TIME.

 BILL MAHER, ON HBO, IS A BLESSING TO THE FREEDOM OF SPEECH. HIS CRITICISM SHOULD BE IN MOST NEWSPAPERS THAT ARE NOT OWNED BY THE RACIST RUPERT MURDOCK ENTERPRISES.

RACIST PAT ROBINSON, FARWELL, AND ALL OF THE KLAN GATHERINGS IN CHURCHES IS LAYING LOW, AND THEY WAS/ WILL NOT GO ON PUBLIC TV TO HELP "THE NIGGERS THAT SHOULD BE IN POVERTY SLAVERY AS THEY SHOULD".

I REALLY WOULD HAVE LIKE TO BE THE FLY ON THE WALL"

ALABAMA NATIONAL GUARD COVER UP, VISITED ALABAMA FIRST, AND FUCK THE NIGGERS, LIVING IN THE CITY WATER. KILL AS MANY OF THEM NIGGERS THAT RECEIVE WELFARE, WELFARE IS FOR ANY WHITE PERSON.

09-07-05

BUSH AND BHENEY'S HOME LAND SECURITY WAS/IS DISAS-TEROUS. FEDERAL EMERGERNCY MANAGEMENT AGENCY (FEMA) HAS BEEN REPLACED WITH POLITICAL PEOPLE OF THE BUSH AND CHENEY ADMINISTRATION'S PEOPLE FOR POLITICAL FAVORS, INSTEAD OF A BUREAU OF DISASTER EXPERIENCE. UNDER HOMLAND SECURITY IT IS ALL POLI-TICS.

GOD PULLS THE COVER OFF OF THE COVERT RACISM IN THIS COUNTRY. PRESIDENT BUSH MOTHER AND FATHER VISITED THE HOUSTON ASTRODOME, WHERE EVAUEES WERE LIVING, AND HIS MOTHER SAID THESE WERE DEPRIVE PEOPLE, SO THEY ARE MAKING OUT BETTER THAN THEY WERE.

09-11-05

BUSH-CHENEY'S ADMINISTRATION ON THE RUN AND DO NOT RECOGNIZE G-D. THE DECENDANTS OF THE ROMANS AND THERE LEAD TO CONQUER BY INVADING AND STRICKING THE RICHES OF THE INVADED LAND (IRAQ). HALIBURTON, VICE PRESIDENTS COVER TO SECURE FUNDS, OIL PRODUCTS, AND RECONSTRUTION., THAT IS THE REASON TO COME OUT OF HIS COMFORT ZONE TO VISIT THE TRENT LOTT'S STATE OF MISSISSIPPI. THEY ARE THE TRUE DEVILS AND ACTIVIST OF RACISM. THEY ARE RACIST TO THE CORE.

HE AND HOMELAND LACKEY CHIEF HAD TO RECALL FEMA'S CHIEF BROWN TO WASHINGTON, AND THE PRESIDENT ORDERES A NO NONE SENSE THREE STAR GENERAL HONORE TO TAKE CHARGE OF OPERATION IN NEW ORLEANS, LOUISIANA, AFTER G-D BLEW HIS DISTANE OF THE LIGHTER HUMANS THAT CONTINUES TO DEPRIVE THE LESS WEALTY.

THE LIGHTER HUMANS WANT TO DO THERE DIRT AND THEN PUT IT IN THE DARK, LIKE INSISTING THE MEDIA NOT COVER THE RETURNING CASKETS FROM THE WAR FOR OIL, JUST AS SADDAM HUSSEIN, THE PRESIDENT OF IRAQ, A SOVERIEN COUNTRY AT THE TIME OF THE BUSH AND CHENEY'S PERSONAL CONTRACT ON A STATESMAN, IN THE NAME OF WEAPONS OF DESTRUCTION.

CNN SUED THE GOVERNMENT TO NOT TO BE BLOCKED FROM FILMING THE DEAD BODIES AS NEWS GATHERING THAT IS COVER UNDER THE UNITED STATES CONTITUTION. IMAGINE THE PRESIDENT AND VICE IS TRYING TO CONTROL THE MEDIA, IN ORDER TO HAVE A RACIST RUPERT MURDOCK AND HIS PAPER COMPANIES AND FOX NEWS ARE AS BIAS AS ANY ONES COMPANY IS OUT TO TRICK AND BE

BIAS OF ALL THE NEWS THAT INVOLVES ALL PEOPLE. LAW SHOULD REQUIRE IT. FREEDOM TO DISAGREE IS GOOD, BUT COMPLETELY BETRAY THE PUBLIC, IN ORDER TO COVER THEIR RACISM.

NOMINEE JUDGE ROBERTS FOR THE UNITED STATES SUPREME COURT, BY THE BUSH ADMINISTRATION IS THE STACKING OF THE COURT TO GO BACK TO PRE EARL WARREN DAYS AS CHIEF JUSTICE THAT GAVE THE CHANCE TO THE DECENDANTS OF SLAVES, AND NOW THE BUSH ADMINISTRATION WANT TO REVERSE THE LAWS, JUST AS TRENT LOTT HAD SAID ABOUT STORM THURMOND'S 1948 PRESIDENTIAL BID, THAT SEGREGATION FOREVER.

WILLIAM REQUIST PASSED THE OTHER DAY, AS HALF MASS FLAGS WERE FLOWEN. RACIST AS THAT OVERTHREW THE UNITED STATES CONSTITUTION THAT HE HAD SWORNED TO UPHOLD, DURNING THE 2000 ELECTION.

THE NEW THING FROM CHENEY'S ADMINISTRATION IS THE BLAME GAME TO COVER THEIR INSENSITIVENESS DURING THE FIRST SUFFERING OF THE BLACK PEOPLE OF HURRICANE KATRINA 2005.

THE AMERICAN RACIST ARE IN THE LIGHT AGAIN THROUGH G-D'S UPSET OF THE CRACKERS GOLD COAST OF THE UNITED STATES. THE IRAQ WAR BROUGHT SHAME ON AMERICA LIKE NO OTHER WAR. THE WANTED TO BE KNOWN WAR PRESIDENT BUSH AND HIS VICE PRESIDENT CHENEY DID THE ENTIRE AMERICAN TO DOOM. THE MAJORITY IN BOTH HOUSES AND THE EXECUTIVE BRANCH WERE ABUSED AND I HOPE IT WILL BE CHANGED AS THE PEOPLE OF AMERICA WILL WAKE-UP AND PUT RACISM ASIDE AND BECOME HUMANISM

10-09-05

MSNBC 'S INVESTIGATES, A SPECIAL PROGRAM OF AMERI-
CANS PRISON SYSTEM, THEY ZOOMED IN ON THE GREAT
STATE OF KENTUCKY, SO CALLED, "THE CASTLE ON THE HILL",
MOSTLY ALL OF THOSE OF AFRICAN-AMERICANS ARE/WERE
DEPRIVED BY BIRTH IN AMERICA. THE WAY THAT ALL BREEDS
OF SOCIETY'S HUMANS THAT WAS DEPRIVED OF HERITAGE,
RELIGION, LANGUAGE, AND NOW THESE ADVANCE TECH-
NOLOGY DAYS, A HUMAN HAS TO HAVE TUDORS TO ASSIST
IN HUMAN DEVELOPMENT, BUT RACISM HAS A RULE, LOCK
THE NIGGER AND ALL THE IGNORANT LIGHTER HUMANS,
AND THROW AWAY THE KEY.

TIA WE WILL CONCENTRATE ON SOME OF THE TITLES AS I
TRIED FROM TIME TO TIME, YOU AND CIARRA HAS SOME
RESEARCH TO DO. THERE IS A LOT OF RESEARCH AVAIL-
ABLE TO ARGUE THE CASE ON THE ROMAN THINKING
JUDGES ARE NOT LIBERAL, AS ALL JUDGES NEEDS TO BE.
CRACKERS DID NOT BELIEVE THE DARK NORTH AFRICAN
HOLY MESSIAH JESUS CHRIST, THE SON OF G-D. IN THE
IMAGE OF THE HUMANS AND NOT YOUR COMPLEXION AS
IT IS TO DAY. REMEMBER HANNIBAL OF CARTAGE, NORTH
AFRICA, A MOOR, AND THREE CENTURIES BEFORE THE
CREATION OF JESUS CHRIST OF NAZARETH, PALESTINE, ARE
AT FOLLOWED THE TRUE PREACHING JESUS AND NOW THEY
CALL IT ISLAM, THAT THE ROMANS PROMISED THEM SELVES
THAT NO AFRICAN WILL CONQUER THEM AGAIN; NOW THEY
CALL THEMSELVES ITALIANS. RUDY, THE FORMER NEW YORK
MAYOR AND NOW A CANDIDATE FOR PRESIDENT OF THE
UNITED STATES, NOW IS THE TIME TO PUBLISH. A NOTE TO
MY FAMILY MEMBER TO EDIT AND PUBLISH THIS BOOK, BUT
THEY WERE NOT ABLE.

"THE AMERICAN WAY" BY LWFS.

LAW ENFORCEMENT, JUDGES, AND DISTRICT ATTORNEY GENERALS ARE NOT JUST.

STRIKELAW INSTEAD OF EDUCATION AND A POSSIBLE LIFE OF INDEPENDENCE IS POSSIBLE. I HAVE SEEN NO EDUCATION AND PETTY CRIMES LEADS TO LIFE SENTENCES AND THAT IS NOT THE PROPER WAY FOR A COUNTRY, WHO IS SUPPOSE TO CRITICIZE OTHER NATIONS OF HUMAN RIGHTS. AFTER THE FORMER GOVERNOR GEORGIA AND FORMER PRESIDENT OF THE UNITED STATES JIMMY CARTER REALIZE THE CHAIN GANGS OF GEORGIA WAS NOT HUMANE IN ANY SENSE OF THE WORD. THE ARIZONA STATE HAS GONE BACK TO CHAIN GANGS AND HARD LABOR FOR THE MOST IGNORANT OF OUR SOCIETY. THE WORD GANG IS MISLEADING AND IS USE MOSTLY AS SOME STREET ELEMENT, WHEN IT IS A NATURAL FOR HUMAN SPIES, JUST AS THE OTHER SPIES OF THE EARTH TO GATHER AND REPRODUCE. IT IS ONLY THE HUMANS WHO TRIES TO SEPARATE AND THAT IS OUR PROBLEM.

JUDGES ARE SUPPOSE NOT TO BE BIAS, BUT IN THIS HUMAN GROWTH HAS PRODUCE MUCH RACISM AND IT HAS LEAD TO THE PRISONS TO BE FILLED, AND THE HUMAN CONSCIOUS-NESS OF G_D'S LAW IS IGNORED. THAT IS ONE OF THE DIFFERENCES IN THE ISLAM SOCIETY, AND THE REASONS FOR PUNISHMENT OF ANOTHER HUMAN. THE AMERICANS LAWS ARE MORE MAN MADE LAWS AGAINST PEOPLE OF COLOR, FOLLOWING THE ROMAN RULE HANDED DOWN THROUGH THE HOMO WORD OF SAINT. GOD SAID HAVE SEX AND BUILD FAMILIES AND THE SAINTS CHURCH WANTED YOU TO BELIEVE IN CELIBACY. IT IS A LIE AND THE ONES CONTINUE TO BELIEVE ARE DEVIL WORSHIPING. IN THIS

MODERN DAY WORLD HAS TO CHANGE, JUST AS THE LIARS GO NATION TO NATION PREACH CHRISTIANITY LIES.

THE BUSH CHENEY ADMINISTRATION HAS PUSHED EVERY-THING UNDER THE RUG, UNDER THE PUBLIC, UNDER THE LAW, AND UNDER THE GOOD OF THE UNITED STATES. WE WERE SUPPOSE TO BE THE LAND OF THE FREE, AND I THINK THAT WE ARE FREER THAN MOST COUNTRIES AND NATIONS OF THE WORLD, BUT THE UNITED STATES HAS A POPULA-TION GAP THAN NEEDS TO BE ADDRESS, IN COMBINATION OF THE GOVERNMENT, INSURANCE INDUSTRY, AND OTHER RESOURCES TO HAVE THIS COUNTRY AS CAPITALIST AND SOCIALIST MIX, BECAUSE OF THE WAY THE UNITED STATES WAS BUILT AND IS CONTINUE TO JAIL AND SEPARATE THE DESCENDANT OF SLAVES IN THE NAME OF EDUCATION TODAY. THEY WANT "PATROIT LAWS" INSTEAD OF HUMAN LAWS FOR THE POOR. THE "PATROIT LAWS" SHOULD NOT BE PERMANENT. IT ERASES THE WARREN COURT LAWS OF PRIVACY AND THE FOURTH AMENDMENT.

THE RACIST ABORTION LAWS ARE WHAT MOST ALL THE KLAN WANTS BECAUSE OF THE LIGHTER POPULATION. IF YOU TAKE THE ASIANS, MEXICANS, AND THE DESCENDANT OF SLAVES POPULATION THEN THE PEOPLE OF COLOR IS THE MAJORITY OF THE UNITED STATES TODAY. I HAVE NEVER SEEN A SO-CALL PRO-LIFER SUPPORT AN UNWANTED BIRTH, AND ESPECIALLY A DARK, OR A BABY OF COLOR. JUST LOOK AT TELEVISION MOST ARE THE LIGHTER IMAGES, THEY OWN IT THEY PROMOTE IT.

MAY G_D BLESS AMERICA FROM SOME OF THE RACIST AND TOTALITARIAN DREAMS OF FORMER PRESIDENT "TRICKY DICK" RICHARD NIXON IN THE UNITED STATES. THIS SYSTEM SEEMS TO WORK IN SOME RESPECTS. THE TWO TERM PRESI-DENT IS OK, THE ELECTION OF CONGRESS AND THE SENIORITY

RIGHTS IS DEBATABLE, AND THE NO TIME LIMIT OF THE FEDERAL JUDICIARY SHOULD BE ALTER WITH A TIME LIMIT. WE CAN NOT HAVE THE EVIL BUILDING WALLS AND FENCES JUST TO KEEP US IN MORE THAN ANY SO-CALL TERRORIST COMING ACROSS THE SOUTHERN BORDER WITH WEAPONS OF MASS DESTRUCTION; THEREFORE, THERE SHOULD NOT BE ANY WALLS OR FENCES TO KEEP THE ORIGINAL PEOPLE SOME ACCESS TO THEIR ANCESTORS LAND. HITLER WANTED TO SEPARATE AND EXTERMINATE AND NOW THE RIGHT WING ESPECIALLY, WANT TO SEPARATE AND ALL OF THE PATRIOT LAWS, THEY CAN EXTERMINATE. RACE CLEANING IS VERY POSSIBLE AS THE RIGHT WINGERS PROMOTE ABOR-TION, PATRIOT LAWS, AND NO RIGHTS FOR THE PEOPLE OF COLOR. THE 2008 ELECTION IS SO IMPORTANT, MORE THAN THE 2004 WHEN THE RIGHT WINGERS STOLE A CHANCE TO STACK THE FEDERAL COURTS WITH RACIST BIAS JUDGES. DON KING HELP WON OHIO AND WHAT DID HE GET? HE SOLD OUT WITH THE ANTI- CHRIST RIGHT WINGERS.

10-10-05

FIRST THING ON THE NEWS TODAY, WAS THAT PRESIDENT BUSH WAS ON IT'S WAY TO NEW ORLEANS, AND THAT THE NEW ORLEANS'S POLICE BEAT THIS AFRICAN –AMERICAN MAN ON PUBLIC TELEVISION AS ONE OFFICER WAS ON HORSE BACK WAS TRYING TO BLOCK THE CAMERAMAN OF CNN'S. A LITTLE LATER A POLICE GRABBED THE CAMERA MAN. POLICE TOLD HIM THAT HE HAS BEEN THERE FOR SIX WEEKS TRYING TO SURVIVE AND YOU SHOULD GO HOME", WHERE WE CAN BEAT THESE NIGGERS BACK INTO SUBMIS-SION.

PAKISTAN HAD AN EARTHQUAKE AND THE BUSH ADMIN-
ISTRATION HAS HELICOPTERS AND ALL TYPE OF SUPPLIES.
PEOPLE ARE ASKING WHY IS IT THAT THE BUSH ADMINIS-
TRATION CAN HAVE HELP IN PAKISTAN AND NOT TO NEW
ORLEANS? THE AMERICAN WAY.

10-14-05

THE POLICE BEATINGS IN NEW ORLEANS OF AN AFRICAN-
AMERICAN WANTS A TRIAL BY A JUDGE. THAT IS AN AMER-
ICAN WAY OF THE WHITE PEOPLE AND ESPECIALLY THE
LAW ENFORCEMENT, THAT THEY CAN KILL, MANE, OR DO
ANYTHING TO MY PEOPLE, DURING SLAVERY, JIM CROW,
AND NOW AS PLAIN OLD NIGGER. A NIGGER CAN NOT
TOUCH A WHITE PERSON, AND DURING MY PARENTS AND
GRANDPARENTS TIME YOU COULD NOT EVEN LOOK AT A
WHITE WOMAN. I FOUGHT THAT AND HAVE CHILDREN OF
MIX BREED AND THAT IS ALSO THE AMERICAN WAY.

WHEN A POLICE DO HAVE TO FACE A COURT IN THESE PAST
TWENTY YEARS THEY WANT TO CHANGE VENUE TO AN ALL
WHITE SUBURB OR FIND THEIR JUDGE WHO WAS A PROS-
ECUTOR AND IS SYMPATHY TO THE KLAN. JUSTIFY ACTION
THEY ALWAYS CLAIM, EVEN THOUGHT, THERE ARE FILMING
THE BEATING OR KILLING OF A BLACK OR LATINOS.

 TIA JUDGES IS THE LAW AND THE LAW IS RACIST.

BUSH2 IS JOKING, ROBBERING THE UNITED STATES TREASURY,
IRAQ, AND IS CONTINUINGLY STAGING AND IS STACKING
THE COURTS WHEN CONGRESS GOES ON RECESS. DICK
CHENEY IS THE ENGINEER AND THE CHIEF OF ALL OF THOSE
TYPES OF MOVES.

10-25-05

THERE IS A LEAK FROM THE BUSH ADMINISTRATION OF THE CIA, A TREASONER'S ACT, AND THE PRESIDENT SAYS HE WILL PUNISH ANYONE WHO MAY HAVE DONE IT.

VICE PRESIDENT CHENEY IS KNOWN TO HAVE BEEN INVOLVED IN THE CIA LEAK OF VALERIE PLAME WILSON, TO THE RIGHT WINGERS EDITOR, ROBERT NOVAK, BECAUSE HER HUSBAND WAS A CLINTON AMERICAN DIPLOMAT OF THE UNITED STATES. ANTI- AMERICAN IS JUST PLAIN AND SIMPLE. WHEN THEY ROB THE TREASURY TO KEEP THE UNITED STATES GOVERNMENT TO RECONCILE THE ACRE AND A MULE LIE, THEY WILL DO ANYTHING. THE GOOD SHEPHERDS ARE ALL-RACIST AND ARE THE ONES TO PROTECT THIS DEMOCRACY, IN THE NAME OF STATUS QUO.

THE REPUBLICAN CONGRESS, WHO IS IN CONTROL OF BOTH HOUSES, WILL NOT SERVE THE WHOLE PEOPLE OF THE UNITED STATES. THEY ONLY SERVE THE CAUCASIANS OF THE BRITISH AND THE ROMAN EMPIRE. THE DEMOCRATS WENT ALONG WITH THE REPUBLICANS TO IMPEACH CLINTON ON LYING ABOUT A SEX ACT, AND NOW THE REPUBLICANS ARE LOCKING THEM OUT OF OFFICES AND MEETINGS. THEN CAME THE EX- CIA CHIEF AND FORMER PRESIDENT GHW BUSH TO PUT HIS SON AS PRESIDENTIAL CANDIDATE, WITH TRICKY DICK" CHENEY AS VICE, AND COLON POWELL AS SECRETARY OF STATE, AND WENT ON TO OVERTHROW THE UNITED STATES CONSTITUTION, BY HAVE CHIEF JUDGE OF THE UNITED STATES COME OUT OF HIS SICK BED AND IN HIS WHEEL CHAIR TO DETERMINE A HANG CHAD WAS NOT A VOTE AND APPOINT BUSH AS THE PRESIDENT OF THE UNITED STATES. I PRAY AND HOPE THAT VOTING MACHINES IN EVERY PRECINCT IN THE NATION, WITH A PAPER RECEIPT AS

TO HOW AND WHO THEY VOTED. NEVER SHOULD THE COST OF SOME COMPUTER AND VOTE FRAUD SHOULD OCCUR AGAIN, IF THIS IS THE MODEL NATION FOR THE DEMOCRACY SYSTEM OF HUMANS. NEVER AGAIN SHOULD THE BUSHES OR ANY OTHER SHEPHERD THROW ANOTHER ELECTION.

TODAY BUSH SPEAKS TO THE RACIST GENERALS OF THE ARMED FORCES' WIVES, ABOUT HIS WAR IN IRAQ AND NOT I AFGHANISTAN, WHERE THE PEOPLE WHO ATTACKED US RESIDES.

HE ALSO GAVE MENTION TO ROSA PARK'S DEATH, THE MOTHER OF THE CIVIL RIGHTS, BECAUSE SHE WOULD NOT SIT IN THE REAR OF A BUS. HE MOST LIKELY MENTIONS HER BECAUSE OF HIS CHIEF OF STAFF CONDOLISA RICE, WHO IS PARKS HOME OF ALABAMA.

BUSH STAGED ALSO STAGED TALK TO THE HAND PICK SOLDIERS LAST WEEK, AND IT WAS ALL OVER THE MEDIA AND BUSH IS STILL LAUGHING, AS EVERYTHING IS A JOKE TO HIM. AMERICA WAS DOING WELL UNDER CLINTON- GORE. GORE DID NOT USE CLINTON, TRYING TO PLEASE THE REPUB-LICANS, AND THEN THEY PUT THE HUGE RAT COMMERCIAL ON THE AIR AND GORE WAS SCARE AND TIMID FROM THEN ON, THE BUSHES ROLLED ON TO THE WHITE HOUSE.

10-26-05

"N.Y. HIGH COURT CUFFS COP IN CONSENT CASE", SECOND CIRCUIT COURT OF APPEALS…6-1,"UNREASONABLE", FOR THE COPS TO INTERPRET THE CONSENT TO MEAN THEY COULD SLICE THROUGH FLOOR CARPETING AND PULL APART THE GAS TANK…" JUDGE SUSAN READ BACKED THE COPS…. WE LIVE IN AN AGE WHERE WE SHOULD BE MOST RELUCTANT

TO CREATE HARD-TO-APPLY RULES THAT HAMSTRUNG POLICE OFFICERS WHO REASONABLY SUSPECT THAT A VEHICLE CONTAINS A HIDDEN COMPARTMENT...ECHOED, BY JOHN GREBERT OF THE STATE CHIEFS OF POLICE ASSOCIATION, WHO SAID: IN A DANGEROUS TIMES SUCH AS THESE, WE'D PREFER TO SEE FEWER RESTRICTIONS ON POLICE-NOT MORE...."

THE NEW YORK DAILY NEWS REPORTED IN THIS MORNING PAPER.

WE CANNOT TRUST THE POWER OF THE POLICE, BECAUSE OF THEIR GUN SLING REPUTATION. THIS IS THE MOST OF ALL THE WATERING DOWN OF THE FOURTH AMENDMENT TO THE CONSTITUTION OF THE UNITED STATES. I WILL BE WILLING TO BET YOU THE JUDGE WAS A FORMER PROSECUTOR. THAT IS WHY THERE SHOULD NOT BE ANY WALLS OR FENCES ACROSS THE SOUTHERN BORDER, UNLESS THEY PUT THEM ACROSS THE NORTHERN BORDER, WHICH I DO NOT THINK THE ABORTIONIST DESCENDANTS WILL NOT GO FOR FENCES AND WALLS. THOSE RACIST TEXANS AND ARIZONANS ARE STILL IGNORANT AND GUN CARRYING EVERYDAY AND EVERYWHERE TO SHOT A NIGGER OR A MEXICAN. THE AMERICAN WAY. INTRUSION THEY WILL FOREGO, BUT NOT THE SECOND AMENDMENT, GIVING THEM THE RIGHT TO BARE ARMS.

STACKING OF COURTS IS NOT AMERICAN AND VOTERS HAS TO VOTE TO STOP THE PATRIOT ACT, NO KNOCK ENTRANCE, AND RACIST PROFILING OF MY PEOPLE AND I HAVE BEEN THERE, THEY VIOLATE YOUR RIGHTS ALL OF THE TIME.

PROFILING WAS BEING ADDRESS WITH THE CLINTON ADMINISTRATION AND NOW THE BUSH CHENEY STACKING OF FEDERAL JUDGES TO OVERTURN THE WARREN COURT

LAWS, EVEN IF A PERSON IS CARRY SOMETHING ILLEGAL THERE SHOULD NOT INTERRUPT FOR ANY CREATED PROBABLE CAUSE OF TRAFFIC LAWS. WHITE PEOPLE GO TO THE DRUG STORE AND OTHER GO TO THE STREETS. WHAT HAPPEN IN GERMANY WITH THAT RACIST ADORF HITLER, WAS BECAUSE THE SO-CALL JEWS THERE WERE PRACTICING AN AFRICAN RELIGION OF HEBREW JUDEA ISRAEL IS NORTH AFRICA, SO TELL ME WHY IS IT ONLY A HAND FULL THERE CONTROLLING THE WEALTH AND MILITARY, BACKED BY THE UNITED STATES MILITARY, BECAUSE THEY ARE THE DESCENDANT OF THE ROMAN EMPIRE. THERE WILL NEVER BE PEACE THERE UNTIL THE PEOPLE BECOME COLOR BLIND AND LIVE TOGETHER AS PEOPLE, WHATEVER IS YOUR RELIGIOUS BELIEF. THAT IS THE SUPPOSE TO BE MODEL OF THE UNITED STATES.

THE GOVERNMENT IS NOT WORKING ON MAKING VOTERS RIGHTS AMENDMENT TO BE PERMANENTLY. MOST PEOPLE THOUGHT THAT THE VOTER RIGHTS BILL OF 1964, SIGNED INTO LAW BY PRESIDENT LYNDON B. JOHNSON, WITH THE REVEREND DOCTOR MARTIN LUTHER KING, JUNIOR AND OTHER CIVIL RIGHTS ACTIVISTS IN ATTENDANCE AT THE WHITE MAN'S WHITE HOUSE, WAS AN EXPERIMENT AND HAD A TIME LIMIT. I WAS SHOCK TO RECENTLY FINDING THAT TO BE A FACT. ONE MAN VOTE AS THE CONSTITUTION ORIGINALLY INSURED THE PEOPLE OF THE UNITED STATES; AND, TO BE FREE FROM A KING JAMES AND THE UNITED KINGDOM IS NOT VALET IN 2005. ELECTORAL COLLEGE OF WHITE PEOPLE, MOSTLY WHITE MEN IS THE RULE TO KEEP THE AFRICAN-AMERICANS FROM ATTAINING THE HIGHEST OFFICES OF THE LAND.

IN 2007 VOTERS RIGHT BILL IS SUPPOSE TO EXPIRE, AND IF IT DOES ALL OF THE NONE WHITE PEOPLE OF THE UNITED

STATES WILL NOT BE ABLE TO VOTE AGAIN. I HOPE IT IS MADE PERMANENT, INSTEAD OF SOME TYPE OF EXTENSION, AND ESPECIALLY AFTER IT HAS MY PEOPLE USE TO VOTING AND FOR THEM NOT TO COULD BRING MORE SHAME ON THE UNITED STATES. I DO NOT THINK THAT YOU CAN TURN THE CLOCK BACK ON VOTING AS THE RIGHT WINGERS ARE CONTINUING TO DO WITH THE FOURTH AMENDMENT AND THE ABORTION RIGHTS OF WOMEN TO HAVE CHILDREN OR NOT.

I REMEMBER BEFORE THE ROE V. WADE ABORTION LAW, A LOT OF TEENAGERS WERE USING COKE COLA BOTTLES, COAT HANGERS, AND OTHER WAYS TO ABORT AND SOME OF THOSE DIED. HOW COULD A JUST SOCIETY AFTER COMING OUT OF THE DARK AGES OF WOMEN RIGHT TO VOTE, ABORT, AND NOW ARE TOLD BY SOME RIGHT WINGER APPOINTED UNITED STATES SUPREME COURT JUSTICE REVERSE THOSE RIGHTS, WITH OUT ORDERING THE GOVERNMENT TO SUPPORT THE BIRTH OF EVERY CHILD THAT IS FOUND NOT WANTED. THOSE WHO WANT A FAMILY AND HAS A FAMILY WOULD NOT BE ELIGIBLE, BUT FOR THE YOUNG GIRL AND BOY WHO ARE TEENAGERS WILL NEED SOME TYPE OF SUPPORT THAT THE SO-CALL "RIGHT TO LIFERS", SHOULD BE WILLING AND ABLE TO SUPPORT THIS POPULATION BUILDING REQUIREMENT THAT THEY ARE CONTINUING TO PUSH IN EACH ELECTION. IT IS THE PEOPLE'S RIGHTS AND NOT SOME ASSHOLE WHITE MAN TO TELL MY BLACK ASS OR SOME WOMAN WHO WANTS TO ABORT WHAT IS RIGHT OR WRONG, WHEN THEY ARE THE MOST IMMORAL HERITAGE ON EARTH IN THE NAME OF JESUS CHRIST. JESUS SAID THAT THEY WERE GOING TO USE HIS NAME IN VAIN, AND TODAY THEY ARE CONTINUINGLY TO USE HIS NAME IN VAIN.

THE ROMAN COURTS OF THE UNITED STATES AND THEIR DESCENDANTS WHO ARE SUPPOSE TO BE THE ELITE REPUBLICAN POLITICIANS, THAT IS, BUSHES, CHENEY, HATCH, LOTT, GINRICHES, HELM, AND ALL OF THE CHRISTIAN CRACKERS WHO HARBORS THE LIE OF THE HOLY MESSIAH JESUS CHRIST OF BETHLEHEM, PALESTINE, WITH A DARK COMPLEXION AND HAIR OF LAMBS WOOL, JUST AS SOLOMON, SHOULD NOT LIVE ANY LONGER. A RAINBOW COALITION OF HUMANS COULD BE THE ANSWER, IF THE AFRICAN DESCENDANTS OF SLAVES ARE INSURE THE BASIC OF OWNERSHIP.

A FEW NOTES TO MY SUPPOSE TO BE EDITOR CHILDREN:

TIA THERE HAS TO BE AWAKENING AND THE CRACKERS WILL BLOW UP THE WORLD AND TRY TO HIDE IN SPACE FOR A SHORT PERIOD, WHILE THEY ARE TAKING OUR TAX DOLLARS TO AFFORD THEIR ESCAPE OF THE EARTH. THE WEALTH IS ALL THEY WORSHIP AND THAT IS WHY G_D CONTINUE TO PUNISH THEM AND THEY REBUILT, BUT THERE IS BLACK BLOOD IN EVERY HUMAN. IT IS ALL GENETICS, THE DARKEST OF HUMAN HAS THE LIGHT AND DARK GENES, AND THE DARK GENES ARE ALWAYS DOMINANT. THE RACIST COMES TO FIGHT AND SEPARATE THE BIRTH OF THE LIGHTER GENE FROM THE DARKEST.

FREEDOM OF SPEECH, PRIVACY TO WALK, DRIVE, AND NOT BE HARASS BY SOME RACIST POLICE, IS SOMETHING I HOPE AND PRAY WILL HAPPEN IN AMERICA, THE SUPPOSE TO BE THE LAND OF THE FREE, WILL NOT GIVE THE POLICE THE BENEFIT OF THE DOUBT, BECAUSE THEY DO NOT ALWAYS DESERVE IT. THESE LAWS WERE BASED ON AFRICAN DESCENDANT HUMANS WERE NOT HUMANS AND UNTIL THAT MENTALITY CHANGES, THE POLICE SHOULD NOT INTERFERE WITH PEOPLE DRIVING DOWN THE STREET FOR NO REASON.

10-27-05

TEE&CEE, NOTES TO MY CHILDREN

ON ABORTION, THE RACISM OF THE LIGHTER HUMAN, ARE POISONING THE WATERS OF AFRICA, CONTINUING TO CREATE DISEASES, VIRUSES, AND WARS IN THE PEOPLE OF COLOR COUNTRIES, TO CONTINUE THEIR DOMINATION AND SUPERIORITY OF THE DARKER HUMANS. THEY ARE NOT GOING TO FEED ONE DARK BABY THAT IS BORN IN POVERTY; BUT, THEY WILL INDEED TAKE CARE OF EVERY WHITE/LIGHT BABY THAT IS BORN, AND ESPECIALLY IN THIS COUNTRY.

IT IS ALL ABOUT POPULATION GROWTH, THAT IS, AND STATISTICS OF MAJORITY AND MINORITY. "THE AMERICAN WAY", LWFS.

LATER

10-30-05

Tee & cee,

Judges are supposed to be liberal/independence; especially post reconstruction of the civil war of the United States, judges has been anything but the above. bush-Cheney should be impeached for treason of the American people.

The word People in our society usually means white people, but they drop the adjective these days. UNITED STATES SUPREME COURT selection is to be demoralizing to women and people of color , if bush-Cheney has their way. Their party is the racist majority in this country's political parties.

10-31-05

KATRINA TWO MONTHS LATER AND THOSE FEDERAL EMER-GENCY MANAGEMENT AGENCY (F.E.M.A) TRAILERS STILL HAS NOT ARRIVED IN NEW ORLEANS, LOUISIANA. THE CAPITAL OF POOR DESCENDANT OF SLAVES: AS WITH RITA AND THIS

LATEST ONE IN THE STATE OF FLORIDA HAS TRAILERS. THE AMERICAN WAY, LWFS.

BUSH NOMINEE IS SAMUEL ALIDO AS UNITED STATES SUPREME COURT NOMINEE, A JUDGE OF FIFTEEN –YEARS, FROM NEW JERSEY. ONLY A FATHER AS A DESCENDANT FROM AMERICA, BUT HIS FATHER HELP BOROUGH EUROPEAN CULTURE TO THESE IGNORANT ASSES THAT WAS RELEASE ON THE WORLD TO BE FREE FROM THE KING RULE OF EURO-PEANS; AND ESPECIALLY THE ENGLISH SPEAKING COUN-TRIES. ENGLISH IS THE LAST OF THE LATIN ROOT WORDS, AND THE LAST OF THE LIGHTEST HUMANS WHOM PAST JUDGMENT ON THE DARKER HUMAN COMPLEXIONS. HE IS A SHY MAN, AS SAMUEL S LUXEMBURG OF NEW JERSEY.

THIS NOMINEE AND EVENTUALLY BECAME THE APPOINTED JUSTICE, AND CHENEY WANTED HIM TO BE CHIEF JUSTICE AND THAT IS WHAT HE BECAME. HE DID NOT HAVE TO START OFF AT THE END OF THE BENCH, HE WAS THE IMME-DIATE APPOINTED CHIEF JUSTICE TO REPLACE THE WILLIAM REHNQUIST JUSTICE THAT GOT OFF HIS DYING BED TO DECLARE THAT TIME WAS OF ESSENCE TO HAVE A PRESIDENT OF AMERICA AND APPOINTED GEORGE W. BUSH. VOTING MACHINES IN EVERY VOTING PRECINCT IN AMERICA HAS TO BE A FEDERAL EXPENSE, BUT THE STATUS QUO WANTS TO PUT IT ON THE STATES, AND THAT IS A PLOY FROM THE BEGINNING OF THE ORIGINAL STATES TO BE SEPARATE FROM THE OTHER, BUT AFTER THE 2000 BREACH OF THE UNITED STATES CONSTITUTION, A NEW PRESIDENT AND CONGRESS SHOULD ABSOLUTELY HAVE THE COMPUTER MACHINE THAT WILL PRINT OUT A RECEIPT OF WHO EACH VOTER VOTED FOR. NO MORE FLORIDA HANGING CHADS, AND THE RURAL COUNTY OF SOUTHERN STATES THREATEN THE IGNORANT BLACK PEOPLE WHO LOSS THE HERITAGE AND LANGUAGE

WAS ORDERED TO SPEAK ENGLISH, JUST AS THE REPUBLICAN RACISTS ARE SAYING TODAY THAT THE MEXICANS HAS TO SPEAK ENGLISH. IT IS ALL-RACIST AND THEY WANT TO OVER HEAR WHAT YOU ARE SAYING, TO KEEP THEIR POWER.

ITALY HAS SEEN THE LIGHT TOO, JUST SPAIN DID AND ARE RETREATING TO THEIR SOLDIERS BACK TO THEIR HOME-LAND. GREAT NEWS FOR THE PEOPLE OF AMERICA, BUT NOT FOR THE DECEIVERS, THE BUSH FAMILIES AND THE SO-CALL REPUBLICAN POLITICAL PARTY OF THE SLAVE MASTERS DESCENDANTS TO ECONOMICAL SEGREGATED FROM PEOPLE OF DESCENDANT OF SLAVES, AND IT WILL ALWAYS MATTER.

THE ENGLISH FOREFATHERS OF THE UNITED STATES WERE NOT/ARE NOT KIND AND HONORABLE MEN THAT FORBIDDEN THEIR WOMEN AND CHILDREN TO PAST ON THE "STAUS QUO". THEY BEAT AND STILL BEATING NIGGERS IN NEW ORLEANS AND THE REST OF AMERICA. THEY WANT THE DESCENDANTS OF SLAVES TO FORGET THEIR HERI-TAGE OF AFRICA, JUST TO UNDERSTAND THEIR CULTURE, IN ORDER, TO CONTROL THEIR SLAVE POPULATIONS FOR FOUR HUNDRED AND FIFTY YEARS, AND COUNTING, NOR MATTER WHAT YOUR EDUCATION LEVEL AS THE MODERN DAY CRACKERS WANT TO PERTRAY IN THIS DAY. THEY HAVE THE BOMBS AND THE GOLD FROM THE BOMBS; THESE CRACKERS ARE IMMINENT TO DIVIDE EVERYBODY EXCEPT THEIR WHITE BABIES.

11-11-05

VETERAN 'S DAY SPEECH BY THE TRICKY DICK NIXON CLONE, GEORGE W. BUSH ADMITS DATA WAS NOT CORRECT AND THAT CONGRESS AND THE SENATE SEEN THE SAME

FALSE DATA, THAT CAUSED THE CENTRAL INTELLIGENCE AGENCY SPY WAS REVEALED AND COVERED UP UNTIL TODAY; NO IMPEACHMENT HEARINGS ARE SCHEDULED. QUOTED SENATOR JOHN KERRY IN HIS REASON TO VOTE FOR THE WAR" ...IF HE HAS IN HIS (SADDAM) HAND..." BUT SADDAM DID NOT HAVE AND EVERYDAY HE WAS GIVING HIS REMAINING MISSILES, AS HE HAD BEEN UNDER A NORTH AND SOUTH NO FLY AND NOT MUCH MOVEMENT ON THE GROUND. WATERGATE, COMMIT TREASON AND ADMITTED LATER AS REASON NOT TO BE PROSECUTED.

11-29-05

STACKING THE COURTS AND CORRUPTION IS STILL PLAQUE IN IRAQ.

I FINAL GOT THE NERVE TO SEND IN TO CNN EMAIL A COMPLAINT ABOUT JIM CROW AND THE CONTINUATION OF PROFILING THE ARABS AND AMERICAN PEOPLE OF COLOR UNDER THE NAME OF ANDY.

BUSH ADMINISTRATION SHOULD BE IMPEACHED.

THIS MONTH WENT TO ASIA. BUSINESS

11-12-06

THE AMERICAN WAY"

THE TRUTH WILL COME TO THE LIGHT".

THE 2006 UNITED STATES ELECTION PROVES AGAIN, AFTER WATERGATE, THAT NIXON DREAM IS STILL ALIVE. THE LATEST OF THE HITLER AND NIXON CLONES IS GEORGE HERBERT WALKER BUSH, TRICKY DICK CHENEY, AND ALL OF THE REST

OF THEM IN THE NAME OF REPUBLICANS, INCLUDING JEB BUSH. THE PEOPLE HAVE SPOKEN. THANK GOD.

BUSH AND CHENEY, THE FRONT MEN IS ADMITTING WHAT I HAVE SAID ALL ALONG, THAT THE WAR WAS ABOUT OIL. THE FORMER ALLIES OF THE UNITED STATES, SADDAM HUSSEIN, WHO WAS RECENTLY FOUND GUILTILY, AND IS SUPPOSE TO BE HUNG SOON ON PUBLIC DISPLAY. EXACTLY THE WAY THE AMERICAN KLU KLUX KLAN HAS DONE THROUGH SLAVERY AND ALL THE "JIM CROW LAW" DAYS IN THE NORTH AMER-ICAN. DRAIN THE UNITED STATES TREASURY, IN THE NAME OF TAX CUTS. CHENEY'S HALLIBURTON HAS GANGSTER ALL OF THE CONTRACTS FROM ANYONE ELSE TO BID TO SUPPLY A VARIETY FOR OUR LOYAL SOLDIERS NEEDS, WHILE FIGHTING TO MAKE CHENEY- BUSHES RICHER AND STACKING THE COURTS WITH KNOWN BIAS JUDGES. NIXON, REAGAN, BUSH, AND BUSH2'S APPOINTMENTS WERE/IS TERRIBLE FOR ALL THE PEOPLE OF THE UNITED STATES, BUT PERFECT FOR THE ARIAN TAKE OVER IN THE NAME JUSTICE.

JOHN KERRY WAS SPEAKING TO COLLEGE STUDENTS A WEEK BEFORE THE VOTERS WAS TO VOTE IN 2006. HE MADE SOME STATEMENT THAT OFFENDED SOME PEOPLE. BUSH AND CHENEY CAMPAIGNED ON IT AS DISRESPECT TO OUR SOLDIERS. KERRY WAS CORRECT AND HIS PARTY, DEMO-CRATS, FORCED HIM TO APOLOGIZED FOR CALLING THE TROOPS NOT VERY EDUCATED AND KERRY WAS CORRECT.

WE WERE NOT EDUCATED, MY FATHER WAS NOT EDUCATED, MY GRAND PARENTS, AND GREAT GRAND PARENTS WERE NOT EDUCATED, BUT BUSH AND CHENEY BLEW KERRY'S WORDS OUT LIKE HE WAS UN-AMERICAN. KERRY WAS IN VIETNAM WITH ME AND VERY POSSIBLE MY COMPANY WAS ON HIS BOAT DOWN IN CAMBODIA AND LAOS. TRICKERY IS AT THE HIGHEST LEVEL OF THE GOVERNMENT. WHITE

SUPREMACY AT IT'S BEST IN THE DARKEST OF THE NIGHT, JUST AS THEY DID TO THE HOLY MESSIAH, JESUS CHRIST OF NAZARETH, BETHLEHEM. BUSH AND CHENEY IS CARRYING ON THE MODERN DAY ROMAN LAW.

FROMER PRESIDENT WILLIAM JEFFERSON CLINTON CAMPAIGN IN VIRGINIA AND HE KNOWS THE POWER OF ALL OF THOSE REPUBLICANS, DOLE, HATCH, HYDE, LOTT, AND ALL OF THE REST OF HITLER, NIXON, REAGAN, BUSH, AND BUSH2'S, NIGGER LOVERS POWER. THIS IS STILL A RACIST SOCIETY THAT IS BEING MORE AND MORE BRAIN WASH. CLINTON SAID THAT IF YOU VOTE FOR THEM THE HAVE YOU SCARE TO VOTE FOR WHITE DEMOCRATS (LIBERALS), SCARE GOES ACROSS THE STREET, CAUSE IT IS A TERRORIST THAT YOU WILL RUN ACROSS. THIS STATEMENT MADE BY THE FROMER PRESIDENT GIVES CAUSE TO THIS BOOK AND THE RESPONSES FROM ME ON THE LATEST CURRENT EVENTS OF TODAY, AND WHAT IS NEEDED TO BRING ATTENTION TO THE NEED OF MY PEOPLE. WE DID NOT COME TO AMERICA VOLUTARYLY; THAT IS, WE WERE KIDNAPPED, BOUND, AND CHAINED LIKE A DOG, PUT ON SHIP AND TOLD YOU COULD NOT PRACTICE YOUR RITUALS AND COULD NOT TAKE A TREE STUMP AND MAKE SOUNDS TO OTHER AFRICANS ON OTHER PLANTATION, AND YOU WERE TOLD NOT TO SPEAK YOUR LANUAGE, YOU HAD TO SHAKE YOUR HEAD, CAUSE YOU THOUGHT THOSE WHITE FOLKS ARE SILLY AND STUPID. THEY HAD THE GUNS, HORSES, AND THE WHIPS, AND WE WERE ACROSS THE ATLANTIC OCEAN. WE NEED TO BE PAID. DR. MARTIN LUTHER KING, JUNIOR SAID THERE HAS TO BE ENOUGH FOR US IF YOU KEEP COMING UP WITH MONIES FOR WAR THAT IS NOT NECESSARY.

WE WILL SEE HOW THIS WORK OUT, BUT I THINK BUSH WILL GET TO USE HIS VETO POWER, SINCE HE DID NOT HAVE TO

WHEN HE AND HIS FAMILY FUCKED AMERICANS BY HAVING ALL THREE POWERS OF THE UNITED STATES CONSTITUTION. THEY LIE AND THEY ARE UN-AMERICAN PEOPLE OF COLOR.

11-16-06

BORN AN ARAB, CAME TO THE UNITED STATES AS AN INFANT, AND NOW HE IS THE ONLY AMERICAN ARRESTED AS AN "EMEMY COMBATANT".

BUSH AND CHENEY HAS GONE AGAINST THE UNITED STATES CONSTITUTION. NOW TRICKY DICK SAYS" FULL STEAM AHEAD IN IRAQ", HE AND HIS FRONT MAN (GWB) HAS ALMOST GOT OUT OF OFFICE WITH NO OVERSIGHT BY ANY REPUBLICAN.

ALL OF THE KNOWN LIES OF THE BUSH ADMINISTRATION AND THERE HAS NOT BEEN A SPECIAL PROSECUTOR AS IT WAS FOR CLINTON'S EMBARRASSED SEX ACT IN THE WHITE HOUSE. THE CONSPIRACY TO HAVE IMPEACHMENT HEARING FOR IRAQ, CIA, AND THE VOTING MACHINES DID NOT HAPPEN AND NOW A LOT OF THE REPUBLICANS DID NOT GET RE-ELECTED AND THAT IS GOOD FOR THIS DEMOCRACY, EVEN THOUGH, IT IS NOT PERFECT AND NO POLITICAL SYSTEM IS PREFER TO PLEASE ALL OF THE PEOPLE ALL OF THE TIME.

THE POWER OF THE MAJORITY SHIFTED TOWARDS THE DEMOCRATS, BUT NOT ENOUGH TO CHANGE OR OVERRIDE CERTAIN LEGISLATION THAT THIS RACIST CONSERVATIVE HITLER CLONE THINKING ADMINISTRATION. REMEMBER GWB CAME INTO OFFICE WANTING TO KNOWN AS A WAR PRESIDENT AND THE SURPLUS WILL BE SPENT AND THROUGH

IT'S STEVE FORBES'S TAX REBATE, AFTER THE TAX BREAKS FOR THE CORPORATIONS, AND NOT THE INDIVIDUAL, THE DEMOCRATS NEED MORE HELP IF THEY WANT TO GET BACK TO HELPING PEOPLE CREATE JOBS AND TO SUSTAIN THE NEEDS OF THE POOR PEOPLE. THOSE RIGHT WINGERS THAT SURVIVE THE 2006 ELECTION ARE BACK TO PROTECT THE BUSH CHENEY ADMINISTRATION. THEIR JOB IS TO BLOCK AND FILIBUSTER LEGISLATION.

TRENT LOTT AFTER HIS RACIST STATEMENT ABOUT WHAT STORM THURMOND SAID IN 1948 PRESIDENTIAL ELECTION, THAT NIGGERS ARE GETTING TOO MANY RIGHTS, AND TRENT SAID THAT IF " WE HAD LISTEN BACK THEN WE WOULD NOT HAVE THE PROBLEMS WE HAVE TODAY", I.E. THE VOTING RIGHTS, BLACK CAUCUS, AND OTHER ACHIEVEMENTS OF THE VICTIMS OF THE UNITED STATES SLAVE SYSTEM; THEREFORE, HE HAD TO STEP DOWN FROM HIS WHIP JOB OF LEADERSHIP IN THE SENATE. HE WAS RE-ELECTED AND HE IS IN THE BACKGROUND MORE THAN BEFORE. HE AND HIS CONSERVA-TIVE HAD TO REGROUP AND CONTINUE THE COVER-UP OF ABUSE OF POWER BY OUR WAR PRESIDENT AND VICE PRESI-DENT CHENEY, WHO ARE TO BE INVESTIGATED.

THE ONLY THING ABOUT THIS GOVERNMENT IT TAKES TURNS TOWARD MAJORITY RULE, BUT THE DIVIDE AND CONQUER RULE STILL APPLY IN THE NAME OF THE HOLY MESSIAH JESUS CHRIST.

 WHEN THE DESCENDANT OF SLAVES WENT TO THE LEAD-ERSHIP OF THE HONORABLE ELIJA MUHAMMAD FOR INDE-PENDENCE FROM THE SHARE CROPPING, AND OTHER DEMEANING JOBS, WITH NO EDUCATION, EXCEPT TO LEARN ONES HISTORY AND TO WORK FOR ONES SELF, WAS LOOKED UPON AS A HATE GROUP. NOW CAN YOU BELIEVE A HATE GROUP WHO HAS KIDNAPPED, CAGED, KILLED, STRIPPED OF

ONES HERITAGE, AND DEMEAN IN ANY MANNER, COULD TELL THE PUBLIC THE LIGHT OF MAN'S NATURE IS TAUGHT THROUGH ISLAM DID NOT WORK FOR SOME WHO WAS LOST IN DRUGS, POVERTY, AND DEMEANED WOULD NOT COME IN TO ELIJAH AND HIS FIGHT TO FREE HIMSELF AND OTHERS AFTER HE AND MY GRANDFATHER SEEN THE LIGHT THROUGH THE MASTER FARD MUHAMMAD. ATLANTA, GEORGIA WAS THE CRADLE OF JIM CROW LAWS AFTER THE EMANCIPATION PROCLAMATION AND GENERAL SHERMAN DEFEATED THE CONFEDRATE, AND BURN DOWN ATLANTA, GEORGIA. G_D HAS AWAY TO FREE HIS CHILDREN FROM BONDAGE, AND IN MANY WAYS THAT WAS ANOTHER MOSES IN A DIFFERENT LAND AND TIME; BUT YOU DO NOT SEE IT IN ANY NEW TESTAMENT OF THE ROMAN CHRISTIANITY, AFTER THEY CRUCIFIED JESUS, AND TOLD THE WHOLE WORLD THAT THE JEWS KILLED JESUS. THAT LIE IS STILL LIVING TODAY.

11-26-06

THE WAR PRESIDENTS, I.E. "TRICKY DICK" CHENEY-BUSH CONSPIRACY TO DEFRAUD THE AMERICAN PEOPLE AND MOST LIKELY TO KEEP DEBT, JUST AS THERE PRECIOUS RONALD REAGAN, WHO MADE GHW BUSH, AND EX- CHIEF CIA SPY HIS VICE PRESIDENT.

TRICKY DICK CHENEY WAR HAS NOT GONE THEIR WAY AND HAS HIM SCRAMMING TO SAUDI ARABIA FOR CONFERENCING WITH THE KING AND FAMILY, AS GW BUSH IS TO MAKE TRIP TO JORDAN TO MEET IRAQ APPOINTED PRESIDENT, THAT WAS ELECTED UNDER STRESS AS SADDAM WAS ON TRIAL. CHENEY IS COORDINATING ALL OF THIS AND IT IS ASHAMED. THE AMERICAN WAY HAS TO CHANGE FOR

ALL OF THE PEOPLE AND NOT JUST THE STATUS QUO, AS BUSH LIKE TO DESCRIBE HIMSELF, FRIENDS, AND FAMILY; THEREFORE, NO VOTING MACHINES THAT WILL HANG CHADS. WITH THE REPUBLICAN CONSPIRACY THEY WOULD NOT SUPPOSE AND MAKE SURE THAT EVERY COUNTY IN AMERICA HAS A VOTING MACHINE THAT WILL GIVE THE VOTE HIS RECEIPT, JUST AS ONE DO AT A GAS PUMP.

THIS MORNING ON CNN'S "SITUATION ROOM" WITH WOLF BLITZER, FORMER NATIONAL SECURITY CHIEFS HENRY KISSINGER AND BRENIV ZIBRENCI, THEY WERE DISCUSSING THE INVASION OF IRAQ AND THEY BOTH AGREED THE INVASION OF IRAQ SHOULD HAVE NEVER BEEN DONE, AND NOW THE COMMANDER IN CHIEF AND CO-CHIEF HAS THE UNITED STATES IN BIG TROUBLE IN THE REGION. THE CONSULTATION OF KISSINGER IS A CONSTANT FOR THE BUSH ADMINISTRATION, JUST TO SHOW THE FORMER NIXONITES, CHENEY AND KISSINGER ARE SCHEMING HOW TO FINISH THE DREAM OF NIXON. NIXON WAS SUCH A RACIST HE WOULD CALL YOU IGNORANT IF YOU WOULD THINK THAT A BLACK MAN HAD THE INTELLIGENT IS BE A QUARTERBACK OF THE NATIONAL FOOTBALL TEAM, WE WERE NOT ABLE TO BE ANY TYPE OF BRAIN, AND BUSH CHENEY AND THEIR FEDERAL COURT JUSTICES ARE VERY MUCH WITH THAT TYPE OF THINKING. A TIME LIMIT FOR FEDERAL JUDGES NEEDS TO BE AMENDED. THE OVERTHROW HAS RUSSIA AND CHINA BEING CLOSELY ALIGNED, BECAUSE THEY KNOW THAT THEY ARE FOOLING THE AMERICAN PEOPLE AND NOT THEM. BLAIR AND BRITISH HAD BUSH CHENEY RUN UP THE OIL, BECAUSE THE BRITISH HAS ALWAYS PAID MORE FOR THE OIL.

ALSO TODAY THE NEW YORK FINEST HAS JUST BEEN DRUNK AT A STRIP CLUB AND FOLLOW SOME YOUNG HARD-WORKING BLACK YOUNG MEN OUT ON A BACHELOR PARTY,

AS SEAN BELL WAS TO BE MARRIED TO HIS HIGH SCHOOL SWEETHEART, AFTER THEY HAVE A BABY SON, BUT NEW POLICE WERE SPYING IN CLUBS DRUNK. THEY FOLLOW SEAN AND HIS FRIENDS LEAVE AND HAD THEIR BACK-UP VICE TO APPROACH THEM WITH GUNS AS IF THEY WERE ROBBERS INSTEAD OF POLICEMEN.

THE POLICEMEN SHOT FORTY-ONE BULLETS AT THESE MEN, AND SHOT AND KILLED SEAN BELL, WHILE WOUNDING HIS FRIENDS WHO WERE ALL IN THE CAR. CANNOT GIVE THE POLICE THE BENEFIT OF THE DOUBT, JUST IN THE SOUTH WHEN ALL OF THE POLICE WERE KLU KLUX KLAN, AND NO WHITE MAN WOUND GO TO JAIL FOR A NIGGRAS. THE DARWIN THEORY THEY WANT TO BELIEVE IS FACT. THE WHITE MAN KNOWS HE IS THE LIGHTER GENETICS GENE OF THE DARK GENETICS GENE OF THE HUMAN BODY, THEY WANT TO SELL IT AS TRUTH AS THEY DID WITH THE CRUCI-FIXION OF THE HOLY MESSIAH JESUS CHRIST. THE AMERICAN WAY AND ALSO IS THE EUROPEAN WAY.

THEY CAME TO PARTY IN OCTOBER AND WAS SHOT AND KILLED, BECAUSE THEY WERE BLACKS AND BLACKS ARE ALWAYS CRIMINALS. THEY ARE TAUGHT IT IN THE ACADEMY. THE HUNDRED BLACK POLICE OFFICERS WHO HAVE A GATH-ERING AND SEPARATE VIEW JUST TO HAVE A JOB FOR THE CITY AND COUNTRY HAVE THE UNITED STATES. MAYOR BLOOMBERG IS ANTI- NIGHT CLUB AND ANYONE WITH AS MUCH MONEY AS HE SHOULD NOT WANT TO BE A POLITI-CIAN, BECAUSE THEY DO NOT RELATE TO THE DISADVAN-TAGE, EXCEPT WHEN IT COMES TO ELECTION. AOL HAD AN ARTICLE THIS AND CITIZENS RIGHTS IN AMERICA. BLOOMBERG WANTS TO BLOCK PARKING AND THE MONIES RECEIVE FOR TERRORIST FROM THE TAX PAYERS WERE USE TO MAKE PARKING ILLEGAL IN THE MIDDLE OF THE NIGHT,

RED LIGHTS WITH ARROWS TO CAUSE CONGESTION IN MID TOWN FIFTH AVENUE, AND CONCRETE OF EXTENDED CURBS TO PREVENT PARKING IN THE NIGHT CLUB DISTRICT THAT THE RACIST RUDY GIULIANI STARTED.

11-27-06

BUSH 43 IS IN THE EASTERN EUROPE, ON HIS WAY TO JORDAN FOR A CONFERENCE WITH THEIR FRONT MAN OF IRAQ, ACTUALLY SOUTH OF BAGHDAD, IRAQ.

ALL NEWS REPORTS A CIVIL WAR, WHEN CHENEY=BUSH STILL IS TRYING TO FOOL THE AMERICAN PEOPLE. HIS RACIST PARTY IS ALL SELLOUTS OF THE AMERICAN PEOPLE. THEY DO NOT WANT TO MENTION CIVIL WAR THAT THEY COMMENCED WITH THE OVER THROW OF IRAQ'S PRESIDENT SADDAM HUSSEIN. THEY WERE OUR ALLIE AND NOW IS THE HOME OF TERRORIST AGAINST THE UNITED STATES. CHENEY BUSH OIL WAR HAS ENRICHED THEM AND THEIR FAMILIES AND REPUBLICANS FRIENDS AND FAMILIES.

SECRET ARIAN VIOLENCE AS THE MEDIA CALLS IT, HAS ESCALATED TO HUNDREDS EVERYDAY WITH THE POOR AMERICAN TROOPS IN THE MIDDLE OF THIS ILLEGAL WAR. THE MODERN DAY ROMAN EMPIRE IS STILL ALIVE AND WELL IN THE NAME OF AMERICA AND BRITISH COALITION. WENT THROUGH AFRICA AND TOOK ALL THE GOLD, DIAMONDS, AND OTHER EARTHLY MINERALS. TODAY IT'S CHENEY BUSH OIL WARS. THEY ADMIT IT NOW AS TO NOT TO BE BLAME FOR A COVER-UP, AS A COVER-UP WILL TRIGGER IMPEACH-MENT HEARINGS. THEY HAD ALL THREE BRANCHES OF THE GOVERNMENT AND ALL THE REPUBLICANS OF BOTH HOUSES

OF CONGRESS PROTECTED THEM WITH THOSE KNOWN LIES OF WEAPONS OF MASS DESTRUCTION. LIES LIES LIES LIES

12-14-06

THE AMERICAN WAY" THE WORLD OF POWERFUL HUMANS",BY.LWFS"
THE 2006 ELECTION BLESSED THE U.S. AMERICAN PEOPLE WITH THE CHANGE OF POWER IN THE SENATE, MEANS DICTATORSHIP IS HALTED, SOMEWHAT.

THE IRAQ REPORT BY BI-PARTISANSHIP LEADERS AS "CO-CHAIR JAMES BAKER AND LEE HAMILTON, PAST AND PRES-ENTLY POWERFUL CAUCASIAN, COMMITTEE THAT INCLUDED VERNON JORDAN", FORMER PRESIDENT OF AFRICAN-AMERICAN CIVIL RIGHTS ORGANIZATION AND PRESIDENT WILLIAM JEFFERSON CLINTON'S CLOSES ADVISOR, THE FORMER UNITED STATES SUPREME COURT JUSTICE SANDRA DAY O'CONNOR, AND POWERFUL CAUCASIAN PEOPLE.

GENERAL PACE, THE JOINT CHIEF OF STAFF AND RUMS-FIELD'S DEPARTURE, AS GATES RETURN TO THE PENTAGON AS RECENT APPROVED REPLACEMENT OF DONALD RUMS-FIELD'S, DEFENSE SECRETARY.

SENATOR'S KERRY, DODD, AND OTHERS ARE ON THEIR WAY DAMASCUS, SYRIA, AND THE BUSH- CHENEY ARE FURIOUS THAT THEY ARE GOING TO DO AS THE "IRAQ STUDY COMMITTEE'S " RECOMMENDATIONS THAT THE WAR IS A DISASTER, AND THE AMERICAN'S SHOULD TALK TO SYRIA AND PERSIANS (IRAN)

THAT SHOWS WHY BUSH-CHENEY IMPEACHMENT HEARING SHOULD COMMENCE. IF SENATOR WARREN HATCH, TRENT LOTT, HYDE, HELMS, AND OTHERS CALL FOR AND RECEIVED

IMPEACHMENT HEARING WITH THE DEMOCRATS WAS IN CONTROL OF CONGRESS, THEY ARE MOSTLY RAISED AS RACIST AND DESCENDANTS OF AMERICAN SLAVERY, AND WOULD RATHER GIVE GRANTS TO ALL TYPE OF GOVERNMENTS AND CAUCASIAN CHARITIES, JUST TO NOT MAKE EDUCATION REQUIRED FOR ALL DESCENDANT OF SLAVES, THAT WAY THESE EMIGRANTS THAT HAS COME IN HERE FROM RONALD REAGAN'S BEGGING U.S.S.R'S MIKHAIL GOVISHHA TO TEAR DOWN THAT WALL THAT HAS HARBORED THE BLEEDING OF THE CAUCASIANS (SO-CALL EUROPEAN'S, THAT ARE REALLY SOUTHERN ASIANS); JUST THE DESCENDANT'S OF THE SPANISH LANGUAGE FORMER SLAVES ARE CALL LATINAS, WHICH IS THE ROMAN LANGUAGE), DECIDES IS THE CON GAME OF THE CRUCIFIERS OF JESUS CHRIST, AND THE THEN BRAIN WASHED THE EUROPEAN WORLD AND THEIR SLAVES THAT THE HEBREW JUDAS, WAS THE SELL OUT, BUT ONLY CONSPIRACY TO SET THE HOLY MESSIAH JESUS CHRIST TO THE ROMANS , AND THEY CRUCIFIED AFTER ONE OF GOD'S DEIFIER'S, JESUS, WHO WAS OF DARK COMPLEXION AND HAIR OF LAMB'S WOOL . RONALD REAGAN WANTED TO FREED THOSE SO-CALL CAUCASIANS ONTO THE FREE WORLD AND HAVE MORE WHITE BABY FROM WHAT THEY CALL PURE WHITE BLOOD, AS THEY WERE SPLIT -UP IN BERLIN.

HANNIBAL OF NORTH AFRICAN CARTAGE IS STILL THE GREATEST MILITARY MIND OF THE LAST TEN THOUSAND YEARS OF HUMAN HISTORY. DESTROY AFRICAN DESCEN- DANTS FOREVER AFTER HANNIBAL CONQUERED ROME, ITALY, FOR TWENTY YEARS.

TODAY IN MIAMI A CAUCASIAN BOY AND FRIEND PULL A GUN ON A POLICE OFFICER AND PULL THE TRIGGER. HIS FOLKS ARE SAYING THAT THE BOY DID NOT KNOW THAT THE PISTOL WAS LOADED", A BLACK CHILD DEATH AND THERE

IS NO PITY. THIS HAPPENS OFTEN ALL OVER AMERICA, AND IT'S COURT SYSTEM.

THE UNITED STATES JUDICIAL BIAS RULINGS HAS TO BE ADJUSTED WITH THE BIAS RACIST RULINGS"

DRUG LAWS HAS TO BE COMPLETELY REVISED AND UNIFORMLY RULES FOR THE COMPLETE COUNTRY. KEEP SEVENTY-FIVE PERCENT OF DARK COMPLEXION, JUST TO CONSPIRE TO KEEP DOWN THE DARK BABIES THAT COULD BE BORN AND IN THIS EUROPEAN COMMON LAW SYSTEM OF MAKE A MISTAKE AND PAY DUES OF SOME JAIL TIME FOR SOME SITUATIONS, THAT IS NOT DEPENDED ON COMPLEXION OF ONES HUMAN BODY, THAT IS DELVED AND RACIST'S LAWS. DARK PEOPLE NEED NOT TO SUFFER FOR PROFIT OR ENJOYMENT ESPECIALLY, SHOULD NOT BE CLASSIFIED AS A TRAFFICKER, WHEN THIS DRUG CULTURE OF THE U.S., AND ALL OF THEIR DRUG STORES TO KEEP THEIR PEOPLE DRUGGED LEGAL.

CBS' REPORTER, RANDALL PINKSTON IN IRAQ WITH A REPORT AFTER SADDAM HUSSEIN, AND THE PEOPLE OF IRAQ SAYS THAT THE U.S. DESTROYED THEIR LIVES. BUSH AND CHENEY HAD THE UNITED NATION'S INSPECTORS TO LEAVE AS THE BOMBING WAS TO BEGIN, BECAUSE CHENEY'S WAR DID NOT WANT THE TRUTH, AND THEY KNEW THAT SADDAM HAD BEEN PUT UNDER A NO FLY ZONE. HOW COULD ANY COUNTRY BUILD WEAPONS OF MASS DESTRUCTION WITH OUT AN AIR FORCE IS UNREASONABLE IN THIS DAY AND TIME.

SADDAM WAS TURNING OVER ALL IT'S MISSILES EVERYDAY AND IT DID NOT MATTER THE BUSH CHENEY HAD LIE TO THE CONGRESS AND THE UNITED NATION, AND NOBODY WANTED TO INVESTIGATE FUTURE, KNOWING THAT IRAQ

WAS UNDER A NO FLY ZONE. CHENEY -BUSH COMMITTED TREASON AND ROBBERY OF ANOTHER DARK NATION IN THE NAME OF TERRORIST. CHENEY-BUSH CAUSED THAT IN THE EARTHLY SUMMIT IN SOUTH AFRICA IN JANUARY OF 2001. THEY SIDED AND WALKED OUT OF EVERY NATION AND GOVERNMENT, JUST FOR THE MEANING AND CHASTISING OF THE ROMAN ISRAELIS. THEY WERE THE ONLY TWO GOVERN-MENTS THAT WALKED OUT OF THE WORLD CONFERENCE.

I BELIEVETHAT LED TO THIS 2001 WORLD TRADE CENTER DISASTER. THEN THEY DRAFTED THAT OTHER RACIST, TONY BLAIR, PRIME MINISTER OF GREAT BRITIAN, WITH THE QUEEN'S BLESSING TO BACK THEIR SISTER AND BROTH-ER'S THAT IS LOST ACROSS THE ATLANTIC OCEAN, AMONG SAVAGES, THEY CALL THE PEOPLE OF THE WORLD'S DARK CHILDREN.

TODAY ON THE HISTORY CHANNEL "THE SEXUAL REVO-LUTION", WHEN THEY GOT TO THE 1980'S, AND ACQUIRED IMMUNE DEFICIENT DISEASE (AIDS), THE WHITE HOUSE IGNORED IT UNTIL 1986, WHEN THEY ACKNOWLEDGE IT.

JERRY FARWELL AND THE CHRISTIAN COALITION'S CON MEN'S WEIGHT IN AFTER THEY WERE ALL PART OF AN CONSPIRACY OF TWENTY CENTURY GENOCIDE OF THE AFRICANS AND THEIR DESCENDANTS IN THE NAME OF HOMOSEXUAL. ALL THESE CENTURIES OF DISEASES IN THE HUMAN COMMUNITIES THAT AIDS IS ONLY RELATED IN THE DARKEST OF THE EARTH.

HALLOWEEN AND THE BLACK CAT STORIES OF FEAR AND DEATH IS TO FRIGHTEN THE EUROPEAN WOMEN OF THE AFRICAN MAN AND THEIR DESCENDANTS.

HISTORY CHANNEL TODAY IS OF THE TRIBE OF THE AZTEC OF, WHAT IS CALL MEXICO.

12-16-06

JUSTICE-COPS TV. SERIES SHOWS THAT THE POLICING IS OF HITLER'S GERMANY AND ALL THE CHECK POINTS. PEOPLE WALK DOWN THE STREET AND GET STOPPED FOR BEING IN A SO-CALL" HIGH CRIME AREA, IS JUST PLAIN OLD ILLEGAL IN THE LAND OF THE FREE".

RACIST IS THAT WHITE PEOPLE MOVE TO THE WOODS OF AMERICAN CITIES, JUST TO BRING THEIR CHILDREN UP AWAY FROM THE BLACKS AND DARKIES OF THIS COUNTRY, AND MOST LIKELY DESCENDANT OF SLAVES. IN THE NAME OF DRUGS MAKE STOPS FOR NO OTHER REASON, ILLEGAL STOPS AND SEARCHES. A LOT OF PEOPLE HAS SOME TYPE OF ARRESTS OF SOME TYPE, AND THEN THE GOVERNMENT USES THAT AS PROBABLE CAUSE. RACIST, THIS SYSTEM IS PURE RACIST. WANT TO ASK PEOPLE QUESTIONS, JUST BECAUSE THEY ARE IN A HIGH CRIME AREA.

POLICE ARE ON A KILLING AFRICAN-AMERICANS ACROSS THE COUNTRY. IN NEW YORK REVEREND AL SHARPTON LEAD A MARCH DOWN FIFTH AVENUE, IN MIST OF ALL OF THE XMAS SHOPPERS, TO PROTEST THIS YOUNG BLOOD THAT WAS OUT IN HIS RUN DOWN NEIGHBORHOOD STRIP BAR, WHEN DRUNK POLICE OFFICERS, WHO WERE ALLOWED TO DRINK ON DUTY, THEN THEY SHOT THESE MEN WITH FIFTY BULLETS INTO THEIR CAR, AND THE YOUNG MAN WHO WAS TO BE MARRIED WITHIN TEN HOURS, BUT WAS KILLED AND IS PARTNERS WERE STILL IN THE HOSPITAL WITH POLICE BULLET WOUNDS.

STRICKLAWS UNCONSTITUTIONAL UNDER THE U.S. CONSTI-
TUTION, BUT NOT THE STATE STATURES THAT ARE USED TO
KEEP IGNORANT THE DESCENDANTS OF SLAVES, AFTER FIVE
HUNDRED YEARS OF HUMAN RIGHTS.

SO-CALL CRACK LAWS ARE BIAS AND SHOULD HAVE BEEN
DISBANDED. THEY ARE ADDICTED TO THE BUTANE AND NOT
THE SUBSTANCE OF COCAINE. COCAINE IS THE SO-CALL
BLACK DRUGS THAT GOD PUT ON EARTHLY GROUNDS, AND
METH IS WHITE FOLKS AND THEY DO NOT LOCK THE KEEP
AND THROW THEM AWAY.

12-17-06

NBC'S "MEET THE PRESS", WITH TIM RUSSELL IS THE MOST
AND TODAY'S LINE-UP OF NEWT GINGRICH, TOM FRIEDMAN,
WASHINGTON POST, AND OTHER GENTLEMEN, THAT HAS
THE REASONS FOR IMPEACHMENT OF THE BUSH-CHENEY.
NEWT GINGRICH IS PRAISING BARACK OBAMA, AS THE
GREAT SENATOR OF THE STATE OF ILLINOIS IS PRAISED BY
ALL BACKGROUND OF AMERICANS AS THE NEXT PRESIDENT
OF THE UNITED STATES, AND IF THAT HAPPENS I MIGHT
CONSIDER VOTING.

DEMOCRACY IS SECOND ON THE MINDS OF IRAQ AND
THE MIDDLE EAST AND ALL BACK FIRED ON THE UNITED
STATES APPOINTMENT OF A PRESIDENT IS NOT TO HAPPEN
AGAIN. THE LAW. U.S. SUPREME COURT REHNQUIST SHOULD
HAVE NEVER HAPPENED, IT WAS A COMPLETE CONFLICT
OF JUSTICE. "TRICKYDICK" CHENEY AND THE JUSTICE WAS
HUNTING PARTNERS ON VACATION FOREVER.

STRIKELAWS HAS TO BE UNCONSTITUTIONAL AND HAS
CAUSED HUMAN RIGHTS VIOLATIONS IT WAS INTENDED TO

CURVE THE SO-CALL "REVOLVING DOOR", "NIGGERS DON'T NEED A REVOLVING DOOR, WHITE ME NEED TO REVOLVED, NOT NIGGERS", BY THE KLAN. BACK IN NEW YORK WHEN IT'S RACIST GOVERNOR DAVID ROCKEFELLER INSTITUTED THE DRUG LAW THAT LOCKED CITIZENS UP FOR FIFTEEN YEARS, FOR TWO OUNCES OF SUBSTANCE, WHEN A PARTY HAS THAT MUCH. HE CONVINCED THE LEGISLATURE THAT IT WOULD GET RID OF DRUGS AND THE DEALERS, WHEN ALL IT DID WAS TO CREATE A BUNCH OF INFORMERS, AND RUIN A LOT OF THE DESCENDANTS OF SLAVES LIVES. THEY WERE MOSTLY NOT EDUCATED THEN AND IT HAS NOT CHANGED MUCH TODAY. THE GOVERNMENT WILL NOT BE HAPPY UNTIL THEY DO AS THEY DID WITH THE BOOTLEGGERS. FORGIVING LAWS OF IT'S CITIZENS AND NOT TO BUILD CRIMINAL RECORDS FROM THE TIME A BLACK CHILD IS BORN. REGIONAL LAWS SHOULD NOT EXIST IN ORDER TO HAVE BETTER ORDER THOUGHT STATE CAN SPEND FOR EDUCATION FOR ALL OF THE UNITED STATES DESCENDANTS OF IT SLAVERY THAT BUILD THE FOUNDATION OF THE WORLD'S ADVANCE NATION. BUSH, CHENEY, STEVE FORBS, AND THE REST OF THE REPUBLICANS THAT PAST AND GANG BANG THOSE TAX CUTS OF THE SURPLUS THAT WAS CREATED, IN PART, BY BILL CLINTON'S BACK TO WORK PROJECT. AND TO GIVE SOME OF THESE LAW ENFORCEMENT JOBS, THOSE ON THE BLACK HAND SIDE AFTER TO BE AWARE OF THE MOSTLY ENCAGED RACIST COMES TO THE PUBLIC. THIS RACIST WHITE BITCH WITH HATRED IS ENFORCING NEW YORK MAYOR BLOOM-BERG; SELF MADE BILLIONAIRE, WHO DOES NOT ACCEPT A CHECK FROM THE CITY, IN THE NAME OF SAVING THE CITY MONEY. THAT IS THE MOST BULLSHIT THAT I HAVE EVER HEARD OF. HE NEEDS TO NOT BE ABLE TO RUN A CITY AS A PRIVATE CORPORATION. BOB SHAFER, CBS' "FACING THE NATION", WITH COLON POWELL, SAYS WE DO NOT HAVE TROOPS", THE FORMER CHIEF OF THE MILITARY. BUSH-

CHENEY-RUMSFIELD SHOULD BE IMPEACHMENT. MORE TROOPS ARE NOT NEED, AS JOHN MC CAIN AND THE BUSH ADMINISTRATION. VICTORY IN IRAQ WHEN WE HAD WON THE GULF WAR, AND NOW A CONTINUATION INVASION IS A TREASONABLE.THERE ARE NO EXCUSES TO CONTINUE THE WAR BUSH HAS CREATED CHAOS. RACIST DICK CHENEY SAID ON FRIDAY OR THURSDAY OF THIS WEEK, AT RUMSFIELD'S GO AWAY PARTY WITH THE DICK AND JUNIOR LEADING THE WAY OF PRAISE. CHENEY SAID RUMSFIELD WAS THE BEST SECRETARY OF STATE EVER. GENERAL COLON POWELL WAS DIPLOMATIC ABOUT THE CROSS-, FROM THE NUMBER ONE CROSS ARTIST AND RACISM BY THE GOOD SHERPERDS. OBAMA MANIA IS ON THE RISE AS ABC'S TALK TODAY. GEORGE WILL AND HIS SON WATCHING "MONDAY NIGHT FOOTBALL", IT HAD TWO MILLION HITS ON THEIR WEBSITE. NEWT GINGRICH SAID ON THE SUBJECT OF HIS INSISTENCE ON THE IMPEACHMENT OF CLINTON WAS ABOUT THE LIES. THEY DID NOT ASK HIM ABOUT ALL OF THE LIES THAT THIS WHITE HOUSE HAS DONE, UNDER THE COVER OF MAJORITY RULE. TOM FRIEDMAN ON MEET THE PRESS", SAID THAT THE IRAQ PEOPLE TELL THE TRUTH ON THE RECORD AND TELL YOU ANYTHING IN PRIVATE, WHILE THE AMERICANS TELL THE TRUTH IN PRIVACY, NOT TELL IT ON THE RECORD. WHAT DOES THAT SAYS ABOUT OUR JUSTICE SYSTEM. IMPEACH-MENT HEARING NEEDS TO COMMENCE.I NEED TO GET THIS PUBLISHED SOONNEWT SAID THAT STUBBORNNESS IS NOT A STRATEGY", THIS SHOULD NOT BE A BUSH WAR, IT SHOULD BE AN AMERICAN WAR", NEWT GINGRICH. IMPEACH THE BUSH ADMINISTRATION AS HIS FATHER CRY FOUL. "MEET THE PRESS" 07-09-07777 WERE- A DAY OF BLESSING AS THERE WERE GIFTS, PASSION, AND THANK GOD. TITLE "THE AMER-ICAN WAY" FEATURING JUDGE'S STRIKELAWS THAT NEEDS ERADICATION, ETC. POLITICS ASIDE ALL THE PROBLEMS OF THE WORLD ARE ALL INHUMANE PROBLEMS, FOR SUPERI-

ORITY OF THE HUMAN FAMILY RACIST), FINANCES, AND VERY LITTLE LOVE FOR ENVIRONMENT, OTHER COMPLEXION OF HUMAN, WHICH IF THE HUMANS ARE IN THE IMAGE OF THE CREATOR, AND THE EARTH WAS IN THE DARK, JUST AS THE LIGHTER HUMANS SCHEME TO FURTHER SPREAD HATRED AND GO TO SPACE, WHERE THERE KNOW NATURE HUMAN ATMOSPHERE, TO GET AWAY WITH THE DIRT OF THE EARTH, AND VERY FEW HUMANS CAN NOT EVEN ATTEMPT TO THINK ABOUT HOW TO LIVE THERE ON EARTHLY PRODUCTS, IT COMES DOWN TO WHO'S FOOLING WHO? GOD DO NOT LIKE UGLY DEEDS OF MASSES OF HIS CHILDREN, NOT EUROPEAN, BRITISH, AMERICAN, BOMBING AND ALL OF THE HATE THAT MY BELOVED UNITED STATES OF AMERICAN TRUSTY POLITICIANS WHO SOLD EVERYONE BY HATING ON HOLY LAND THAT YOU PRETEND TO GO TO CHURCH TO HATE AND COVER -UP WHAT HAS BEEN DONE, IN THE NAME OF JESUS, IS NOTHING BUT THE LIGHTER HUMAN BEING SEPARATE TO STAY LIGHT AFTER ALL OF THE CABALISM THAT THE END OF THE EARTH PEOPLE, WHO MINE AND SOUL TO SURVIVE THE COLDEST OF THE EARTH HUMANS (CAUCASIANS) ,IS GOING ALL OF A SUDDEN THAT THEY ARE NOT SUPPRESSION THEIR DESIRE TO MOVE IN THE WOODS TO CONTINUE THE MASTER PLAN , TO BE THE LIGHT , BRIGHT, AND RIGHT ATTITUDE, AND WITH MORE FINANCE POWER , THE HAVES HAVE TO HELP SOME OF THE WEAK OF HOUSING , FOOD, AND MAYBE IT WILL SURVIVE A LITTLE LONGER ON GOD'S EXPERIMENT OF CREATION OF THE EARTH, AS THEY ARE THE UNIVERSE. THE HUMAN SPACE HOUSE WILL NOT PUT THE ALMIGHTY HUMAN FROM SEARCHING FOR THEIR CREATOR, WHEN THE DESCENDANTS OF AFRICANS ARE JUST AS THE ROSWELL, NEW MEXICO, SO-CALL ALIENS WERE THERE AND THEY LOOK LIKE AFRICANS AND THE DEVILS DO NOT WANT TO ADMIT THE CREATOR DID RETURN AFTER THE CRUCIFION. THE AMERICAN POLITI-

CIANS AND THE MILITARY, WHO SAYS WHAT TO BE SAID AND NOT BE SAID, IS ALL A COVER-UP. THE MILITARY HAS LIE AND COVER-UP THE FACTS TO KEEP THE INFORMATION OF THE HUMAN SUPPRESSORS OF AMERICA, THE WHITE MAN AND HIS ARMY, AND ARE CRIMINALS WHO BECOME LAWFUL. THAT IS THE LAW OF THE WORLD. DETERRENTS ARE NEEDED FOR MORE NATIONS THAN THE CAUCASIAN CONTROL NUCLEAR OF THE WORLD. THE LIGHTER HUMAN HAS DONE SO MUCH TO GAIN POWER AND THEY HAS TO HONOR THE NEED TO RESPECT EACH OTHERS BEING AFTER THE HUMAN HAS ACCOMPLISHED A LOT. WE WERE CREATED TO BE SUPREME OF THE EARTH AND NOW BEING IN DEEP SPACE, WITH A SPACE SUIT AND A TUBE WITH HUMAN AIR TO REST AND PREPARE SOMETHING ELSE TO GO DEEPER IN SPACE, JUST AS WE HAVE TO THE OCEAN FLOOR, WE CAN NOT RELATE TO GOD UNIVERSE, AND HE BREATH THOUGHT ALL OF US. THE UNIVERSE AIR IS WHAT US HUMANS LIVE ON. THEY USE TO CALL ME A MAD SCIENCTIST. THIS MORNING NEWS BREAKING THE DECLINE OF THE IRAQ WAR, PEOPLE HERE THE RACIST CONTROLLER OF EARTHY AFFAIRS, IS SCREAMING "WHAT ARE WE GOING TO DO WHEN WE PULL OUT", THEY ARE RETURNING TO WASHINGTON AFTER THE PEOPLE OF AMERICAN WILL VOTE FOR SOME OTHER CANDI-DATE, THEY NEED TO BE REPLACE FOR TREASON, WENT ALONG WITH ANY AND ALL THEY THE BUSHES-CHENEY WORDS THAT THEY KNEW WERE FALSE WORDS. I KNEW AND THEIR IS NO WAY THEY ARE THE MEDIA CARED FOR THE OIL, TREASON TO ROB THE AMERICAN POOR PEOPLE, THE AFRICAN-AMERICAN REPARATION WAS NOT GOING TO HAPPEN, NOT WITH TRICKY DICK CHENEY'S POWER AND FAMILIARITY OF THE UNITED STATES SUPREME COURT JUSTICES, THAT THEIR MISSION WAS TO DESTROY THIS MECCA OF HOLY PEOPLE'S LAND, JUST TO SHOW THAT THEY ARE WORSHIP COMPLEXION SUPERIORITY, THEY DESTROY

THE PALACES, TOOK OVER THE PALACES OF THE IRAQ PEOPLE
, CAUSING THEM TO BECOME DESTITUTE OVER NIGHT AND
WILL THEY CAR SOME OF THEIR SNITCHES, JUST THE AMER-
ICAN INDIAN GERONIMO AND THE REST OF THE INDIANS
OF THIS LAND, MEXICAN LAND AND WE IN THE UNITED
STATES RACIST GOVERNMENT , HAS GOT TO TAKE CARE OF
ALL OF THE EDUCATION OF ALL THE SLAVE DESCENDANTS
OF THE UNITED STATES, AS WELL AS ANY AMERICAN HOSPI-
TALS, FOOD, AND HOUSING COULD BE DONE AS THE GREAT
WILLIAM JEFFERSON CLINTON , AND AL GORE WAS WEAK
AND SCARE OF THE BUSH CHENEY'S NOT TO USE HIS PARTNER
AND PRESIDENT HELP HIM AND THE AMERICAN PEOPLE
CONTINUE WHAT HAD TO A HUNDRED AND FIFTY YEARS
TO COME TO THE POINT OF REPARATIONS, WHICH WILL
START WITH BARAK OSAMA'S PRESIDENT OR THE VICE PRES-
IDENT , AT THE VERY LEASE. THERE SHOULD BE TIME LIMITS
TO THAT ONLY INSTITUTION THAT HAS THE MOST DRAMATIC
POWER OF THIS DEMOCRACY IS THE FEDERAL JUDGES WHO
ARE NOT WILLING TO ADAPT TO THE HUMAN NEEDS FOR
THE AMERICAN PEOPLE. THERE SHOULD BE ONLY TWO OR
THREE PRESIDENTIAL TERMS AT THE MOST. PROSECUTION
IS NOT TO BE LIBERAL AS GOD INTENDED, BUT CONSERVA-
TIVE FOR SEPARATION OF LIGHTER HUMAN AND ALL OF
THE DARKER ONES, WHO NEWT GINGRICH, BUSH-CHENEY,
CALL STATUS QUO. 07-10-07LAST YEAR BUSH FIRST STOP WAS
IN ROME TO CONSULT THE NAZI POPE BEFORE HE LANDED
IN TURKEY. THIS YEAR HE MADE ROME HIS FINIAL STOP
BEFORE RETURNING TO THE UNITED STATES, AND TODAY
AND SINCE BUSH CHENEY OVER TOOK THE ELECTION 2000,
NIXON DREAM OF DOMINATION OF THE FOURTH REIGN IS
IN LINE, AS THE NAZI POPE SO-CALL BENEDICT,HAD TO BE
A DICK DICT, IT IS ALL THE SAME , THE FUCKERS. THIS WORLD
OF HUMANS HAS TO GET AWAY FROM THE SEPARATION IN
THE NAME OF JESUS, THE FOLLOWING IS SOME TYPE OF

CONSPIRACY TO SUPPRESS THE POOR AND BRAIN WASHED PEOPLE. GOD SAID MAKE LOVE AND HAVE MANY DECENDANTS, AND THE ROMANS SAYS LISTEN TO A BUNCH OF CELEBRACY MEN, WHO DO NOT LIKE WOMEN INTIMATE, IN THE NAME OF JESUS, AND IT HAS TO CHANGE. THE NEWS IS THERE TODAY AND NOW THEY DO NOT WANT OTHERS TO HAVE NUCLEAR ARMS, OR THE RICHES OF THEIR LANDS, THE DARK PEOPLE'S LAND IS WHAT PRODUCE ALL OF THE RICHES OF THE HUMANS. THIS WHAT THE NAZI POPE SAID TODAY: VATICAN CITY (Reuters) -- The Vatican on Tuesday said Christian denominations outside the Roman Catholic Church were not full churches of Jesus Christ.The Vatican said other churches are "wounded" since they do not recognise the primacy of the Pope.

A 16-page document, prepared by the Congregation for the Doctrine of the Faith, which Pope Benedict used to head, described Christian Orthodox churches as true churches, but suffering from a "wound" since they do not recognize the primacy of the Pope.

But the document said the "wound is still more profound" in the Protestant denominations -- a view likely to further complicate relations with Protestants."Despite the fact that this teaching has created no little distress ... it is nevertheless difficult to see how the title of 'Church' could possibly be attributed to them," it said.The Vatican text, which restates the controversial document "Dominus Iesus" issued by the then Cardinal Joseph Ratzinger in 2000, said the Church wanted to stress this point because some Catholic theologians continued to misunderstand it.Ratzinger was elected Pope in April 2005. The document is his second strong reaffirmation of Catholic tradition in four days, following a decree on Saturday restoring the old Latin Mass alongside the modern liturgy.The document stressed that dialogue with other Christians remained "one of the priorities of the Catholic Church".The document, issued by Benedict's successor in doctrinal matters, Cardinal William Levada, complemented the Latin Mass decree in aiming to correct what it called "erroneous or ambiguous" interpretations of the Second Vatican Council, which took place from 1962 to 1965.Church modernizers interpreted the Council as a break from the past while conservatives, like Benedict, see it in continuity with 2,000 years of Catholic tradition.The document said the Council's opening to other faiths recognized there were "many elements of sanctification and truth" in other Christian denominations, but stressed only Catholicism had all the elements to be Christ's Church fully.The text refers to "ecclesial communities originating from the Reformation", a term used to refer to Protestants and Anglicans. Father Augustine Di Noia, Under-Secretary for the Congregation for the Doctrine of the Faith, said the document did not alter the commitment for ecumenical dialogue, but aimed to assert Catholic identity in those talks. GIVE ME A BREAK. GENOCIDE IS STILL THE PLAN. DISEASE, BOMBINGS, HANGING, DRUGS, RELIGION, OR ANYTHING ELSE TO MAKE HUMAN SUFFERING CONTINUE. GOD SAYS THE WELL TO DO HAS TO PROVIDE FOR THE LESS WELL TO DO. 07-23-07THE DEMOCRATIC PRESIDENTIAL DEBATE TODAY IN SOUTH CAROLINA, HOSTED BY CNN TELEVISION NETWORK. THE QUESTIONS BY ORDINARY AMERICANS AND NOT SOME FIXED QUESTIONS FROM SOME MEDIATOR, AS BUSH CHENEY ALWAYS DEMANDED, BECAUSE THEY HAD A TRICK FOR THIS BELOVED COUNTRY. THEY THOUGHT IT WAS/IS THEIRS ONLY. THE NEWS IS THAT BUSH CHENEY SOLD AMERICA AND IT'S PEOPLE OUT. PAKISTAN PRESIDENT MUSHARRAF TOOK THE MONEY AND SHUT -UP ABOUT THE COVER-UP TO INVADE SADDAM AND THE IRAQ PEOPLE, A HOLY COUNTRY OF ABRAHAM. THE BUSH CHENEY KNEW THAT THE PEOPLE RESPONSIBLE FOR THE SEPTEMBER 11,2001 WERE IN PAKISTAN AND NOT IN IRAQ. THEY USED THE JUSTICE SYSTEM TO GET IN OFFICE, CAUSE OF G.H.W BUSH AND TRICKY" DICK CHENEY WENT TO CHIEF JUSTICE REHNQUIST AND SCYLLA TO JUSTIFY HALF PUNCH CHATS

(PUNCH CARDS), WHEN THEY ALL KNEW THAT THE TECH-
NICALITY THAT THEY WERE PUSHING WAS DENYING VOTERS
THEIR VOTE: THEREFORE, THE JUSTICES THROUGH OUT THE
HALF PUNCHED CARDS, MOSTLY IN DEMOCRATIC AREAS,
AND ORDER BUSH CHENEY AS PRESIDENT AND VICE PRESI-
DENT OF THE UNITED STATES. THEY CREATED ONE OF THE
GREAT CONSPIRACIES TO DEFRAUD THE UNITED STATES OF
AMERICAN PEOPLE; AND, THEY ARE THE GREAT CRIMINALS
THAT MADE AMERICA AS IT IS TODAY. WE NEED A LOT OF
HELP AFTER WHAT BUSH, CHENEY, AND THE REST OF THE
RIGHT WING CREW WHO ARE LAYING LOW. THE MORMONS
AND HATCH SHOULD NEVER BE ELECTED AGAIN, AFTER HE
FUCKED THE PEOPLE HE WAS REPRESENTING. "TRICKY"
DICK CHENEY AND HIS COMPANY HALLIBURTON GANG-
STERED THE NO BIDS AND DICTATED THAT HALLIBURTON
HAS CONTROL OF ALL THE GOODS, FOOD, COMMISSARY,
CLOTHS, AND MANY MORE MONEY MAKING VENTURE. TO
FEED EVERY SOLIDER EVERYDAY WITHOUT SOME TYPE OF
MINORITY OWNERSHIP IS CRIMINAL. TODAY IN THE NEWS
A SO-CALL CHRISTIAN TOWN AND CHURCH IN THE STATE
OF FLORIDA WAS BUILT TO SEPARATE THEMSELVES FROM
BLACK AND COLORFUL PEOPLE OF THIS COUNTRY, AND IS
OWNED BY THE OWNER OF DOMINO PIZZA. SEPARATE BUT
EQUAL LAWS OF JIM CROW AND THE UNITED STATES
SUPREME COURT LAWS THAT WAS OVERTURNED DURING
THE CIVIL RIGHTS YEARS, AND NOW SOME WHITE MAN HAS
RECEIVED A LOAN AND PURCHASED A FRANCHISE AND
HAS BUILT A NEIGHBORHOODS FOR CHRISTIANS ONLY, AND
IS PROMOTING RACISM IN THE NAME OF JESUS CHRIST. THE
CIVIL LIBERTY UNION PROMISE TO SUE, AND THEY WILL
WIN. IT IS CLEARLY DISCRIMINTORY AND WE WILL SEE IF IT
GETS TO THE HIGHEST COURT OF THE LAND.THE RESIDENCE
OF THE TOWN SAY THEY WOULD MOVE AGAIN TO STAY
AWAY FROM BLACKS, ABORTIONIST, NUDITY, AND ALL OF

THE OTHER HUMAN VICES THAT THE GOVERNMENT TRIES TO REGULATE. RACIST AT IT'S HIGHEST LEVEL IN AMERICA, BUSH CHENEY TYPE OF PEOPLE: THEREFORE, HITLER AND TRICKY DICK RICHARD NIXON. THERE HAS TO BE A AMENDMENT TO TIME LIMITS FOR JUDGES AND THE FEDERAL JUDICIARY. CHIEF JUSTICE WILLIAM REHNQUIST IN A WHEEL CHAIR PULL THE PLUG ON THE UNITED STATES CONSTITUTION THAT HE WAS SWORN IN TO PROTECT AS A NON BIAS, BUT THAT IS NOT WHAT IS NOMINATED AND APPROVED BY BOTH PARTY MEMBERS. NON-BIAS JUSTICES ARE NEED TO REPEAL THE RIGHTS OF THE AFRICAN-AMERICANS AND THERE POOR PEOPLE OF THE UNITED STATES. PRIVACY, SEARCH AND SEIZURE LAWS ARE JUSTIFIED FOR A DICTATOR AND THEIR POLICE FORCE, WHETHER LOCAL, STATE, OR FEDERAL LAW ENFORCEMENT. THE OWNER OF THE LAND THAT BUILD THE NEW HOUSES, ROMAN CATHOLIC CHURCH (DEVIL SANCTUARY), AND ALL THE OTHER BUSINESSES ARE SUPPOSE TO HELP WHITE PEOPLE GET TO HEAVEN, WHICH IS A MYTH. A HUMAN AND HELL IS HERE ON EARTH AS LONG AS ONE LIVE, AND THE ONLY REINCARNATION IS THROUGH A MAN AND A WOMAN TO BIRTH IN THE SPERM THAT WILL FORM INTO AN HUMAN. I HAVE NEVER SEEN A SO-CALL PRO LIFE WHITE PERSON AND IT IS DEFINITELY A RACIST ISSUE TO HELP POPULATE THE EARTH WITH CAUCASIANS, THE LIGHTER HUMAN, AND POISON THE RIVERS OF AFRICA, SPREAD DISEASE, AND DOMINATE THE GUN POWDER THAT THEY LEARN FROM COLORFUL NORTH ASIA, SOUTHERN ASIA IF THE END OF THE EARTH AND THE GENOCIDE CAPITAL OF THE EARTH THAT THE CAUCASIANS CALL EUROPE TODAY. MAY GOD BLESS US ALL CALL GOD DO NOT LIKE THE UNITED STATES, BRITAIN AND ALL OF THE BACKERS OF INVASION OF INDISANT PEOPLE TO BE KILLED FOR LAND AND IT'S RICHES. SOUTH AFRICA, ISRAEL, THE NOW OIL RICH STATES, AND THE UNITED STATES, WHO WANTS TO SUPPRESS

ALL OF IT'S MISDEEDS OF HER SLAVE DESCENDANTS, BUT SAYS LOOK AT CONDOLISA RICE AND COLIN POWELL, WHO HAS SOLD OUT THE DARK PEOPLE, JUST TO BE LOYAL TO HATRED AND DECEIT. TONIGHT'S YOU TUBE .COM DEBATE, ON CNN, WAS THE BEST NONE BIAS DEBATE I HAVE SEEN. THESE TYPE OF DEBATES SHOULD HAVE BEEN WITH THE CONTROL ENVIRONMENT THAT TRICKY DICK" CHENEY AND GOOD TIME GEORGE W. BUSH'S LAST TWO ELECTION, THEN AL GORE WON AS ONE MAN ONE VOTE, BUT THE ELECTORAL COLLEGE SHOULD BE ILLEGAL. IT WAS STARTED AFTER THE CIVIL WAR TO KEEP THE POWER OF THE SLAVE OWNERS AND THEIR DESCENDANTS. SENATOR DODD SAYS THE REPUB-LICANS HAS BEEN COMMITTING VOTER FRAUD ALL THE TIME, NOW AS A NATION WE HAVE TO SUFFER FOR THEIR NARROW IDEOLOGY, JUST AS HITLER, REAGAN, NIXON, BUSH 1 &2. NO MATTER WHAT DID HAPPEN IN 2000 ELECTION AL GORE FUCKED - UP BY PASSING UP SENATOR JOHN EDWARDS FOR A RACIST JOE LIEBERMAN, WHO IS ALL PRO ISRAEL, AND AMERICA STILL IS NOT READY FOR A JEWISH PRESIDENT, NOR A VICE PRESIDENT. I AM A VIETNAM VETERAN AND WAS PLEASE TO SEE A WILLIAM JEFFERSON CLINTON'S TOWN HALL MEETINGS GOT HIM ELECTED, AND HE CAME CLOSEST TO KEEPING HIS WORD OF HAVING AFRICAN-AMERICANS IN HIS CABINET. AL GORE WAS THE RIGHT CHOOSES, BUT THE KLAN SCARED HIM AND THAT WAS ASHAMED. OUR COUNTRY WAS GOING IN A DIRECTION THAT I COULD HARDLY BELIEVE, AND HE WAS AFRAID TO USE BIG BILL CLINTON, BECAUSE OF SOME SEXUAL AFFAIR IN THE BIG SLAVE MASTER'S HOUSE, AND WAS HATED FOR ALL OF THE AFRICAN-AMERICANS THAT WAS CONSTANTLY THEIR ON THE GROUNDS AS DIGNITARIES, AND NOT MAIDS, BUTLERS, OR ANY OTHER SERVITUDES OF THE BIG WHITE HOUSE. HOW COULD GORE DOUBT EDWARDS BECAUSE HE WAS YOUNG SENATOR, AND THOUGHT A LITTLE WEAK MAN LIKE JOE

LIEBERMAN WOULD BE ABLE TO HANDLE TRICKY DICK CHENEY. AL SHOULD HAVE KNOWN THAT DICK WAS PATTING JOE ON THE BUTT ALL THE TIME IN THE SENATE. NOW JOE IS TALKING JUST LIKE BUSH CHENEY. AFTER THE OVERTHROW OF OUR GOVERNMENT THROUGH THE UNITED STATES SUPREME COURT IN 2000, ALL HOPE VANTAGE BACK TO THE JIM CROW LAW DAYS THAT I GREW UP IN AMERICA.   I THOUGHT THAT BARACK OBAMA WON THIS DEBATE TONIGHT, WITH SENATOR HILLARY CLINTON VERY CLOSE SECOND. I THINK THAT THE DREAM TICKET FOR THE WHITE HOUSE AND AMERICA SHOULD OBAMA CLINTON, OR CLINTON OBAMA, EITHER WAY THEY BOTH NEED TO BE THERE TO INSURE THAT WE AS A COUNTRY TRY TO GET BACK TO THE LAWS BEFORE BUSH CHENEY'S INVASION OF THE SURPLUS AND THE LAWS OF THIS MELTING POT OF TODAY'S EARTH. DENNIS WAS STRONG AND I LIKE HIS VIEWS AND HIS HEART. JOE BIDDEN AND THE REST ARE FINE, BUT BARACK CLINTON WOULD BE A DREAM TICKET.   THE ILLI-NOIS STATE RURAL WHITE PEOPLE ELECTED BARACK OBAMA AND I BELIEVE HE IS THE CLASS OF VERY FEW STATE SENA-TORS IN AMERICA, SINCE THE INSTITUTION OF THE UNITED STATES, AND THAT SAYS A LOT ABOUT HOW THIS COUNTRY CAN BE. WE SHOULD GIVE THANKS TO THE PEOPLE OF ILLI-NOIS FOR THEIR INSIGHT OF A CANDIDATE AND NOT THE COLOR OF HIS SKIN, AS WAS THE CASE IN TENNESSEE, FORD AND HIS KLAN OPPOSITION.I HOPE THIS WILL MAKE OUR COUNTRY AND THE WORLD A BETTER PLACE TO LIVE IN. EDUCATION AND HEALTH CARE SHOULD BE UNIVERSAL FOR ALL AMERICANS, AND THAT WILL GO CLOSER TO THE REPARATIONS THAT THIS SO-CALL RICH NATION OF OURS. RELIGION IS A ROUGH OBSTACLE BUT I BELIEVE AFTER THE INITIAL SHOCK OF THE ROMAN CATHOLIC CHURCH PHILOS-OPHY THEN PEOPLE COULD BE MORE TOLERANT THAN ANYTIME AFTER HANNIBAL OF CARTHAGE, NORTH AFRICA

LEFT SPAIN WITH HIS ELEPHANTS AND CONQUER THE ROMAN AND NOW ITALIANS. THAT IS WHY THEY WANT TO KILL ALL OF THE ELEPHANTS OF THE WORLD TODAY, IN THE NAME OF THE IVORY TUSSLE. OUR IVORY HUMAN TEETH IS NOT ENOUGH IN SOME CASES. Privacy advocates, prepare thy letter writing hands. A student at Timberline High School, outside Seattle, Washington, has recently been arrested for calling in repeated bomb threats. That, you should have no problem with.

The scary part is the manner in which he was caught and convicted. Josh Glazebook, 15, taunted authorities via e-mail and even created a MySpace profile called Timberlinebombinfo (shown), which used the alias Doug. It's through this profile that the FBI was able to track down Josh. Using a fake profile, the FBI sent a message to Timberlinebombinfo that installed a hacker-style trojan horse on his PC. The FBI spyware collected a wide range of information including the computer's IP address, MAC address, open ports, a list of running programs, the operating system type, version and serial number, preferred Internet browser and version, the computer's registered owner and registered company name, the current logged-in user name, the last-visited URL and the IP Address of every computer it connects to. Phew...

The FBI was able to install this program without a suspect or wiretap warrant because "under a ruling this month by the 9th U.S. Circuit Court of Appeals ... Internet users have no 'reasonable expectation of privacy' in the data when using the Internet."

So note: Simply using the Internet disqualifies you from normal expectations of privacy and safety of your data.

See

Wired

for the full story.

PRIVACY SHOULD NOT EVER BE COMPAMIZE FOR ANY REASON, BUT EVEN BEFORE THE IRAQ FOR MY PEOPLE WERE NOT EXPECTED TO HAVE GUNS, AS THE SECOND AMENDMENT GIVES IT'S CITIZENS, AND THE FOURTH AMENDMENT IS BEING WATERED DOWN MORE AND MORE BY THE COURTS, IN THE NAME OF BELIEVING THE LAW ENFORCEMENT OFFICERS WHO ARE CONSTANTLY LYING FOR THE PROSECUTORS TO HAVE CONVICTION STATISTICS FOR POLITICAL REASONS. THERE ARE A GREAT MAJORITY OF THE JUDGES ON ALL THE COURTS OF THE UNITED STATES WERE PROSECUTORS, AND WHEN THEY ARE APPOINTED, OR ELECTED TO THE BENCH, THEY TEND TO RULE WITH THE STATE AND THAT IS A SETBACK TO THE LAW OF FACTS. THERE ARE SICK PEOPLE OUT THERE AND THEY HELP INFRINGING ON OUR LIBERTIES BY CONCOCTING FEAR, JUST AS THE BUSH CHENEY ON THE AMERICAN PEOPLE. AS I CLOSE OUT TONIGHT AND CLOSE TO ENDING MY PROTEST OF THE 2000 ELECTION, THIS IS JUST WHAT I HAVE BEEN SAYING ALL THE TIME. IF YOU CAN NOT HAVE PRIVACY TO DRIVE IN YOUR VEHICLE IN THE CITY, BUT IN RURAL AREAS THAT DOES NOT HAVE CAMERAS AND GET HOMELAND SECURITY MONEY, JUST TO GET REELECTED, NO EXPECTATION OF PRIVACY IN YOUR HOME, NO KNOCK WARRANTS, OR A QUICK KNOCK, AND ALL OF THE KILLINGS OF DARK PEOPLE IN THE NAME OF THE LAW. JUST CNN HAD TO FILE SUITE AND RECEIVED RECENTLY THAT THE POLICE LIED ABOUT A SHOOTING IN NEW ORLEANS, AS A BLACK MAN CAME TO THE POLICE FOR HELP AND WAS SHOT IN THE BACK, AS THEY CLAIM THAT HE ATTACKED THEM IN THEIR PATROL CAR. BLACK POLICE CANNOT SAY A THING, BECAUSE THEY NEED BACK UP IN FUTURE ACCIDENTS. JUDGE'S NEED TO STOP BEING PROSECUTORS THEN TURN JUDGE OF THE BENCH TO RULE UNBIAS, IT HAS TO BE DIFFICULT TO TAKE

THAT PROSECUTOR'S HAT OFF ON THE BENCH. THEY ARE STILL IN FAVOR THEIR POLICE FRIENDS AND COLLEAGUES THAT LIED FOR THEM AS PROSECUTORS, JUST FOR STATIS-TICS. THANK GOD FOR THE DNA ATTORNEY'S OF BARRY SCHECK AND COMPANY, SHOWS YOU CANNOT ALWAYS TRUST PEOPLE'S VISIONS AND ESPECIALLY QUICK VISIONS OF A WITNESS TO SOME CRIME.THE DISTRICT COURT IS WRONG AND I HOPE THAT THIS U.S. SUPREME COURT JUSTICES WILL NOT LET THIS STAND AND HAVE TO SHOW PROBABLE CAUSE. I FOUND THIS ARTICLE RECENTLY AND IT IS PROOF OF HOW MANY, AND MOSTLY AFRICA-AMERICAN LIVES THAT HAS BEEN LOST ON SOME HAVE BLIND AND NERVOUS ACT THAT NO HUMAN CAN DO IS TO IDENTIFY A STRANGE FACE. TODAY WITH CAMERAS THERE ARE PROBLEMS WITH IDEN-TIFICATION OF PEOPLE COMMITTING CRIMES. REPARATIONS ARE A MUST FOR THE UNITED STATES TO Its DESCENDANT OF SLAVES. THE FOLLOWING ARTICLE I AM POSTING:

Posted: 2007-12-12 14:23:55

ATLANTA (AP) - A man enjoyed freedom Tuesday for the first time in nearly three decades after a DNA test proved he did not commit a 1979 rape. John Jerome White, 48, left Macon State Prison on Monday evening." I'm just thankful that this is behind me," White said at a news conference Tuesday morning with the Georgia Innocence Project, which had worked to free him." When I first started out, I wondered why this happened to me," he said, breaking into tears. "I just saw it as something that had to happen because I wasn't living a moral life." White is the seventh Georgia convict to be cleared by DNA evidence, said Aimee Maxwell, director of the Atlanta-based Georgia Innocence Project. In every case, the men were wrongly convicted on the basis of eyewitness accounts." This case does point out the fallibility of eyewitness identification," Maxwell said. White was convicted in 1980 of breaking into a 74-year-old woman's home and raping and robbing her. The woman has since died. At the urging of the Innocence Project, authorities tested DNA from hairs found at the scene of the 1979 rape, using tests that weren't available at the time. District Attorney Peter Skandalakis of the Coweta Judicial District said authorities found that the DNA matched DNA on file in the Georgia Bureau of Investigation database, leading to an investigation of a new suspect. No arrests have been made yet, the GBI says. Maxwell said her organization is working with state lawmakers and authorities to require all law enforcement agencies to develop and follow clearly written procedures for doing eyewitness identification with a victim, Maxwell said. The organization says 82 percent of the 355 Georgia law enforcement agencies surveyed do not have any type of written eyewitness standards. White was joined at the news conference by his wife, three sisters and his mother, Florence White." When they called to tell me that he was getting out, I didn't know whether to shout, cry or holler," said his mother, who lives in Merewether County. "I'm so glad to have him back home one more time before I leave this world."

07-24-07TODAY POLITICS IS WHAT CARRY THIS ADMINISTRATION AND IT'S REPUBLICAN PARTY. AFTER THE DEBATE IN SOUTH CAROLINA AIR FORCE BASE SPEECH BY BUSH, THERE BEATING HIS WAR DRUM. BUSH'S SO-CALL COMPASSIONED SPEECH TO THE AIR FORCE PLOTS THAT THEYMUST WIN THE WAR IN IRAQ. HE CAME IN TO THE OFFICE OF PRESIDENT PROMISING THE PEOPLE OF AMERICA THAT HE WANTED TO BE KNOW AS A WAR PRESIDENT AND TOOK THE SURPLUS OF TREASURY AND GAVE IT BACK TO THE STEVE FORBS AND THE REST OF THE FORTUNE 500 FAMILIES. HE DID NOT MAKE A NOTION TO USE THE SURPLUS TO ENHANCE THE SCHOOLS IN THE POOR AND RURAL AREAS OF AMERICAN, AND TO BUILD NEW ONES IN THE POOR SECTIONS WITH AN INCREASE OF TEACHERS SALARIES. HE WANTED TO GIVE BACK AND TO MAKE THE AMERICAN PEOPLE CONTINUE TO SUFFER AND

FORCE TO COMMIT MORE CRIMES TO SUPPORT THEIR FAMI-
LIES, AND ESPECIALLY MY PEOPLE, THE DESCENDANTS OF
SLAVES. CNN THIS MORNING AFTER THE PRESIDENT SPEECH
ON BEING ABLE TO "MUST WIN IN IRAQ" SPEECH IS AN ILLU-
SION. MICHAEL WARE, A COMMENTARY ON IRAQ, AS HE
KNOWS THE PEOPLE OF IRAQ, AS HE HAS LIVED THEIR FOR
MANY YEARS BEFORE THIS CONFLICT WITH IRAQ. HE SAID
BUSH IS POLITICKING MORE THAN REALTY. 07-26-07AMER-
ICAN KLANSMEN JOINTING ALL OF AMERICA'S POLICE FORCE
OF BLUE INSTEAD OF THE WHITE SHEET, AMERICA HAS TO
RECOGNIZE AND ALL OF THE WELL TO DO'S SHOULD
CONTRIBUTE TO THE WELFARE OF THE DESCENDANTS OF
SLAVES, IN LIGHT OF ALL OF THE BRUTALITY THAT WAS
SHOWN BY THE LAW ENFORCEMENT IN NEW ORLEANS,
AFTER GOD WENT AND VISITED HIS CHILDREN IN
GUANTAMO BAY, CUBA. THE FIGHTERS WERE DEFENDING
THEMSELVES AGAINST THE UNITED STATES INVASION OF
IRAQ. THAT WAS LIKE THE ROSWELL ALIENS, AND THEY DO
NOT HAVE NARROW NOSES, AS THE JEWISH AND EURO-
PEANS IMAGE OF AN ALIEN TELEVISION SERIES. THE SAME
GOES WITH THE IMAGE OF JESUS, WHO WAS LIKE SOLOMON,
A HEAD OF HAIR OF LAMBS WOOL. THE ETHIOPIANS HAS
THE DESCENDANTS OF DAVID AND KING SOLOMON'S TYPE
HAIR. MOSES PEOPLES THAT ESCAPE THE ROMANS ACROSS
THE RED SEA, WERE MOSTLY PEOPLE WHO HAD HAIR OF
LAMBS WOOL TEXTURE. TODAY'S NEWS WAS ABOUT THE
UNITED STATE DEPARTMENT'S "WORLD LARGEST EMBASSY",
IS SAID TO CONGRESS WAS BUILT ON THE BACK OF SLAVERY.
TO THE POOR AND DARK PEOPLE OF THE MIDDLE EAST AND
INDIA, THEY WERE KIDNAPPED, NO SHOES, AND TERRIBLE
WORKING CONDITIONS. THE CONTRACTORS, MOST LIKELY
HALLIBURTON AND Its SUBSIDIARIES WERE THE CULPRITS,
AND THEY WANT TO CONTROL THE WORLD. THE SAME
AMERICANS THAT LIVE IN THE MANSIONS AND BUILDING

ALL OF THOSE SUBDIVISIONS IN THE WOODS AND MOUN-
TAINS TO STAY AWAY FROM ANY PEOPLE OF COLOR. "THE
AMERICAN WAY". THE SAME PEOPLE WHO GAVE AND PUSH
TERRIBLE INTELLIGENCE FOR INVADING AND CONQUERING
IRAQ TODAY THE CRUCIFION OF MICHAEL VICK COMMENCE
IN RICHMOND, VIRGINIA FEDERAL COURT HOUSE. THEY
HAVE CONVICTED BY SOME RACIST DOG LOVER, CALL THE
HUMANE SOCIETY. IF THEY RAISED AS MUCH HELL ABOUT
THE POOR SLEEPING ON DOOR STEPS OF CHURCHES ACROSS
THE UNITED STATES, THEN I WOULD THINK THAT THEY ARE
HUMANE, AND THEY ARE NO WHERE CLOSE. THEY ARE JUST
AS RACIST AS THE WHITE POWER PEOPLE, WHO CALL THEM-
SELVES "RIGHT TO LIFE" ADVOCATES. I HAVE NEVER SEEN
THE FEED ANY BABIES, CLOTH, OR MEDICAL INSURANCE
FOR ANYONE, EXCEPT A FEW FERTILITY DRUG WHITE BABIES.
THEY WANT LAWS TO DRIVE WOMEN BACK TO CLOTH
HANGER, COKE BOTTLES, AND ANYTHING ELSE TO ABORT
AN UNWANTED CHILD. IT EVEN CAUSED MANY WOMEN
THEIR LIVES DURING MY EARLY YEARS, UNTIL ROE VS. WADE,
THE ONLY MAKE SENSE LAW THAT GIVE A WOMAN THE
FREEDOM AS GOD CREATED, THEY ARE THE ANTI-CHRIST,
IN THE NAME OF JESUS CHRIST. FOR ANY JUDGES PROVE TO
BE MORE FAVORABLE TO ONE POLITICAL PARTY OR ANOTHER
SHOULD NOT BE APPROVE, AND THOSE THAT ARE ON THE
BELOVED UNITED STATES FEDERAL JUDGES FOR LIFE SHOULD
AMEND THE CONSTITUTION, JUST AS THEY AMENDED IT IN
FAVOR OF ELECTORAL COLLEGE. THE UNITED STATES CONSTI-
TUTION OF THE RACIST FOUNDING EUROPEAN FATHERS,
SAID "ONE MAN ONE VOTE", AND IT WOULD BE TODAY IF IT
WERE NOT FOR THE UNITED STATES CIVIL WAR. THIS 2008
BARACK OBAMA SHOULD BECOME PRESIDENT. GOD BLESSES
AMERICA. 8-15-07THE NEW YORK DAILY NEWS, YESTERDAY
HAD AN ARTICLE ON RETIREMENT OF KARL ROVE, PRESI-
DENT GEORGE W. BUSH'S CHIEF OF STAFF, CHIEF OF DIRTY

TRICKS, AND WITH TRICKY DICK CHENEY THE AMERICAN PEOPLE HAS BEEN FUCKED AND THE UNITED STATES SUPREME COURT AND THE REPUBLICAN CONGRESS SHOULD BE NOT ELECTED AGAIN AND THE BUSH ADMINISTRATION SHOULD BE PUT ON TRIAL FOR WAR CRIMES. BUSH'S BRAINS THEY CALL ROVE, THE ENGINEER OF THE 2004 SWIFT BOAT COMMERCIAL THAT PUT LESS TRUST IN KERRY, EVEN THOUGH, IT CAME DOWN TO THE ELECTORAL COLLEGE. THEY GIVE A CHRONOLOGY OF ROVE'S LIFE AND ACHIEVE-MENTS AND IT ASTOUNDING THAT HE WAS A CRIMINAL AS HE BROKE INTO THE ILLINOIS DEMOCRATIC OFFICE CANDI-DATE FOR TREASURE TO STEAL LETTERHEADS TO PRINT UP WITH MISLEADING TO HAVE THE REPUBLICAN CANDIDATE WIN IN 1970, AFTER HE HAD DECLARE HE'S FOR NIXON, AT THE AGE OF 10.HE WAS GEORGE W. H. BUSH'S SPECIAL ASSIS-TANT, IN 1973 AND 1992 IN THE WHITE HOUSE, WHERE HE WAS FIRED FOR LEAKING INFORMATION, THE SAME WITH THE TREASON OF THE UNITED STATES CENTRAL INTELLI-GENCE AGENCY'S SPY VALERIA PLAME'S COVER AND THE PRESIDENT KNEW IT AS DID CHENEY, AND THEY LIE THEN AND NOW. BUSH SAID IF IT IS IN HIS WHITE HOUSE HE WOULD PUNISH AND FIRE WHOEVER IT IS, WHEN IT WAS THE PRESI-DENT. IMPEACH HIM AND WAR CRIMES. POST JUSTICE?09-23-07THE IRANIAN PRESIDENT SPEECH TO THE UNIVERSITY OF COLUMBIA, IN NEW YORK, WAS BEAUTIFUL AND VERY EDUCATIONAL, EVEN THOUGHT, THE PRESIDENT OF THE UNIVERSITY INSULTED THE LEADER AND SHOWED HIS IGNO-RANCE OF BIAS RACISM. THE JENA 6 MARCH OF BLACK CIVIL RIGHTS VIOLATION IN THE STATE OF LOUISIANA WAS HUGE AND IT BROUGHT ATTENTION TO THE NOOSES THAT WERE DISPLAYED AT A HIGH SCHOOL THAT CAUSE THE SIX BLACK STUDENTS TO BEAT-UP THE YOUNG KLANSMEN, AND THEIR PARENTS WERE NOT HAPPY. THE CHILDREN WERE CARRYING THE HATE THAT THEIR PARENTS WERE TAUGHT. THERE

SHOULD BE NO WALLS IN AMERICA. LOU DOBBS IS FEEDING INTO THOSE SOUTHERN TEXAS AND ARIZONIANS TO PROTECT NORTH OF THE RIO GRAND RIVER, WHICH IS THE LINE DRAWN AS ENOUGH OF MEXICO AFTER THE MEXICAN-AMERICAN WAR AND THE ALAMO. NOW BECAUSE OF THE ILLEGAL INVASION OF IRAQ HE WANTS PEOPLE TO SEAL OUR BORDERS AS IF AN ARMY OF TERRORIST ARE GOING TO COME AN ATTACK THE AMERICAN TERRORIST. HE HAS TURNED ME OFF. HE IS IN LINE WITH THE SKIN HEADS AND THE NEO-NAZI OF THE UNITED STATES OF AMERICA AFTER THE DAMAGE TO WHOLE RACE OF PEOPLE, THAT WERE KIDNAPPED AND BROUGHT HERE TO OTHER PEOPLES LAND WITH THE GUN, LIQUOR, AND THE HORSE, TO HAVE A PLACE TO LIVE INSTEAD OF THE BRITISH PRISONS, NOW WHAT THE AFRICAN-AMERICANS TO BELIEVE THAT THIS WALL AND FENCE IS TO PROTECT AMERICA FROM TERRORIST. THEY ARE PROFILING MY PEOPLE HERE AND MY FAMILY HAS BEEN HERE SINCE THE 1690'S. DOBBS DOES NOT BEAT THE DRUMS TO HAVE THE BUDGET OF THE UNITED STATES TO SUPPORT THE INSTITUTION OF EDUCATION, HOUSING, AND OTHER THINGS THAT WOULD BE PROSPER FOR THE DESCENDANTS OF THE UNITED STATES SLAVE SYSTEM, WHO PEOPLE ARE IN THE BACK GROUND IN SHATY TOWNS, JUST AS IN SOUTH AFRICA, UNTIL THOSE RULERS RELOCATED TO THE UNITED STATES AND HAS TEAMED UP WITH THE IGNORANT AMER-ICAN KLANSMEN TO PROTECT THE WHITE WOMAN. IN ATLANTA, GEORGIA THERE ARE A WHITE ONLY CIRCLE OF CLUBS PREACHING WHAT I WITNESS BACK IN THE FIFTIES, AND NOW THE SOUTH AFRICAN BRITISH DESCENDANTS, WHO CALL THEMSELVES JEWS TODAY ARE THE LARGEST THREAT TO THE AMERICAN SOCIETY THAN A FEW MEXICAN INDIANS WHO COME TO WORK AND SEND MONEY BACK TO THEIR FAMILIES. THEY ARE THE NEW AMERICAN SLAVES AND THEY TALK ABOUT IMMIGRATION. THE BERLIN WALL

THAT WAS TORN DOWN TO FREE THE EASTERN EUROPEANS TO ADD TO THE CAUCASIAN POPULATION, THAT WERE SO-CALL PURE WHITE PEOPLE WITH LESS BLACK BLOOD AFTER WORLD WAR TWO, NOW THE AMERICAN GOVERNMENT WITH THE ISRAELI GOVERNMENT IS BUILDING WALLS TO SEPARATE AND ATTACK THE DARK PEOPLE OF THE NATIONS THAT IS INVOLVE, THAT IS, THE MEXICAN, AFRICAN-AMERI-CANS, THE PALESTINIANS, AND OTHERS IN THE AFFECTED AREAS. HURRICANE KATRINA TRAILERS WERE INFECTED AND LAWSUIT ARE IN THE COURTS. BARBARA BUSH THE CURRENT PRESIDENT MOTHER SAID DURING THE RECOVERY AFTER THE HURRICANES THAT THOSE PEOPLE (BLACK) DID NOT HAVE ANYTHING BEFORE THE STORMS, SO WHY SHOULD THE AMERICAN GOVERNMENT HELP THEM. HER FATHER AND GRAND FATHER WERE PRESIDENT AND POLITICIANS AND THE WHOLE FAMILY IS RACIST. THE AMERICAN WAY. LOCK THE BLACK ASS UP AND THROW AWAY THE KEY. GOD SENT HIS SPELL ON THE GULF COAST AND THE REPUBLI-CANS ESPECIALLY COULD NOT BELIEVE THAT THE WHOLE GULF COAST OF THE UNITED STATES, AFTER GOD WENT TO GUANTAMO BAY, CUBA TO VISIT HIS DEPRIVED CHILDREN OF THE TWENTY- FIRST CENTURY, TO TEAR DOWN THE SHACKS IN THE MISSISSIPPI, FULL OF DESCENDANTS OF AMERICAN SLAVE SYSTEM. IN THE NEXT INTERSTATE EXIT THERE ARE CASINOS THAT PORTRAYS PROSPERITY. THE AMERICAN WAY. KU KLUX KLAN, WHO RUNS MOST LAW ENFORCEMENT IN AMERICA WAS KILLING EVERY BLACK MAN THEY COULD BEFORE KATRINA, THEY JUST ESCALATED IT AFTER KATRINA AND NOW SOME LOCAL JUDGE AND THEIR JURORS JUST FREED THIS POLICEMAN AFTER KILLING DANNY BRUMFIELD, 45, WAS KILLED BY OFFICER RONALD MITCHELL EARLY SEPT.3, 2005, JUST BEFORE THE NATIONAL GUARD ARRIVED TO EVACUATE THE CONVENTION CENTER. A SHOT GUN BLAST FROM BACK TO FRONT OF BRUMFIELD'S

BODY, NOT FROM THE FRONT AS THE OFFICERS TRY TO COVER
-UP THE DEATH. THEY ARE THE GANG THE LEGAL GANG OF
HUMANS, WHO DOES NOT LOOK AT THE SELVES AS GANG-
STERS.YOU SEE BIRDS OF A FEATHER FLOCKS TOGETHER,
WHY HUMANS CANNOT FLOCK TOGETHER. IF YOU ARE THE
AMERICAN KLAN YOU CAN FLOCK TOGETHER AND GO OUT
ON THE RANGE AND TARGET PRACTICE TO KILL BLACKS OR
COLOR PEOPLE NOT CALLED GANG MEMBERS. GOD SAID
THAT WE ARE TO HAVE SEX AND POPULATE TOGETHER, BUT
THE RACIST PROTECTORS OF THIS SO-CALL DEMOCRACY. I
LIKE BILL MAHER'S OPINION ON BEING AMERICANS AND
NOT WHAT THE REPUBLICAN RACIST WHO ARE HARD NOTE
TO KEEP THE DIVIDE AND CONQUER IT'S DESCENDANTS OF
SLAVES. BARACK OBAMA SHOULD HAVE A CHANCE TO
CHANGE AMERICA FOR THE GOOD OF AMERICA. I HAVE
BEGUN TO SEE THAT HE HAS THE BALLS TO BE RIGHTEOUS
AND TRUST WORTHINESS. THIS IS DEDICATED TO A BETTER
AMERICA, MY DAUGHTER CC AND MY FRIEND GOOD OL BOY
EDDIE FOXX, A MAN EVEN THOUGH, HIS HERITAGE AS
DESCENDANT OF SLAVE MASTERS HE IS A RIGHTEOUS
FRIEND AND DEDICATE INDIVIDUAL. THAT MEANS ASS
HOLES YOU HAVE TO WATCH MORE BECAUSE THEY DO NOT
LIKE DEDICATION, AND ESPECIALLY DEDICATION TO A
BLACK MAN. JJ MY LITTLE MAN WILL BE BETTER FOR ALL OF
US. HE IS TOUGH FOOTBALLER AT A YOUNG AGE, AND HOPE
HE CONTINUE HIS EXCELLENCE, AND SHELISA. THE FINAL
CALL JULY EDITION HEADLINE," GANG WARS REPORT:
RACIAL TARGETING OF BLACK MALES", SAY IT LOUD AND
CLEAR THAT WE DO NOT HAVE JUDICIAL REFORM, AND
THAT WOULD TAKE THE FREE HIGH EDUCATION FOR
DESCENDANT OF SLAVES; THEREFORE, NEW COLLEGES AND
UNIVERSITIES NEEDS TO BE BUILT, NO MATTER WHAT NEWT
GINGRICH AND THE BUSHES AND CHENEY SAYS THAT IS
NOT WHAT THE "STATUS QUO" CAN AFFORD. IT IS A MUST

IF WE ARE TO BE HUMANE. THE PEOPLE OF AMERICA I HOPE ARE READY FOR A MORE MULTI - COLOR SOCIETY. I HOPE THE SONS AND DAUGHTERS OF THIS DEMOCRACY DOES NOT BRING MARSHALL LAW TO KEEP THEM PURE BLOODED. THE LARGEST GANG IS THE MILITARY. IN COURTS AND POLICE ACROSS AMERICA USE THIS WORD AS TROUBLE AND SOME CASES MIGHT BE SO, BUT WHEN IN CHURCH THAT GANG IS A GOOD HUMAN GATHERING. A FEW GANG OF ENGLISHMEN TOOK OVER AND TRICKED THE INDIANS FOR THEIR LAND, WHICH LATER BECAME THE UNITED STATES OF AMERICA. THE PURITANS PURIFIED THE INDIAN'S LAND OF THEIR LAND, AND NOW CALL IT THEIR UNITED STATES OF AMERICA, AND THEY SATISFIED SOME OF THE INDIANS, BY SECTIONING OUT CERTAIN UNCROPABLE LAND AS INDIAN RESERVA-TIONS. GOT THEM DRUNK IN THE NAME OF JESUS, THEN CAME IN AND DESTROYED THEIR WHOLE FAMILY AT NIGHT. TODAY CHILDREN ARE SO UNAWARE OF HISTORY, THAT THEY HAVE ACHIEVED SOME SUCCESS AND ARE GETTING DRUNK.   12-05-07THE NUCLEAR AGENCY'S REPORT THAT IRAN DOES NOT HAVE A NUCLEAR WEAPON, NOR HAS ATTEMPTED ONE SINCE 2003 AND BUSH IS HARD NOSE AND CONTINUE TO KEEP ALL OPTION OPEN TO ATTACK IRAN, WHO IS SUPPOSE TO BE A THREAT TO ISRAEL, THE SAME ATTITUDE ABOUT IRAQ. EVERY DAY ON ALL NEWS STATIONS SADDAM WAS BRING FORTH EVERY SMALL WEAPON THAT HE HAD LEFT FROM THE IRAN AND IRAQ WAR, AND THE NO FLY ZONES THAT WAS INSTITUTED BY HIS FATHER AND COLIN POWELL BUSH CHENEY BETRAYED THEIR LOYAL AFRICAN- AMERICAN SOLDIER TO BOMB IRAQ. THE PRESI-DENT ELECTION IS BECOMING MORE INTENSE AS THE IOWA VOTE IS ONLY THREE WEEKS AWAY. OPRAH IS TO CAMPAIGN FOR BARRACK OBAMA, AS SENATOR CLINTON HAS HER HUSBAND DOING THE SAME FOR HER, IN IOWA AND SOUTH CAROLINA.   12-08-07THE LIGHT IS SHINING AGAIN ON THE

ILLEGAL ADMINISTRATION OF BUSH AND CHENEY. ANOTHER COVER-UP THAT SENATOR JAY ROCKEFELLER, SAID HE COULD HOLD HEARING AND INVESTIGATION NEXT WEEK. IT IS DIFFERENT WITH THE RIGHT WINGERS OF THE REPUBLICANS WHO COVER-UP AND FOUGHT, CLOSED SENATE DOORS AND ROOMS TO THE DEMOCRATS. THE GREAT GRAND DRAGON SENATOR FROM THE GREAT STATE OF MISSISSIPPI TRENT LOTT IS RETIRING AFTER THE SENATE DISMISS FOR CHRISTMAS, AFTER HIS BROTHER IN LAW IS BEING TRIED FOR CORRUPTION. YOU CAN BELIEVE LOTT DID NOT WANT TO RETIRE AFTER ALL HE DID TO STAY IN THE SENATE AFTER HIS RACIST STORM THURMOND SPEECH OF SEGREGATION NOW AND FOREVER. GOOD BYE TRETT AND AMERICA WILL NOT MISS YOU, HYDE, BUSH, HATCH, CHENEY, AND MOST THAT ARE REPUBLICANS IN OFFICE TODAY; NOT TO MENTION ALL THE RACIST LAWMAKERS OF THE PAST. AL SHARPTON IS A DIRECT DESCENDANT OF STORM THURMOND.AS I TRY TO HASTILY FINISH THIS BOOK IT IS PROVING THAT EVERYTHING FROM A DESCENDANT OF THE AMERICAN SLAVERY. THERE WERE MORE NOOSE STORIES IN THE NEWS THIS WEEK AND ONE FROM THE LONG SHOREMAN'S QUARTERS IN LONG BEACH, CALIFORNIA. THE MENTALLY STILL EXIST AND A FENCED IN AMERICA IS NOT THE RIGHT THING TO DO. IT WAS NOT CORRECT FOR CHINA, IT WAS NOT CORRECT FOR GERMANY, AND IT DIVIDED THE PEOPLE OF THE NATIVE ANCESTOR OF THIS LAND OF AMERICA. THERE AN ARTICLE ON THE INTERNET TODAY FROM A LADY FOXXY-FATIMAL17 :THE FIRST WEEK OF DECEMBER 2007 HAS BEEN A LOT MORE DENIAL FROM THE BUSH ADMINISTRATION AND Its CENTRAL INTELLIGENT AGENCY METHODS OF INTERROGATIONS, AND IT IS ALL AGAINST THE GENEVA'S CONVENTION RULES. WE DO NOT HAVE ANYTHING TO COMPLAIN ABOUT IF FOR SOME REASON ONE OF OUR AGENTS ARE INTERROGATED AS THE BUSH CHENEY HAS AUTHORIZED

TO DO TO THE AFRICAN-DESCENDANTS OF THE MIDDLE EAST, PARTICULAR THE IRAQ DETAINEE AND BIN LADEN'S SOLDIERS. BUSH CHENEY WENT AGAINST WHAT HIS FATHER'S LIFE OF CIA OPERATIVE AND CHIEF OF CIA, THAT WAS WHY RONALD REAGAN HAD CHOSEN HIM AS VICE PRESIDENT, AFTER JIMMY CARTER'S HAD OPEN UP THE RESERVES TO KEEP THE PRICE OF GAS DOWN FOR THE AMERICANS, BUT BUSH CHENEY ARE OIL MEN AND HAS INVESTMENTS IN OIL, THEREFORE, WHY SHOULD THEY OPEN THE RESERVES? THE BUSH ADMINISTRATION AND JUSTICE DEPARTMENT CAN NOT COVER -UP FOREVER, AND NOW WATERGATE 2 COULD BE JUST AROUND THE CORNER, THE ONLY DIFFERENCE IS THE JUSTICE DEPARTMENT IS PART OF THE COVER-UP, WHEN THE WATERGATE INCIDENT HAPPEN, NIXON DID NOT HAVE THEM TO DENY CONGRESS AS THESE NEW TRAITORS ARE DOING TODAY. THEIR ATTORNEY GONZALEZ JUST RETIRED TO COVER-UP THE LIES OF THE IRAQ WAR AND THE CIA SCANDAL OF VALERIE PLAME, WHO THE RIGHT WINGERS COULD NOT INVESTIGATE AND HAVE AN INDEPENDENT PROSECUTOR APPOINTED, AS THE DEMOCRATS WHO WORKS WITH THEM, BUT THEY NEVER, OR VERY RARELY WORK WITH ANY SO-CALL LIBERAL DEMOCRAT. THE FOLLOWING I THOUGHT MIGHT HELP DRAW THE POINT FROM A PRIVATE CITIZEN VIEW AND I AM WILLING TO BET A DRINK THAT NOT ANY, OR AT THE LEASE ARE OF AFRICAN -DESCENDANT. THE AMERICAN WAY.

Justice Department spokesman Erik Ablin said Bush has granted 142 pardons and commuted five sentences since taking office in 2001 — lagging far behind the pace set by most modern presidents. The list was issued with little fanfare Tuesday afternoon by the Office of the Pardon Attorney at the Justice Department. Bush was not expected to issue any more pardons this year. In July, Bush commuted Libby's 2 1/2-year sentence, sparing Vice President Dick Cheney's former chief of staff from serving any prison time after being convicted of perjury and obstructing justice. Libby, who recently dropped appeals to have his convictions overturned, has paid a $250,000 fine and remains on two years probation. Libby was the only person to face criminal charges in the case of the 2003 leak of then-CIA operative Valerie PLAME'S identity. PLAME, who has since left the CIA, contends the White House was trying to discredit her husband, a critic of Bush's Iraq policy. A pardon amounts to federal forgiveness for one's crime, while a commutation cuts short an existing prison term. Nearly all of those to win pardons this year were small-time crooks that at most were imprisoned for five years. Many of them never served time at all, and instead were fined or put on probation. On the list this year was William Charles Jordan Jr., a 64-year-old retiree from Dover, Pa., who was pardoned for his role in a college and NFL football gambling ring that federal authorities shut down on Super Bowl Sunday in 1997.Jordan said he did not want his eight grandchildren to know he was a felon, so he obtained the necessary paperwork through his congressman. He learned Tuesday the pardon came through." It's a nice Christmas present," Jordan said. "I didn't know what the odds were on getting one. I just sent the stuff in and hoped."

BUSH AND CHENEY KNEW WHO INFORMED THE COLUMNIST ROBERT NOVAK OF VALERIA PLAME WILSON'S IDENTITY, THEREFORE, COMMITTED TREASON. THEY ARE STILL HIDING KARL ROWE, AS HE WENT ON TO RESIGN TO KEEP SOME OF THE HEAT OFF OF THE BUSH CHENEY'S WHITE-HOUSE, AND TO PROTECT THE PRESIDENT AND VICE PRESIDENT, JUST AS KEN LAY DID IN THE ENRON SCANDAL, AND THE REAGAN'S CIA CHIEF CASEY DID TO PROTECT THE REAGAN BUSH ADMINISTRATION; EVEN THOUGH, OLIVER NORTON TOOK ENOUGH OF THE WEIGHT OFF OF THE REAGAN BUSH ADMINISTRATION. BUSH DID NOT PARDON LIBBY, BUT HE DID NOT GO TO JAIL AND PAID A FINE THAT

DID NOT MOST LIKELY COME FROM HIS POCKET. BUSH CHENEY ESPECIALLY DID NOT LIKE HER CLINTON AMBASSADOR'S HUSBAND. WHAT LIBBY WAS CONVICTED FOR IS NOW AN INVESTIGATION OF DESTROYED VIDEO OF THE BUSH CHENEY ADMINISTRATION. GOD IS IN CONTROL AND HE DOES NOT LIKE THE LIES OF THE SO-CALL EUROPEAN DESCENDANTS OF HATE IN A SO-CALL RELIGIOUS SETTINGS. THE SONAMY, HURRICANE KATRINA, THE ICE STORMS AND THE HUMANS STILL DOES NOT WANT TO BELIEVE THAT THE STORIES OF THEIR BIBLE, KORAN, AND OTHER BOOKS NEEDS TO BE UPDATED AND POSSIBLY THIS COULD BE A START. I CONSIDER MYSELF A MAN OF GOD AND I AM NOT PERFECT. I HAVE BE INVOLVED IN ALL OF THE HERBS OF THE EARTH AND WE SHOULD NOT BE PUNISH FOR THEM. THE GORILLAS, MONKEYS, AND THE OTHER SPIES LIVE AND THRIVE ON THE STIMULANTS OF THE JUNGLE, WHY IS IT THAT THE EUROPEANS WANT TO CREATE PROHIBITION LAWS ON SOME OF THE HERBS, BECAUSE THEY HAVE REMOVE THEMSELVES FROM THE JUNGLES THROUGH GENOCIDE OVER MILLION OF YEARS OR MORE TO CREATE THE LIGHTER GENE OF THE HUMAN MALE BODY, BY DESTROYING THE DARKER GENE IN A PARTICULAR POPULATIONS IN THE NORTH OF AFRICA, IN WHAT IS CALL EUROPE IN MODERN TIMES. 12-17-07 THE REPUBLICAN SENATORS ON THE INTELLIGENCE COMMITTEE ARE FEED UP WITH THE BUSH CHENEY COVER-UPS AND ARE WITH THE DEMOCRATS TO ISSUE SUBPOENAS FOR THE DESTROYING THE INTERROGATION TAPES, WHICH WAS ILLEGAL AND THE JUSTICE DEPARTMENT IS TRYING TO FIGHT IT. WHY SHOULD THE JUSTICE DEPARTMENT PROTECT THE PRESIDENT AND NOT DO AS CONGRESS WANT? THE SENATOR SAID THAT HE IS FEED UP WITH THE EXCUSE TO PROTECT THE INTERROGATORS, AND EXPRESSLY WHEN THE TAPE EXISTED FOR THE THREE PREVIOUS YEARS. IT IS GOOD FOR THIS BOOK ON THE BUSH AND CHENEY'S ADMINISTRATION,

MOSTLY CHENEY IN THE NAME OF BUSH. JOHN MCCANN TRIED TO EXPLAIN THE EXPERIENCE FACTOR AND IT DOES NOT COME OUT GOOD WHEN HE WAS ONE OF THOSE REPUBLICANS WHO MISLEAD THE WORLD OF THE SADDAM HUEISEIN AND IRAQ AND THE ILLEGAL APPOINTMENT OF THE BUSH ADMINISTRATION IN 2004 IN THE NAME OF TIME AND THE CONSTITUTION. THAT IS WHY AMERICA IS HATED MORE TODAY THAN WHEN CLINTON LEFT THE OFFICE. THE SO CALL ISRAEL PROTECTOR SENATOR JOE LIEBERMAN, FORMER VICE PRESIDENT AL GORE'S CHOOSE FOR 2000 VICE PRESIDENT OVER JOHN EDWARDS, AND THAT WAS A GREAT MISTAKE, AS HE STILL GOT MORE VOTES THAN BUSH, BUT A JEW UP AGAINST DICK CHENEY, AND HE SUPPOSED TO HAVE HAD MORE EXPERIENCE THAN EDWARDS, WHICH WAS NOT CORRECT, CAUSE I BELIEVE EDWARDS WOULD HAVE NOT COLLABORATED WITH CHENEY AS LIEBERMAN DID AND LOSE THE DEBATES, NOW THIS PAST WEEKEND HE ENDORSED SENATOR JOHN MCCANN FOR PRESIDENT. LIEBERMAN IS A SELL-OUT AND THE DEMOCRATS NOMINATED ANOTHER TO REPRESENT CONNECTICUT AND LIEBERMAN COULD NOT TAKE THE REJECTION, AS HE THOUGH HE HAD TO STAY IN CONGRESS TO VOTE WITH BUSH AND THE IRAQ WAR, SO HE WENT ON TO BE INDEPENDENT, WHICH THE REPUBLICANS VOTED FOR HIM AS AN INDEPENDENT AND NOT THE SO-CALL LIBERAL DEMOCRAT. THE CONSPIRACY IS CONTINUING AS I TRY TO FINISH THIS BOOK. 12-18-07THE BUSH CHENEY ADMINISTRATION IS UNDER ORDERS TO SHOW IN COURT, BECAUSE OF THE DESTROYED VIDEO TAPES THAT WERE DESTROYED, WHEN THE FEDERAL JUDGE HAD TOLD THEM NOT TO DESTROY THE VIDEO. TODAY THEY REFERRED ALL QUESTIONS TO THEIR JUSTICE DEPARTMENT, AND THE EXECUTIVE BRANCH IS NOT WORKING WITH CONGRESSIONAL BRANCH, OR THE JUDICIAL BRANCH OF THE CONSTITUTION OF THE UNITED STATES. THIS IS "TRICKY " DICK CHENEY'S

BABY AND BABY BUSH IS GOING DOWN WITH THIS. IF THE LIES THAT THE WHITE AND THE JUSTICE DEPARTMENT DOES NOT PLEASE THIS ANGRY FEDERAL JUDGE THIS FRIDAY, THEY SHOULD BE IN PLENTY HOT WATER AFTER DOING THEIR DIRT, AND THEN ADMITTING TO IT AS NOT TO COVER-UP. CONGRESS IS PRECEDING WITH THEIR SUBPOENAS, AND I WANT TO HOLD THIS BOOK UP JUST TO SEE THIS COME TO A FULL EIGHT YEARS CONCLUSION, AFTER THE ILLEGAL APPOINTMENT OF BUSH CHENEY AS PRESIDENT OF THE UNITED STATES. IT AND THE INVASION OF IRAQ WAS THE INSPIRATION FOR THESE CRITICISMS AND COMMENTS ON THE HISTORY AND HOPE TO BE SOLUTIONS TO MAKE THIS A NEW MELTING POT OF HUMAN DIGNITY AT IT'S BEST, GIVING THERE IS ALWAYS ROOM FOR THE LESS TO FIND A WAY TO HAVE MORE. MY FAMILY AND FRIENDS WAS ALSO INSPIRA-TION FOR THEM TO HAVE ENDURED THE BEST AS POSSIBLE AS MY CHILDREN OF MINES AND CIARRA, TIA, NICK, RJ, STEVE, ALL HAVE TO CARRY ON THE KNOWLEDGE AND PRIDE OF ME AND THEIR DESCENDANTS WHO DID NOT ASK TO COME HERE, NOR DID THEY WANT TO SPEAK THE ENGLISH LANGUAGE, BUT WE ARE HERE AND WE ARE CONSIDERED MEN AND WOMEN, WHEN IN THE PAST WE WERE NOT EVEN CONSIDERED HUMAN TO THE IGNORANT ENGLISH AND THE REST OF THE CONQUERORS. ONE OF THE SLOGANS OF THE SECOND STATE TO HAVE PRIMARY TO VOTE IS NEW HAMPSHIRE, AND THEIR STATE SLOGAN IS "LIVE FREE OR DIE", AND MAY GOD BLESS AMERICA. THE AMERICA WAY. MAY PEACE BE UPON US? 12-26-07 THE PRESIDENTIAL IOWA ELECTION FOR SO-CALL CAUCUS VOTER FOR THE NEXT PRES-IDENT, THAT SHOWS THAT ONE MAN ONE VOTE IS NOT THE PRIORITY OF THIS DEMOCRACY AND IT HAS TO REVERT BACK TO THE ONE MAN ONE VOTE, EVEN THOUGH, TODAY WOMEN HAVE RIGHTS THAT WAS NOT PERMITTED, JUST AS THE SLAVES, AND THEIR DESCENDANTS UP UNTIL THE 1964

VOTING RIGHTS LAW. WE ALL HAVE A LONG WAY TO GO. THERE IS ANOTHER RACIST PRESIDENTIAL CANDIDATE, JOHN PAUL, WHO IS ADVOCATING NO INCOME TAXES AND A LOT OF OTHER RIDICULES LAWS TO STOP THIS REPARATION, BUT THAT KIND OF THINKING AND PREACHING THIS IS NOT IN THE BEST INTEREST OF OUR NATION PROTECTION, AND THE EMERGENCY NEEDS THAT IS GOING TO ARRIVE; NOT TO MENTION HOW ARE WE GOING TO PAY THE DEBT THAT HAS US SOLD OUT TO OTHER NATIONS. 12-27-07BARRON HILTON THE GRANDFATHER OF PARIS HAS SAID HE IS CUTTING HIS GRANDCHILDREN OUT OF HIS WILL. THERE IS A HILTON FOUNDATION THAT ONE OF HIS SONS WILL CONTINUE IN CONRAD HILTON'S NAME. HEMPSELY, TRUMP, HILTON, AND OTHERS SHOULD HAVE THE CONSCIOUS TO MAKE LANDS, HOUSING, AND OTHER THINGS THAT WOULD DIRECTLY SUSTAIN THE DESCENDANT OF SLAVES. 01-02-08HAPPY NEW YEARS AND I AM TRYING TO GET THIS BOOK FINISH THE PRESIDENTIAL ELECTION, SINCE IT WAS SENT BACK FOR EDITING AND IT HAS BEEN GREAT AS A CONCLUSION OF THE ILLEGAL BUSH CHENEY ADMINISTRATION TO USE THE LEGAL SYSTEM TO FORCE THE POOR AND MIDDLE BUSINESS PEOPLE TO THE WELFARE LINE, OR AT LEASE NOT IN BUSINESS ANY MORE BECAUSE OF EMINENT DOMAIN, WHICH IS A RACIST INTERPUTATION TO MAKE THE LARGE CITIES AND THERE SUBURBS WITH LESS AFRICAN-AMERICAN BUSINESS MEN BECAUSE MOST BANKS ONLY ASSISTED THE WHITE BUSINESS PEOPLE FIRST AND THE CRUMBS GO TO THE SO- CALL MINORITY OF THE UNITED STATES POPULATIONS. MAYOR BLOOMBERG OF NEW YORK IS SO WEALTHY THAT HE DOES NOT ACCEPT HIS MAYOR'S SALARY, BECAUSE HE THINKS HE CAN RUN IT LIKE ONE OF HIS CORPORATIONS. EMINENT DOMAIN, CHANGING THE PARKING RULES TO MAKE CONGESTION AND THE STATE FEED INTO IT, JUST TO RECEIVE BILLIONS OF TAX DOLLARS, IN THE NAME OF

GREENHOUSE EFFECT MYTH. IT IS ONLY THE SPACE SHUTTLE AND THE AIRPLANE TRAFFIC THAT IS CAUSING ANY EARTHLY MELT DOWN. SIMPLE SCIENCE WHEN YOU HEAT THE ICE SPACE THEN YOU WILL HAVE A MELT DOWN. THEY SHOULD GIVE A NOBEL PEACE PRIZE INSTEAD OF AL GORE'S VISION THAT IT ALL COMES FROM THE EMISSION OF THE AUTOMOBILE, AND ANTIQUE FACTORIES. THEY DO NOT COMPARE TO THE SPACE PROGRAM AND THE EMERGING OF AIRPLANES, JET AIRPLANES AND THERE IS NO STOPPING THAT, THEREFORE, THEY SAY, WE HUMANS WILL HAVE OTHER LANDS TO FLOCK. THE BANKERS AND THE WELL TO DO WILL BE BUILDING IN THE AN ARTIC VERY SOON. THE FOLLOWING ARTICLE SHOWS THAT SOME OF THESE LAWS THAT BUSH APPOINTMENT OF THE YOUNGEST JUSTICE ALIDO AS THE CHIEF JUSTICE WITHOUT COMING THROUGH THE RANKS, CAUSE " TRICKY DICK" CHENEY IS A DEMON AND HIS RACISM IN THE NAME OF WHITE SUPREMIST HAS PUT OUR UNITED STATES ON A BACKWARDS MOVEMENT AND WE AS A PEOPLE HAS TO REVIVE SOME OF THE WARREN COURT PROTECTION FOR THE FOURTH AMENDMENT AND THE PRIVACY ISSUE SHOULD BE ENFORCED, BY AUTOMATI-CALLY REVERSING THE PATRIOT ACT THAT HAS VIOLATED EVERY AMERICAN RIGHTS IN THE NAME OF TERRORIST. OHIO REPRESENTATIVE DENNIS KOCINDIS WAS ABSOLUTELY CORRECT AND HE WOULD BE A GOOD VICE PRESIDENT.

Does the Supreme Court's latest ruling on eminent domain pose an eminent threat to African American communities? Anytime a law OKs "taking property that's rightly one individual's for the benefit of another, that's not good," says Rep. Bennie G. Thompson (D-Miss.). In Kelo v. New London, the Supreme Court on June 23, 2005 ruled against homeowners in a 5-4 decision that upheld local governments' ability to condemn homes for private development purposes. The Court affirmed that it was a permissible "public use" under the Fifth Amendment. It's especially a concern when "a lot of land located in the inner city and urban areas is prime for the taking" says Thompson, ranking Democrat on the Homeland Security Committee. This year, Thompson expects more bipartisan debates and resolutions calling to restrict the use of eminent domain for private development. "Eminent domain has been used both to destroy and build black communities," says Sheena Wright, president and CEO of Abyssinian Development Corp. in Harlem. "On one hand, it has been used to undermine our communities and displace us wholesale for private business interests." But in some areas, she says, it has removed blight and provided affordable housing, and commercial revitalization. Damon Dorsey, president of the North Avenue Community Development Corp. in Milwaukee, agrees that eminent domain "expands the capacity to improve communities" by adding value and jobs to the area. Beulah White, executive director of Five Rivers Community Development Corp. in Georgetown, South Carolina, worries, "African American landowners will become extinct due to escalating taxes, dubious court rulings, and land sales transactions."

THE NEW JUSTICE DEPARTMENT HAS FINALLY COME AROUND AND HAS LAUNCHED AN INVESTIGATION OF DESTROYING VIDEO OF INTERROGATION OF SUSPECTS FROM THE MIDDLE EAST AND DENIED THE COMMISSION ACCESS TO EVERYTHING AS THE CIA WAS TO DO BUT CHENEY TOLD THEM NOT TO COOPERATE. HE SHOULD COME UP FOR WAR CRIMES AND HIS HEART WILL DIE. THE COVER-UPS OF THE BUSH ADMINISTRATION HAS FINALLY COME TO THE LIGHT AND THAT IS GREAT FOR THE UNITED STATES. THEY DID NOT LEARN FROM THE WATERGATE SCANDAL THAT BROUGHT DOWN " TRICKY DICK" NIXON. GOD BLESSES AMERICA. THE SO-CALL COMMISSION THAT BUSH CHENEY HAD APPOINTED TO FIND ABOUT WHAT TO DO TO WIN THE IRAQ WAR, AFTER THEY IGNORED THE PEOPLE WHO ATTACK AMERICA, AND WENT

INTO IRAQ INSTEAD AFGHANISTAN, BECAUSE BUSH AND CHENEY WANTED ALL OF THE BLACK GOLD, LIKE HITLER WANT THE GOLD OF ALL OF THE BANKS OF COUNTRY HE HAD CONQUERED. HALLIBURTON IS OFFSHORE, BUT CHENEY AND BUSH IS NOT.

01-04-08BARACK OBAMA, A AFRICAN-AMERICAN MAN WHO HAD BECAME THE STATE SENATOR OF A MIDDLE AMERICAN ILLINOIS STATE SENATOR AND NOW IS THE UNITED STATES SENATOR OF ILLINOIS. HE HAS NOW WON THE IOWA CAUCUS VOTE, AND NOW ON TO NEW HAMPSHIRE. A CHANGE HAS CAME AND AS HE SAYS, WE ARE CHOOSING HOPE OVER FEAR, AND I HAVE SOME DEEP FEELING THAT IS COMING OVER ME TO SEE THIS DAY IN AMERICA, IN MY LIFE TIME IS SHOWING THE YOUNG PEOPLE AND THE MEDIA, COMPUTER, AND THE EVIL OF THE REPUBLICANS WHO IGNORED THE COUNTRY AND SIDE WITH KLANISHSHIP OF BUSH CHENEY. I HOPE THERE IS SOMEONE TO RUN AGAINST HATCH OF UTAH AND OTHER BUSH SENATORS WHO DIE HARD BACKED AN ILLEGAL WAR AND SENT THEM ON TO PRIVATE LIFE, JUST HIS PARTNER TRENT LOTT. GOD BLESSES AMERICA. BARACK SAYS A CHANGE IS COMING TO AMERICA. I WILL SEE AND HOPE THERE WILL NOT BE THE RACIST PLOTS OF THE REPUBLI-CANS, AS IT WAS IN TENNESSEE'S SENATE RACE WITH FORD, THE BLACKMAN WHO TRIED TO DO WHAT OBAMA DID IN ILLINOIS. I TRULY AND REALLY HOPE THAT THIS BECOME THE NEW AMERICAN WAY. IN FIVE DAYS WE WILL SEE IF BARACK OBAMA CAN WIN THERE, AND IF SO HE WILL BECOME THE PRESIDENT. THE ABORTION RIGHTS, THE RELIGIOUS RIGHT, AND THE CONSERVATIVES CAN NOT CONTINUE TO BE ANTI-AMERICAN, IN THE NAME OF WHITE AND BLACK.HILLARY MADE A DOUBLE MISTAKE BY VOTING WITH THE REPUBLI-CANS TO DECLARE IRANIANS MILITARY AS TERRORIST, JUST TO SHOW YOU HOW THE REPUBLICANS ARE STILL PLAYING

THE FEAR GAME ON MIDDLE AMERICA. RONALD REAGAN WAS ONE OF THE BEST AT THAT AND HIS VICE PRESIDENT BUSH'S SON AND REAGAN'S SECRETARY OF DEFENSE DICK CHENEY NOT TO DESTROY THE CHANGE IN AMERICA TO GIVE THE DESCENDANT OF SLAVES THE BENEFIT OF THEIR HERITAGE, THAT WAS DESTROYED BY THE BRITISH DESCENDANTS AS SLAVE MASTERS OF FREED JUNGLE HUMANS. THE WHOLE WORLD WAS AND IS A JUNGLE WHETHER IT HAS BECOME CONCRETE, AND NOW THEY ARE WORKING ON A JUNGLE IN SPACE.A MARYLAND ESCAPE CONVICT WAS CAPTURED, KILLED, AND DISPLAY IN THE MEDIA WITHOUT COVERS. BIG BLACK MAN LAYED DEAD AND PARADED LIKE THEY DID DOING SLAVERY, IN ORDER, TO SEND A MESSAGE THAT NIGGERS IF YOU WANT TO BE FREE WE WILL CAPTURE YOU AND KILL YOU. THE FEAR FACTOR IS HOW THE PEOPLE OF THE AMERICAN SLAVE SYSTEM SCARE THEIR SLAVES TO WORK SUN UP TO SUN DOWN EVERYDAY OF EVERY WEEK. AMERICA OWES THE DESCENDANTS OF THOSE AFRICANS WHO WERE KIDNAPPED, BOUND, AND CHAINED JUST TO BUILT AND FIELD FOOD FOR THE IGNORANT ENGLISHMEN, WHO WERE RELEASE FROM THE OVER CROWDED GREAT BRITIAN'S PRISONS. THE COMMON LAWS OF BRITIAN WERE USE TO INSTITUTE THE FREE FROM A KING DOCUMENT, CALLED THE UNITED STATES CONSTITUTION AND THOSE PEOPLE DESCENDANTS HAS TO END THE PROVERITY OF THE UNITED STATES PERMAMENTLY. G_D'S LAW STATES THAT THE WELL TO DO HAS THE OBIGATION TO SEE THAT THE LESS WELL TO DO HUMANS WILL HAVE AT LEASE THE BASIC LIVING CONDITIONS WITH PAY. THE LAND OF THE FREE AND THERE ARE MANY OF MY PEOPLE STILL LIVING SHACKS ALL ACROSS ALL OF THE EASTERN COAST LINE COMMUNITIES OF THE UNITED STATES. THEY GO AROUND THE WORLD BRAGGING THAT WE ARE THE RICHES NATION IN THE WORLD AND ALL OF THOSE RICHES DID NOT COME FROM THIS LAND,

MOST OF THE RICHES ARE STILL COMING FROM AFRICA, JUST AS IT HAS BEEN SINCE THE THIEVERY OF THE AMERICAN INDIAN LANDS.THE KIDNAPPING LAWS WERE MADE TO STRICK FEAR INTO THE DARK MAN OF TRYING TO DO WHAT THEY HAD DONE AND DISPLACE A WHOLE PEOPLE, JUST AS BUSH AND CHENEY HAS DONE TO THE NORTH AFRICANS, CALLED MIDDLE EASTERN AND TERRORIST IN QUANTAMO BAY, CUBA TODAY. THEY WANT TO KEEP THE SAME PRICIPALS TODAY IN THE NAME OF TERRORIST AND OUR GOVERNMENT HAS TERRORISTED MANY PEOPLE AND COUNTRY IN THE NAME OF TERRORIST. PRAY TO GOD THAT THESE CONSERVATIVE, ABORTIONIST, RIGHT WINGERS DO NOT DESTROY THE NEW PEOPLE OF THE UNITED STATES. MY PEOPLE WERE LESS THAN DOGS, AND TODAY THOSE RIGHT WINGERS GIVE A DOG MORE RIGHTS THAN AN AFRICAN-AMERICAN, AND THE OTHER DARK PEOPLE, MORE RIGHTS AND THAT IS BECAUSE A DOG IS THE CAUCASIAN MAN'S BEST FRIEND AND NOT MAN'S BEST FRIEND. THE WHITE PEOPLE OF EUROPE ATE DOGS AND THE DARK HUMANS IN ORDER TO SURVIVE THE ALMOST YEAR ROUND FREEZING COLD OF THE SO- CALL EUROPEAN CONTINENT THAT THEY CREATE. THAT IS ANOTHER LIE THE LIGHTER HUMANS IS STILL PROTRAYING TO THE WORLD HISTORY THAT IS ALL BIAS AND IS NOT THE ABOSOLUTELY MYTHS, JUST AS THE JEWS KILLED JESUS CHRIST.

01-04-08

THERE ARE MANY CASES COMING OUT BECAUSE OF MAN'S TECHNOLOGY INTO GENETICS. ONE OF O.J. SIMPSON'S DREAM TEAM GROUP HAS THIS DESTINY TO FREE CONVICTED PEOPLE, WHO DID NOT DO THE CRIME, AND IN THE AMERICAN COURT SYSTEM VICTIMS LIE AND CAN NOT RECOG-

NIZE THEIR OFFENDER IN A LINE UP. SOME WHITE VICTIMS
BLAME A CRIME ON THE FIRST BLACK PERSON THEY SEE,
AND THEY KNOW IT WAS A WHITE MAN WHO DID THE RAPE
AND MURDER.CHARLES CHATMAN DID 27 YEARS IN PRISON,
IN DALLAS, TEXAS, FOR AN ASSAULT ON SOME LADY, WHO
PICKED HIM OUT OF A LINE –UP AND BELIEVE ME TODAY
IN TEXAS IS NOT A GREAT PLACE FOR ANY AFRICAN-AMER-
ICAN, WHO MOST ARE POOR OR JUST ABOVE POOR, THEY
ARE RAILROAD MORE THAN ANY STATE IN THE UNION
SINCE THEY WERE ANNEX INTO THE UNITED STATES. THIS
FOLLOWING ARTICLE PROVES SOME OF MINE MENTALITY
ABOUT THE UNITED STATES OWES EVERY DESCENDANT OF
THE UNITED STATES SLAVE SYSTEM, AND AN APOLOGETIC
GESTURE WILL NOT DO. A STATE RECENTLY APOLOGIZE BUT
I BELIEVE THEY ALL HAVE GOT A VIEW OF THIS BOOK, AS IT
SAT IN THE PUBLISHER'S OFFICE FOR THREE MONTHS AND
LISTENING TO SOME OF THE PRESIDENTIAL CANADATES IS
VERY APPEALING, BARACK OBAMA WILL BRING NEW HOPE
, JUST JOHN F . KENNEDY DID IN 1960. I THINK HE IS VERY
SENSITIVE TO THE POOR AS WELL AS THE ELITE. OPRAH
WINFRED, WHO HAS USE THE MENTALITY OF MASTER FARD
MUHAMMAD PREACHING INDEPENDENCE, THEN HELP
YOUR PEOPLE THEN ALL OF THE REST OF THE PEOPLE. GOD
BLESSES. THE FOLLOWING ARTICLE SHOWS THE GOVERN-
MENT PUT YOU THERE AND YOU DIE THERE UNLESS YOU
ADMIT TO YOUR CRIME OF CONVICTION, AND IN MOST
CASES IN AMERICAN THE SENTENCE IS 2-3 TIMES OF WHAT
SHOULD BE DONE FOR THE CRIME. THE MAN DID OVER
TWENTY –YEARS AND THE PAROLE BOARD WANTED SOME-
TYPE OF ADMISSION AFTER YOU HAVE DONE THE TIME, AND
THAT SYSTEM NEEDS TO BE ABOLISHED. IT IS NOT A FAIR
SYSTEM OF PAROLE RELEASE, THEY RESENTENCE YOU JUST
BECAUSE YOU DO NOT ADMIT TO THE CRIME, JUST SLAVE
TIME OF PAST AND THE PENAL SYSTEM IS SLAVERY OF TODAY

IN THE NAME JUSTICE AND PEACE FOR WHITE PEOPLE IN THE SUBURBS.

The release of Chatman, 47, added to Dallas County's nationally unmatched number of wrongfully convicted inmates.

"Every time I'd go to parole, they'd want a description of the crime or my version of the crime," Chatman said. "I don't have a version of the crime. I never committed the crime. I never will admit to doing this crime that I know I didn't do."

District Judge John Creuzot, whom defense lawyers credited with shepherding Chatman's case for exoneration through the legal system, recommended that Texas' Court of Criminal Appeals find Chatman not guilty. With several relatives dabbing at their eyes with tissues and cheering, Chatman was released.

"I really can't tell you how I feel," said his aunt, Ethel Bradley. "But I can tell you it is a different feeling than I have had in a long time, just to be holding his own hand."

Before the crime is officially cleared from Chatman's record, the appeals court must accept the recommendation or the governor must grant a pardon. Either step is considered a formality after Creuzot's ruling.

Chatman became the 15th inmate from Dallas County since 2001 to be freed by DNA testing. He served more time than any of the other inmates, four of whom were in court Thursday to show their support.

Dallas has freed more inmates after DNA testing than any other county nationwide, said Natalie Roetzel of the Innocence Project of Texas. Texas leads the country in prisoners freed by DNA testing, releasing at least 30 wrongfully convicted inmates since 2001, according to the Innocence Project.

What's Your Take?

One of the biggest reasons for the large number of exonerations is the crime lab used by Dallas County, which accounts for about half the state's DNA cases. Unlike many jurisdictions, the lab used by police and prosecutors retains biological evidence, meaning DNA testing is a viable option for decades-old crimes.

District Attorney Craig Watkins also attributes the exonerations to a past culture of overly aggressive prosecutors seeking convictions at any cost. Watkins has started a program in which law students, supervised by the Innocence Project of Texas, are reviewing about 450 cases in which convicts have requested DNA testing to prove their innocence.

"It is time we stop kidding ourselves in believing that what happened in Dallas is somehow unique," said Jeff Blackburn, the founder of the Innocence Project of Texas. "What happened in Dallas is common. This is Texas."

The hearing attracted a standing-room-only crowd that included Watkins, who was greeted warmly by two wrongly convicted Dallas men who have since won their freedom. Also there was state Rep. Terri Hodge, a member of the criminal jurisprudence committee, who promised unspecified reforms when the Legislature convenes in 2009.

Chatman was 20 when the victim, a young woman in her 20s, picked him from a lineup. Chatman said he lived five houses down from the victim for 13 years but never knew her.

She identified him in court as the attacker, and serology tests showed that the type of blood found at the crime scene matched that of Chatman - along with 40 percent of other black males.

Chatman said he was working at the time of the assault, an alibi supported by his sister, who was also his employer. Nevertheless, Chatman was convicted of aggravated sexual assault in 1981 and sentenced to 99 years in prison. He said his faith kept him from giving up.

Chatman said he believes his race led to his arrest and conviction. The jury, he said, had one black member.

"I was convicted because a black man committed a crime against a white woman," Chatman said. "And I was available."

Chatman said he wants to work with the Innocence Project of Texas to support other people exonerated or wrongly convicted.

"I believe that there are hundreds, and I know of two or three personally that very well could be sitting in this seat if they had the support and they had the backing that I have," Chatman said. "My No. 1 interest is trying to help people who have been in the situation I am in."

01-09-08

THE UNITED STATES "WAR PRESIDENT" BUSH IS IN ISREAL AND THE MIDDLE EASTERN STATES SUPPOSINGLY FOR A PEACE TRIP. THE MEDIA AND THE HEADS OF STATES ARE SAYING TOO LITTLE TO LATE, AND HE IS NOT MEETING WITH ANY PALESTINAN LEADER. THEY ASK QUESTION TODAY AND ISREAL PRIME MINISTER GAVE SOME LAME EXPLANATION, OF THEIR MEETING IN ANNAPALOIS MARYLAND A MONTH AGO. BUSH IS A RACIST AND HE CAN NOT ACT THAT HE LIKE ANY PALESTINAN LEADER. HE DID NOT WOULD NOT UNDER ANY CIRCIMSTANCES MEET WITH YASSAR ARAFAT, THEN ARAFAT DIED AND HE PRETENTED ALL OF HIS YEARS

OF PRESIDENT THAT HE IS NOT GOING TO MEET WITH ANY TERRORIST. HIS FATHER , NIXON, REAGAN, AND ALL UPHOLD US AS COMMUNIST AND THAT DID NOT MAKE SENSE WHEN WE HARDLY KNEW WHAT THE WORD MEANT , AND NOW WE LOOK LIKE TERRORIST AND THE GAME OF DENIAL OF AFRICAN DESCENDANT PEOPLE ARE A THREAT TO DO ALL THE WORST THINGS IN OUR SOCIETY AND THE WHITE PEOPLE ARE THE CREDIABLE PEOPLE OF THE BRITISH AND NOW ANY EUROPEAN PERSON IN AMERICA.

THE BUILDING OF WALLS AND FENCES ARE PLEASING THE AMERICAN SKIN HEADS AND KLANSMEN WHO WANTS TO REVOLT AGAINST ANY MAN OR WOMEN OF COLOR IN AMERICA. THE GANGS SERIES OF THE HISTORY CHANNEL IS MAKING IT CLEAR TO ALL YOUNG WHITE PEOPLE OF SEPARTISM AND THE LYNCHING PARTY OF WHITE KIDS IN NEW YORK, WHO CAME TO TERRORIST MR. WHITE AND HIS SON AT HIS HOUSE ,AFTER HE WORKED HARD ALL OF HIS LIFE AND TO MOVE TO THE SURBURBS OF NEW YORK, THEN WITH HIM AT HIS HOME AS SOME GANG OF WHITE MEN AND WOMEN ONE WAS SHOT, AND A PROSECUTOR JUST HAD A JURY CONVICT THIS BLACK MAN OF MURDER, IT IS ABSO-LUTELY RIDICULOUS. THE JURY SAYS THE JUDGE THREATEN THEM TO COME TO A VERDICT BEFORE CHRISTMAS, IN ORDER FOR HIM/HER TO GO HOME FOR CHRISTMAS, AND THE JURY PROTESTED AND COMPLAINED TO THE MEDIA. PRESIDENT GEORGE W. BUSH IS THE ONLY PRESIDENT SINCE JIMMY CARTER, THAT DID NOT MAKE ANY ATTEMPT TO SOLVED THE ISREAL AND PALESTINAN DIFFERENCIES, EVEN LESS THAN REAGAN AND HIS FATHER, CHENEY POISON HIM ON THE SITUATION OF PROTECTING ISREAL OVER PROTECTING ANYTHING ELSE IN THE WORLD. REMEMBER THEY WALKED OUT OF THE 2001 WORLD CONFERENCE IN AFRICA WITH ISREAL, AND THEN CAME THE WORLD TRADE CENTER

DIASTER. IT WAS STUNNING THEN WHEN THEY WALKED OUT BECAUSE OF ONE PROVISION, AND IT REFLECKED THE HATE ON US BECAUSE OF ISREAL.

AL SHARPTON HAS JUST FINISHED A RALLY FOR THIS MR. WHITE'S CONVICTION LAST WEEK. THIS 2008 AN AMERICA HAS A LONG WAYS TO GO AND WE HAVE TO RID THE SO-CALL CONSERVATIVES WHO ARE CONSTANTLY PUSHING THE POLITICANS TO PROTECT THE WHITE PEOPLE FROM THESE INTERRELATIONSHIPS. TODAY THE SAME MENTALLY AS I GREW UP UNDER THE "JIM CROW" LAWS OF SOUTHERN UNITED STATES, AND CONDONED BY THE UNITED STATES SUPREME COURT. WE HAVE TO CHANGE SOME OF THE UNDER HAND JUDGESHIPS APPOINTMENT OF THE BUSH CHENEY ADMINISTRATION, WHILE CONGRESS IS ON VACA-TION. THOSE ACTS SHOWS HOW DEVIAS THE CONSERVATIV ES=CONFEDRATE. AMERICA HAS TO CHANGE AND EVERY SINCE WATERGATE, GOD HAS SAVE AND DELAID WHAT THE CONSERVATIVES WANT TO LOCK US UP IN ANY AND EVERY POSSIBLE, TO GIVE THE STATE SO-CALL "PROBABLE CAUSE". THEY ARE TRYING TO FOREGO THE CONSTITUTION TO KEEP THE STATUS QUO IN ISOLATION FROM THE FORMER SLAVES OF THE UNITED STATES. THERE MANY AND EVERY TYPE OF PEOPLE IN THIS COUNTRY TODAY, AND THE BANKS AND GOVERNMENT WILL GIVE THEM ANY AND ALL TYPES OF GRANTS AND WILL NOT HONOR THE DESCENDANT OF THE UNITED STATES SLAVE SYSTEM. ISREAL DOES THE SAME WITH THE PALESTINANS.

THE JEWISH INFLUENCE IN AMERICA IS ONE THAT IS RACIST. THEY ALWAYS TALK ABOUT HILTER, BUT THEY ARE QUICK TO PARTNERSHIP WITH THE KLAN IN AMERICA, WHO DO NOT LIKE THEM, AND LOOK DOWN ON THE AFRICAN AMER-ICANS. THEY DO NOT WANT TO HONOR ALL OF THE LIVES

OF MY PEOPLE WHO WERE EXTERMINATED IN AMERICA. THE COUNTRY OF THEIR ADOPTION. IT DOES NOT MAKE SENCE TO ME, BUT THAT IS AN AMERICAN WAY. THEY WANT THE WHOLE WORLD TO HONOR THEIR HOLACUST , BUT NOT HONOR THE HOLACUST OF THE KIDNAPPED, CHAIN, BOUND, HUNG, AND SOME OF THE WORSE DEATH OF AN AFRICAN PEOPLE, THAT IS NOT CORRECT OR POPULAR FOR THE UNITED STATES TO HONOR THOSE HELLISH DAYS OF WORLD WAR 2, AND NOT SHOW ANY KIND OF REDEMPTION TO MY PEOPLE OF THE UNITED STATES SLAVE SYSTEM. NO MATTER HOW MANY ARE MORE EDUCATED IN THE ENGLISH LANUAGE AND WAYS, THE UNITED STATES CORPORATIONS AND THE GOVERNMENT OWES A DEBT AND IT SHOW WE NEED TO BE PAID, AND IT SHOULD BE SHOWN ON THE UNITED NATIONS FLOOR, AS A CONTINUED HUMAN RIGHTS VIOLATIONS. THEY TO HONOR THE JAPANESE, VIETNAMESE, KOREANS, IRAQUIS,SO WHY NOT TAKE CARE OF THE UNITED STATES OF AMERICA'S OWN DESCENDANT OF SLAVES?

AL SHARPTON HAS JUST FINISHED A RALLY FOR THIS MAN'S CONVICTION LAST WEEK. THIS 2008 AN AMERICA HAS A LONG WAYS TO GO AND WE HAVE TO RID THE SO-CALL CONSERVATIVES WHO ARE CONSTANTLY PUSHING THE POLITICANS TO PROTECT THE WHITE PEOPLE FROM THESE INTERRELATIONSHIPS.

NEW HAMPSHIRE PRIMARY ENDED LAST NIGHT WITH HILLARY CLINTON WINNING , OBAMA, AND EDWARDS SECOND. THE RACIST JOHN MCCANN WON, ROMNEY, HUCK-ABEE, THESE ARE GOING TO " YES WE CAN' TIME IN AMERICA , AS OBAMA SPEECH WAS "YES WE CAN". ANY DEMOCRAT NOT ANY REPUBLICAN FOR AMERICAN PRESIDENT, WE CAN NOT HAVE ANOTHER WAR PRESIDENT.

THE WEST COAST AND MIDDLE OF AMERICA IS CRYING OF UNPRESIDENT SNOW, WIND, AND TORNADOS THIS TIME OF THE YEAR. I BET YOU GOD IS PUNISHING THEM AS THEY WERE LOOKING DOWN ON ALL OF THE POOR BLACKS AND THE WHITES OF KATRINA AND THE OTHER HURRICANE , THAT IS NOT TOOK CARE OF TODAY. NOW I WANT TO SEE IF THE F.E.M.A MOVE TO HELP THEM MORE THAN THE ONES IN NEW ORLEANS THAT HAS NOT BEEN TAKEN CARE OF BY THE UNITED STATES. A LOT OF THE MONEY WAS STOLEN BEFORE IT GOT TO THE PEOPLE, AND MOST OF IT WAS TAKEN BY SO-CALL TRUSTED WHITE PEOPLE. RED CROSS, SALVATION ARMY AND OTHER HELPERS EXECUTIVES ALL GET A PIECE OF THE PIE BEFORE IT GETS ANYWHERE. THE AMERICAN WAY. THEY ARE THE CRIMINALS WHO NEVER SEE THE INSIDE OF A COURT , JAIL, OR ANY OTHER PUNISHMENT, INSTEAD THEY ARE LOOKED UPON AS CHARITABLE NEIGHBORS. THE AMERICAN WAY.

CNN'S SPECIAL, "GOD'S WARRIORS", CHRISTIAN ARMAN-POUR, WAS VERY EDUCATING RECENTLY AND UNBIAS REPORTING.

THE INJUSTICE OF THE RIGHT WINGERS HAS STRUCK WITH THE DECISION BY THE APPOINTED CHIEF JUSTICE OF THE UNITED STATES SUPREME COURT, WITH A 5-4 DECISION TO WATER DOWN ROE V. WADE'S ABORTION LAW. THEY WANT WOMEN WHO DO NOT WANT A PREGNANCY TO GO TO EXTREME TO RID THEMSELVES OF A BABY, AND THOSE RIGHT TO LIFERS DO NOT SUPPORT NOT ONE UNWANTED BABY AND ESPECIALLY AN BABY OF COLOR. THE COURT SHOULD NOT AND THEY CANNOT REVERSE THIS LAW , IT WOULD BE INHUMANE.

THE LAWSUIT BY DAN RATHER, AGAINST THE "CBS" CORPO-RATION, HAS BEEN ORDER TO PRODUCE THE DOCUMENTS

AND WITNESSES TO CLEAR HIS NAME. THE STORY FOR A SUPPOSE TO BE FLAWED STORY ON PRESIDENT BUSH'S DAYS IN THE TEZAS AIR NATIONAL GUARD,"TO PACIFY THE WHITE HOUSE". RATHER WAS REMOVED FROM HIS LOGTIME ANCHOR POST …". IT SHOW BUSH'S LIES AND DECIET. HE 'S NOT THE FIRST AND PROBABLY WILL NOT BE THE LAST, BUT THESE DAYS IS HIS LAST AS PRESIDENT OF THE AMERICAN PEOPLE AND THE AMERICAN CORPORATIONS.THEY NEED TO HELP IN MAKING GOOD ON THE REPARATIONS DEAL, ONE ACRE AND A MULE. THERE CANNOT BE A STATUE OF LIMITATIONS WHEN THERE WERE NOT ANY STATUE OF OWNING.

TAXATION WITHOUT REPRESENTATION OF THE DISTRICT OF WASHINGTON, DC IS NOT A DEMOCRACY AND THE RIGHT WINGERS ESPECIALLY WOULD NOT WANT TO BE FAIR TO THE CONSTITION AND IT'S TAXATION LAWS. A REPRESEN-TATIVE FROM WASHINGTON WOULD ALWAYS BE A BLACK AND NOW THESE DAYS THERE ARE A FEW BLACK FACES IN THE HOUSE OF REPRESENTATIVES, AND BARACK OBAMA IS THE FIRST AND ONLY BLACK FACE IN THE UNITED STATES SENATE. AMERICA IS CHANGING FOR THE GOOD, BUT THIS COUNTRY IS WAKING UP TO SOME OF TRICKS OF THE REPUB-LICANS TO ALL AMERICANS, AND A DEMOCRAT WILL LEVEL THE PLAYING FIELD A LITTLE, TO STOP THIS ROLLER BALL OF RACIST CONSERVATIVES APPOINTMENT OF THE FEDERAL COURTS AND THE INSENSITIVENESS OF THE DESCENDANT OF THE UNITED STATES SLAVE SYSTEM. THEY CALL US THE UNDER CLASS, THE IGNORANT, AND IT IS TRUE IN A LOT OF SENSE; THEREFORE, THE UNITED STATES AND IT'S CORPORA-TIONS HAS TO PAY FOR THE PAIN AND SUFFERING FOR ALL OF THE YEARS. THERE IS A WAY IF THEY WANT TO GENERATE REVENUE TO HELP THE PEOPLE OF IRAQ, THEN THE BUSH AND IT'S CONSERVATIVE POWER HAS TO MAKE GOOD TO AMERICANS, AND SOME ARE FIGHTING TODAY IN IRAQ.

THE AFRICAN-AMERICANS DESCENDANT OF SLAVES HAS TO BE PAID THE EQUAL FOR AN ACRE AND A MULE, AT THE VERY LEASE. IT WAS A CONTRACT THAT HAS NEVER MADE GOOD ON AND THE COURTS CAN MAKE THE DECISION TO START THE CONGRESS, INSURANCE , COTTON, AND OTHER INDUSTRY THAT HAS BENIFITED THROUGH THE CENTURIES.

I HOPE THAT THIS BOOK WILL ENLIGHTEN THE PEOPLE IN THE DARK, BUT IT WILL NOT BE EASY , ESPECIALLY HONORING A NAZI POPE PREACHING SEPARATION AND THE DISREGART OF A WOMEN RIGHTS TO CONTROL EVERY ASPECT OF HER BODY, AND THAT INCLUDE WHETHER OR NOT FOR HER TO ABORT A CHILD. CLONING OF THE HUMANS SHOULD NOT TAKE PLACE, EVEN THOUGH, I THINK THE TRICKERY OF THE ARIAN SCIENTIST HAVE DONE THIS . THEY ALWAYS PORTRAY THE MOON LANDING IN MOVIES, AS THEIR PRACTICE FOR WHERE THEY ARE HEADED. THE CLONING OF HUMANS WOULD ONLY SERVE THE CACASIAN POPULATION, AS THEY ARE THE LIGHTER AND THE MINORITY OF THE HUMANS. THEY WOULD NEVER THINK OF CLONING ANY AFRICANS, AS THEY ARE STILL COMMITTING GENOCIDE OF THE AFRICANS AND OTHER DARK HUMANS, SO WHY WOULD ONE THINK THAT YOU CAN TRUST ANY WHITE GOVERNMENT OFFICIAL AND MOST OF THEIR FELLOW PEOPLE. CLONING OF THE COWS, PIGS, AND SHEEPS IS A LITTLE TOO MUCH, BUT THE POPULATION GROW OF THE HUMANS PROBABLY WILL NEED HELP, BUT THEY ARE ALREADY STEROIDING THOSE ANMIALS AND THERE STEROID MILK HAS THE BABIES GROWING LARGER AND TALLER.

SENATOR HILLARY CLINTON SAID AMERICA HAS CHANGE WITH A WHITE WOMAN AND AN BLACK MAN LEADING THE DEMOCRATIC PRIMARIES, THE GLASS CEILING IS BUSTED

OPEN, THAT IS , BLACKS AND WOMEN HAS A CEILING IN THE CORPORATE WORLD AND NOW WE ARE ON THE VERGE TO CHANGE AMERICA FOR THE BETTER OF AMERICA.

IN CONCLUSION, I HOPE THE AMERICAN CONTINENT IS GOING TO CHANGE FOR THE BETTER THAN WHEN I STARTED TAKING NOTES OF CURRENT EVENTS THAT LEAD TO THE HISTORY OF THE HUMAN NATURE:

THESE THOUGHTS, NOTES, AND REFERENCES ARE IN RESPONSE TO HOW THE REPUBLICAN PARTY OF THE UNITED STATES, HEADED BY GEORGE HERBERT WALKER BUSH AND TRICKY DICK CHENEY DECIDED TO OVERTHROW THE UNITED STATES CONSTITUTION BY RIGGING THE 2000 PRESIDENTIAL ELECTION. ALL OF "TRICKY DICK" NIXON'S MEN WAS TO CONTINUE WHAT NIXON WANTED AND THAT WAS DICTA-TORSHIP, JUST AS ADOLPH HITLER IN THE THIRTIES. THE RIGHT WINGER'S CONSPIRACY TO COMMITTED TREASON HAVE THE UNITED STATES OF AMERICA, AND THERE IS NOTHING THE PEOPLE OF AMERICA CAN DO, AND THAT IS THE AMERICAN WAY.

WE HAVE WENT FROM KING GEORGE OF ENGLAND'S WAR ON THE UNITED STATES AND GENERAL GEORGE WASH-INGTON AND HIS CONTINTAL ARMY. HE HAD HIS PARTNER AND SLAVE RIDING WITH HIM DURING EVERY EVENT HE ATTENDED. NOW WE HAVE ALMOST FINISHED THROUGH TWO MORE GEORGE'S IN THE BUSHES AS PRESIDENT AND THE LAST GEORGE W. BUSH HAS DID WHAT HIS FATHER AND CHENEY WANTED AND THAT WAS TO DESTROY OUR REPU-TATION TO THE WORLD AS LEADER OF THE FREE WORLD. THE INVASION OF IRAQ WAS A BAD DECISION THAT HAS CAUSED US HATRED ALL OVER THE WORLD. THANK GOD FOR OBAMA AND HILLARY AND WE MIGHT COULD CLEAN UP SOME OF THE HATE, AS LONG AS WE CAN GET ISREAL

AND THE PALESTINANS TO LIVE TOGETHER AS IN THE UNITED STATES. IT IS SO RACIST IN ISREAL, BECAUSE THEY WOULD AUTOMATICALLY BECOME THE MINORITY OF THEIR COUNTRY, SO WE WILL SEE HOW THIS GOES. THEY USE TO TELL US THAT WE COULD NOT GO TO LUNCH COUNTERS WITH WHITES AND NOW WE CAN GO BUT WE CAN NOT AFFORD THE PRICES. IT IS ECONOMIC RACISM IN NEW YORK AND THE REST OF THE UNITED STATES.GEORGE H. W. BUSH, NIXON'S CENTRAL INTELLIGENCE AGENCY'S (CIA) CHIEF, THE PRESENT GEORGE W. BUSH'S FATHER, RONALD REAGAN'S WASHINGTON, D.C. INSIDE MAN, AND THE VICE PRESIDENT TO RONALD REAGAN, SENOR PRESIDENCY. A CONSPIRACY TO FOOL THE MIDDLE OF AMERICAN PEOPLE WITH FEAR THAT THEIR COUNTRY WAS BEING TAKEN OVER BY ALIENS, MEXICAN, AFRICAN-AMERICAN DESCENDANTS OF SLAVES, AND ALL OTHER PEOPLE OF COLOR. THEY LIED AND LIED SOME MORE. RONALD REAGAN HOLDS A SPEECH TO THE AMERICAN PEOPLE AT NINE O'CLOCK SPEECH, THEN WHEN THE MORNING AND NOON NEWS SHOWS THERE WAS ALWAYS A RETRACTION, BUT THE HARM WAS DONE, THE LIE WAS TOLD, THEN THE WATERGATE RULE APPLIES, I.E, DO YOUR DIRT AND THEN ADMITTED, THEREFORE, THEY CAN NOT BE ACCUSED OF A COVER-UP, AND THE AMERICAN PEOPLE ARE STILL SUCKERED IN, UNTIL THE 2006 ELECTION. THE RIGHT WING RELIGIOUS DEVILS ARE ONLY CONTINUING THE SO-CALL STATUS QUO OF THE SLAVE MASTER'S DESCEN-DANTS.I AM A COMBAT VIETNAM WAR VETERAN WHO COULD NOT TAKE IT ANYMORE AND DECIDED TO PUT DOWN MY THOUGHTS AT A TIME IN MY LIFE THAT I WAS ELEVATING TO ATTAIN A PATENT GRANT. I HAD SOME TIME TO THINK AND I SEEN WHAT HAPPEN IN FLORIDA DURING THE 2000, THEN THE INVASION INTO IRAQ, I HAD TO EXPRESS MYSELF AS AN AMERICAN, WHO SO HAPPENS TO BE BORN AFRICAN DESCENDANT OF THE UNITED STATES SLAVE TRADE. I KNEW

THAT IT COULD NOT BE POSSIBLE FOR SADDAM HUSSEIN AND IRAQ COULD NOT HAVE ANY WEAPONS OF MASS DESTRUCTION THAT MATTERED. AT THE END OF THE GULF WAR HE USED ALL HE HAD TO ISRAEL AND THEN HE AND HIS PEOPLE WAS PUT UNDER A NO FLY ZONE, AND THERE IS NOTHING KNOW ONE COULD TELL ME HAD WEAPONS THAT MATTERED AND I WAS CORRECT. GEORGE W. BUSH AND TRICKY DICK CHENEY INSPIRED ME TO PUT DOWN MY THOUGHTS AS THIS INVASION WENT ON, CAUSE IT WAS A PERSONAL VENDETTA, BECAUSE HIS FATHER WAS SUPPOSE TO HAVE SOME TYPE OF DEATH THREAT PUT ON HIM BY SADDAM. SADDAM AND BUSH 1 WAS ALLIES IN THE WAR AGAINST IRAN THAT IRAQ LOST AND TODAY HIS SON AND CHENEY ARE TRYING TO HAVE WAR WITH IRAN TO AVENGE WHAT HAPPEN TO THE SHAW DURING THE CARTER ADMIN-ISTRATION AND THE ALLATOYA, THE EXILE ISLAMIC LEADER WHO WAS IN PARIS AND RETURN TO HAVE AN ISLAMIC RULE COUNTRY, NOT A PUPPET FOR THE UNITED STATES. BUSH SAID TWO THINGS TO THE PUBLIC, AFTER HE AND CHENEY PULLED OFF THE OVER THROW, IN THE NAME OF HANGING CHADS, PUNCH CARDS THAT WAS NOT FULLY PUNCH, WAS TO BE THROWN OUT , THEREFORE, THEY RIGGED THE ELEC-TION WITH THE HIGHEST COURT OF THE LAND, WHICH CHENEY HAD IN HIS HAND, WHEN THIS OLD RACIST CHIEF JUSTICE OF ALL JUDGES OF THE UNITED STATES DECIDED TO VOID THE VOTERS INTENT. IF IT WAS PUNCH, WHETHER IT WAS CUT ALL THE WAY THROUGH OR NOT , IT WAS WHAT THOSE VOTERS WANTED, AND MOST ALL OF THEM WAS IN A DISTRICT THAT WAS DEMOCRATIC, WAS THAT THE FUNDS SURPLUS OF THE CLINTON ADMINISTRATION "WILL BE SPENT" , AND THAT HE WANTED TO BE KNOWN AS A WAR PRESIDENT. KATHLEEN HARRIS, THE FLORIDA SECRETARY OF STATE WAS PAID FOR HER EFFORTS TO LIE AND DEFRAUD THE FLORIDA VOTERS, WHEN SHE WAS APPOINTED TO A

BUSH2 ADMINISTRATION JOB IN WASHINGTON, D. C. THEY ALL SHOULD BE IMPEACHED AND SENT UP FOR WAR CRIMES. EVENTUALLY THEY WERE RE-ELECTED AND NOW THE MEDIA IS COMING AROUND, BUT THE COURTS HAS BEEN STACKED AND CONTINUE TO BE STACKED.THIS PAST WEEKEND ANOTHER DICTATOR MUSHARRAF OF PAKISTAN IMPOSED MARSHALL LAW AGAIN AND SUSPENDED THEIR CONSTITU-TION. THEY ARE LOCKING UP ALL OF THEIR ATTORNEYS AND SO-CALL DEMOCRATIC OPPOSITION TO DICTATORSHIP. BUSH AND CHENEY HAS SENT THAT MAN AND HIS COUNTRY TEN BILLION UNITED STATES DOLLARS AND THEY DO NOT WANT TO FUND THE HEALTH CARE BILL THAT WAS VETOED TWO WEEKS AGO, AS TOO EXPENSIVE. THEY DO NOT WANT TO HELP THE COMBAT VETERANS WITH PTSD CHECKS TO LIVE ON AND TRY NOT TO GET INTO ARGUMENTS THAT COULD CAUSE HARM TO SOMEONE, ALL THEY WANT IS TO THROW AWAY THE KEY TO THE UNEDUCATED DESCENDANT OF SLAVES, WHO SHOULD BE RECEIVING REPARATION PAY. IF THE UNITED STATES CAN SEND ALL OF THIS MONEY TO HELP MILITARIES OF THE WORLD, HELP IRAQ PEOPLE SPEAK ENGLISH, JUST THEY REQUIRE THE AFRICAN SLAVE, AND IS REQUESTING THE MEXICANS TO SPEAK ENGLISH IS THE SAME OLD STORY EVERY SINCE THEY ESCAPE THE KING OF ENGLAND'S RULE.THE SENTENCES GUILD LINES ARE JUST DISCUSSING. WHEN THE SLAVES WERE NOT CONSIDERED HUMAN, THE IGNORANT ENGLISHMAN WAS GIVEN A SECOND CHANCE, AND NOT SINCE THE JIM CROW KLU KLUX KLAN RULES OF THE UNITED STATES SUPREME COURT, KILL THEM, CHAIN GANG THEM TO BREAK THEIR STRONG WILL AND THEIR WISDOM AS EDUCATED AFRICANS BEFORE THEY WERE CAPTURE AND CHAINED TO A SLAVE SHIPS, IN THE NAME OF COLUMBUS AND ANYBODY ELSE. TODAY WE ARE BEING ECONOMIC DEPRIVE IN THE NAME OF FREEDOM. AND A EUROPEAN PERSON COME TO AMERICA, MIDDLE EASTERN,

ASIAN, AND SOME AFRICANS THEY ARE GIVEN BANK LOADS AND OTHER THINGS THAT MOST UNEDUCATED BLACKS CAN NOT ATTAIN, BECAUSE THEIR HERITAGE WAS TAKEN AWAY AND THEIR DESCENDANTS WERE MADE TO SPEAK ENGLISH, AND WORK TO MAKE THE LAND OWNER RICH. IGNORANCE IS IN ALL CITY AND RURAL AREAS OF THE NATION, EVEN THOUGHT, IT IS NOT AS PREVALENT AS WHEN MY PARENTS AND MY PEERS WAS/IS, BECAUSE OF THE RACIST SYSTEM OF MISS EDUCATION. PRISON SHOULD BE EDUCA-TIONAL FACILITIES AND THE SO-CALL REVOLVING DOOR WOULD NOT BE REVOLVING AS MUCH, AND I AM PROOF OF THAT. THE AMERICAN WAY. THIS BOOK TRACES AND RELATED TO THE HUMAN NATURE OF FAMILIARITY. HUMAN ARE TO CONGREGATE JUST AS GOD CREATED HIS LAST SUPREME BEING. THE RACIST WANTS TO DIVIDE AND CONQUER IN THE NAME OF GANGS, BUT THE TRUE GANGS ARE THE MILI-TARY AND THE POLICE FORCES OF THE HUMAN SPECIES. WE WERE CREATED TO STAND ON TWO FEET WITH OUT TAILS, AND IT ALL STARTED IN THE DARK WITH THE BLACK HUMAN, BLACK ELEPHANTS, AND MOST OTHERS OF DARK SEA AND OCEANS OF THE WORLD, NOT TO MENTION THE DARKNESS OF UNIVERSAL UPPER SPACE. THE SPACE RACE IS TO TRY AND FIND THE CREATOR, WHICH GOD SAID THE HUMAN IS THE IMAGE OF THE CREATORS, THEN THE ROSWELL, NEW MEXICO LANDING HAPPENED AND THEY LOOK LIKE THE SHORT AFRICANS AND NOT THE WHITEN TV NARROW NOISE WHITE IMAGE, JUST TO SHOW YOU HOW THE BRAINWASHING IS CONTINUING, EVEN WHEN THE INTERNET AREA IS RISING, SO THEY WANT TO KILL OR BLOW UP THE PEOPLE OF THE EARTH AND ESCAPE TO SPACE WITH THEIR WHITE WOMEN AND MAKE BABIES TO BECOME THE MAJORITY HUMAN. THIS BOOK IS TO ENLIGHTEN THE INTELLECT AND THE RACIST SCIENTIST WILL TRY TO DISAPPROVE THE FACTS AS THEY COME OUT MORE AND MORE OVER THE NEXT FEW GENERA-

TIONS. ROB THE OIL COUNTRIES, GOLD, DIAMOND, COAL, AND ALL OF THE OTHER MINERALS OF THE EARTH AND CLAIM THEY OWN IT ALL AND THEY DO TODAY WITH THE HELP OF THE MILITARY. MAY GOD BLESS AMERICA? THIS 2008 PRESIDENTIAL ELECTION IS BECOMING MORE AND MORE WEIRD AS THE DAYS PAST. RON PAUL A RACIST WANTS TO ELIMINATE THE SOCIAL SECURITY TAX AFTER FRANKLIN D. ROOSEVELT SAVE THE PEOPLE FROM THE FOOD LINES IN THE THIRTIES, NOW THIS NARROW MINDED MAN HAS RISEN FOUR MILLION DOLLARS IN TWELVE HOURS OVER THE INTERNET. THEY ARE CHECKING THE STORY, BUT IF IT IS HALF THAT IT IS TROUBLING FOR THE HUMAN RELATION AFTER THE CLINTON GORE HAD ALL PEOPLE GETTING ALONG BETTER THAN EVER. THE BUSHES ARE THE EVIL PEOPLE OF THE WORLD, EVEN THE MOTHER BARBARA BUSH SAYS OF KATRINA VICTIMS IN NEW ORLEANS AND MISSIS-SIPPI THAT THEY DID NOT HAVE ANYTHING AND THE FEMA SHOULD NOT HELP THEM, AND THEY DID NOT. THEY WENT TO ATLANTA AND OTHER CITIES AND NOW THEY STILL DID NOT GET ANY ASSISTANT OR VERY LITTLE, WHEN THE CALI-FORNIA FIRES THE WHITE FOLKS GET WHATEVER IS NEEDED. THE AMERICAN WAY.

ARE REFERENCES THAT A READER CAN VENTURE FURTHER INTO A CERTAIN SUBJECT OR MY OPINION AS AN AFRICAN-AMERICAN FROM THE SOUTHERN UNITED STATES?

01-11-08AS I CONTINUE TO CONCLUDE THERE ARE OTHER FACTORS TO COME OUT ABOUT MY COUNTRY'S UPCOMING PRESIDENTIAL ELECTION FROM THE EUROPEANS. THERE WAS A STORY ON NBC NEWS EVENING STATING THAT THEY HOPE AMERICA WILL ELECT A DEMOCRAT, BECAUSE THEY SEE THE REPUBLICANS AS EXTENTION TO GEORGE W. BUSH AND HIS "TRICKY DICK" CHENEY"S ADMINISTRATION.

BUSH'S TOUR OF ISREAL HAS AWAKEN THE PRESIDENT TRIP TO THE MIDDLE EAST BEFORE HIS TERM ENDS THIS YEAR, AND PEACE WILL HAPPEN IF THE JEWS HONOR JEREWSALEM AS THE PALESTINA CAPITOL AS IT WAS BEFORE THE 1967 WAR, AND THE JEWS CAN LIVE THERE BUT THEY WILL HAVE TO PAY TAXES TO THE PALESTINAS. THERE ARE PRIVACY ISSUES THAT AMERICA IS TRYING TO INSTITUTE WITH INDENTIFICATION FOR DRIVER LICENCES, AND THEY ARE DENYING THE POOR AND THE ELDERLY THE RIGHT TO VOTE, BECAUSE THE CONSERVATIVES WANT ONE TO HAVE INDEN-TIFICATION, WHICH IS ANOTHER CLEAN WAY TO DENY VOTERS IN HIGHLY DEMOCRATIC AREAS, AS WAS DONE IN FLORIDA'S HANGING CHADS DESTROYING CITIZENS VOTE, IN THAT CASE FOR AL GORE. GORE STILL HAD MORE VOTES, BUT THE ELECTORIA COLLEGE NEEDS TO BE ELIMINATED. IT IS A STATUS QUO SYSTEM OF CHOOSING A PRESIDENT AND OTHER ELECTIONS. THESE BOOK WILL RUB SOME THE WRONG WAY, AS THEY WILL CONTINUELY WANT THE PUBLIC AND ALL OF THE CHRISTIAN BRAIN WASHING SERMONS IN BLACK ISLANDS PREACHING LIES ABOUT JESUS CHRIST, AND THIS IS AN AWAKENING WITH WHAT MAN HAS ACHIEVE SINCE THE CREATION OF THE HUMAN SPICIES, BUT WE HAVE COME FULL CIRCLE AS FAR AS THE DIFFERENT HUMAN COMPLEX-IONS AND THE LANUAGES; BUT, WE HAVE TO WORK HARDER TO GET ALONG UNDER THE CAPITALIST SYSTEM OF ATTAINING THE BEST LIFE FOR OUR FAMILIES IN EVERY PART OF THE WORLD. THE UNITED STATES PUBLIC OFFICIALS ON THE LOCAL AND THE FEDERAL LEVEL HAS TO MAKE A WAY TO HELP THE DESCENDANT OF SLAVES INSTEAD OF HOUSING, FEEDING, AND NATION BUILDING ALL AROUND THE WORLD, AFTER THE WARS HAS ENDED, THEN THERE ARE PLENTY FOR MY LOST PEOPLE OF AFRICA, TO THE BACKBONE OF THE BUILDING OF THE UNITED STATES OF AMERICA. BEING BLACK IS WHAT KEEPS ALL OF THE TURMOIL IN THE WORLD GOING

AFTER ALL OF THE FROMER COLONIES OF EUORPE POWER STATES, HAS NOT OVERCOME THE FREEDOM AND INDEPEN-DENCE AS IS NEEDED. AFRICANS FIGHTING AFRICANS AND THERE ARE NOT ANY EUOPEANS AND THEIR DESCENDANTS FIGHTING EACH OTHER; THEREFORE, THE GENOCIDE OF THE DARK MAN CONTINUES AT THE HANDS OF THE EUOPEANS AND THEIR DESCENDANTS, AND OF THE AFRICANS AND THE AFRICAN-DESCENDANTS ARE HELPING IN THE DESTRUC-TION OF THE AFRICANS THROUGH DISEASES AND THE GUN POWER. WE ARE ALL HUMANS AND I HOPE THAT THE ENTIRE COMPEXIONS OF THE HUMAN SPECIES CAN COMES TOGETHER, AS GOD WANTS, BUT THE DEVILISH SIDE IS WINNING AND GOD IS NOT HAPPY. STORM AFTER STORM AND THE AMERICAN GOVERNMENT CAN REBUILD, BUT THAT IS ONLY A WARNING AND THE EUOPEANS CANNOT RUN TO OUTER SPACE TO GET AWAY FROM THE HATE AND THE DECIET THEY HAVE PROTRAYED TO WEAKEST OF THE HUMANS. IF FOR SOME REASON BARACK OBAMA WIN THE NOMINATION AND THEN OVERCOME THE TERRIBLE HATE OF THE CONSERVATIVES OF THE UNITED STATES, THEN WE MIGHT HAVE A CHANCE IN THE ENTIRE HUMAN POPULA-TION.   01-12-08AS I FINALLY TO CONCLUDE , I THINK THAT I HAVE FINALLY CAME CLOSE TO A FULL CIRCLE WITH WHAT HAS BEEN DONE BEFORE AND DURING THE ILLEGAL APPOINTMENT OF A PRESIDENT IN 2000, A POPE JOHN PAUL TRAVELING AROUND THE WORLD, AND EVEN HAD THE STATE OF ISREAL ISSUING SOME TYPE COHESIVE RELATION-SHIP, AND THE ILLEGAL INVASION OF IRAQ THAT JUST SENT ME OVER THE EDGE FOR OIL; AND, THEY TRIED TO PUT IT ON WEAPONS OF MASS DESTRUTION AND SOME TERRORIST WHO ATTACK US ON SEPTEMBER 11,2001, AND ME AND MY COMPUTER ASSISTANCE WAS WORKING WHEN THE BUSH ADMINISTRATION DECIDED TO GO AGAINST THE UNITED NATION'S INSPECTORS, AND TOLD THEM THAT THEY HAD

TWENTY-FOUR HOURS TO FLEE IRAQ BEFORE THE BOMBING IS TO BEGIN. WITH THE WANTED TO BE KNOW "WAR PRESIDENT" THAT GEORGE W. BUSH GOT IN FRONT OF THE CONGRESS AND THE NATION HIS INTENT AS AN APPOINTED PRESIDENT OF THE UNITED STATES, AND NOT ANYONE IN THE MEDIA, CONGRESS, OR ANYONE ELSE INQUIRED INTO THIS APPOINTED PRESIDENT, AND ONE OF THE WORST PRESIDENT OF THE UNITED STATES' HISTORY. PUSHING WAR IN THE NAME OF DEMOCRACY IS NOT UNDERSTANDING BY ME AND THE PEOPLE OF THE WORLD, WHO IS NOT PART OF ANY GOVERNMENT. IN BAHRAIN, ONE OF THE LAST STOP OF HIS MIDDLE EASTERN TRIP OF PROGANDA OF PEACE AND DEMOCRACY IS VERY HIPOCRITICAL AND HAS PUT AN IMAGE OF AMERICA THAT IS NOT HEALTHY FOR THE WORLD. THE EUOPEANS IN BRITIAN AND OTHERS SAID THEY HOPE AMERICA ELECT A DEMOCRAT, INSTEAD OF AN EXTENTION OF THE PRESENT PRESIDENT BUSH'S WAR MENTALITY. JOHN MC CAIN STILL ON THE WAR BEAT IN THE NAME OF WINNING SOMETHING THAT WAS WON WITH THE OVERTHROW OF SADDAM AND DESTROYED THE PALACES, MASIONS, AND ALL OF THE PROSPERITY OF THE PEOPLE OF IRAQ, AND NOW WANT TO TAKE OUR TAX DOLLARS TO REBUILD, WHEN THE MILITARY HAS TESTED ALL OF THERE NEW WEAPONS ON THE DARK NATION OF IRAQ. PRESIDENTIAL CANDIDATE MIT ROMNEY, SAID THIS MORNING, TRYING TO COUNTER SENATOR JOHN MC CAIN'S SURGE TACTICS, THAT THIS PRESIDENT HAS KEPT US SAFE AND THE CONSERVATIVES IS TRYING TO JUSTIFY THE WAR IN IRAQ AS KEEPING US SAFE, WHEN ACTUALLY THERE WAS A SPECTACULAR ATTACK AND THERE ARE NOT TOO MANY MORE ATTACKS THAT COULD TOP THAT, AND THAT 9/11 ATTACK WAS AN EXCEPTION AND THEY WANT US TO GIVE UP OUR PRIVACY, LIBERTIES, AND RIGHT TO NOT BE PROFILE IS ANOTHER TRICK OF THE RIGHT WINGERS. FROMER PRESIDENT CLINTON SAID IT BEST, WHEN

HE SAID IN A VIRGINIA SPEECH LAST YEAR, THAT THE RIGHT WINGERS WANT US TO THINK THAT A TERRORIST IS BEHIND EVERY STREET CORNER, AND THAT IS A FEAR TACTIC THAT IS INTENTED TO KEEP THE SO-CALL PATRIOT ACT, WHICH WILL NOT LAST, IT CANNOT LAST. IT HAS TO END FOR THE LIFE, LIBERTY, AND JUSTICE FOR ALL AMERICANS. IF THEY TRY AN ELIMINATE POVERTY LIKE THEY KEEP THE WAR MACHINE GOING THEN WE WILL BE A GREAT COUNTRY. THEY DO NOT WANT A BLACK IMAGE IN AMERICA, AND AS IN SLAVERY THEY HAVE ALWAYS KILLED THE HEAD LIKE A SNAKE, AND THEN THE OTHER BLACK PEOPLE WILL SEE, AND THE BODY JUST DIE OFF, BUT THIS IS A HUMAN AND IT DOES NOT DIE OFF JUST LIKE THAT. KNOWING "TRICKY DICK" CHENEY'S INTELLECT AND SCHEMING GANGSTER THAT HE IS, THAT BABY GEORGE HAD TO GO TO SEE WHAT HALIBURTON HAS DONE THERE AND THE WAR OF IRAQ IS AND IS GOING TO CONTINUE TO BENEFIT THE BUSHES, CHENEY, BAKERS, AND A LOT OF TOP CONSERVATIVE SENA-TORS AND CONGRESSMEN WHEN THEY RETIRE. THE PRESI-DENT AND VICE IS BENIFITING FROM THE WAR AND THEY NEED TO BE KNOW AS THE MISLEADINGEST ADMINISTRA-TION EVER. HALIBURTON I SHOULD HAVE BROUGH ME SOME STOCKS. THE SPEECH THIS MORNING IN BAHRAIN WAS ABOUT IRAN AND THEIR SUPPORT FOR DIFFERENT GOVERN-MENT GROUPS OF PALESTINANS, WHO IS DEFENDING THEIR TRUE HOME LAND, AND BUSH IS SUPPOSING TO DEFENDING OUR HOMELAND, AFTER TAKING IT FROM THE INDIANS, AND IT DOES NOT MAKE SENSE, WHEN WE ARE SUPPORTING ISREAL. PROBABLY IF WE DO NOT SUPPORT ISREAL, THEN MAYBE IRAN WILL NOT SUPPORT THE PALESTINANS. I DO NOT THINK THAT IT WILL HAPPEN; THEREFORE, I CANNOT SEE PEACE WITH THOSE ANGRY WHITE YOUNG ISREALIS WHO LOVE THEIR JERUESALEM APARTMENTS ON PALESTI-NANS HOME LAND. WITH THE NEW MOVIE "NATIONAL

TREASURY BOOK OF SECRETS", IT IS CLEAR AFTER ALL OF THESE YEARS THAT THE QUEEN OF ENGLAND WAS ON THE SIDE OF THE CONFERATE AND , WITH THE HELP OF THE ESCAPE SLAVES TO FIGHT FOR THE NORTHERN UNITED STATES AND ABRAHAM LINCOLN AS PRESIDENT ACCEPTED THE NEEDED HELP, AND WON WITH SHERMAN BURNING DOWN OF ATLANTA, AFTER DEFEATING GENERAL ROBERT E. LEE, IN RICHMOND, VIRGINIA, IT WAS CLEAR THAT PRESIDENT LINCOLN HAD TO DIE FOR UNITED THE UNITED STATES AS ONE NATION UNDER GOD. THE SAME HAPPEN WITH PRESIDENT CARTER AND ANDREW YOUNG, PRESIDENT CLINTOALL OF HIS AFRICAN- AMERICAN INTELLECTUALS IN AND OUT OF HIS CABINET IS WHY THE RIGHT WING CONSERVATIVES (CONFEDERATS) WANT AND GOT A SPECIAL PROSECUTOR FOR LYING ABOUT A SEX ACT IN THE OVAL OFFICE, AS WELL AS MANY, IF NOT ALL OF THE PRESIDENTS HAS DONE, AND NOT WANT TO DO ANYTHING BUT LOCK THE DEMOCRATS OUT OF THE HALLS OF CONGRESS ROOM IS PROOF THAT WE HAVE CAME A LONG WAY, BUT NOTHING HAS CHANGE WHEN IT COMES DOWN TO PROTECTING THE CONFEDERATE, AS SENATOR JOHN WARNER AND SENATOR TRENT LOTT HAS DONE FOR SO MANY DECADES, AND NOW THEY AND OTHER HAS RESIGNED OR DIE WITH THE SECRETS OUT IN THE OPEN FOR EVERY ONE TO SEE. WAR CRIME TRIALS IS NOT OUT OF THE QUESTION WITH ALL OF THE TRUTH ABOUT THE INVASION OF IRAQ IS OUT AND NO APOLOGIES SHOULD BE DONE WITH THEM AND HALIBURTON RICHES AND NOT ONE DIME FOR THE AMERICAN PEOPLE. THE ECONOMY IS WORST THAN ANY TIME AS WITH THE DEPRESSION WHEN THEY WERE JUMPING OFF OF BUILDINGS. PRESIDENT BUSH SPEECH TODAY IN BAHARAIN ABOUT THE STATUE OF LIBERTY HISTORY TO A PART OF THE WORLD THAT HE HAS CAUSED MORE CHAOS AND HATE TOWARDS MY COUNTRY AND IT'S WHITE MAJORITY, WE NEED A BARACK

OBAMA AND HILLARY CLINTON, BUT OBAMA WILL PLEASE
THE WORLD TO BE HONEST AND BE A JOY BETTER THAN
WITH THE NINETEEN SIXTY PRESIDENT JOHN F. KENNEDY,
BECAUSE THE WHOLE WORLD LIKES OBAMA, AND WITH ALL
OF THE SECRETS OF THE PRESIDENTS ARE OUT IN MOVIES
AND ALL HE WOULD BE THE FIRST TO BE BLACK AND PRESI-
DENT OF THE UNITED STATES. IF FOR SOME REASON HILLARY
WINS THE NOMINATION, THEN IT WOULD SERVE THE
COUNTRY WELL TO HAVE OBAMA AS VICE PRESIDENT; BUT
WITH THE FEEL OF THE COUNTRY AND KERRY'S ENDOR-
MENT OF OBAMA THERE IS A CHANCE FOR A NEW START
FOR AMERICA. OBAMA AND KERRY WOULD BE AN EXCEL-
LENT TICKET TO GET THIS COUNTRY BACK CLOSE TO WHAT
IT WAS WHEN PRESIDENT CLINTON LEFT OFFICE. SENATOR
JOHN F KENNEDY CHOSE JOHNSON, REAGAN CHOSE GHW
BUSH, CLINTON CHOOSE GORE, AND ALL OF THEM WAS
GREAT PRESIDENTS. GENERAL EISENHOWER CHOOSE NIXON,
SO OBAMA DO NOT NEED TO HAVE BEEN NOTHING BUT
LOVE BY THE PEOPLE, AND I BELIEVE SINCE HE IS A HARVARD
GRADUATE, HE CAN MEND FENCES WITH WHAT IS LEFT OUT
OF THE OLD CONFEDERATE HATCH AND COMPANY TO
MAKE A GREAT UNITED STATES SUPREME COURT THAT IS
FOR THE PEOPLE AND NOT FOR THE STATUS QUO AS THE
CONSERVATIVE CONFEDERATS HAS BEEN ATTEMPING EVERY
SINCE PRESIDENT REAGAN CONTINUATION OF THE TRICKY
DICK NIXON ADMINISTRATION, WHO PULLED THE 2000 ELEC-
TION. THE VOTES OF CONFIDENCE WAS WHAT HILLARY SAID
ON NBC'S "MEET THE PRESS", AS THE REPUBLICANS HAD
BOTH HOUSES AND THE WHITE AND THEY SOLD THE
COUNTRY DOWN THE DRAIN, AND HELP FOOL THOSE DEMO-
CRATS TO VOTE AND TRIED TO TRUST THAT THE BUSH
ADMINISTRATION, WHICH PROOF THEY COULD NOT BE
TRUSTED AFTER THE WORLD TRADE CENTER DIASTER. THEY
USED OUR MILITARY ON FALSE PRETENSE, THEN SAID THE

IRAQ PEOPLE IS BETTER OFF WITH OUT SADDAM, WHEN IN REALITY WE CAUSE PAIN AND SUFFERING AND DISPAIR BEYOND REPAIR, NO MATTER HOW MUCH MORE BILLIONS ALMOST TRILLIONS OF AMERICAN DOLLARS THERE AND EUROPE. THE FALL OF THE DOLLAR IS FROM THE BUSH ADMINISTRATION AND THE AFRICAN AMERICAS HAS MORE SUFFERING TO DO AS THEY INTENTED TO DO. THE FEW WHITES THAT WILL SUFFER IS JUST TOO BAD, BUT THAT MAKES IT LOOK LIKE IT IS ACROSS THE BOARD. THEY HAVE SCARE WOMEN NOT TO TRUST NO BLACK ASS AND FOR THE WHITE WOMEN TO FALL IN LOVE WITH ANOTHER WOMAN, HOMOSEXUAL, OR TO GET A DOG TO MAKE LOVE TO INSTEAD OF A BLACK MAN IF YOU CANNOT FIND A SUITABLE WHITE MAN. GINGRICH, DICK CHENEY, AND MANY MORE SCARE THEIR CHILDREN INTO THE HOMO WORLD, EVEN THOUGHT, CHENEY'S DAUGHTER HAS HAD A BABY BY MOST LIKELY A HOMO, AND THAT IS THE AMERICAN WAY. 01-14-08   AS WE PREPARE TO GO TO PRESS THE CHARLOTT BOBCATS BASKETBALL OWNER, AND FROMER FOUNDER CAMPAIGNING FOR HILLARY CLINTON, GIVING THE WELL DESERVE PROPS TO HER AND HER HUSBAND, FROMER PRESIDENT CLINTON AND THEIR DEEPLY INVOLVEMENT IN IMPORTANT ISSUES OF THE BLACK COMMUNITIES, WHEN BARACK WAS LIKE SO MANY AMERICAN, INCLUDING, THE PRESENT PRESIDENT BUSH, CLINTON, GORE, FORDS, AND YOU CAN GO DOWN THE LINE THAT THERE HAS BEEN SOME TYPE OF DRUG EXPERIMENT OF SOME KIND, WHETHER OVER THE COUNTER OR NOT, ONE IS LEGAL AND THE OTHERS ARE NOT, BUT THEY ARE DRUGS. IF YOU COULD NOT HOLD IT AGAINST ANY OF THE ABOVE MENTION THERE IS NO WAY THAT ONE CAN HOLD A TEENAGER'S EXPERIMENTS AGAIST THEM AS THEY ARE RUNNING FOR THE HIGHEST OFFICE OF THE LAND. BARACK IS FREE AND CLEAR ABOUT HIS LIFE AND THE PEOPLE OF ILLINOIS, IOWA, AND THE REST OF THE UNITED

STATES ARE READY TO GIVE A SITTING FRESHMAN SENATOR OBAMA A CHANCE. SOME WOULD WANT TO KILL HIM AS THE MILIATARY KILLED CLINTON'S COMMERCE SECRETARY AFTER HIS DANCING IN AFRICA TRIP TO BRING COMMERCE COMMUNTIES OF AFRICA AND AMERICA TOGETHER AS IS IN CHINA, KOREA, AND OTHER SO –CALL THIRD WORLD COUNTRIES. THERE IS A SURGE OF TROOPS TO BE DEPLOYED TO AGANISTAN TO COVER THE OFFENSE OF THE TALIBAN, WHO MOST DEMOCRATS GAVE THE BUSH ADMINISTRATION THE GO AHEAD TO ATTACK AND FREE THAT NATION OF THE SO-CALL REBELS, BUT INSTEAD HE WANTED TO GET SADDAM FOR A FAIL HIT ON HIS FATHER, AFTER HIS FATHER TRICKED SADDAM INTO KUWAIT INVASION, THEN WE HAD TO COME TO KUWAIT DEFENSE, IN WHAT IS KNOWN AS THE GULF WAR AND WE HAVE BEEN IN IRAQ EVERY SINCE. PRESIDENT BUSH IS IN THE KINGDOM OF SAUDI ARABIA WITH THE GREAT KING ABDULLA AND IS SUPPOSE TO END IN EGYPT. THERE ARE WEAPONS DEALS AT MOSTLY EVERY STOP. BUSH IS AT THE END OF HIS PRESIDENCY AND HE IS CONSTANTLY BEATING THE WAR DRUM OF IRAN CONFLICT, WHEN IRAN IS GIVING THE UNITED NATION ALL THAT IS NEEDED TO ADD ON TO OUR CIA REPORT THAT IRAN WAS NOT PURSUING A NUCLEAR BOMB. PAKISTAN, INDIA, AND POSSIBLY CHINA HAS ONE AND WHY NOT AFTER WHAT WE DID TO JAPAN. WITH THE CATHOLIC CHURCH ALWAYS CHOOSING SOME EASTERN EUROPEAN NAZI AS POPE, HOW COULD THE AMER-ICAN GOVERNMENT CONTINUE TO HONOR ALL THAT IS DONE THERE, AND IS PACIFING THE JEWS, WHO THE CATHO-LICS SPEAD THE LIE ABOUT JESUS. THE GOVERNMENT LIE TO THE WORLD OF THE MOON WALK AND THAN IS THE AMER-ICAN WAY TO KEEP THEIR SUPERIOR WHITE HUMAN IMAGE TO THE WORLD. THEY HID NAZI SOLIDERS HERE FROM THE JEWS, AND THEY ARE PROTECTING ISREAL BECAUSE THEY ARE ROMAN DESCENDANT, WHO IS DISTORTING THE WORDS

OF THE ORIGINAL HEBREWS, WHO WERE ALL BLACK. ISREAL IS NORTH AFRICA AND SO IS EGYPT, SO THEY WERE UNDER THE ROMAN SLAVE SYSTEM, UNTIL AND A LITTLE AFTER THE ROMANS CRUCIFIES THE HOLY MESSIAH JESUS CHRIST OF NAZARRETH. POPE BENIDICT IS ON HIS WAY TO AMERICA TO SPREAD THE HATE OF SEPARATION OF THE HUMANS; AND, ONE LIGHT WHO IS SUPPOSES TO BE SUPERIOR, BECAUSE OF THEIR HOLD ON THE MILITARY, BANKS, AND THE PEOPLE. WITH THIS ELECTION IS GOING TO BE MEAN, BUT THE CITIZENS OF THE UNITED STATES ARE WAKING UP AND VOTING FOR THE BEST CANDIDATE THAT WILL UNITED ALL OF THE PEOPLE, AND NOT JUST THE CONSERVATIVE CONFEDERATES OF THE UNITED STATES. WHATEVER A ACRE AND A MULE WAS WORTH FOR EVERY SLAVE, THAT MOST BECAME SHARE CROPPERS TO EARN A PLACE TO REST THEIR HEADS AND FAMILY, BECAUSE OF AGE AND THE SLAVE SYSTEM THAT HAD THEM LOSE EVERYTHING FROM THEIR ANCESTORS. THE CARRIBEAN NATIONS HAS CARRIED ON THE AFRICAN MUSIC FROM AFRICAN MUSIC PIECES. CUBA, JAMACA, AND OTHERS CARRY ON THERE AFRICAN HERTIAGE, AS WE WERE HELD IN BONDAGE FOR CENTURIES LONGER THAN MOST OF THE ISLANDS. WE AFRICAN-AMERICANS AND THE AFRICANS HAS TO CEASE BLACK ON BLACK CRIME IN AMERICA, AND THAT CAN BE SLOWED IF THE DESCENDANTS OF THE UNITED STATES SLAVE MASTERS CORPORATIONS AND THE GOVERNMENT OF THE UNITED STATES SLAVE SYSTEM, AND DISPERSE CHECKS TO THE DESCENDANTS OF SLAVES. THE CONSERVATIVE CONFEDERATES ALWAYS WANTS TO KEEP THE WAR MACHINE GREASED WITH LARGE CHECKS TO DEFENSE CONTRACTORS, IT KEEP JOBS FOR SOME AND COST OVER RUNS IS A REGULAR, AND WE HAVE TO KEEP THE BEST MILITARY, BUT THAT AND ALL OF THE NATION BUILDING, THERE HAS TO BE INCLUDED INTO THE BUDGETS MORE FOR THE VETERANS OF COMBAT AND THE DESCENDANTS OF

SLAVES COST OF LIVING EXPENSES. OBAMA WAS MENTIONING SOMETHING ABOUT SOME TYPE OF TAX CREDIT OF TWO HUNDRED AND FIFTY DOLLARS TO HELP THE POOR PEOPLE WHO HAS LOST THEIR JOBS AND IS CLOSE TO LOSING THEIR HOUSE OR HAVE LOST THEIR HOMES, WHILE THE FARM LANDS ARE TURNING INTO SUBURBS FOR THE WELL TO DO AND THE SO-CALL MIDDLE CLASS. ONLY AFRICAN-AMER-ICAN THERE ARE THE LOST BALL PLAYERS, WHO IS WORRIED ABOUT THERE GENTIALS BEING MASSAGED, AND IS NOT FIGHTING THE POLITICANS TO HELP THERE OLD NEIGBOR-HOODS, ELIMINATE PROVERTY IN THE UNITED STATES. THE UNITED STATES HAS TO HAVE THOSE COMPUTER UNIFORM VOTING MACHINES IN EVERY VOTING PRECINT IN AMERICA, THAT PRINTS OUT THE VOTER'S VOTE AS PROOF OF THE VOTE. WE AS A NATION SHOULD NEVER HAVE ANOTHER FLORIDA PRESIDENTIAL ELECTION OF THE UNITED STATES COURTS IS TO APPOINT A PRESIDENT; THEREFORE, THEY SHOULD HAVE HAD A REVOTE AT THE VERY LEASE. GORE AND THE DEMOCRATIC BRAINS WAS THROWN COMPLETELY OF THE TRICKERY OF THE CONSERVATIVE CONFEDERATES OF THE UNITED STATES. THEY ARE DEFINITELY AT IT AGAIN IN 2008 PRESIDENTIAL ELECTION AND THIS TIME THEY WILL NOT DISINFRANCHISE VOTERS. THERE ARE POOR PEOPLE IN MISSISSIPPI, ALABAMA, LOUISIANA, TEXAS, VIRGINIA, AND A FEW MORE WHO ARE LIVING IN SHANTY TOWNS, JUST WE WERE RAISING HELL FOR THOSE IN SOUTH AFRICA'S SHANTY TOWNS, WITH NO PLUMING, RUNNING WATER, AND NO TRANSPORTATION TO A VOTING BOOTH. THESE ARE SOME OF THE PEOPLE THAT INSPIRE ME TO FIGHT FOR, AND IF OBAMA OR CLINTON WINS THE PRESIDENCY, I HOPE AND PRAY THAT THEY ADDRESS THESE PEOPLE AND LIFT THEM UP AFTER THERE ANCESTORS WERE BROUGHT HERE AND SCRIPTED OF THERE DIGINITY AND HERITAGE. THESE ARE THE PEOPLE OF THE UNITED STATES, AND WITH THESE

EXISTING CONDITIONS, THE UNITED STATES ARE IN THE
WORLD'S HUMAN RIGHTS VIOLATION AND IT NEEDS TO BE
ADDRESS IN THE UNITED NATIONS AND THE HALLS OF
CONGRESS. GIVE ME LIBERTY OR GIVE ME DEATH AND WE
CANNOT STILL STAND BY THE STATUE OF LIBERTY WITH MY
PEOPLE LIVING IN THESE CONDITIONS IN 2008. DOG EAT DOG
WORLD, BUT ALL OF THE CIVIL RIGHTS GROUPS NEEDS TO
KEEP THIS ON THE FRONT BURNER IN EVERY STATE HOUSE,
AND THE CONGRESS OF THE UNITED STATES CONGRES-
SIONAL SECTION. IT SHOULD BE IN EVERY NEWS MEDIA, I
KNOW MURDOCKS AND FRIENDS WILL CONTINUE TO TRY
AND KEEP THIS ON THE BACK BURNER OF THEIR NEWSPA-
PERS AND NEWS TELEVISION SHOWS. WE DEFINITELY
CANNOT HAVE A BARRY GOLDWATER CLONE FROM ARIZONA
BECOME PRESIDENT FOLLOWING HIS KLANSMEN OF THE
BUSH CHENEY ADMINISTRATION. I AM VERY INCLINE TO SEE
THAT THE EUROPEANS RECOGNIZES AND ARE SPEAKING TO
THE AMERICAN PEOPLE. IT WOULD BE A DIASTER TO THE
WHOLE WORLD. TRICKERY IS THE WAY OF AMERICANS TO
PAY TAXES AND THE REPUBLICANS TAX THE PEOPLE IN
MANY WAYS, AS THEY TRY TO FOOL THE PEOPLE NOT,
BECAUSE OF THE INCOME TAX, BUT WITHOUT SOME REASON-
ABLE TAX THE NEEDS OF OUR SOCIETY WILL CRUMBLE MORE,
AS THE POLITICIANS ARE GETTING THERE STATES MONIES
THAT USUALLY NEVER GET TO HELP THE POOR AND THE
JUST ABOVE POOR PEOPLE OF THE UNITED STATES. WE HAVE
TO HAVE A NEW PRESIDENT THAT WE CAN TRUST TO DO
THIS AND AS WE GO TO PRESS, AND ALL OF THE DEBATING
ABOUT DOCTOR M.L. KING, JR., BETWEEN OBAMA AND
CLINTON, I AM GOING TO ENDORE BARACK OBAMA FOR A
COMPLETE CHANGE, AND AMERICANS OF ALL RACES AND
NATIONALITY CITIZENS HAVE TO VOTE HIM. WE CANNOT
AFFORD TO ELECT ANOTHER CONSERVATIVE CONFEDERATE
TO THE WHITE MAN'S HOUSE. A CHANGE THAT I THINK

THAT CAN LAST, FOR THE GOOD OF THE NEW UNITED STATES WITH NO WALLS AND FENCES, AND PEACE IN THE WORLD HOT SPOTS, I BELIEVE OBAMA"WE CAN' DO IT WITH A VICE PRESIDENT SENATOR JOHN KERRY. I LIKE THE KERRIES EVEN MORE SINCE HE AND HIS WIFE'S ENDORMENT OF OBAMA. WITH BUSH IS IN THE END MIDDLE EAST SO-CALL PEACE AND WAR TRIP AND MORE BOMBS ARE BEING EXPLODED AS HE ENDS HIS TRIP. PREACHING PEACE AND DEMOCRACY IN ISREAL AND PALESTINE, THEN LEAVE AND CONTINUE TO BEAT THE WAR DRUMS FOR IRAN. WE USE SADDAM TO GO TO WAR WITH IRAN, AND THE IRANIANS WON. WE CANNOT GET OVER THE OVERTHROW OF THE SHAW OF IRAN, BACK IN 1977. WE NEED TO GET OVER IT AND TRY TO GET ALONG WITH PEOPLE INSTEAD OF TRYING TO PUSH THESE BRITISH AND AMERICAN TYPES OF SOCIETIES ON AFRICAN NATIONS WHERE THE RULES OF DEMOCRACY STARTED THOUSANDS OF YEARS AGO. WHEN WE DO THAT THEN WE MIGHT BE ABLE TO GET SOME RESPECT IN THE AFRICAN AND MIDDLE EASTERN NATIONS. HOPE ALL WILL ENJOY AND HELP MAKE THIS A BETTER WORLD WITH THE KNOWLEDGE OF HISTORY THAT CAN BE RECTIFIED AND IMPROVED. ELECT BARACK OBAMA AND THE DEMOCRATS, REPUBLICANS, AND THE INDEPENDANTS CAN MAKE US HAVE A TEAM OF OBAMA AND KERRY. KERRY IS ONE VIETNAM VETERAN WHO DROPPED MY COMPANY OFF IN THE MUDDY CANALS IN SOUTH VIETNAM AND CAMBODIA ON RECON MISSIONS. GETTING OFF THOSE LITTLE BOATS IN MUD UP TO MY KNEES WAS NO FUN. HE IS NOT LIKE THE JOHN MC CAIN AND HIS RACIST VIEWS, EVEN THOUGH, HIS WIFE MADE HIM ACCEPT AN ADOPTION OF A BLACK TAIWANESE, AND SHE HAS TO THINK WHITE, EVEN THOUGH, HER COMPEXION IS VERY DARK. May 27, 2008SINCE THERE WAS A PUBLISHER'S MISTAKE AND THE PRIMARIES ARE OVER NINETY- PERCENT DONE, WITH SENATOR BARACK OBAMA NEEDING APPROXMINGLY

SEVENTY VOTES FOR THE NOMINATION OF THE DEMOC-
RACTIC PARTY, AND FROMER PRESIDENT WILLIAM JEFFERSON
CLINTON'S SOUTHERN RACIST BACKGROUND HAS HIS WIFE
AND HE NOT TO RESPECT THE ORIGNAL RULES OF THE
DEMOCRATIC PARTY, THAT SHOULD NOT HAVE HAPPEN,
AND THE REBEL STATES OF FLORIDA AND MICHGAN, SHOULD
HAVE ABIDED BY THOSE RULES. I AM ONE TO BELIEVE IN
EVERY VOTE COUNT AND CLINTON, AND ALL OF THE OTHER
DEMOCRATIC CANADATES WHOM WERE IN THE RACE FOR
UNITED STATES PRESIDENT, SHOULD HAVE MADE SOME TYPE
OF DEAL WITH THOSE TWO REBELOUS STATES IN A MUCH
TOO IMPORTANT TIME IN UNITED STATES HISTORY, WHEN
TWO OIL MEN AND THEIR FAMILIES, ALONG WITH ALL OF
UNITED STATES RIGHTWING SENATORS AND HOUSE OF
REPRESENTATIVES SOLD OUT THE UNITED STATES, JUST TO
WIDEN THE GAP OF THE RICH AND POOR. THE CONSPIRACY
TO DENY THE DECENDANTS OF THE UNITED STATES SLAVE
SYSTEM WAS THE MAIN OBJECTION AS IT HAS BEEN DURING
AND SINCE THE EMANCIPATION PROCAMATION, THAT
SPUNG A NEW SOUTHERN UNITED STATES LAW INTO AFFECT,
CALL "THE SEPARATE BUT EQUAL LAW." THIS LAW EVENU-
ALLY WAS CALL SOME SOUTHERN "JIM CROW LAWS", WHICH
I WAS BORN UNDER AND HEARD MANY STORIES OF HANG-
INGS IN DOWNTOWN ATLANTA, GEORGIA, WHERE MY
GRANDFATHER WAS A FAMILY MAN THAT I GREW-UP UNDER,
MORE SO THAN MY BIOLOGICAL FATHER. BOTH WERE GOOD
MEN, EVEN THOUGH, MY FATHER WAS NOT A BUSINESS
MAN, BUT HE TRIED TO DO THE BEST A DESCENDANT OF
SLAVE CHILD COULD BEING RAISED DURING THE 1920'S ON
UP UNTIL HE DIE IN DECEMBER 1998. MY GRANDFATHER HAD
THE MOST AFFECT ON MY LIFE AND HE LIVE TO SEE ME
RETURN FROM VIETNAM IN ONE PIECE PSYCIALLY, BUT
MENTALLY NEVER WILL BE THE SAME AS I WAS WHEN I
ENTER THE ARMY. THE WAR IN IRAQ IS STILL GOING ON AND

THERE HAVE BEEN SOME TYPE OF SO-CALL SURGE INCREASE OF AMERICA'S CHILDREN IN A SELFISH VENDETTA WAR FOR GREED AND AS PRESIDENT GEORGE W. BUSH SAID, SADDAM HAD TRIED TO KILL MY FATHER, AND AMERICA YOU SHOULD GO ALONG WITH ME TO GET THIS PRESIDENT OF IRAQ, WHO WAS NOT IN ANY WAY A THREAT TO THE AMERICAN PEOPLE OR ISREAL. THE TRICKY DICK BUSH ADMINISTRATION IS BLAMING FLAWED INTELLENCE, WHEN THEY AND THE COUNTRY KNEW THAT THE UNITED NATION WERE IN EVERY PART OF IRAQ AND KNEW IRAQ BETTER THAN ANY AMER-ICAN MILITARY OFFICIAL, BUT THE FORMER TRICKY DICK NIXON AND ADMIRAL OF ADOLF HITLER, RICHARD "TRICKY DICK" CHENEY UNDER THE NIXON ADMINISTRATION AND THE REAGAN ADMINISTRATION CLONE, JUST THE FROMER PRESIDENT GEORGE HERBERT WALKER BUSH, THE CURRENT PRESIDENT FATHER, WHO ORGISTRATED THE OVERTHROW OF THE 2000 PRESIDENTIAL ELECTION, AND NOW THEY ARE NOT SAYING TOO MUCH ABOUT PUTIN'S NEW POST AFTER SOME TYPE OF ELECTION IN RUSSIA. THEY DID EXACTLY WHAT WAS DONE HERE, TO KEEP REPARATION OUT OF THE SPOT LIGHT, GAIN ACCESS TO SADDAM'S PALACES, AS THESE RACISTS DO NOT LIKE ANY BLACK MAN ON EARTH TO HAVE MORE THAT THEY DO SINCE THEY CAME OUT OF WESTERN ASIA SURVIVE ON EAT ING BLACK BABIES AND DOGS, NOW THEY CALL THEMSELVES ARISTICRACTS OF EUROPE. MY GOD HOW MAN HAS SURVIVED ON EARTH USING EACH OTHER IN SUCH TERRIBLE MEANS. DIVIDE AND CONQUER IS STILL THE WAY AFTER ALL OF THE GREEK AND ROMAN HISTORY THAT HAS BEEN DISTORTED AND IMAGES DESTROYED AND COVERED-UP FOR THE SUPERIOR HUMAN BEING, WHO IS OUT IN THE UNIVERSE LOOKING FOR THE CREATORS WHO HAS ALWAYS BEEN FLYING AROUND, BUT THE WHITE MAN AND IT'S SO-CALL FREE MEDIA COVER THIS UP EVERYDAY, BUT TODAY THERE ARE TOO MANY SIGHTING OF THE SHIPS

THAT THEY TRAVEL AROUND IN. THE UNITED STATES GOVERNMENT AND IT'S END OF THE EARTH PEOPLE, WHO SOME ARE COMING AROUND, BECAUSE OF TECHNOLOGY. I AM A GOD FEARING MAN, AND TO SEE PEOPLE VOTING FOR A BLACK AMERICAN, WHO ALSO A DESCENDANT OF AN AFRICAN, AND NOT LIKE MOST OF MY PEOPLE WHO CAME THROUGH THE SLAVE SYSTEM OF YESTERDAY AND IS LIVING THROUGH THE MODERN DAY SLAVERY OF MOSTLY AFRICAN DESCENDANTS OF ALL TYPES OF COMPLEXIONS AND LANU-AGES FIGHTING EACH OTHER OVER SURVIVAL TO HAVE THE RICHES OF THE EARTH, AND THE SO-CALL STATUS QUO, WHO IS DESPERATELY COMMITING GENOCIDE AROUND ALL OF THE DARK NATIONS OF GOD'S EARTH. THE HUMAN, MONKEY, AND GORRILLAS WERE THE LAST OF GOD'S MASTER PLAN. IT IS ALL IN THE GENES AND THE HUMANS WERE MADE TO BE SUPERIOR BEINGS OF EARTH. THEY ARE STILL PREACHING ABOUT THE BLACK CAT AND HOW IT IS NOT TO BE TRUSTED, WHEN THE BLACK CAT WAS THE ORIGNAL, AS IS THE HUMAN BEING WHEN THE WHOLE EARTH WAS DARK LIKE IT IS IN THE UNIVERSE TODAY. GOD SAID LET THERE BE LIGHT AND WE HAVE LIGHT TO SEE FURTHER AND TO SEE WHAT EACH OTHER'S COMPLEXION, AND WE ARE CONTIN-UINGLY ABUSING EACH OTHER. IF WE DID NOT HAVE LIGHT THERE WOULD MOST LIKELY BE LOVE, BUT WE HAVE LIGHT AND THE STRONGEST SURVIVE. AFTER THE AMERICAN ECONOMY HAS FAILED SO RAPIDLY UNDER THE RIGHTWING CONSPIRACY, AS IT STILL COVERING UP THEIR DECEIT TO THE AMERICAN PEOPLE, THAT FROMER CONGRESSMAN NEWT GINGRICH, WHO FOOLED PRESIDENT CLINTON ON ALL ISSUES IN FRONT OF A CAMERA, TODAY ON THE NEWS MORNING WANTS TO BLAME THIS CONGRESS OF NOT DURING ENOUGH TO HELP LESSER THAN THE WELL TO DO, TO BUY GAS, PAY THEIR MORTGAGE, FEED THE CHILDREN, OTHER RESPONSIBILIES TO TRAVEL AS WE HAVE BECOME

ACCUSTOM TO, BUT HE WOULD NOT DARE MENTION THE BUSH ADMINISTRTION'S SOUTHERN THOUGHTFULNESS AND OIL MEN WHO SHOULD BE BROUGHT UP ON WAR CRIMES AND TREASONABLE ACT OF THE AMERICAN PEOPLE'S TREASURY AND SOCIAL ACTS THAT WE AS A PEOPLE DESERVE. THE DESCENDANT OF THE UNITED STATES SLAVE SYSTEM SHOULD BE PROUD TO RAISE HOUSE, FEED, AND EDUCATE EVERY DESCENDANT OF SLAVE CHILDRE FROM TODAY UNTIL ETERNITY, BUT THE COLOR OF ONES COMPLEXION IS THE PROBLEM. THE ARE THREATING SENATOR BARACK OBAMA AND HIS FAMILY, JUST AS THEY DID THE REVERN DOCTOR MARTIN LUTHER KING JUNIOR, AS THEY ARE GOING TO BUILD A TRIBUTE TO HIM AROUND THE WASHINGTON MALL, WHERE ALL OF THE SLAVE ONCE LIVED AND NOW WE POSSIBLLY COULD HAVE A YOUNG BLACK AMERICAN WHO HAS NO BAD BAGGAGE, AND IS THE ONLY ONE WHO CAN CLEAN UP A LOT OF THIS MESS THAT THE BUSH-CHENEY ADMINISTRATION HAS GOTTEN OUR BELOVE UNITED STATES IN TROUBLE, AFTER THE CLINTON YEARS OF RELAXATION AND RESPECT HAD RETURN, BUT TODAY HE HIS HOT FUMING RED NECK UPSET ABOUT A BLACK MAN GETTING VOTES OUT OF MIDDLE AMERICA WHITE PEOPLE AND ALL TYPES OF YOUNG AMERICANS WHO SEE THE LIGHT AND KNOWS THEIR HISTORY AS IT UNFOLDS WITH SATTELITE TELEVISION. NOW WE AS NATION HAVE TO WATCH OUT THAT OUR BELOVE MILITARY DOES NOT TURN INTO THE FOURTY REICH, AFTER HITLER'S GENERALS WERE PERMITTED TO ENTER THE AMERICAS, AND THOSE SO-CALL JEWS HAD BETTER WATCH OUT CAUSE HISTORY CAME REPEAT ITSELF WITH THEM AND THE AMERICAN DESCEN-DANTS OF UNITED SLAVERY, WHO EVERYONE IN AMERICA TRY TO USE THE PHASE THAT 'IT (SLAVERY) WAS IN THE PAST", AND AMERICA SHOULD NOT HONOR IT AS THE FORMER ROMANS WHO CARRY ON THE LIE OF WHO WAS

THE TRUE DESCENDANT OF ABRAHAM AND RUTH, AND THEY DO NOT LOOK LIKE ANYONE YOU SEE ON TELEVISION, BECAUSE IT IS STILL THE HIDDEN SECRET THAT IS SLOWLY COMING TO THE LIGHT. THEY ARE THE ONLY CACASIANS IN THE MIDDLE EAST AND THE PALESTIANS THEY HAVE TO CONTINUE TO TAKE THEIR LAND AS THEY HAVE DONE SINCE CIRA FOUR B.C. (BEFORE CHRIST). AS I TRY TO BRING A QUICK SYNOPSIS OF THE CURRENT EVENTS OF THE INJUSTICES IN AMERICAN AND HOPEFULLY SOME TYPE OF DIALOG TO CHANGE THE WORLD AS HUMANS, BUT THE RACISM CONTINUES WITH THE BLACK PEOPLE KILLING EACH OTHER IN AMERICA AND AFRICA, AND THE LAW ENFORCEMEN ARE KILLING BLACK AMERICAN AND GET AWAY WITH IT IN COURTS, UNDER FORMER PROSECUTOR JUSTICES, WHO HAS HAD THE LAW ENFORCEMENT TO LIE ON MANY DEFENDANTS, JUST FOR STATISTICAL REASON OF CONVICTION FOR POLITICS AND IT'S SOCIAL CIRCLES. THE SEAN BELL WAS KILLED ON HIS WEDDING DAY, WHEN HE AND HIS FRIENDS AND BLACK AMERICANS CAN NOT GO OUT AND HAVE FUN WITHOUT THE POLICE UNDERCOVER AND THEIR SPIES WANTING TO KNOW EVERYTHING THAT GOES ON IN THE PUBLIC AND PRIVATELY. WHEN THE SO-CALL FOUNDING FATHERS CREATED THE FOURTH AMENDMENT TO THE UNITED STATES CONSTITUTION, SLAVES DID NOT HAVE ANY PRIVACY, AND NOW TODAY THE SLAVE MASTER'S CHILDREN WHO ARE CARRING ON AND TRYING TO KEEP PRIVACY FOR THEMSELVES AND NOT THE DARK PEOPLE OF THIS NATION, THESE TYPE OF KILLINGS ARE CONTINUING. THE BLACK MAN IN NEW YORK HAD WORKED AND RAISED HIS FAMILY, THEN MOVED TO THE SUBURBS, JUST TO ACCIDENTLY KILLED THIS WHITE TEENAGER MOB GUY WHOM CAME TO THIS MAN'S HOUSE TO GET HIS TEENAGE SON, WHO HAD BEEN AT SOME PARTY THAT TURNED RACIST, MOST PROBABLY OVER SOME WHITE GIRL, AND THE GANG OF TEEN-AGER

SCARE MR.WHITE IN THE MIDDLE OF THE NIGHT, AS HIS GUN WENT OFF ON HIS PROPERTY AND UNFORTUNATELY KILL ONE OF THE RACIST TEEN AGER, WHO WAS MOST LIKELY RAISED IN A RACIST FAMILY HAD TO SUFFER. MR. WHITE WAS CONVICTE AND IS IN JAIL TODAY AND THE REVERN AL SHARPTON IS PREACHING ALL OF HIS INJUSTICES AND MARCHES AS MUCH AS POSSIBLE, BUT WE AMERICANS STILL HAS A LONG WAY TO GO. THE RIGHTWINGERS CAME UP WITH THE REVERN JEREMY WRIGHT, WHO IS/WAS HIS PASTOR IN CHICAGO, BUT HIS MINISTERY IS THE SAME AS THE REVERN DOCTOR MARTIN LUTHER KING, JUNIOR, BUT WANT TO TRY AND POISON THE ELECTORAL COLLEGE AND THE AMERICAN PEOPLE NOT TO VOTE SENATOR OBAMA, BUT TO VOTE FOR SENATOR, BUT THAT DID NOT WORK. I WILL ALWAYS RECOGNIZE MY AFRICAN- AMERICAN PEOPLE. I GREW UP ADMIRING AND EVENTUAL GOT TO ASSOCIATE WITH MUHAMMAD ALI, KING FAMILY, AND ALL OF MY FAMILY AND I ARE MINISTERS. MOST HAD ROOTS IN ATLANTA, GEORGIA AND I FEEL BLESSED TO KNOW WHO I AM, AND THE HISTORY OF THE HUMAN RACE, AND IS STILL FIGHTING FOR MY FREEDOM, AS I HAVE FOUGHT FOR THE AMERICAN DURNING THE VIETNAM WAR. YOU ARE NOT GOING TO TELL THE STATUS QUO IN AMERICA NOT TO ATTEND A KLAN RALLY ON SUNDAY MORNING, THEN I AM PROUD TO BE AND AMERICAN, AND I GROWN OLDER TO REALLY UNDERSTAND IT A LITTLE BETTER. THEY WANTED TO CALL MY PEOPLE COMMUNIST, MARTIST, AND ANYTHING THEY COULD TO DISCREDIT DUBOIS OR ANY OTHER INTEL- LECTUAL AFTER THE EMANCIPATION PROGAMATION, BEFORE THEN THEY WOULD FIND OUT A SLAVE COULD READ YOU WERE HUNG AT THE NEAREST TREE, SHOT, BURNED, OR CRUCIFIED ON A CROSS. THEY WANT TO CALL THE MINIS- TERS EMENY COMBATAN, WHEN WE ARE USING THE FREEDOM OF SPEECH. REVERN JEREMY WRIGHT, FARRA-

KHAN, REVERN AL SHARPTON, REVERN JESSE JACKSON, AND THE LIST GOES ON, AND FROMER BILL CLINTON TRYING TO LINK SENATOR OBAMA TO ALL OF US DESCENDANT OF SLAVES AND IT DID NOT WORK. GOD BLESS AMERICA AND SENATOR OBAMA, THIS COULD TRULY BECOME THE AMERICAN WAY. THEY ALWAYS WANT THE AFRICAN-AMERICANS NOT TO ASSOCIATE WITH EACH OTHER, JUST AS IT WAS DURING SLAVERY, WHEN THE SLAVE OWNERS KNEW THE ISLAND PEOPLE IN THE CARRIBEAN WERE REVOLTING AND THE WHITE PEOPLE LEFT AND WENT BACK TO EUROPE OR CAME TO THE UNITED STATES. WE COULD NOT TAKE A HOLLOW LOG AND MAKE A DRUM, BECAUSE THE SLAVE OWNERS KNEW THAT MESSAGES COULD BE SENT THROUGH MUSIC, BECAUSE THEY ARE STILL SCARE WHEN BLACK GET TOGETHER IN AMERICA, MIDDLE EAST, AFRICA, CHINA, AND OTHER DARK COMPLEXED HUMANS. THEY SAY ON THING AND DO ANOTHER, IN OTHER WORDS, TRICK YOU AND ANYBODY TO GATHER YOUR LAND, MONEY, GOLD, OIL, IVORY, AND ANY OTHER THINGS TO MAKE MONEY. THAT IS THE AMERICAN AND EUROPEAN WAY. THE EASTERN EUROPEANS CAME OVER WITH ALL OF THE LOVE OF THE REAGAN ADMINISTRATION, AND ALL OF THE FOLLOWING ADMINISTRTIONS OF THE UNITED STATES, THE LAND OF THE FREE AND RICH WELL TO DO COUNTRY WHO DOES NOT WANT TO TAKE CARE OF THE DESCENDANTS OF SLAVES. SENATOR HILLARY CLINTON KNEW HER NAME WAS WELL KNOWN AND IT DOES NOT MATTER WHETHER SHE RECEIVED THE MOST POPULAR VOTE WHEN THERE WAS NO CONTEST IN FLORIDA AND MICHGAN. CLINTONS GOING ALL OUT IN RURAL EASTERN STATES WITH THE RACIST ARMISH, NEO-NAZIS, KLU KLUX KLAN, AND OTHER CHILDREN OF THE CONFEDERATE WHO TRIES TO BE INCLUDED IN ALL THAT AMERICA CAN BRING, BUT AMERICAN HAS CHANGED IN THE NAME OF HAVING NO KING, DICTATOR, OR GENERAL'S

RULE OF LAW. WE ARE THE PEOPLE AND THE YOUNG PEOPLE
HAS COME TO SEE THE LIGHT THAT WE ARE HUMANS AND
THE RACIST RIGHTWING BUSH ADMINISTRATIION HAS PUT
AMERICAN IN DISTRESS. WHY NOT SENATOR OBAMA? CBS'
60 MINUTES RECENTLY HAD AN INTERVIEW OF UNITED
STATES SUPREME JUSTICE ANTONIN SCALIA WAS ENLIGHT-
ENING IN MANY WAYS, BUT HE WAS BROUGHT TO THE LAND
OF FREE, AFTER GROWING –UP UNDER THE ITALIAN
DICTATOR MUSSALINI, ADOLF HITLER'S MAIN COMRADE
AND RACIST INSTITUTION OF THE ROMANS. HE WANT TO
JUSTIFY HIS BELIEF OF NO ABORTION ON HE BEING A CATH-
OLIC. ACTIVIST JUSTICES HE IS ONE OF THEM IN THE NAME
THAT THE ENGLISH FOUNDING FATHER DID NOT PRECEIVE
ABORTION RIGHTS AND FREE SLAVES, AND HE HAS OUR
PEOPLE'S LIFE IN HIS HAND BECAUSE HE CAME TO WHITE
AMERICAN SPEAKING MULTI LANUAGES, AND WAS THE
HEAD OF HIS CLASS, BECAUSE MOST OF THE EUROPEANS
THINK AND KNOW FOR A FACT THAT THE AMERICANS ARE
NOT AS SMART AS THEM, BECAUSE THEY ARE NOT IN EUROPE.
HE IS HERE AND JOIN THE RACISM OF THE AMERICAN KLAN
AND THE NEO-NAZIS, AS HE IS REALLY A NEO-NAZI. HOW
COULD HE BE A HIGH JUSTICE OF THE LAND, WHEN HE
LOOKS DOWN ON DESCENDANT OF SLAVES? HE IS JUST LIKE
THE RACIST PRESIDENT RONALD REAGAN SAYING HE WAS
NOT PREJUDICE, WHEN THE ONLY BLACKS THAT WAS
AROUND HIM WAS THE BLACK SERVANTS, AND MY GRAND-
MOTHER SERVED HIS CALIFORNIA PARTIES TO CLOTH ME. 60
MINUTES INTERVIEW THE ONLY BLACK ON THE HIGH COURT,
JUSTICE CLARENCE THOMAS. HE AND I HAD MORE SIMU-
LARIES THAN I KNEW, BUT HE WAS FROM EASTERN GEORGIA.
HIS GRANDFATHER HAD GREAT INFLUENCE ON HIM, AND
HE LIVE DURING THE SAME TIME THAT I DID. I WAS SURPRISE
TO LEARN HOW MILITANT HE HAD TO BE WHEN GROWING
UP, AND THEN TRYING TO APPEASE THE CONFEDERATE

CONSERVATIES OF AMERICAN POLITICS, BUT HE WAS SUPPOSE
TO REPLACE THE GREAT UNITED SUPREME JUSTICE THUR-
GOOD MARSHALL, WHO IS ANOTHER OF MY ADMIRERS, JUST
AS ALI, BUT ALI AND I WAS IN THE JUNGLE AND THURGOOD
WAS MORE INTELLECTUAL ORPORTUNIES THAT ALI AND I.
JUSTICE THURGOOD FOUGHT AND WON THE BOARD OF
EDUCATION LAW TO FREE BLACK TO ENTER INTO WHITE
AMERICAN SCHOOLS, THEREFORE, LEADING TO THE INTER-
GATION LITTLE ROCK ARKANSAS, FROMER BILL CLINTON'S
HOME STATE, BUT FROM GHWBUSH APPOINTED HIM TO
REPLACE JUSTICE MARSHALL, BUT I BELIEVE AFTER SEEING
THE 60 MINUTES INTERVIEW THAT HE WILL LEAVE THE
THOUGHT THAT THE FOUNDING FATHERS HAD TO THINK
OF EVERYTHING THAT THIS DEMOCRACY WOULD BRING.
THE CONFEDERATE EQUALS CONSERVATIVES WANTS TO
PREACH ABOUT ACTIVIST JUDGES AND JUSTICES, JUST TO BE
LIKE THE MORMONS, ARMISH, KLAN, AND THE NEO-NAZIS
TO KEEP THE BLACKS IN THE CITIES WHILE THEY GO OUT IN
THE WOODS/ RURAL AMERICA AND SHOOT THE WILD LIFE
TO MAKE WAY FOR THEM TO LIVE IN AMERICA WITHOUT
THE ASSOCIATION OF THE INDIANS, BLACKS, OF THE MEXI-
CANS, AND THAT IS WHY THE OVERTHROW OF THE 2000
PRESIDENTIAL ELECTION THAT JUSTICE SCALIA TOLD LESLIE
STALL TO "GET OVER IT", NOW I COULD NOT BELIEVE WHAT
HE HAD SAID TO KEEP REPARATIONS AND VICE PRESIDENT
AL GORE FROM BECOMING THE PRESIDENT OF AMERICA. IN
THE NAME OF DEMOCRACY WE CAN NOT HAVE THE CONFED-
ERATES WHO LOST THE CIVIL WAR BECAUSE THE RUN AWAY
SLAVES AND THE UNION ARMY ARE STILL TRYING TO
CONTINUE THEIR SEPARATE BUT EQUAL MENTALITY, WHEN
IT IS SEPARATE IT CAN NEVER BE EQUAL. THEY ARE THE LAW
AND THE LAW BREAKERS. STACKING OF THE COURTS IN THE
NAME OF THE CONFEDERATE CONSERVATIVES HAS LEAD TO
THE OVERTHROW OF THE 2000 PRESIDENTIAL ELECTION

AND THE ILLEGAL INVASION OF THE SOVERIGN COUNTRY OF IRAQ, JUST TO ASSASINATE THEIR LEADER SADDAM HUESEIN. YOU CAN NOT BELIEVE ANYTHING SENATOR JOHN MC CAIN, NEWT GINGRICH, BUSH-CHENEY ADMINISTRATION, AND ALL OF THE RIGHTWINGERS, WHO ARE DEPRIVING THE AFRICAN-AMERICAN CITIZENS THEIR RIGHT TO THE FRUITS OF THE LAND THAT THEY CULTIVATED, DIE, KILLED, ENSLAVED, AND BUILD THE INFRASTRUTURED OF THE UNITED STATES. THE ENGLISHMEN FREED THEMSELVES FROM KING GEORGE OF ENGLAND, JUST TO TRICK, KILL, AND EVENTUALLY PUT THE ORIGINAL PEOPLE ON RESERVATION HERE, SOUTH AFRICA, AUSTRALIA, AND THE ISLAND PEOPLE ON RESERVATIONS; BUT THE DESCENDANT HAD LOST THEIR LIVES, LANUAGE, RELIGION, AND HERITAGE TO THE ENSLAVER OF EUROPE, THE ESPECIALLY THE UNITED KINGDOM OF GREAT BRITIAN. WE ARE THE LOST CHILDREN OF THE LAND JUST AS THE HEBREW JEWS THAT THE ROMANS WAS CRUCIFYING AND IMPRISONING THEM, UNTIL A HALF BREED CALL MOSES CAME ALONG TO HELP FREE GOD'S CHILDREN CRYING OVER CENTURIES TO BE FREE, AND NOW THE BUSH-CHENEY ADMINISTRATION KIDNAPPED THE ARABIC SO-CALL ENEMY COMBATANS INTO CUBA COMPLETELY AWAY FROM THE MIDDLE EAST, JUST AS THEY DID THE FOURTEEN HUNDRED AND ENTER WHAT IS NOW CALLED JAMES TOWN, VIRGINIA. GOD CAME WITH KATRINA AND MANY MORE TYPE OF STORMS TO ALL OF THE DEVIL WORSHIPING NATIONS OF THE EARTH. IN THE NAME OF JESUS CHRIST USING HIS NAME IN VAIN AND HE HAS RETURNED MANY TIMES TO THE EARTH, AND HE IS ALWAYS BLACK, THEREFORE, THE CATHOLICS AND THEIR NAZI POPE LEADER WILL BE UNVEILED LITTLE BY LITTLE, THROUGH THEIR HOMOSEXUAL PRACTICES AND BELIEFS. THEY HAVE PAID BILLIONS OF DOLLARS TO COVER-UP THEIR SO-CALL PRIESTS, NOW THE CHURCHES ARE CLOSING AS THE TRUTH

BECOME THE LIGHT. THE CREATOR CARL ROVE AND ONE OF THE CONSPIRACY TO TAKE THE 2000 ELECTION WITH KATHRINE HARRIS AS THE SECRETARY OF THE STATE OF FLORIDA TOOK A BIAS SIDE OF THE REPUBLICANS INSTEAD OF THE PEOPLE OF FLORIDA, SHE LISTEN AND FOLLOW GOVERNOR JEB BUSH ORDERS TO IGNORE THE HALF PUNCH CARDS OF THE VOTERS IN THE BLACK AND DEMOCRACTIC AREAS OF FLORIDA. THIS WAS JUST AS TERRIBLE AS KLAN RIDING AROUND WITH GUNS INTIMINDATING SHARE CROPPER AND OTHER AFRICAN DESCENDANTS NOT TO VOTE, WHEN THEY CAN NOT READ AND WRITE, EVEN TODAY WHEN THE RACIST UNITED STATES SUPREME COURT JUSTIFYING WHY PEOPLE WHO DO NOT HAVE A CAR, EDUCATION, AND VERY MONEY TO LIVE ON HAVE TO FINE A WAY TO OBTAIN SOME TYPE OF IDENTIFICATION TO VOTE. CARL ROVE IS FINALLY UNDER INVESTIGATION. A NEW BOOK BY FROMER PRESS SECRETARY SCOTT MC CLELLAN "WHAT HAPPEN" IS OUT AND IN THE NEWS TODAY. IT SHOWS THAT IT WAS/ IS A WAR AND INVASION THAT SHOULD NOT HAVE HAPPEN AND THAT MAKES MY VIEWS TRUE AND ON THE MONEY ABOUT THE 2000 ELECTION AND THE INVASION OF IRAQ. WAR CRIMES SHOULD BE IN ORDER FOR BUSH AND CHENEY. MR. ROVE IS PRESIDENT BUSH'S MAIN MAN NEEDED TO BE , PROTECTED, AND COVERED-UP THE UNCOVERING ONE OF THE CIA'S COVERT AGENTS, VALERIE PLANE WILSON, BECAUSE HER HUSBAND WAS AN IRAQ DIPLOMATE DURING THE CLINTON ADMINISTRATION. I KNEW WHEN IT CAME OUT THAT IT CAME FROM THE WHITE HOUSE AND PRESIDENT BUSH GOT IN FRONT OF THE CAMERA AND SAID HE WOULD FIRE AND PUNISH ANYONE IN HIS ADMINISTRATION, WHEN HE AND TRICKY DICK CHENEY WAS THE ENGINEER OF THE MOVE. TREASON WAS THEIR AND NOW AS THE LIGHT HAS COME OUT BUSH AND CHENEY ARE TRYING TO GET OUT OF TOWN WITH THEIR TAIL BETWEEN THEIR LEGS, AS THE DEMOCRATS

COULD NOT GET ENOUGH REPUBLICANS TO BRING AN INDE-
PENDENT PROSECUTOR, JUST AS THEY DID WHEN CLINTON
ONLY COMMITTED A SEX ACT IN HIS PRIVATE OFFICE AND
LIED ABOUT IT. BUSH AND CHENEY ADMINISTRATION IS/
WAS ALL LIES AND NO SPECIAL PROSECUTOR, BECAUSE OF
PRESIDENT RICHARD NIXON IMPEACHMENT, REPRESENTA-
TIVE TOM DELAY FAIL, TRENT LOTT FAIL, ORRIN HATCH
WENT IN HIDING TRYING TO GET RE-ELECTED TO COME
BACK AND BACKED SOME OTHER RIGHT WING STATUS QUO
JUSTICE, AND ALL OF THE OTHERS WHO WAS REPLACED IN
2006 ELECTION AND THE ONES WHO ARE STILL THERE AND
QUIET AS A LAMB. THEY ALL ARE PUBLIC OFFICIALS AND
THE PUBLIC SHOULD KNOW EVERYTHING THEY DO IN
PUBLIC LIFE. MEDIA AND ALL SHOULD CONTINUE TO WRITE
AND SHOW THE PEOPLE HOW THEY PASS LAWS TO PROTECT
THEIR PERSONAL AFFAIRS INSTEAD OF ALL OF THE PEOPLE.
"TRICKY DICK" CHENEY'S MAIN MAN AND CHIEF OF STAFF
HAS BEEN CONVICTED AND PARDON AT THE SAME TIME.
THEY MAKE THE LAW AND BREAK THE LAW AS THEY ARE
SUPPOSE TO UPHOLD THE LAW OF THE LAND. THIS IS A
PERFECT EXAMPLE OF WHY I AM WRITING THIS BOOK AND
NAMING IT "THE AMERICAN WAY NOSTRICK LAWS-RIGH-
TWINGERS CONSPIRACY ROMAN STYLE WAR. IRAQ IS A
ROMAN STYLE WAR, ATTACK A COUNTRY OR NATION WITH
OVERWHELMING POWER AND CONFISCATE THE RICHES OF
THE LAND, IN THIS CASE IT IS OIL, AND HALIBURTON AND
OTHER BUSH-CHENEY FRIENDS SHOULD NOT BE ABLE TO
HAVE CONTRACTS WITH THEIR PUPPET GOVERNMENT TO
ENRICH THEMSELVES, AND ESPECIALLY WHEN IT IS AGAINST
THE LAW TO HAVE NO BID CONTRACT, BUT GANGTER VICE
PRESIDENT AND PRESIDENT CHENEY THOSE RULES DOES
NOT APPLY. THEY MAKE MONEY ON ALL COMMISSARY,
MEALS SERVE, AND EVERYTHING ELSE THERE THAT A
SOLIDER HAS TO SPEND THEIR PAY THE LITTLE COMFORTS

BEING AWAY FROM HOME. I THINK A LOT OF THE MONIES SHOULD GO TO THE TREASURY AND DISPENSE TO HELP POOR AMERICANS. THE AMERICAN WAY. THERE IS NO PERSON WHO KNOWS WHAT THE FUTURE WILL BRING. SENATOR JOHN MC CAIN CAN NOT BE A BETTER PRESIDENT THAN SENATOR BARACK OBAMA. PRESIDENT BUSH AND CHENEY DID NOT HAVE THAT MUCH EXPERIENCE. WE HAVE PRISONERS IN CUBA, JUST WHERE WE CAN NOT GIVE THEM A HABAES CORPUS RIGHTS, BUT MC CAIN, BUSH, AND OTHERS DO NOT WANT THE AMERICAN CUBAN COMMUNI-TIES TO TRAVEL TO THEIR HOME LAND NINETY MILES ACROSS THE UNITED STATES BORDER. THAT IS THE ARGU-MENT THAT MC CAIN AND OBAMA ARE DISPUTING FOREIGN POLICIES. MC CAIN WHAT SENATOR OBAMA TO VISIT IRAQ WITH HIM, I WOULD NOT WANT TO VISIT IRAQ WITH JOHN MC CAIN THE NOMINEE OF THE REPUBLICAN, WHO WOULD BE TRYING TO PICK SENATOR OBAMA'S BRAIN, THE CLASSIC KLAN MANNER OF KNOWING WHAT THE BLACKS AND THE RIVAL IS THINKING. SENATOR OBAMA IS MORE TRUST WORTHY THAN ANY REPUBLICAN, AND ESPECIALLY THE RACIST JOHN MC CAIN. SENATOR OBAMA IS YOUNG LIKE PRESIDENT KENNEDY AND HE WILL CHOOSE A VICE PRESI-DENT WHO WILL HELP GUILD HIM THROUGH, JUST AS PRES-IDENT REAGAN DID WHEN HE CHOOSE THE CIA CHIEF GEORGE HERBERT WALKER BUSH, AND THE REST IS HISTORY. THEY DID NOT WANT TO LISTEN TO MY PEOPLE IN SLAVE HUTS, AND THEY DO NOT WANT TO LISTEN TODAY, EVEN THOUGHT, THEY DO LISTEN THEN GO AWAY AND CRITICIZE THE BLACK ASS WAY OF LIVING IN A SLAVE MASTER'S CHIL-DREN DOMAIN. I JUST CANNOT BELIEVE HOW A RACIST NAZI HOMO POPE COMES TO NEW YORK AND THE WHOLE WORLD BOW DOWN TO HIS FEET LIKE HE IS SO PURE, WHEN HE IS CARRYING ON DECEIT. JESUS CHRIST THE HOLY MESSIAH OF NAZARETH, SAID AND IS REPHASE MANY TIMES

IN THE DELUTED KING JAMES VERSIONS OF THE SO-CALL NEW TESTAMENT, THAT PEOPLE OF EARTH WILL BE DECEIVED IN HIS NAME. HE SAID WORSHIP AND HONOR GOD ALMIGHTY CREATOR OF THE UNIVERSE AND THE EARTH, BUT MAN NATURE WILL TAKE CREDIT FOR ANYTHING THAT IS GOOD AND WILL DECEIVE AND ENSLAVE ANYONE WHO DOES NOT BELIEVE IN THE GREATEST LIE THAT MAN HAS TO BE CELE-BRATE. GOD SAID HAVE SEX AND POPULATE THE EARTH, AND THE WELL TO DO SHOULD SEE THAT THE LESS THAN WELL TO BE FEED, HOUSED, AND TREATED HUMAN AS POSSIBLE. REVERN HOSEA WILLIAMS FEED THE HUNGRY PROGRAM IN ATLANTA, GEORGIA SHOULD BE A NATIONAL EFFORT, JUST AS MINISTER ELIJAH MUHAMMAD DID WHEN HE WAS ENLIGHTEN IN ATLANTA, GEORGIA AND PULL IN THE POOR DESCENDANTS OF SLAVES THAT HAD BEEN DISPLACED FROM SLAVERY AND THEIR SHARECROPING HOMES, THEN TURN TO THE UNITED STATES CITY STREETS AS ALCOHOLICS AND DOPE ADDICTS. ONE OF MY GRANDFA-THER'S MAIN HELPERS WAS A MAN WE CALL L.C. NEVER KNEW WHAT IT MEANT, BUT HE WORK HARD EVERYDAY AND ON THE WEEKEND HE PARTY AND BECAME DRUNK ON DECATUR STREET, JUST TO BE TAKEN TO JAIL TO SLEEP IT OFF. MY GRANDFATHER ALWAYS HAD TO GO GET HIM OUT OF JAIL. HE COULD NOT READ OR WRITE HIS NAME, THAT IS WHAT AMERICA HAD DONE TO MY PEOPLE AND KNOW ONE CAN TELL ME WHO I AM TO ASSOCIATE WITH, EVEN THOUGHT, YOU HAVE TO WATCH ALL OF YOUR WHITE FRIENDS, BECAUSE THEIR FRIENDS ALWAYS SORT OF BRING THEM BACK TO THEY HAVE TO BE SUPERIOR AND THAT ATTI-TUDE ALWAYS CAUSES PROBLEMS WITHIN A RELATIONSHIP. YOUR OWN PEOPLE WILL DECEIVE YOU FASTER THAN SOME OTHER PEOPLE, SO A PERSON HAS TO BE AWARE, AND ESPE-CIALLY IF YOU ARE A SUCCESSFUL MAN OR WOMAN. THE GOVERNMENT LOOKS DOWN ON THE POOR PEOPLE TODAY

AS THEY SLEEP ON CITY STREETS AND BYWAYS OF AMER-
ICAN STREETS. THE GOVERNMENT SAYS IT IS SOCIAL AND
THIS IS A CAPITALIST SOCEITY, UNTIL YOU GO TO PRISON,
THEN YOU WILL KNOW WHAT COMMUNISM AND DICTA-
TORS DO. I HAD A VERY CLOSE CUBAN FRIEND WHO CAME
HERE DURNING THE EARLY 1980'S AND HE USE TO TELL ME
ABOUT FIDEL CASTRO AND THE COMMUNISM, AND NOT TO
HAVE CHOOSES IS NOT GREAT. THERE IS A LAWSUIT IN THE
STATE OF FLORIDA AGAIN BASED ON THE FOURTEETH
ADMENDMENT THAT EVERY CITIZEN HAS A RIGHT TO VOTE,
AND IN THIS CASE FOR THE VOTE TO COUNT. FROMER PRES-
IDENT CLINTON UPSETS ME THESE DAYS ABOUT LOSING THE
NOMINATION OF THE DEMOCRATIC PARTY FOR HIS WIFE, IT
IS AMAZING HOW ELECTIONS CAN TURN AROUND. SENATOR
OBAMA CAME OUT OF NOWHERE AND BEAT EVERYONE
WHO WAS RUNNING IN JANUARY AND BEYOND. THE
CLINTON THOUGHT THAT THEY HAD THE NOMINATION
WON BEFORE A VOTE WAS COUNTED AND NOW ALL OF THE
RACISM HAS COME FROM HIM AND HILLARY, AND THE
PARTY IS VERY UPSET WITH HIM AND HILLARY, THAT MIGHT
END UP CAUSING HER SENATE SEAT IN NEW YORK. CALI-
FORNIA MOVE UP AND A NUMBER OF STATES MOVED UP
AFTERWARDS WITH THE INTENTION OF HAVING AN IMPACT
ON WHO THE NOMINEE WILL BE, BUT THEY CAN NOT COME
BEFORE IOWA AND NEW HAMPSHIRE AND THEY WERE AT
THE END OF JANUARY. FLORIDA SET THEIR DATE FOR
JANUARY ANYWAY AND IT CAUSED THEM TO BE SANCTION;
THEREFORE, THE CLINTONS SHOULD HAVE BEEN AT THE
DEMOCRATIC PARTY IN FLORIDA AND MICHGAN THEN
BEFORE ANY ELECTION MAKING SURE THAT THEY COMPLY
WITH THE RULES OF THE PARTY, AND ESPECIALLY WHEN
THEY WERE BECOMING THE ELDERS IN THE PARTY, BUT THEY
JUST KNEW THAT BIDDEN, RICHARDSON, EDWARDS, AND
OTHERS WERE NOT GOING TO COME CLOSE TO THE CLIN-

TONS, BUT THERE IS A FRESMAN SENATOR OBAMA WHO IS
YOUNG AND FRESH FOR AMERICA AND HE IS A BLACK MAN.
THE CLINTON'S NAME CARRIED THEM, BUT THE CANADATES
WERE NOT ALLOWED TO CAMPAIGN IN FLORIDA, IF THEY
WOULD HAVE BEEN ALLOWED TO CAMPAIGN IN FLORIDA,
THEY WOULD NOT HAVE GOTTEN AS MANY VOTES AS SHE
ENDED UP WITHOUT CAMPAIGNING, BUT THE CLINTONS
WAS NOT SCREAMING BLOODY MARY THEN AND NOW THEY
ARE LOSING TO A BLACK MAN THEY ARE TRYING TO COUNT
THE VOTES OF FLORIDA AND MICHGAN; THEREFORE, THOSE
VOTES SHOULD NOT COUNT AND FLORIDA SHOULD HAVE
FILED A LAWSUIT IN JANUARY. SENATOR OBAMA HAS WON
MOST SUPER DELEGATES AND HAS THE MOST POPULAR
VOTE, CAUSE FLORIDA AND MICHGAN CANNOT COUNT,
BECAUSE EVERYWHERE SENATOR OBAMA HAS CAMPAIGNED
HE HAS WON OVER FOURTY PERCENT, EXCEPT IN RACIST
JERRY FALWELL COUNTRY. WITHOUT WINNING THOSE OVER
FOURTY PERCENT IN THOSE EASTERN STATES HE STILL
LEADS HILLARY; THEREFORE, SHE NEEDS TO HAVE THE LOVE
OF THE PARTY AND I THINK SHE WILL AFTER THESE LAST
THREE OR FOUR UPCOMING ELECTION, AND OBAMA ONLY
NEEDS A FEW MORE POPULAR VOTES AND HE HAS MOST OF
THE SUPER DELEGATES. THE CLINTONS ARE PLENTY UPSET
THAT SHE HAS LOST AND THE BLACKS IN AMERICA HAS
BEEN AND IS MORE DEPRIVED THAN ANY SECT OF PEOPLE
IN THE UNITED STATES AND THE WOMEN AND ALL SHOULD
VOTE FOR OBAMA FOR THE GOOD OF AMERICAN. SENATOR
KENNEDY, EDWARDS, RICHARDSON, AND OTHERS HAVE
ENDORSED OBAMA AND HE IS LOOKING FOR A RUNNING
MATE. MAY GOD BLESS AMERICA? I SENT AN EMAIL TO THE
CLINTON THAT THE DEMOCRATIC PARTY SHOULD SEAT THE
DELEGATES HALF AND HALF, THEN OBAMA WOULD STILL
WIN AND BE THE NOMINATION. IT WAS THE DEMOCRACTIC
PARTY THAT SHOULD HAVE FILED THE LAWSUIT TO PREVENT

THE LOCAL PARTY FROM VOTING IN JANUARY AND WE WOULD NOT BE WHERE WE ARE AS COUNTRY IN SUCH AN IMPORTANT ELECTION. THE REPUBLICANS HAS DECEIVE THE OATH AND THEIR LOVE OF COUNTRY, BECAUSE OF RACISM AND ABORTION IS ALL A RACISM ISSUE, AND THE UNITED STATES SUPREME COURT CANNOT CONTINUE WITH THIS OUT OF DATE EXCUSE OF WHAT THE FOUNDING FATHERS WOULD THINK AND DO, WHEN THEY COULD NOT VISION ONE FLYING IN AIRPLANES, DRIVING AUTOS, SLAVES BEING CITIZENS, AND OTHER ISSUES. WHITE RACIST AMERICA YOU GET OVER IT, AS THEY ARE TRYING TO TELL THE YOUNG AFRICAN-AMERICANS, WHO ARE DESCENDANTS OF THE HOLUCAST OF UNITED STATES SLAVE SYSTEM.   PRESIDENT BUSH FIRST SPEECH TO THE CONGRESS AND THE AMERICAN PEOPLE HE SAID THAT HE WANTED TO BECOME A WAR PRESIDENT AND THAT HE WILL ROB AND SPEND THE SURPLUS OF THE UNITED STATES TREASURY FROM THE CLINTON ADMINISTRATION. AFTER THE APPOINTMENT BY THE HIGH COURT OF THE LAND I KNEW MY COUNTRY WAS IN BIG TROUBLE, AFTER I HAD STARTED ADMIRING THE CLINTON ADMINISTRATION AND ALL OF THE NONE HELP TYPE OF DIGNITARIES WHO HAD ACCESS TO THE WHITE MAN'S BIG HOUSE, BUILT ON THE BACK OF UNITED STATES SLAVES. THE MILITARY KILLED THE COMMERCE SECRETARY RON BROWN, AFTER HE WAS IN AFRICA DANCING AND HAVING FUN, WHEN HE WAS FORCED ON A PLANE IN THE MIDDLE OF A RAIN STORM AT NIGHT. BUSH FATHER AND ALL OF NIXON'S MEN NEED TO LEAVE OUR COUNTRY ALONE, BUT NOW THEY ARE PRESENTING SENATOR JOHN MC CAIN, BECAUSE HE WAS PROMISE TO BE THE NEXT REPUBLICAN NOMINEE, IF HE BOWS OUT AND DO NOT CONTEST BUSH AND CHENEY PRESIDENCY. RIGHT WING CONSPIRACY CONTINUES TODAY LIKE NEVER BEFORE, BECAUSE THEIR TOTAL FORCUS IS ON STACKING OF THE COURTS WITH SOUTHERN BIAS JUDGES

TO DO JUDIUARY DUTIES TO KEEP THE STATUS QUO IN POWER AND NOT BE RESPONSIBLE FOR THEIR HARM TO WORKERS AND THE ORDINARY PEOPLE OF THE UNITED STATES. A LAWSUIT KEEPS THEM ON THE RIGHT TRACK, OTHERWISE THEY WILL CONTINUE TO HARM PEOPLE. JOHN MC CAIN SPEAKS OF IRAQ AND WINNING A WAR THAT SHOULD NOT HAVE HAPPEN THAT HE SUPPORT. WE DO NOT NEED ANY POLITICANS WHO WANTS TO TEST NEW WEAPONS ON BLACK NATIONS. THEY NEVER TEST WEAPONS ON ANY EUROPEAN NATION. AFTER GENERAL HANNABLE THEY PROMISE THEIR WILL NEVER BE ANOTHER BLACK TO CONQUER ANY EURO-PEAN NATION AND THAT IS WHY THEY CRUCIFIED THE HOLY MESSIAH JESUS CHRIST OF NAZARETH, BECAUSE HE WAS BLACK AND THERE ARE OTHERS IN THE WORLD WHO ARE HUMANS POSSESSES POWERS AS JESUS. LISTEN TO THE POPE JESUS IS COMING, WHEN JESUS HAS CAME AND HE HAS COME THROUGH THE POOR AND HE WAS/IS BLACK TODAY. I HAD INTENTED FOR THIS BOOK TO BE OUT, BUT SINCE I HAVE ANOTHER CHANCE TO REVISE SOME AND UPDATE SOME EVENTS AND MY THOUGHTS OF THE SITUATIONS THAT INSPIRED AND ANGERED ME, THERE IS A RECENT MOVIE OUT ABOUT THE 2000 PRESIDENTIAL ELECTION, CALL "RECOUNT", AND THE RIGHTWINGERS ACHIEVED THEIR OBJECTIVES TO CONTINUE TO STACK THE COURTS AS THEIR LEADER FROMER PRESIDENT RICHARD "TRICKY DICK" NIXON MOVEMENT TO KEEP THE DESCENDANTS OF SLAVES IN THE BACKGROUND OF AMERICAN LIFE. HE WAS SO RACIST HE DID NOT BELIEVE THE A BLACK HAD THE INTELLEGENCE TO QUARTERBACK A NATIONAL FOOTBALL LEAGUE TEAM. HOPE THAT THIS NEVER HAPPEN AGAIN WITH THE TECHNOLOGY FOR VOTING MACHINES SHOULD BE FEDERAL PROJECT THAT EVERY MACHINE IN EVERY VOTING PRECINT BE THE SAME. NOT MORE IN THE SUBURBS AND LESS IN THE CITIES, FOR PEOPLE TO BE DISCOURAGE FROM VOTING BECAUSE OF LONG

LINES. WE HAVE CAME A LONG WAY AND WE HAVE EVEN A LONGER WAY, AND HOPE THERE ARE ADMENDMENTS TO THE CONSTITUTION TO BE SURE EVERY DESCENDANT OF SLAVES ARE TAKEN CARE OF FROM BIRTH UNTIL HIGHER EDUCATION, JUST AS WHITE AMERICA IS DOING WITH THE WHITE EUROPEAN CHILDREN. IT IS A RIGHT THAT WE HAVE INHERITED AND THE UNITED STATES AND IT'S LARGEST CORPORATION THAT WERE BUILD ON COTTON PICKERS AND OTHER LABOR DURNING SLAVERY AND AFTER. WITH ALL THAT IS SAID AND DONE I THINK THE HISTORY OF THIS HIGHEST COURT OF THE LAND IS FITTING TO ALL THAT HAS HAD THE OPENING OF MIND TO READ MY FIRST NON-FICTIONAL BOOK. THANKS The history of the Supreme Court is frequently described in terms of the Chief Justices who have presided over it.Initially, during the tenures of Chief Justices

Jay, Rutledge, and Ellsworth (1789–1801), the Court lacked a home of its own and any real prestige.

That changed during the Marshall Court (1801–1836), which declared the Court to be the supreme arbiter of the Constitution (see Marbury v. Madison) and made a number of important rulings which gave shape and substance to the constitutional balance of power between the federal government (referred to at the time as the "general" government) and the states. In Martin v. Hunter's Lessee, the Court ruled that it had the power to correct interpretations of the federal Constitution made by state supreme courts. Both Marbury and Martin confirmed that the Supreme Court was the body entrusted with maintaining the consistent and orderly development of federal law.

The Marshall Court ended the practice of each judge issuing his opinion seriatim, a remnant of British tradition, and instead one majority opinion of the Court was issued. The Marshall Court also saw Congress impeach a sitting Justice, Samuel Chase, who was acquitted. This impeachment was one piece of the power struggle between the Democratic-Republicans and the Federalists after the election of 1800 and the subsequent change in power. The failure to remove Chase is thought to signal the recognition by Congress of judicial independence. The Taney Court (1836–1864) made a number of important rulings, such as Sheldon v. Sill, which held that while Congress may not limit the subjects the Supreme Court may hear, it may limit the jurisdiction of the lower federal courts to prevent them from hearing cases dealing with certain subjects. However, it is primarily remembered for its ruling in Dred Scott v. Sandford, the case which may have helped precipitate the Civil War. In the years following the Civil War, the Chase, Waite, and Fuller Courts (1864–1910) interpreted the new Civil War amendments to the Constitution, and developed the doctrine of substantive due process (Lochner v. New York; Adair v. United States). Under the White and Taft Courts (1910–1930), the substantive due process doctrine reached its first apogee (Adkins v. Children's Hospital), and the Court held that the Fourteenth Amendment applied some provisions of the Bill of Rights to the states through the Incorporation doctrine. During the Hughes, Stone, and Vinson Courts (1930–1953), the court gained its own accommodation and radically changed its interpretation of the Constitution in order to facilitate the New Deal (West Coast Hotel Co. v. Parrish, Wickard v. Filburn), giving an expansive reading to the powers of the Federal Government. The Warren Court (1953–1969) made a number of alternately celebrated and controversial rulings expanding the application of the Constitution to civil liberties, leading a renaissance in substantive due process. It held that segregation in public schools is unconstitutional (Brown v. Board of Education); the Constitution protects a general right to privacy (Griswold v. Connecticut); public schools cannot have official prayer (Engel v. Vitale), or mandatory Bible readings (Abington School District v. Schempp); many guarantees of the Bill of Rights apply to the states (e.g., Mapp v. Ohio. Miranda v. Arizona); an equal protection clause is not contained in the Fifth Amendment (Bolling v. Sharpe); and that the Constitution grants the right of retaining a court appointed attorney for those too indigent to pay for one (Gideon v. Wainwright). The Burger Court (1969–1986) ruled that abortion was a constitutional right (Roe v. Wade), reached controversial rulings on affirmative action (Regents of the University of California v. Bakke) and campaign finance regulation (Buckley v. Valeo), and held that the implementation of the death penalty in many states was unconstitutional (Furman v. Georgia), but that the death penalty itself was not unconstitutional (. Georgia). [5]The Rehnquist Court (1986–2005) will primarily be remembered for its revival of the concept of federalism, which included restrictions on Congressional power under both the Commerce Clause (United States v. Lopez; United States v. Morrison) and the fifth section of the Fourteenth Amendment (City of Boerne v. Flores), as well as the fortification of state sovereign immunity (Seminole Tribe v. Florida; Alden v. Maine). It will also be remembered for its controversial 5 to 4 decision in Bush v. Gore which ended the electoral recount during the presidential election of 2000 and led to the presidency of George W. Bush. In addition, the Rehnquist court narrowed the right of labor unions to picket (Lechmere Inc. v. NLRB); altered the Roe v. Wade framework for assessing abortion regulations (Planned Parenthood v. Casey); and gave sweeping meaning to ERISA pre-emption (Shaw v. Delta Air Lines, Inc.; Egelhoff v. Egelhoff), thereby denying plaintiffs access to state courts with the consequence of limiting compensation for torts to very circumscribed remedies

(Aetna Health Inc. v. Davila;CIGNA Healthcare of Texas Inc. v. Calad); and affirmed the power of Congress to extend the term of copyright (Eldred v. Ashcroft). The Roberts Court (2005–present) began with the confirmation and swearing in of Chief Justice John G. Roberts on September 29, 2005, and is the currently presiding court. Though still too early to call it a definite trend, the Court under Chief Justice Roberts is perceived [6] as moving towards the conservative end of the spectrum. Some of the major rulings so far have been in the areas of abortion (Ayotte v. Planned Parenthood;

Gonzales v. Carhart); anti-trust legislation (Leegin Creative Leather Products, Inc. v. PSKS, Inc.); the death penalty (Kansas v. Marsh;Baze v. Rees); the Fourth Amendment (Hudson v. Michigan); free speech (Garcetti v. Ceballos; Morse v. Frederick); school desegregation (Parents v. Seattle); and voting rights (Crawford v. Marion County Election Board). The Roberts Court, with Chief Justice Roberts recusing himself, ruled in favor of some constitutional protections for non-citizen Guantanamo detainees in Hamdan v. Rumsfeld. The Court heard oral arguments on the Guantanamo habeas corpus case Al Odah v. United States on December 5 of the 2007-2008 term, and a decision is expected by the end of the term.

AUTHOR: FAST EDDIE X

www.ingramcontent.com/pod-product-compliance
Lightning Source LLC
Chambersburg PA
CBHW061342280526
45784CB00001B/103